CliffsTestPrep™

SAT I®/PSAT™

WILEY

Wiley Publishing, Inc.

About the Author

Dr. Jerry Bobrow, Ph.D., is a national authority in the field of test preparation. As executive director of Bobrow Test Preparation Services, he has been administering the test preparation programs at over 25 California institutions for the past 27 years. Dr. Bobrow has authored over 30 national best-selling test preparation books, and his books and programs have assisted over two million test-takers. Each year, Dr. Bobrow personally lectures to thousands of students on preparing for graduate, college, and teacher credentialing exams.

Publisher's Acknowledgments

Editorial

Project Editor: Christine Meloy Beck

Copy Editors: Rebecca Whitney, Janet M. Withers, Gregg Summers

Editorial Assistants: Melissa Bluhm, Laura Jefferson, Carol Strickland

Production

Proofreaders: Vicki Broyles, Jennifer Mahern

Wiley Indianapolis Composition Services

CliffsTestPrep™ SAT I®/PSAT™

Published by:
Wiley Publishing, Inc.
909 Third Avenue
New York, NY 10022
www.wiley.com

Copyright © 2000 Jerry Bobrow, Ph.D.

Published by Wiley Publishing, Inc., New York, NY

Published simultaneously in Canada

Library of Congress Control Number No.: 00-102522

ISBN: 0-7645-8611-4

Printed in the United States of America

10 9 8 7 6 5 4 3 2

1X/SS/QR/QT/IN

Author's Acknowledgments

I would like to thank Michele Spence and Linnea Fredrickson, for their many hours of editing the original manuscript, and Christy Beck, of Wiley, for her assistance and careful attention to the production process. I would also like to thank my office staff of Joy Mondragon, Cindy Hadash, Allison Drucker, and Deena Mondragon for their assistance. Finally, I would like to thank my wife, Susan; daughter, Jennifer (22); and sons, Adam (19) and Jonathan (15), for their patience, moral support, and comic relief.

Table of Contents

PART II: PRACTICE-REVIEW-ANALYZE-PRACTICE

PART III: ABOUT THE PSAT/NMSQT

Preface

Your SAT I: Reasoning Test or PSAT Score Can Make the Difference!

And because of this fact, you can't afford to take a chance. Prepare with the best! Because better scores result from thorough preparation, your study time must be used most effectively. *CliffsTestPrep SAT I/PSAT* has been designed by leading experts in the field of test preparation to be the most comprehensive guide that you can realistically complete in a reasonable time. In keeping with the fine tradition of Cliffs Notes, this guide is written for the student. It is direct, precise, compact, easy to use, and thorough. The testing strategies, techniques, and materials have been researched, tested, and evaluated and are presently used in SAT I test preparation programs at many leading colleges and universities. This book emphasizes the Bobrow Test Preparation Services approach, developed over the past 27 years with thousands of students in preparation programs. The Bobrow approach focuses on the six major areas that should be considered when preparing for the SAT I:

1. Ability Tested
2. Basic Skills Necessary
3. Understanding Directions
4. Analysis of Directions
5. Suggested Approaches with Samples
6. Practice-Review-Analyze-Practice

This guide combines introductory analysis sections for each exam area with lots of practice — four full-length practice tests (three SAT and one PSAT). These practice tests have complete answers, in-depth explanations, analysis charts, and score range approximators to give you a thorough understanding of the SAT I and PSAT.

CliffsTestPrep SAT I/PSAT was written to give you the edge in doing your best by giving you maximum benefit in a reasonable amount of time and is meant to augment, not substitute for, formal or informal learning throughout junior high and high school.

Don't take a chance. Be prepared! Follow the Study Guide Checklist in this book and study regularly. You'll get the best test preparation possible.

SAT I Study Guide Checklist

❑ 1. Read the SAT I: Reasoning Test information bulletin.

❑ 2. Become familiar with the test format, page 1.

❑ 3. Familiarize yourself with the answers to Questions Commonly Asked about the SAT I, page 3.

❑ 4. Learn the techniques of the Successful Overall Approaches, pages 5–7.

❑ 5. Carefully read Part I: Analysis of Exam Areas, beginning on page 11.

❑ 6. Strictly observing time allotments, take Practice Test 1, section by section (take Section 1 and then check your answers; take Section 2 and then check your answers, and so on), beginning on page 109.

❑ 7. Review the answers and explanations for each question on Practice Test 1, beginning on page 156.

❑ 8. Analyze your Practice Test 1 answers by filling out the analysis charts, page 155.

❑ 9. Review your math skills as necessary.

❑ 10. Review or reread Part I: Analysis of Exam Areas, beginning on page 11, to see whether you applied some of the strategies.

❑ 11. Strictly observing time allotments, take Practice Test 2, beginning on page 189. Take a very short break after each hour of testing.

❑ 12. Check your answers and use the Score Range Approximator (page 345) to get a very general score range.

❑ 13. Analyze your Practice Test 2 answers by filling out the analysis charts on page 236.

❑ 14. While referring to each item of Practice Test 2, study all of the answers and explanations that begin on page 238.

❑ 15. Selectively review some basic skills as necessary.

❑ 16. Strictly observing time allotments, take Practice Test 3, beginning on page 271. Take a very short break after each hour of testing.

❑ 17. Check your answers and use the Score Range Approximator (page 345) to get a very general score range.

❑ 18. Analyze your Practice Test 3 answers by filling out the analysis charts on page 313.

❑ 19. While referring to each item of Practice Test 3, study all of the answers and explanations that begin on page 316.

❑ 20. Again, selectively review Part I: Analysis of Exam Areas, beginning on page 11, and any other basic skills or exam areas you feel are necessary.

❑ 21. Carefully read "Final Preparation" on page 419.

PSAT Study Guide Checklist

❑ 1. Read the PSAT/NMSQT free Information Bulletin available from your high school counselor or the College Board.

❑ 2. Familiarize yourself with the PSAT/NMSQT by reading the General Description on page 352.

❑ 3. Review the format of a recent test, page 351.

❑ 4. Learn the techniques of the Successful Overall Approaches, pages 5–7.

❑ 5. Carefully read Part I: Analysis of Exam Areas, beginning on page 11.

❑ 6. Review Verbal and Math sections, page 352.

❑ 7. Read about the Writing Skills section, page 353.

❑ 8. Strictly observing time allotments, take the practice PSAT/NMSQT starting on page 357.

❑ 9. Review the answers and explanations for each question on page 397.

❑ 10. Analyze your practice test by filling out the analysis charts, page 392.

❑ 11. Use the PSAT/NMSQT Score Range Approximator (page 394) to get a very general score range.

❑ 12. Review your math skills as necessary.

❑ 13. Review the list of prefixes, suffixes, and roots starting on page 43.

❑ 14. If you have time for extra practice, work the problems on Practice Test 1 (page 109).

❑ 15. Review the answers and explanations for each question on page 156.

❑ 16. Analyze your Practice Test 1 answers by filling out the analysis charts, page 153.

❑ 17. For additional practice, work as many of the additional practice tests as you want.

❑ 18. Be sure to review your answers and explanations for each test.

❑ 19. Carefully read "Final Preparation" on page 419.

General Format of the SAT I: Reasoning Test		
Section 1	**Verbal Reasoning**	**30 Questions**
30 Minutes	Sentence Completions	9 Questions
	Analogies	6 Questions
	Critical Reading (2 passages)	15 Questions
Section 2	**Mathematical Reasoning**	**25 Questions**
30 Minutes	Multiple Choice	25 Questions
Section 3	**Verbal Reasoning**	**35 Questions**
30 Minutes	Sentence Completions	10 Questions
	Analogies	13 Questions
	Critical Reading (1 passage)	12 Questions
Section 4	**Mathematical Reasoning**	**25 Questions**
30 Minutes	Quantitative Comparisons	15 Questions
	Grid-ins	10 Questions
Section 5	**Verbal Reasoning**	**13 Questions**
15 Minutes	Critical Reading (paired passages)	13 Questions
Section 6	**Mathematical Reasoning**	**10 Questions**
15 Minutes	Multiple Choice	10 Questions
Section 7	**Verbal or Math**	**25–35 Questions**
30 Minutes		25–35 Questions
Total Testing Time 180 Minutes = 3 Hours	**Approximately 163–173 Questions**	

Note: The **order** in which the sections appear and the **number of questions** may vary, and there may be many forms of the test. Only three of the verbal sections — two 30-minute sections and one 15-minute section (about 78 questions) — and three of the math sections — two 30-minute sections and one 15-minute section (about 60 questions) — actually count toward your SAT I score.

One 30-minute section is a *pretest,* or *experimental,* section that does not count toward your score. The pretest or experimental section can be a verbal or math section and can appear **anywhere** on your exam. It does **not** have to be section 7. **You should work all of the sections as though they count toward your score.**

General Description

The SAT I is used along with your high school record and other information to assess your competence for college work. The test lasts three hours and consists of mostly multiple-choice type questions, with some grid-in questions. The verbal sections test your ability to read critically, to understand word relationships, and to understand words in context. The math sections test your ability to solve problems using mathematical reasoning and your skills in arithmetic, algebra, and geometry.

A Close Look at the SAT I	
Verbal	**Approximate Number of Questions**
Sentence Completions	19
Analogies	19
Reading	40
Total Verbal Questions	78
Math	
Multiple Choice	35
Quantitative Comparisons	15
Grid-Ins	10
Total Math Questions	60

The problems in each section of the SAT I are slightly graduated in difficulty within each question type, except for Critical Reading, which is not in order of difficulty. Many students make simple mistakes because they rush through the easy questions to get to the difficult ones. *Keep in mind that each question within a section is of equal value, so getting an easy question right is worth the same as getting a difficult question right.*

Special Notes for the SAT I

- Calculators may be used.
- On grid-in questions, there is no penalty for guessing.

- Verbal sections are reading and reasoning oriented.
- Math sections are reasoning oriented.

Questions Commonly Asked about the SAT I

Q: WHO ADMINISTERS THE SAT I?

A: The SAT I is part of the entire Admissions Testing Program (ATP), which is administered by the College Entrance Examination Board in conjunction with Educational Testing Service of Princeton, New Jersey.

Q: IS THERE A DIFFERENCE BETWEEN THE SAT I AND THE SAT II?

A: Yes. The SAT I assesses general verbal and mathematical reading and reasoning abilities that you have developed over your lifetime. The SAT II measures your proficiency in specific subject areas. The SAT II tests how well you have mastered a variety of high school subjects.

Q: CAN I TAKE THE SAT I MORE THAN ONCE?

A: Yes. But be aware that ATP score reporting is cumulative. That is, your score report will include scores from up to five previous test dates. It is not uncommon for students to take the test more than once.

Q: WHAT MATERIALS MAY I BRING TO THE SAT I?

A: Bring your registration form, positive identification, a watch, three or four sharpened Number 2 pencils, a good eraser, and your calculator. You may not bring scratch paper or books. You may do your figuring in the margins of the test booklet or in the space provided.

Q: IF NECESSARY, MAY I CANCEL MY SCORE?

A: Yes. You may cancel your score on the day of the test by telling the test center supervisor, or you may write, fax, or e-mail a cancellation to College Board ATP. See specific instructions for canceling your score in the *Student Bulletin*. Your score report will record your cancellation, along with any completed test scores.

Q: SHOULD I GUESS ON THE SAT I?

A: If you can eliminate one or more of the multiple-choice answers to a question, it is to your advantage to guess. Eliminating one or more answers increases your chance of choosing the right answer. To discourage wild guessing, a fraction of a point is subtracted for every wrong answer, but no points are subtracted if you leave the answer blank. On the grid-in questions, there is no penalty for filling in a wrong answer.

Q: HOW SHOULD I PREPARE FOR THE SAT I?

A: Understanding and practicing test-taking strategies helps a great deal, especially on the verbal sections. Subject-matter review is particularly useful for the math section. Both subject matter and strategies are fully covered in this book.

Q: WHEN IS THE SAT I ADMINISTERED?

A: The SAT I is administered nationwide six times during the school year, in November, December, January, March, May, and June. Some special administrations are given in limited locations.

Q: WHERE IS THE SAT I ADMINISTERED?

A: Your local college testing or placement office will have information about local administrations; ask for the *Student Bulletin*. The SAT I is administered at hundreds of schools in and out of the United States.

Q: HOW AND WHEN SHOULD I REGISTER?

A: A registration packet, complete with return envelope, is attached to the *Student Bulletin*. Mailing in these forms, plus the appropriate fees, completes the registration process. You should register about six weeks prior to the exam date.

Q: IS WALK-IN REGISTRATION PROVIDED?

A: Yes, on a limited basis. If you are unable to meet regular registration deadlines, you may attempt to register on the day of the test. (An additional fee is required.) You will be admitted only if space remains after preregistered students have been seated.

Q: CAN I GET MORE INFORMATION?

A: Yes. If you require information that is not available in this book, write or call one of these College Board regional offices.

Middle States:	3440 Market Street, Suite 410, Philadelphia, Pennsylvania 19104-3338. (215) 387-7600. Fax (215) 387-5805. or 126 South Swan Street, Albany, New York 12210-1715. (518) 472-1515. Fax (518) 472-1544.
Midwest:	1560 Sherman Avenue, Suite 1001, Evanston, Illinois 60201-4805. (847) 866-1700. Fax (847) 866-9280.
New England:	470 Totten Pond Road, Waltham, Massachusetts 02451-1982. (781) 890-9150. Fax (781) 890-0693.
South:	100 Crescent Centre Parkway, Suite 340, Tucker, Georgia 30084-7039. (770) 908-9737. Fax (770) 934-4885. or HighPoint Center, Suite 900, 106 East College Avenue, Tallahassee, Florida 32301-7732. (850) 222-7999. Fax (850) 224-3077.
Southwest:	4330 South MoPac Expressway, Suite 200, Austin, Texas 78735. (512) 891-8400. Fax (512) 891-8404.

West: 2099 Gateway Place, Suite 480, San Jose, California
95110-1017. (408) 452-1400. Fax (408) 453-7396.
or
Capitol Place, 915 L Street, Suite 1200, Sacramento,
California 95814. (916) 444-6262. Fax (916) 444-2868.

Taking the SAT I: Successful Overall Approaches

I. The "Plus-Minus" System

Many who take the SAT I won't get their best possible score because they spend too much time on difficult questions, leaving insufficient time to answer the easy questions. Don't let this happen to you. Because every question within each section is worth the same amount, use the following system, marking on your answer sheet:

1. Answer easy questions immediately.

2. Place a "+" next to any problem that seems solvable but is too time-consuming.

3. Place a "−" next to any problem that seems impossible.

Act quickly; don't waste time deciding whether a problem is a "+" or a "−."

After working all the problems you can do immediately, go back and work your "+" problems. If you finish them, try your "−" problems (sometimes when you come back to a problem that seemed impossible, you suddenly realize how to solve it).

Your answer sheet should look something like this after you finish working your easy questions:

```
  1. Ⓐ ● Ⓒ Ⓓ Ⓔ
+2. Ⓐ Ⓑ Ⓒ Ⓓ Ⓔ
  3. Ⓐ Ⓑ ● Ⓓ Ⓔ
−4. Ⓐ Ⓑ Ⓒ Ⓓ Ⓔ
+5. Ⓐ Ⓑ Ⓒ Ⓓ Ⓔ
```

Make sure to erase your "+" and "−" marks before your time is up. The scoring machine may count extraneous marks as wrong answers.

II. The Elimination Strategy

Take advantage of being allowed to mark in your testing booklet. As you eliminate an answer choice from consideration, make sure to mark it out in your question booklet as follows:

(A)
? (B)
(C)
(D)
? (E)

Notice that some choices are marked with question marks, signifying that they may be possible answers. This technique helps you avoid reconsidering those choices you have already eliminated and helps you narrow down your possible answers. These marks in your testing booklet do not need to be erased.

III. The "Avoiding Misreads" Method

Sometimes a question may have different answers depending upon what is asked. For example,

If $6y + 3x = 14$, what is the value of y?

The question may instead have asked, "What is the value of x?"

Or   If $3x + x = 20$, what is the value of $x + 2$?

Notice that this question doesn't ask for the value of x, but rather the value of $x + 2$.

Or   All of the following statements are true EXCEPT . . .

Or   Which of the expressions used in the first paragraph does NOT help develop the main idea?

Notice that the words EXCEPT and NOT change the above questions significantly.

To avoid "misreading" a question (and therefore answering it incorrectly), simply circle what you must answer in the question. For example, do you have to find x or $x + 2$? Are you looking for what is true or the exception to what is true? To help you avoid misreads, mark the questions in your test booklet in this way:

If $6y + 3x = 14$, what is the value of y?
If $3x + x = 20$, what is the value of $x + 2$?
All of the following statements are true EXCEPT . . .
Which of the expressions used in the first paragraph does NOT help develop the main idea?

And, once again, *these circles in your question booklet do not have to be erased.*

IV. The Multiple-Multiple-Choice Technique

Some math and verbal questions use a "multiple-multiple-choice" format. At first glance, these questions appear more confusing and more difficult than normal five-choice (A, B, C, D, E) multiple-choice problems. Actually, once you understand "multiple-multiple-choice" problem types and technique, they are often easier than a comparable standard multiple-choice question. For example,

If x is a positive integer, then which of the following must be true?

I. $x > 0$
II. $x = 0$
III. $x < 1$

A. I only
B. II only
C. III only
D. I and II only
E. I and III only

Because x is a positive integer, it must be a counting number. Note that possible values of x could be 1, or 2, or 3, or 4, and so on. Therefore, statement I, $x > 0$, is always true. So next to I on your question booklet, place a T for *true*.

T   I. $x > 0$
     II. $x = 0$
     III. $x < 1$

Now realize that the correct final answer choice (**A, B, C, D,** or **E**) *must* contain *true statement I*. This eliminates **B** and **C** as possible correct answer choices, because they do *not* contain true statement I. You should cross out **B** and **C** on your question booklet.

Statement II is *incorrect*. If x is positive, x cannot equal zero. Thus, next to II, you should place an F for *false*.

T   I. $x > 0$
F   II. $x = 0$
     III. $x < 1$

Knowing that II is false allows you to eliminate any answer choices that contain *false statement II*. Therefore, you should cross out **D**, because it contains false statement II. Only **A** and **E** are left as possible correct answers. Finally, you realize that statement III is also false, as x must be 1 or greater. So you place an F

next to III, thus eliminating choice **E** and leaving **A,** I only. This technique often saves some precious time and allows you to take a better educated guess should you not be able to complete all parts (I, II, III) of a multiple-multiple-choice question.

A Summary of General Strategies

- *Set a goal.* Remember that an average score is about 50% right.

- *Know the directions.*

- Go into each section *looking for the questions you can do and should get right.*

- *Don't get stuck* on any one question.

- Be sure to *mark your answers in the right place.*

- Be careful. *Watch out for careless mistakes.*

- *Don't make simple mistakes by rushing through the easy questions* to get to the difficult ones.

- *Know when to skip a question.*

- *Guess only if you can eliminate* one or more answers.

- Don't be afraid to *fill in your answer or guess on grid-ins.*

- Practice using the *"Plus-Minus" System,* the *Elimination Strategy,* the *"Avoiding Misreads" Method,* and the *Multiple-Multiple-Choice Technique.*

- *Remember to erase* any extra marks on your answer sheet.

PART I

ANALYSIS OF EXAM AREAS

INTRODUCTION TO VERBAL REASONING

The Verbal Reasoning sections of the SAT I consist of three basic types of questions: sentence completions, analogies, and critical reading.

One Verbal Reasoning section is 30 minutes in length and contains 30 questions—sentence completions, analogies, and two critical reading passages. Another verbal section is 30 minutes in length and contains 35 questions—sentence completions, analogies, and one longer critical reading passage. And finally, a third verbal section is 15 minutes in length and contains 13 to 15 critical reading questions based on two related (paired) passages. Some questions concern one passage or the other, and some questions concern both passages.

Although the order of the sections and the number of questions may change, at this time the three sections total about 78 to 80 questions that count toward your score. These three sections generate a scaled verbal score that ranges from 200 to 800. About 50% right should generate an average score.

The questions within each of the sentence completion and analogy sections are arranged in slight graduation of difficulty from easier to more demanding questions. Basically, the first few questions are the easiest; the middle few are of average difficulty; and the last few are difficult. There is no such pattern for the critical reading passages or questions.

Analogies

You will have approximately 10 analogy questions on each of two verbal sections on your exam, for a total of about 20 questions. In each section, the analogy questions are generally arranged in order from easier to more difficult.

Ability Tested

The analogy sections test your ability to understand logical relationships between pairs of words.

Basic Skills Necessary

The basic skills necessary for this section are a strong twelfth-grade vocabulary and the ability to distinguish relationships between words and ideas.

Directions

In each question below, you are given a related pair of words or phrases. Select the lettered pair that best expresses a relationship similar to that in the original pair of words.

Analysis of Directions

It is important that you focus on understanding the relationship between the original pair because this is really what you are trying to parallel. Notice that you are to select the best answer or most similar relationship. The use of the word *best* implies that there may be more than one good answer.

Suggested Approach with Samples

To begin, make sure you know just what both words in the first pair mean. A simple word like run may be a noun or a verb. As a noun, it may mean the act of running, or a score in a baseball game, or a flaw in panty hose. As a verb, it may be intransitive (without an object) and mean to move rapidly—to run in a race. Or it may be transitive (taking an object) and mean to control or direct—to run a business.

To determine what parts of speech the words in the original pair are, look at the five answer choices. All of the choices will be the same parts of speech as the original pair. So if you're not sure about a word in the first pair, the words in the choices will tell you what parts of speech are being used.

Sample

1. BOARDS : ROWBOAT ::

   A. disembarks : airplane

   B. enters : account book

   C. gets on : bus

   D. refuses : time

   E. hopes : fear

The word *boards* may be a verb meaning gets into or a noun describing the lumber from which *rowboats* are constructed. The best answer is **C.** The choices make clear that *boards* is a verb. The relationship between *boards* and *rowboat* is the same as the relationship between *gets on* and *bus*.

To help determine the relationship between the original pair, construct a sentence explaining how the two words are related.

Samples

2. SONNET : LITERATURE ::

    A. rhythm : poetry

    B. football : sport

    C. dancing : ballet

    D. research : biology

    E. acting : actor

The best answer is **B.** In this case, you might say to yourself, "A *sonnet* is a type of *literature*" and therefore recognize that the relationship here is between an example and the larger category. Now, doing the same thing with the answer choices, you will find that the correct answer **B** shows the same relationship. *Football* is a type of *sport*. This sentence can be expressed as "*Sonnet* is to *literature* in the same way as *football* is to *sport*."

3. ANONYMOUS : NAME ::

    A. careful : measurement

    B. quick : importance

    C. formless : shape

    D. large : body

    E. colorful : hue

The best choice is **C.** Your sentence should go something like this, "An *anonymous* person or thing is lacking a *name*." Choice **C** is best because it correctly completes the sentence: "*Anonymous* describes the lack of a *name* in the same way as *formless* describes the lack of *shape*."

Remember the standard analogy sentence: "A is to B in the same way as C is to D."

Try to make your sentence as precise as you can. Because some of the choices may be generally the same, a precise relationship may be required.

Sample

4. HEART : HUMAN ::

    A. tail : dog

    B. hand : child

    C. kitchen : house

    D. brick : wall

    E. engine : car

The best choice is **E.** While a *heart* is part of a *human,* a more precise relationship is that the *heart* is the essential, life-giving part of a *human.* Therefore, while every answer satisfies the part-whole relationship, **E** is the best answer, as the *engine* is the essential, life-giving part of the *car.*

> **Be sure to keep the order of the first pair like the order of your answer. Wrong answers may present a correct relationship but in the wrong order.**

Sample

5. SLEEPER : SMOKE ALARM ::

    A. snake : hiss

    B. air raid : siren

    C. car horn : driver

    D. sailor : lighthouse

    E. crossing : bell

The best choice is **D.** Here a *sleeper* is warned by a *smoke alarm* in the same way as a *sailor* is warned by a *lighthouse.* Choice **C** is incorrect because the order is reversed.

> **Occasionally, you will need to consider not only the primary relationship between the original words, but also a secondary relationship.**

Sample

6. VANDALIZE : PROPERTY ::

    A. judge : murderer

    B. criticize : creativity

    C. incinerate : combustibles

    D. slander : reputation

    E. courage : villainy

The best choice is **D.** "To *vandalize* is to destroy *property.*" This sentence tells you that the original relationship is between an action and its object: *Property* is the object of *vandalism.* Beyond this primary relationship, there are secondary relationships to consider. First, notice that destruction is the object of vandalism. Second, notice that it is unlawful destruction. Scanning the choices, you see that to *judge* can destroy (condemn to death) a *murderer;* to *criticize* can destroy (by discouraging) *creativity;* and *courage* can (under certain conditions) destroy *villainy.* But in none of these choices—**A, B,** or **E**—is the relationship between the terms typically or necessarily one of destruction. In choice **C,** to *incinerate* necessarily destroys *combustibles* (flammable objects); and in choice **D,** *slander* typically destroys *reputation.* So both of these are possible choices. However, only one of them refers to a typically unlawful act as well, choice **D.** Thus, taking the secondary relationships of the original pair fully into account, you should conclude that **D** is the best choice.

> **Remember that the second pair of words does not have to be from the same category, class, or type as the first pair of words.**

Sample

---

7. PUPPY : DOG ::

    A.   sapling : tree

    B.   canine : feline

    C.   cat : lion

    D.   poodle : terrier

    E.   collie : mutt

The best choice is **A.** Because in both pairs the first word is a youthful version of the second word, *sapling : tree* makes for a good analogy. It is not important that the first pair are animals and the second pair are plants. What is essential is the relationship.

Some Types of Relationships

The more practice you have working analogy problems, the more quickly you'll recognize some of the common relationships. Some relationships are given below. There are many other possibilities as well.

CLASSIFICATIONS: sorts, kinds, general to specific, specific to general, thing to quality or characteristic, opposites, degree, etc.

A broad category is paired with a narrower category

RODENT	:	SQUIRREL	::	fish	:	flounder
(broad category)		(narrower category)		(broad category)		(narrower category)

A person is paired with a characteristic

GIANT	:	BIGNESS	::	baby	:	helplessness
(person)		(characteristic)		(person)		(characteristic)

The general is paired with the specific

PERSON	:	BOY	::	vehicle	:	bus
(general)		(specific)		(general)		(specific)

A word is paired with a synonym of itself

VACUOUS	:	EMPTY	::	seemly	:	fit
(word)		(synonym)		(word)		(synonym)

A word is paired with an antonym of itself

SLAVE	:	FREEMAN	::	desolate	:	joyous
(word)		(antonym)		(word)		(antonym)

A word is paired with a definition of itself

ASSEVERATE	:	AFFIRM	::	segregate	:	separate
(word)		(definition)		(word)		(definition)

A male is paired with a female

COLT	:	FILLY	::	buck	:	doe
(male)		(female)		(male)		(female)

A family relationship is paired with a similar family relationship

FATHER	:	SON	::	uncle	:	nephew
(family relationship)		(family relationship)		(family relationship)		(family relationship)

A virtue is paired with a failing

FORTITUDE	:	COWARDICE	::	honesty	:	dishonesty
(virtue)		(failing)		(virtue)		(failing)

An element is paired with a greater degree

WIND	:	TORNADO	::	water	:	flood
(element)		(extreme)		(element)		(extreme)

A lesser degree is paired with a greater degree

HAPPY	:	ECSTATIC	::	warm	:	hot
(lesser)		(greater)		(lesser)		(greater)

The plural is paired with the singular

WE	:	I	::	they	:	he
(plural)		(singular)		(plural)		(singular)

STRUCTURALS: part to whole, whole to part, part to part, etc.

A part is paired with a whole

LEG	:	BODY	::	wheel	:	car
(part)		(whole)		(part)		(whole)

A whole is paired with a part

TABLE	:	LEGS	::	building	:	foundations
(whole)		(part)		(whole)		(part)

OPERATIONALS: time sequence, operations, stages, phases, beginning to ending, before to after, etc.

One element of time is paired with another element of time

DAY	:	NIGHT	::	sunrise	:	sunset
(time element)		(time element)		(time element)		(time element)

A time sequence relationship is expressed

START	:	FINISH	::	birth	:	death
(beginning)		(ending)		(beginning)		(ending)

A complete operation is paired with a stage

FOOTBALL GAME	:	QUARTER	::	baseball game :		inning
(operation)		(stage)		(operation)		(stage)

OVERLAPPING: Many analogies will overlap into more than one of the preceding basic types and will have to be analyzed by their purpose, use, cause-effect relationship, etc.

A user is paired with his or her tool

FARMER	:	HOE	::	dentist	:	drill
(user)		(tool)		(user)		(tool)

A creator is paired with a creation

ARTIST	:	PICTURE	::	poet	:	poem
(creator)		(creation)		(creator)		(creation)

A cause is paired with its effect

CLOUD	:	RAIN	::	sun	:	heat
(cause)		(effect)		(cause)		(effect)

A person is paired with his or her profession

TEACHER	:	EDUCATION	::	doctor	:	medicine
(person)		(profession)		(person)		(profession)

An instrument is paired with a function it performs

CAMERA	:	PHOTOGRAPHY	::	yardstick	:	measurement
(instrument)		(function)		(instrument)		(function)

A symbol is paired with an institution

FLAG	:	GOVERNMENT	::	cross	:	Christianity
(symbol)		(institution)		(symbol)		(institution)

A reward is paired with an action

MEDAL	:	BRAVERY	::	trophy	:	championship
(reward)		(action)		(reward)		(action)

An object is paired with an obstacle that hinders it

AIRPLANE	:	FOG	::	car	:	rut
(object)		(obstacle)		(object)		(obstacle)

Something is paired with a need that it satisfies

WATER	:	THIRST	::	food	:	hunger
(thing)		(need)		(thing)		(need)

Something is paired with its natural medium

SHIP	:	WATER	::	airplane	:	air
(thing)		(natural medium)		(thing)		(natural medium)

Something is paired with something else that can operate it

DOOR	:	KEY	::	safe	:	combination
(thing)		(operator)		(thing)		(operator)

An object is paired with the material of which it is made

COAT	:	WOOL	::	dress	:	cotton
(object)		(material)		(object)		(material)

Practice with Word Pairs

The following exercises are designed to increase your skill in determining the relationship between two words. This skill will help you predict the necessary relationship for a second pair of words in an analogy question.

For each item in this exercise, write a short sentence telling the relationship between the two words.

Example — PAW : CAT A paw is part of a cat.

1. PAPER : WOOD _____

2. ROOF : HOUSE _____

3. DETAIN : RELEASE _____

4. SLITHER : SNAKE _____

5. HEART : PUMP _____

6. SPY : COVERT _____

7. OASIS : DESERT _____

8. COLD : SHIVER _____

9. TYPEWRITER : RIBBON _____

10. MAGNET : IRON _____

11. TIRE : RUBBER _____

12. BINDERY : BOOKS _____

13. PEBBLE : BOULDER _____

14. METAL : ANVIL _____

15. DICTIONARY : MEANING _____

Possible Answers for Word Pairs

1. PAPER is made from WOOD.

2. The ROOF is the upper covering of a HOUSE.

3. DETAIN (hold up) is the opposite of RELEASE (let go).

4. SLITHER is the way a SNAKE travels.

5. The HEART performs the same function as a PUMP.

6. The activities of a SPY are COVERT.

7. An OASIS is a fertile area in a DESERT.

8. COLD makes people SHIVER.

9. A TYPEWRITER uses a RIBBON.

10. A MAGNET attracts IRON.

11. A TIRE is made mostly of RUBBER.

12. A BINDERY is a place where BOOKS are produced.

13. A PEBBLE is a very, very small BOULDER.

14. METAL is forged or shaped on an ANVIL.

15. A DICTIONARY is used to find the MEANING of words.

A Summary of Strategies for Analogy Questions

- Make sure you know what both words mean.

- Check the choices to see whether the words are being used as nouns, verbs, and so on.

- Construct a sentence explaining how the two words are related.

- Try to make your sentence as precise as you can.

- Be sure to keep the order of your answer like the order of the first pair.

- Sometimes you will need to consider the secondary relationship between the words, not only the primary relationship.

- Remember that the second pair of words does not have to be from the same category, class, or type as the first pair of words.

Sentence Completion

You will have approximately 10 sentence completions on each of two verbal sections of the exam for a total of about 20 questions. In each section, the sentence completions will basically be arranged in order from easy to difficult.

Ability Tested

This section tests your ability to complete sentences with a word or words that retain the meaning of the sentence and are structurally and stylistically correct.

Basic Skills Necessary

Good reading comprehension skills help in this section, as does a good twelfth-grade vocabulary.

Directions

Each blank in the following sentences indicates that something has been omitted. Consider the lettered words beneath the sentence and choose the word or set of words that best fits the whole sentence.

Analysis of Directions

Note that you must choose the best word or words. In cases where several choices might fit, select the one that fits the meaning of the sentence most precisely. If the sentence contains two blanks, remember that both of the words corresponding to your choice must fit.

Suggested Approach with Samples

After reading the sentence and before looking at the answer choices, think of words you would insert and look for synonyms of them.

Sample

> **1.** Money _____ to a political campaign should be used for political purposes and nothing else.
>
> *How would you fill in the blank? Maybe with the word given or donated? Now look at the choices and find a synonym for given or donated.*
>
>   **A.** attracted
>
>   **B.** forwarded
>
>   **C.** contributed
>
>   **D.** ascribed
>
>   **E.** channeled

The best choice is **C** *contributed*. It is the nearest synonym of given or donated and makes good sense in the sentence.

Look for signal words. Some signal words such as *however, although, on the other hand, but, instead, despite, regardless, rather than,* and *except* connect contrasting ideas.

Samples

> **2.** Most candidates spend _____ they can raise on their campaigns, but others wind up on election day with a _____.
>
>   **A.** all ... debt
>
>   **B.** whatever ... liability
>
>   **C.** everything ... surplus
>
>   **D.** every cent ... deficit
>
>   **E.** nothing ... war chest

The best choice is **C.** *But* signals that the first half of the sentence *contrasts* with the second half. The fact that most candidates spend *everything* (and end up with nothing) contrasts with those who end up with a *surplus*.

3. Can public opinion be influenced so that it _____ rather than encourages the proliferation of the sale of firearms?

   A. redoubles

   B. advances

   C. inverts

   D. impedes

   E. amplifies

The best choice is **D**. The clue here is *rather than encourages*. You need a verb whose object is *proliferation* and which means the opposite of *encourages*. The best choice is *impedes,* which means obstructs or retards. To *invert* is to turn upside down.

4. The critic praised the scenery of the film enthusiastically, but _____ her enthusiasm when she discussed its plot and characterizations.

   A. expanded

   B. established

   C. augmented

   D. declined

   E. tempered

The best choice is **E**. The *but* signals that you need a verb denoting something different from the enthusiasm of the first part of the sentence. Choices **A, B,** and **C** contradict the *but*. The verb *tempered* (moderated, reduced in intensity) is both more suitable in meaning and more idiomatic than **D**.

Other signal words such as *in other words, besides, and, in addition, also, therefore, furthermore,* and *as often* connect similar ideas or lead to a definition of the missing word.

Samples

5. The tools found in the New Mexico excavation are _____ as a single implement might have several edges, each with a different use.

   A. ancient

   B. primitive

   C. ferrous

   D. versatile

   E. reliable

The best choice is **D**. The tools the sentence describes have several edges and several uses, and the missing adjective should fit these conditions. *Versatile* means capable of many things.

---

6. This treatise is concerned only with the process unique to the period in question; therefore, no attempt has been made to _____ phenomena _____ to that era.

    A. include ... unrelated

    B. omit ... irrelevant

    C. re-create ... germane

    D. discuss ... essential

    E. evaluate ... pertinent

The best choice is **A**. The words in the first half of the sentence that are especially related to those to be filled in in the second half are *is concerned only* and *unique to the period.* The verb in the first blank is parallel to *is concerned* and describes the contents. Choices **A** *include,* **D** *discuss,* and possibly **E** *evaluate* are possible. The second blank needs an adjective that will make the phrase *to that era* parallel to *unique to the period.* Choice **B** *irrelevant* would work, but only **A** has the correct first word.

> **Watch for contrasts between positive and negative words. Look for words like *not, never,* and *no.***

Samples

---

7. A virtuous person will not shout _____ in public; he or she will respect the _____ of other people.

The first blank is obviously a negative word, something that a good person would not shout; the second blank is a positive word, something that a good person would respect. Here are the choices:

    A. obscenities ... feelings

    B. loudly ... comfort

    C. anywhere ... presence

    D. blessings... cynicism

    E. insults ... threat

The best choice is **A**. Choice **B** is neutral-positive; **C** is neutral-neutral; **D** is positive-negative; **E** is negative-negative. Only choice **A** offers a negative-positive pair of words.

8. The chairperson was noted for not being obstinate; on the contrary, the members praised her _____.

   A. resistance

   B. experience

   C. coherence

   D. verbosity

   E. flexibility

The best choice is **E**. The correct answer must describe a praiseworthy quality opposite to *obstinacy*. Although **B** and **C** are good qualities, only *flexibility* **E** means pliancy, the quality of being flexible.

Negative words can change the direction of the sentence, sometimes making the logic of the sentence more difficult to follow.

Sample

9. Tamino's choice of the quest to rescue Pamina is _____ not accidental, and he undertakes it with _____ and steadfastness.

   A. considered ... trepidation

   B. circumstantial ... valor

   C. intentional ... reluctance

   D. deliberate ... courage

   E. fortuitous ... ardor

The best choice is **D**. The adjective must be the opposite of *accidental*. The better choices are the synonyms of **A, C,** and **D**—*considered, intentional,* and *deliberate*. **B** and **E** do not fit this context. The second blank requires a noun that is like *steadfastness* or describes a sterling quality. Choice **A** *trepidation* means fear or hesitancy, and choice **C** *reluctance* means unwillingness. Neither will do, but **D** *courage* is what is needed.

Sample

> **10.** The _____ predictions of greatly decreased revenues next year have frightened lawmakers into _____ budget reductions.
>
>   **A.** encouraging ... sizeable
>
>   **B.** convincing ... minute
>
>   **C.** alarming ... negligible
>
>   **D.** optimistic ... huge
>
>   **E.** dire ... drastic

The best choice is **E.** Notice that trying the first word will help you eliminate answer choices **A, B,** and **D.** If the predictions are of decreasing funds and frightening to lawmakers, the first adjective must be either *alarming* **C** or *dire* **E** (fearful, dreadful). Now try the second choice to get the correct answer. Since the lawmakers have been scared into action, you can infer that the reductions are *drastic* **E** rather than *negligible* **C.**

Sometimes it is more efficient to work from the second blank first.

Samples

> **11.** Her parents were _____ when, despite losing the first three games, Sally _____ to win the set by a 6-3 score.
>
>   **A.** surprised ... failed
>
>   **B.** relieved ... came back
>
>   **C.** puzzled ... refused
>
>   **D.** alarmed ... attempted
>
>   **E.** delighted ... was unable

The best answer is **B.** There are no clues here to tell you which of the first words describes the reaction of the parents. Any of the five might work. But if you deal with the second blank first, you can see that the word *despite* makes it clear that Sally must *win the set*. Choice **B** *came back* looks like the best choice, although **D** is possible. That **B** is better is confirmed by the first word, as *relieved* is better than *alarmed.*

12. The merger will eliminate _____ and provide more _____ cross-training of staff.

    A. profit ... and more

    B. paperwork ... or less

    C. duplication ... effective

    D. bosses ... wasteful

    E. competitors ... aggressive

The best choice is **C.** The second blank is something that is provided. Chances are that the something provided is a positive word, and *effective* seems like a good choice. Reading choice **C** into the sentence, you will find that it makes good sense and is stylistically and structurally correct.

> If you don't spot any signal words or you don't know the meaning of some of the choices (or if you're just stumped), quickly read each answer choice in and see which sounds best. Sometimes this last method will help you at least eliminate some of the choices so that you can take an educated guess.

Sample

13. The fertile and productive fields are located at the _____ of the Gila and the Arizona Rivers and are _____ by waters from both.

    A. junction ... desiccated

    B. confluence ... irrigated

    C. bank ... drained

    D. source ... submerged

    E. end ... inundated

The best choice is **B.** The first word probably refers to the place where the rivers are close, since the fields are watered by both. Except for **C,** any of the four nouns is possible. *Confluence* means a flowing together, the place where two waterways come together. The past participle must refer to the watering of these fertile lands. So *desiccated* (dried up) or *drained* can be eliminated. If the fields are productive, *irrigated* (supplied with water) makes better sense than *inundated* or *submerged,* which suggest destructive flooding.

> A special reminder: Always read your answer into the sentence to make sure it makes sense. This will often help you avoid oversights or simple mistakes.

A Summary of Strategies
for Sentence Completion Questions

- After reading the sentence and before looking at the choices, think of words you would insert and look for synonyms of them.

- Look for signal words like *however, although,* and *but* that connect contrasting ideas.

- Look for signal words like *and, in other words,* and *therefore* that often connect similar ideas or lead to definitions of missing words.

- Watch for contrasts between positive and negative words.

- Negative words can change the direction of the sentence, sometimes making the logic of the sentence difficult to follow.

- Questions with two words missing should be attempted one word at a time.

- Sometimes it is more efficient to work from the second blank first.

- If you're stumped, quickly read each answer choice into the sentence and see which sounds best.

- Always read your answer into the sentence to make sure it makes sense.

Critical Reading

Critical reading appears in all three verbal sections—on two occasions, along with sentence completions and analogies as 30-minute sections and once alone as a complete 15-minute section. In one section, there are two passages—one 400 to 550 words in length, one 500 to 700 words in length—with from 5 to 9 questions following each passage. In another section, there is one longer passage, 750 to 850 words in length, followed by 12 or 13 questions. And in one section, there are two related, or paired, passages—totaling about 750 to 900 words in length—with 13 to 15 questions following the "double passage." There are questions on each of the two passages and questions on both of the passages. In total, there are four sets of questions on five passages. Each exam will contain about 40 critical reading questions.

Ability Tested

This section tests your ability to understand, interpret, and analyze reading passages on a variety of topics. The passages on each exam will come from four content areas: humanities, social sciences, natural sciences, and narrative (fiction or nonfiction).

The common types of questions are those that ask you

- about the meaning of a word or phrase in the passage.
- about the main idea, main point, purpose, or even a possible title of the passage.
- about information that is directly stated in the passage.
- about information that is assumed, implied, suggested, or can be inferred.
- to recognize applications of the author's opinions or ideas.
- to evaluate how the author develops and presents the passage.
- to recognize the style or tone of the passage.

Basic Skills Necessary

Students who have read widely and know how to read and mark a passage actively and efficiently tend to do well on this section.

Directions

Questions follow each of the passages below. Using only the stated or implied information in each passage and in its introduction, if any, to answer the questions.

Analysis of Directions

1. If you don't know the answer, take an educated guess or skip it.

2. Use only the information given or implied in a passage. Do not consider outside information, even if it seems more accurate than the given information.

Suggested Approaches with Sample Passages

- Base your answer on what you read in the passage, the introduction to the passage, or footnotes given following the passage. The passage must support your answer. All questions can and should be answered from information given or implied in the passage.

- Some good or true answers are not correct. Make sure that the answer you select is *what the question is asking for* according to the passage.

- Be sure to read all of the choices to make sure you have the best of the ones given. Some other choices may be good, but you're looking for the best. Watch out for "attractive distractors."

- Pace yourself. Don't get stuck on the passage or on any one question. If you have difficulty with one question, either take an educated guess by eliminating some choices or leave it blank and return to it briefly before you read the next passage (if there is more than one passage).

- When more than one reading passage is given, you may wish to first read the passage that is of more interest or familiarity to you and answer those questions before reading the next passage. But be careful if you skip a passage to mark your answers in the proper place on your answer sheet.

- You may wish to skim a few questions first, marking words which give you a clue about what to look for when you read the passage. This method can be especially helpful on unfamiliar passages. Try it on a variety of passages to see how it works for you.

- Read the passage actively, marking main points and other items you feel are important such as conclusions, names, definitions, places, and numbers. Make only a few such marks per paragraph. Remember, these marks are to help you understand the passage.

- On paired passages, the first questions will refer to Passage 1, the next group will refer to Passage 2, and the final group will refer to both passages as they relate to each other.

Sample Single Passage

The following sample passage is the length of the shortest passage on the exam, 400 to 550 words.

Questions 1–5 are based on the following passage.

Woodrow Wilson is usually ranked among the country's great presidents in spite of his failures to win Senate approval of the League of Nations. Wilson had yearned for a political career all his life; he won his first office in 1910 when he was elected governor of New Jersey. Two years later he was elected
(5) president in one of the most rapid political rises in our history. For a while Wilson had practiced law but found it both boring and unprofitable; then he became a political scientist of great renown and finally president of Princeton University. He did an outstanding job at Princeton but lost out in a battle with Dean Andrew West for control of the graduate school. When he was asked by the Democratic
(10) boss of New Jersey, Jim Smith, to run for governor, Wilson readily accepted because his position at Princeton was becoming untenable.

Until 1910 Wilson seemed to be a conservative Democrat in the Grover Cleveland tradition. He had denounced Bryan in 1896 and had voted for the National Democratic candidate who supported gold. In fact, when the Democratic machine
(15) first pushed Wilson's nomination in 1912, the young New Jersey progressives wanted no part of him. Wilson later assured them that he would champion the progressive cause, and so they decided to work for his election. It is easy to accuse Wilson of political expediency, but it is entirely possible that by 1912 he had changed his views as had countless other Americans. While governor of New
(20) Jersey, he carried out his election pledges by enacting an impressive list of reforms.

Wilson secured the Democratic nomination on the forty-sixth ballot after a fierce battle with Champ Clark of Missouri and Oscar W. Underwood of Alabama. Clark actually had a majority of votes but was unable to attract the necessary two-thirds. In the campaign, Wilson emerged as the middle-of-the-road candidate—between
(25) the conservative William H. Taft and the more radical Theodore Roosevelt. Wilson called his program the New Freedom, which he said was the restoration of free competition as it had existed before the growth of the trusts. In contrast, Theodore Roosevelt was advocating a New Nationalism, which seemed to call for massive federal intervention in the economic life of the nation. Wilson felt that the
(30) trusts should be destroyed, but he made a distinction between a trust and a legitimately successful big business. Theodore Roosevelt, on the other hand, accepted the trusts as inevitable but said that the government should regulate them by establishing a new regulatory agency. The former president also felt that a distinction should be made between the "good" trusts and the "bad" trusts.

1. The author's main purpose in writing this passage is to

   A. argue that Wilson is one of the great U.S. presidents.

   B. survey the differences between Wilson, Taft, and Roosevelt.

   C. explain Wilson's concept of the New Freedom.

   D. discuss some major events of Wilson's career.

   E. suggest reasons that Wilson's presidency may have started World War I.

The best choice is **D**. Choices **A** and **E** are irrelevant to the information in the passage, and choices **B** and **C** mention secondary purposes rather than the primary one.

2. The author implies which of the following about the New Jersey progressives?

   A. They did not support Wilson after he was governor.

   B. They were not conservative Democrats.

   C. They were more interested in political expediency.

   D. Along with Wilson, they were supporters of Bryan in 1896.

   E. They particularly admired Wilson's experience as president of Princeton University.

The best choice is **B**. In the second paragraph, Wilson's decision to champion the progressive cause after 1912 is contrasted with his earlier career, when he seemed to be a conservative Democrat. Thus, it may be concluded that the progressives, whom Wilson finally joined, were not conservative Democrats, as was Wilson earlier in his career. Choices **A** and **D** contradict information in the paragraph, while choices **C** and **E** are not suggested by any information given in the passage.

3. The passage supports which of the following conclusions about the progress of Wilson's political career?

   A. Few politicians have progressed so rapidly toward the attainment of higher office.

   B. Failures late in his career caused him to be regarded as a president who regressed instead of progressed.

   C. Wilson encountered little opposition once he determined to seek the presidency.

   D. The League of Nations marked the end of Wilson's reputation as a strong leader

   E. Wilson's political progress was aided by Champ Clark and Oscar Underwood.

The best choice is **A.** This choice is explicitly supported by the third sentence in the first paragraph in which we are told that Wilson *was elected president in one of the most rapid political rises in our history.*

---

4. At the end of the first paragraph in the phrase *his position at Princeton was becoming untenable* (line 11), the meaning of *untenable* is which of the following?

   A. Unlikely to last for ten years

   B. Filled with considerably less tension

   C. Difficult to maintain or continue

   D. Filled with achievements that would appeal to voters

   E. Something he did not have a tenacious desire to continue

---

The best choice is **C.** Although choice **E** may attract your attention because *tenacious* looks similar to *tenable,* the correct choice is **C,** which is the conventional definition of untenable.

---

5. From the passage, which of the following can be inferred about the presidential campaign of 1912?

   A. Woodrow Wilson won the election by an overwhelming majority.

   B. The inexperience of Theodore Roosevelt accounted for his radical position.

   C. Wilson was unable to attract two-thirds of the votes but won anyway.

   D. There were three nominated candidates for the presidency.

   E. Wilson's New Freedom did not represent Democratic interests.

The best choice is **D.** Choices **A, B,** and **C** contain information that is not addressed in the passage and can be eliminated as irrelevant. Choice **E** contradicts the fact that Wilson was a Democratic candidate. The discussion of Taft and Roosevelt as the candidates who finally ran against Wilson for the presidency supports choice **D.**

Related, or Paired, Passages

Questions 1–13 are based on the following passages.

The following two passages, written in 1960 and 1980, discuss some limitations of television programs.

Passage 1

Despite all this increase in commercialization some—but not all—advertising men have wanted still greater control of the total content of the shows they sponsor. One producer, John E. Hasty, who had made shows for both Hollywood and television, was quoted as arguing that television could reach its full potential as
(5)   an advertising medium only when advertising men produced the shows. "TV viewers cannot be regarded as an audience to be entertained," he said. "They are prospects . . . for what the sponsor has to sell. This fact constitutes the show's reason for being. . . . Thus in a TV production the selling motive stands as the dominant factor."

(10) He granted that showmen from Broadway and Hollywood might possess certain important skills that affect scripts, talent, music, and choreography, and that they might be generously endowed with skill and imagination. But, he asked, "Does this overbalance a seasoned adman's experience in mass selling?"

Many sponsors tend to view their television vehicles as total advertisements. The
(15) Institute for Advertising Research has begun offering a new measuring technique called Television Program Analysis which weights the total value of a program as an ad for the company. And an advertising trade journal in 1960 observed, "From all indications, a better tailoring of program type to advertiser, and commercial to program, is in the making. Taken together, commercials and programs in many
(20) cases accentuate the values of a high-consumption economy."

Marketing consultant Victor Lebow summed up the powerful appeal television has as a selling medium when he pointed out: "It creates a new set of conditions, impelling toward a monopoly of the consumer's attention. For the first time, almost the entire American consuming public has become a captive audience. . . . Television
(25) actually sells the generalized idea of consumption." Cases in point to support this theory that television sells "the generalized idea of consumption" might be the squeals and ahs of television audiences on panel shows when prizes such as stoves, refrigerators, rotisseries, and matched luggage are unveiled amid fanfare.

One might speculate also on what it does to a people's sense of values—espe-
(30) cially to children's—when discussions of significant events are followed on television by announcers who in often louder and more solemn voices announce a great new discovery for a hair bleach. Or, to consider another kind of juxtaposition, a broadcast appeal to aid hungry children in mid-1960 was followed immediately by a dog-food commercial.

Passage 2

(35) A story's "newsworthiness" is often determined by geography. Journalist Thomas Griffith describes how he and his colleagues used to argue over "how many people would have to be killed where to make news—three people in an auto wreck in your own town? Ten people drowning in a shipwreck in the English Channel; twenty-five in an avalanche in the Alps—and now the numbers increase sharply—

(40)   one hundred in an earthquake in Turkey; three hundred in the collapse of a bridge in Bolivia; one thousand in a typhoon off Calcutta; fifteen hundred in a fire in China?" News, it appears, is what happens in your own backyard.

This kind of reporting helps to magnify our provincialism. The average American, asked to draw a map of the world, would probably show the U.S.A. occupying
(45)   half of the land surface, with Europe and Russia and China and Africa tucked off in some untidy, insignificant corner of the globe.

Television news dissolves meaning in a wash of flashy images. The takeover of Afghanistan is summed up with a close-up view of a weeping widow, the problem of inflation with an image of the interior of a supermarket with a tight shot of the
(50)   price of hamburger, the importance of gold price fluctuations with footage of gold traders frantically jostling each other to get their orders in. A typical half-hour news broadcast has fifteen to twenty stories. Allowing time for commercial interruptions, that leaves an average of one minute per story. Congressman Michael Synar says this makes for a simple-minded electorate: "When I go home I have to
(55)   deal with people, and all they know of a four-hundred-page bill is one paragraph in the Sunday paper or a thirty-second TV spot. Issues don't break that way, but people just don't grasp the complexity."

The criterion for how much time a story gets, or whether it appears at all, is not its relative importance in world affairs. "We like stories that have wiggle," one net-
(60)   work executive says. "Sexy stories. Iran has wiggle. Defectors from the Bolshoi have wiggle. Stories about government agencies have no wiggle."

In the mind of many network news executives, the difference between a good news story and Marilyn Monroe's posterior is undetectable. Reporters are told to go after the human interest angle to a story—the "people factor"—rather than to
(65)   explore the how or why of a particular event. Researcher David Altheide once accompanied a reporter assigned to do a story on proposed alternatives to achieve racial integration. As they left the studio, the reporter explained how he planned to do the story: "Just barely give a background as to what these alternatives are. Explain the story over film of kids, bless their little hearts, who have no say in the
(70)   matter whatsoever, caught in a game of politics between their parents and the school board." The dramatic peg for the story was thus determined before the reporter had even arrived at the scene!

> **Notice that the line numbers of the passages continue from the first to the second passage. The first group of questions is typically about Passage 1.**

---

1. Which of the following best fulfills the ideal of the producer quoted in the first two paragraphs of Passage 1?

    A. Music television

    B. Educational television

    C. Home-shopping television

    D. Twenty-four hour television news

    E. Situation comedy

The best answer is **C**. Because the producer believes that selling is the real reason for television and sees the audience only as buyers, his ideal would be realized by home-shopping television where there is no pretense about buying and selling.

---

2. In line 13, *seasoned* means

    A. improved in quality.

    B. experienced.

    C. softened.

    D. flavored.

    E. changed in ability.

The best choice is **B**. Although a dictionary would list all five of these definitions of *seasoned*, here it means experienced or mature.

---

3. According to Passage 1, television programs may be expected to become

    A. increasingly dependent on comedy and games.

    B. more carefully crafted to sell a product.

    C. more dependent on Broadway and Hollywood directors.

    D. less dependent on depicting sex and violence.

    E. more carefully edited to suit children's viewing.

The best choice is **B**. The third paragraph speaks of *a better tailoring of program type to advertiser, and commercial to program.*

4. The sentence *Television actually sells the generalized idea of consumption* (lines 24–25) is best understood to mean that

    A. the more people watch television, the more likely they are to buy an advertised product.

    B. television is by and large indifferent to the ecological needs of the modern world.

    C. television, more than any other medium, is suited to the selling of products to a mass audience.

    D. game and panel programs which feature costly prizes pander to the greed of the audience.

    E. by reflecting the consumer values of society, television encourages its viewer to consume more.

The best choice is **E.** Although some of the statements here may be true or may express ideas that the passage is in sympathy with, only **E** specifically paraphrases or interprets the quotation of the question. By showing consumer products and luxury, television programs make the idea of owning more attractive to viewers.

5. In lines 32–33, the word *juxtaposition* means

    A. placing side by side.

    B. sequence of events.

    C. misunderstanding.

    D. unintentional joke.

    E. inappropriate comparison.

The best choice is **A.** A *juxtaposition* is a placing side by side.

The next group of questions is usually about Passage 2.

6. Which of the following best answers the question of the first paragraph of Passage 2, *how many people would have to be killed where to make news* (lines 36–37)?

    A. A small number of deaths will not make news.

    B. The number killed in an earthquake must be at least four times greater than the number killed in an avalanche.

    C. Local accidents are not news.

    D. The smaller the number of deaths, the closer to home they must be.

    E. Ten deaths in an air crash in East Africa would be more likely to make news than ten deaths in an explosion in West Africa.

The best choice is **D.** The question asks both *how many* and *where.* The passage makes clear that news, on television, *is what happens in your own backyard,* so a small number of local deaths would make news, but in distant areas, the size and spectacle would have to be much greater.

---

7. In the second paragraph of Passage 2, the point of describing the world map an average American would draw is to show that

   A. Americans know less about geography than the citizens of other countries.

   B. the United States occupies half of the world's land surface.

   C. Americans have a false notion of the importance of the United States.

   D. Americans are usually unable to identify the capital cities of other nations.

   E. Americans' knowledge of geography has improved since television became popular.

The best choice is **C.** The paragraph is about the provincialism, that is, the narrowness of outlook, of most Americans, and the map most Americans would draw reveals how little they know about the rest of the world and how much they overestimate their own importance. The passage does not tell us whether or not people elsewhere are more or less provincial.

---

8. In Passage 2 (line 55), the word *bill* means

   A. a statement of charges for services or goods.

   B. any written document with a seal.

   C. a list of things offered.

   D. a draft of a law.

   E. a bank note.

The best choice is **D.** As it is used here, *bill* means the draft of a law. The speaker is a Congressman speaking of his constituents' ignorance of legislation in Congress.

---

9. The phrase to *have wiggle* used in the fourth paragraph of Passage 2 is best taken to mean to

   A. have popular appeal.

   B. have overt sexual interest.

   C. involve stars of film or theater.

   D. move sinuously.

   E. have serious implications.

The best choice is **A.** As it is used here, *wiggle* is figurative, not literal, since *Iran has wiggle*. It stands for what has popular appeal.

---

10. Of the following aspects of television mentioned in Passage 2, which does the author believe should be foremost in news broadcasting?

    A. *flashy images* (line 47)

    B. *wiggle* (line 59)

    C. *the human interest angle* (line 64)

    D. *the 'people factor'* (line 64)

    E. *the how or why of a particular event* (line 65)

The best choice is **E.** The author would favor television news that deals with the how or why of events, although television programmers have preferred the four other options.

---

11. From Passage 2, it can be inferred that a news story on which of the following topics would be least likely to appear on television news broadcasts?

    A. The computer systems of the Internal Revenue Service.

    B. A local woman's entry in the Miss America contest.

    C. The marriage of a rock star and a soap opera actress.

    D. The effect of flooding on the Mississippi.

    E. Espionage in New York City.

The best choice is **A.** The computers of the IRS have little drama, human interest, or local appeal, so they are less likely to be considered newsworthy.

The last group of questions usually relies on both passages, comparing and contrasting general ideas and specific points.

---

12. Unlike Passage 2, Passage 1 is an attack upon television chiefly for its

    A. parochialism.

    B. materialism.

    C. superficiality.

    D. anti-intellectualism.

    E. lack of objectivity.

The best choice is **B.** The focus of Passage 1 is on materialism, television as a vehicle for selling. Passage 2 attacks the parochialism, superficiality, and anti-intellectualism of television news broadcasts.

13. Which of the following best describes the primary difference between the two passages?

    A. Passage 1 is serious in tone, while Passage 2 is comic and colloquial.

    B. Passage 1, on the whole, approves of television programming, while Passage 2 is harshly critical.

    C. Passage 1 is concerned with the way that television harms the moral values of all viewers, while Passage 2 is concerned with the failure to report world events accurately.

    D. Passage 1 is chiefly concerned with the influence of advertisers on television, while Passage 2 is chiefly concerned with the superficiality of television news programs.

    E. Passage 1 is concerned with the audience of television programs, while Passage 2 is concerned with the programs.

The best choice is **D.** Passage 2, though colloquial, is very serious in tone. Neither passage approves of television as it is. Passage 1 mentions value in only one paragraph. Both passages are concerned with audience and programs. Choice **D** is a reasonable summary of the two passages.

A Summary of Strategies
for Critical Reading Questions

■ Base your answer on what you read in the passage, the introduction to the passage, or footnotes given following the passage.

■ The passage must support your answer.

■ Some good or true answers are not correct. Make sure the answer you select is "what the question is asking."

■ Be sure to read all of the choices to make sure you have the best of the ones given.

■ Pace yourself. Don't get stuck on the passage or any one question.

■ When more than one reading passage is given, you may wish to first read the passage that is of more interest or familiarity to you and answer those questions first. When skipping, be extra careful to mark your answers in the proper place on your answer sheet.

■ You may wish to skim a few questions first, marking words which give you a clue about the passage before you read the passage.

■ Read the passage actively, marking main points and other items you feel are important.

■ On paired passages, the first questions will refer to Passage 1, the next group of questions to Passage 2, and the final group to both passages as they relate to each other.

Common Prefixes, Suffixes, and Roots

The following list should help you to arrive at definitions of unfamiliar words in the verbal sections of the SAT I and PSAT. These prefixes, suffixes, and roots apply to thousands of words.

Prefixes		
Prefix	**Meaning**	**Example**
pre-	before	precede
de-	away, from	deter
inter-	between	interstate
ob-	against	objection
in-	into	instruct
mono-	alone, one	monolith
epi-	upon	epilogue
mis-	wrong	mistake
sub-	under	submarine
trans-	across, beyond	transcend
over-	above	overbearing
ad-	to, toward	advance
non-	not	nonentity
com-	together, with	composite
re-	back, again	regress
ex-	out of	expel
in-	not	insufficient
pro-	forward	propel
anti-	against	antidote
omni-	all, everywhere	omniscient
equi-	equal, equally	equivalent
homo-	same, equal, like	homogenized
semi-	half, partly	semicircle
un-	not	unneeded
bi-	two	bicycle

Prefix	Meaning	Example
poly-	many	polymorphous
retro-	backward	retrograde
mal-	bad	malfunction
hyper-	over, too much	hyperactive
hypo-	under, too little	hypodermic

Suffixes		
Suffix	Meaning	Example
-able, -ible	able to	usable
-er, -or	one who does	competitor
-ism	the practice of	rationalism
-ist	one who is occupied with	feminist
-less	without, lacking	meaningless
-ship	the art or skill of	statesmanship
-fy	to make	dignify
-ness	the quality of	aggressiveness
-tude	the state of	rectitude
-logue	a particular kind of speaking or writing	prologue

Roots		
Root	Meaning	Example
arch	to rule	monarch
belli	war, warlike	belligerent
bene	good	benevolent
chron	time	chronology
dic	to say	indicative
fac	to make, to do	artifact
graph	writing	telegraph
mort	to die	mortal
port	to carry	deport
vid, vis	to see	invisible

INTRODUCTION TO MATHEMATICAL REASONING

The Mathematical Reasoning sections of the SAT I consist of three basic types of questions: regular multiple-choice questions, quantitative comparisons, and grid-ins.

One Mathematical Reasoning section is 30 minutes in length and contains 25 multiple-choice questions. Another math section is 30 minutes in length and contains 15 quantitative comparisons and 10 grid-ins (25 total questions). And finally, a third math section is 15 minutes in length and contains 10 multiple-choice questions. Although the order of the sections and the number of questions may change, at this time, the three sections total 60 math questions that count toward your score. These three sections generate a scaled math score that ranges from 200 to 800. About 50% right should generate an average score.

The math sections are slightly graduated in difficulty. That is, the easiest questions are basically at the beginning and the more difficult ones at the end. If a section has two types of questions, usually each type starts with easier problems. For example, a section starts with easy quantitative comparisons, and the last few quantitative comparisons become difficult before you start the grid-ins. The grid-ins start with easy questions and move toward the more difficult ones at the end.

- You will be given reference information preceding each Mathematical Reasoning section. You should be familiar with this information.

- You may use a calculator on the SAT I. Bring a calculator you are familiar with.

Using Your Calculator

The new SAT I allows the use of calculators, and the College Board (the people who sponsor the exam) recommends that each test taker take a calculator to the test. Even though no question will require the use of a calculator—that is, each question can be answered without a calculator—in some instances, using a calculator will save you valuable time.

You should:

- Bring your own calculator, because you can't borrow one during the exam.

- Bring a calculator even if you don't think you'll use it. Make sure that you are familiar with the use of your calculator.

- Make sure that your calculator has new, fresh batteries and is in good working order.

- Practice using your calculator on some of the problems to see when and where it will be helpful.

- Check for a shortcut to any problem that seems to involve much computation. But use your calculator if it will be time effective. If there appears to be too much computation or the problem seems impossible without the calculator, you're probably doing something wrong.

- Before doing an operation, check the number that you keyed in on the display to make sure that you keyed in the right number. You may wish to check each number as you key it in.

Be careful that you:

- Don't rush out and buy a sophisticated calculator for the test.

- Don't bring a calculator that you're unfamiliar with.

- Don't bring a pocket organizer, handheld mini-computer, laptop computer, or calculator with a typewriter-type keypad or paper tape.

- Don't bring a calculator that requires an outlet or any other external power source.

- Don't bring a calculator that makes noise.

- Don't try to share a calculator.

- Don't try to use a calculator on every problem.

- Don't become dependent on your calculator.

Take advantage of using a calculator on the test. Learn to use a calculator efficiently by practicing. As you approach a problem, first focus on how to solve that problem and then decide if the calculator will be helpful. Remember, a calculator can save you time on some problems, but also remember that each problem can be solved without a calculator. Also remember that a calculator will not solve a problem for you by itself. You must understand the problem first.

Basic Skills and Concepts You Should Be Familiar With

Arithmetic

- Operations with fractions
- Applying addition, subtraction, multiplication, and division to problem solving
- Arithmetic mean (average), mode, and median
- Ratio and proportion
- Number properties: positive and negative integers, odd and even numbers, prime numbers, factors and multiples, divisibility
- Word problems, solving for: percents, averages, rate, time, distance, interest, price per item
- Number line: order, consecutive numbers, fractions, betweenness

Algebra

- Operations with signed numbers
- Substitution for variables
- Working with algebraic expressions
- Word problems
- Solving equations
- Solving inequalities
- Basic factoring
- Working with positive exponents
- Working with positive roots
- Elementary quadratic equations

Geometry

- Vertical angles
- Angles in figures
- Perpendicular and parallel lines

- Perimeter, area, angle measure of polygons
- Circumference, area, radius, diameter
- Triangles: right, isosceles, equilateral, angle measure, similarity
- Special triangles: 30°-60°-90°, 45°-45°-90°
- Pythagorean theorem
- Volume and surface area of solids
- Coordinate geometry: coordinates, slope

Other Topics

- Interpreting graphs, charts, and tables
- Sequence problems
- Probability
- Special symbols or false operations
- Reasoning problems

The Mathematical Reasoning sections do NOT include:

- Time-consuming and tedious computations
- Fractional exponents
- Use of quadratic formula
- Complicated roots and radicals
- Geometric proofs

Multiple-Choice Questions

You should have a total of about 35 multiple-choice questions — 25 in one 30-minute section and 10 in a 15-minute section.

Ability Tested

The Mathematical Reasoning multiple-choice section tests your ability to solve mathematical problems involving arithmetic, algebra, geometry, and word problems by using problem-solving insight, logic, and the application of basic skills.

Basic Skills Necessary

The basic skills necessary to do well on this section include high school algebra and intuitive geometry. No formal trigonometry or calculus is necessary. Logical insight into problem-solving situations is also necessary.

Directions

Solve each problem in this section by using the information given and your own mathematical calculations, insights, and problem-solving skills. Then select the one correct answer of the five choices given and mark the corresponding circle on your answer sheet. Use the available space on the page for your scratchwork.

Notes

- All numbers used are real numbers.

- Calculators may be used.

- Some problems may be accompanied by figures or diagrams. These figures are drawn as accurately as possible EXCEPT when it is stated in a specific problem that a figure is not drawn to scale. The figures and diagrams are meant to provide information useful in solving the problem or problems. Unless otherwise stated, all figures and diagrams lie in a plane.

- A list of data that may be used for reference is included.

Analysis of Directions

1. All scratchwork is to be done in the test booklet; get used to doing this because no scratch paper is allowed into the testing area.

2. You are looking for the *one* correct answer; therefore, although other answers may be close, there is never more than one right answer.

Suggested Approach with Samples

Take advantage of being allowed to mark on the test booklet by always underlining or circling what you are looking for. This will ensure that you are answering the right question.

Samples

1. If $x + 6 = 9$, then $3x + 1 =$

   A. 3

   B. 9

   C. 10

   D. 34

   E. 46

You should first circle or underline $3x + 1$ because this is what you are solving for. Solving for x leaves $x = 3$ and then substituting into $3x + 1$ gives $3(3) + 1$, or 10. The most common mistake is to solve for x, which is 3, and *mistakenly choose* **A** as your answer. But remember, you are solving for $3x + 1$, not just x. You should also notice that most of the other choices would all be possible answers if you made common or simple mistakes. The correct answer is **C.** *Make sure that you are answering the right question.*

2. Together, a hat and coat cost $125. The coat costs $25 more than the hat. What is the cost of the coat?

   A. $25

   B. $50

   C. $75

   D. $100

   E. $125

The key words here are *cost of the coat*, so circle those words. To solve algebraically,

$$x = \text{hat}$$

$$x + \$25 = \text{coat (cost \$25 more than the hat)}$$

Together they cost $125.

$$(x + 25) + x = 125$$

$$2x + 25 = 125$$

$$2x = 100$$

$$x = 50$$

But this is the cost of the *hat*. Notice that $50 is one of the answer choices, **B.** Since $x = 50$, then $x + 25 = 75$. Therefore, the coat costs $75, which is choice **C.** *Always answer the question that is being asked.* Circling the key word or words will help you do that.

Substituting numbers for variables can often be an aid to understanding a problem. Remember to substitute simple numbers, since *you* have to do the work.

Samples

3. If $x > 1$, which of the following decreases as x decreases?

   I. $x + x^2$

  II. $2x^2 - x$

  III.

  A. I only

  B. II only

  C. III only

  D. I and II only

  E. II and III only

This problem is most easily solved by taking each situation and substituting simple numbers. However, in the first situation (I. $x + x^2$), you should recognize that this expression will decrease as x decreases. Trying $x = 2$ gives $2 + (2)^2 = 6$. Now, trying $x = 3$ gives $3 + (3)^2 = 12$. Notice that choices **B, C,** and **E** are already eliminated because they do not contain I. You should also realize that now you need to try only the values in II. Since III is not paired with I as a possible choice, III cannot be one of the answers.

Trying $x = 2$ in the expression $2x^2 - x$ gives $2(2)^2 - 2$, or $2(4) - 2 = 6$. Now, trying $x = 3$ gives $2 + 3^2 = 12$ or $2(9) - 3 = 15$. This expression also decreases as x decreases. Therefore, the correct answer is **D.** Once again, notice that III was not even attempted because it was not one of the possible choices. Be sure to make logical substitutions. Use a positive number, a negative number, or zero when applicable to get the full picture.

4. If x is a positive integer in the equation $12x = q$, then q must be

    A. a positive even integer.

    B. a negative even integer.

    C. zero.

    D. a positive odd integer.

    E. a negative odd integer.

At first glance, this problem appears quite complex. But let's plug in some numbers, and see what happens. For instance, first plug in 1 (the simplest positive integer) for x.

$$12x = q$$

$$12(1) = q$$

$$12 = q$$

Now try 2,

$$12x = q$$

$$12(2) = q$$

$$24 = q$$

Try it again. No matter what positive integer is plugged in for x, q will always be positive and even. Therefore, the answer is **A.**

Trying simple numbers in word problems can also be effective. Remember to select numbers that are easy to work with such as 1, 2, 10, or 100.

5. A corporation triples its annual bonus to 50 of its employees. What percent of the employees' new bonus is the increase?

    A. 50%

    B. 66⅔%

    C. 100%

    D. 200%

    E. 300%

The correct answer is **B.** Let's use $100 for the normal bonus. If the annual bonus was normally $100, tripled it would now be $300. Therefore, the increase ($200) is ⅔ of the new bonus ($300). Two-thirds is 66⅔%.

Sometimes you will immediately recognize the proper formula or method to solve a problem. If this is not the situation, try a reasonable approach and then work from the answers.

Samples

> **6.** Barney can mow the lawn in 5 hours, and Fred can mow the lawn in 4 hours. How long will it take them to mow the lawn together?
>
>   A.   5 hours
>
>   B.   4½ hours
>
>   C.   4 hours
>
>   D.   2⅖ hours
>
>   E.   1 hour

Suppose that you are unfamiliar with the type of equation for this problem. Try the "reasonable" method. Since Fred can mow the lawn in 4 hours by himself, it will take less than 4 hours if Barney helps him. Therefore, choices **A, B,** and **C** are ridiculous. Taking this method a little further, suppose that Barney could also mow the lawn in 4 hours. Then, together it would take Barney and Fred 2 hours. But since Barney is a little slower than this, the total time should be a little more than 2 hours. The correct answer is **D** 2⅖ hours.

Using the equation for this problem would give the following calculations:

$$\frac{1}{5} + \frac{1}{4} = \frac{1}{x}$$

In 1 hour, Barney could do ⅕ of the job, and in 1 hour, Fred could do ¼ of the job. Unknown $\frac{1}{x}$ is that part of the job they could do together in one hour. Now solving, you calculate as follows:

$$\frac{4}{20} + \frac{5}{20} = \frac{1}{x}$$

Cross multiplying gives $\qquad 9x = 20$

Therefore, $\qquad\qquad x = {}^{20}\!\!/_{9}$ or 2⅖

7. Circle O is inscribed in square ABCD as shown above. The area of the shaded region is approximately

   A. 10

   B. 25

   C. 30

   D. 50

   E. 75

The correct answer is **A.** Using a reasonable approach, you would first find the area of the square: $10 \times 10 = 100$. Then divide the square into four equal sections as follows:

Since a quarter of the square is 25, then the shaded region must be much less than 25. The only possible answer is choice **A** 10.

Another approach to this problem would be to first find the area of the square: $10 \times 10 = 100$. Then subtract the approximate area of the circle:

$$A = \pi\left(r^2\right) \cong 3\left(5^2\right) = 3\left(25\right) = 75.$$

Therefore, the total area inside the square but outside the circle is approximately 25. One quarter of that area is shaded. Therefore, $^{25}\!/_4$ is approximately the shaded area. The closest answer is **A** 10.

> **"Pulling" information out of the word problem structure can often give you a better look at what you are working with; therefore, you gain additional insight into the problem.**

Samples

---

8. If a mixture is ⅗ alcohol by volume and ⅘ water by volume, what is the ratio of the volume of alcohol to the volume of water in this mixture?

  A. ⅗

  B. ⅘

  C. ¾

  D. ⁴⁄₃

  E. ¼

The first bit of information that should be pulled out should be what you are looking for: *ratio of the volume of alcohol to the volume of water*. Rewrite it as *A:W* and then into its working form: ᴬ⁄w. Next, you should pull out the volumes of each: $A = ⅗$ and $W = ⅘$.

Now the answer can be easily figured by inspection or substitution. Using (⅗) ÷ (⅘), invert the bottom fraction and multiply to get ⅗ × ¼ = ¾. The ratio of the volume of alcohol to the volume of water is 3 to 4. The correct answer is **C**.

When pulling out information, actually write out the numbers and/or letters to the side of the problem, putting them into some helpful form and eliminating some of the wording.

---

9. Bill is ten years older than his sister. If Bill was twenty-five years of age in 1983, in what year could he have been born?

  A. 1948

  B. 1953

  C. 1958

  D. 1963

  E. 1968

The key words here are *in what year* and *could he have been born*. Thus the solution is simple: 1983 − 25 = 1958, answer **C**. Notice that you pulled out the information *twenty-five years of age* and *in 1983*. The fact about Bill's age in comparison to his sister's age was not needed, however, and was not pulled out.

> Sketching diagrams or simple pictures can also be very helpful in problem solving because the diagram may tip off either a simple solution or a method for solving the problem.

Samples

10. If all sides of a square are halved, the area of that square is

    A. halved

    B. divided by 3

    C. divided by 4

    D. divided by 8

    E. divided by 16

One way to solve this problem is to draw a square and then halve all its sides. Then compare the two areas.

Your first diagram

Halving every side

Notice that the total area of the new square will now be one-fourth of the original square. The correct answer is **C.**

11. If P lies on $\overline{ON}$ such that $\overline{OP} = 2\overline{PN}$ and Q lies on $\overline{OP}$ such that $\overline{OQ} = \overline{QP}$, what is the relationship of $\overline{OQ}$ to $\overline{PN}$?

    A. ⅓

    B. ½

    C. 1

    D. ²⁄₁

    E. ³⁄₁

A sketch would look like this:

It is evident that $\overset{\frown}{OQ} = \overset{\frown}{PN}$, so the ratio is ⅟₁, or 1. Or you could assign values on $\overset{\frown}{ON}$ such that $\overset{\frown}{OP} = 2\overset{\frown}{PN}$: $\overset{\frown}{OP}$ could equal 2, and $\overset{\frown}{PN}$ could equal 1. If Q lies on $\overset{\frown}{OP}$ such that $\overset{\frown}{OQ} = \overset{\frown}{QP}$, then $\overset{\frown}{OP}$ (2) is divided in half. So $\overset{\frown}{OQ} = 1$, and $\overset{\frown}{QP} = 1$. So the relationship of $\overset{\frown}{OQ}$ to $\overset{\frown}{PN}$ is 1 to 1. The correct answer is **C**.

---

12. What is the maximum number of milk cartons, each 2" wide by 3" long by 4" tall, that can be fit into a cardboard box with inside dimensions of 16" wide by 9" long by 8" tall?

    A. 12

    B. 18

    C. 20

    D. 24

    E. 48

The correct answer is **E**. Drawing a diagram, as shown below, may be helpful in envisioning the process of fitting the cartons into the box. Notice that 8 cartons will fit across the box, 3 cartons deep, and two "stacks" high:

$8 \times 3 \times 2 = 48$ cartons

---

13. If points P(1, 1) and Q(1, 0) lie on the same coordinate graph, which must be true?

    I.   P and Q are equidistant from the origin.

    II.   P is farther from the origin than P is from Q.

    III.   Q is farther from the origin than Q is from P.

    A. I only

    B. II only

    C. III only

    D. I and II only

    E. I and III only

First draw the coordinate graph and then plot the points as follows:

The correct answer is **B.** Only II is true. P is farther from the origin than P is from Q.

> **Marking in diagrams as you read the questions can save you valuable time. Marking can also give you insight into how to solve a problem because you will have the complete picture clearly in front of you.**

Samples

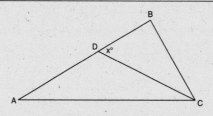

14. In the triangle above, CD is an angle bisector, angle ACD is 30°, and angle ABC is a right angle. What is the measurement of angle x in degrees?

   A. 30°

   B. 45°

   C. 60°

   D. 75°

   E. 80°

You should have read the problem and marked as follows: In the triangle above, CD is an angle bisector (*Stop and mark in the drawing*), angle ACD is 30° (*Stop and mark in the drawing*), and angle ABC is a right angle (*Stop and mark in the drawing*). What is the measurement of angle x in degrees? (*Stop and mark in or circle what you are looking for in the drawing.*)

Now, with the drawing marked in, it is evident that, since angle ACD is 30°, then angle BCD is also 30° because they are formed by an angle bisector (divides an angle into two equal parts). Since angle ABC is 90° (right angle) and angle BCD is 30°, then angle x is 60° because there are 180° in a triangle.

$$180 - (90 + 30) = 60$$

The correct answer is **C**. *Always mark in diagrams as you read descriptions and information about them. This includes what you are looking for.*

15. If each square in the figure above has a side length of 3, what is the perimeter?

    A. 12

    B. 14

    C. 21

    D. 30

    E. 36

Mark the known facts.

We now have a calculation for the perimeter: 30 *plus* the darkened parts. Now look carefully at the top two darkened parts. They will add up to 3. (Notice how the top square may slide over to illustrate that fact.)

The same is true for the bottom darkened parts. They will add up to 3.

Thus, the total perimeter is $30 + 6 = 36$, choice **E**.

If it appears that extensive calculations are going to be necessary to solve a problem, check to see how far apart the choices are and then approximate. The reason for checking the answers first is to give you a guide to how freely you can approximate.

Sample

16. Which of the following is the best approximation of $\dfrac{(.899 \times 55)}{9.97}$ to the nearest tenth?

   A. 49.1

   B. 7.7

   C. 4.9

   D. 4.63

   E. .5

Before starting any computations, take a glance at the answers to see how far apart they are. Notice that the only close answers are **C** and **D**. But **D** is not possible, since it is to the nearest hundredth, not tenth. Now, making some quick approximations, $.899 \cong 1$ and $9.97 \cong 10$, which leaves the problem in this form:

$$\frac{1 \times 55}{10} = \frac{55}{10} = 5.5$$

The closest answer is **C**. Therefore, it is the correct answer. Notice that choices **A** and **E** are not reasonable. You could also have used your calculator to obtain an exact answer and then rounded to the nearest tenth.

In some instances, it will be easier to work from the answers. Do not disregard this method because it will at least eliminate some of the choices and could give you the correct answer.

Sample

17. What is the approximate value of $\sqrt{1596}$?

    A. 10

    B. 20

    C. 30

    D. 40

    E. 50

Without the answer choices, this would be a very difficult problem, requiring knowledge of a special procedure to calculate square roots. By working up from the answer choices, however, the problem is easily solvable. Since $\sqrt{1596}$ means *what number times itself equals 1596*, you can take any answer choice and multiply it by itself. As soon as you find the answer choice that when multiplied by itself approximates 1596, you've got the correct answer. You may wish to start working from the middle choice, since the answers are usually in increasing or decreasing order. In the problem above, start with choice **C** 30. Since $30 \times 30 = 900$, which is too small, you could now eliminate **A, B,** and **C** as too small. But $40 \times 40 = 1600$, approximately 1596. Choice **D** is correct. If your calculator computes square roots, you could have used it and then rounded off.

18. If $x/4 + 2 = 22$, what is the value of x?

    A.   40

    B.   80

    C.   100

    D.   120

    E.   160

If you cannot solve this algebraically, you may use the *work up from your choices* strategy. But start with **C** 100. What if $x = 100$?

$$\frac{x}{4} + 2 = 22$$

$$\frac{100}{4} + 2 \overset{?}{=} 22$$

$$25 + 2 \overset{?}{=} 22$$

$$27 \neq 22$$

Note that since 27 is too large, choices **D** and **E** will also be too large. Therefore, try **A**. If **A** is too small, then you know the answer is **B**. If **A** works, the answer is **A**.

$$\frac{x}{4} + 2 = 22$$

$$\frac{40}{4} + 2 \overset{?}{=} 22$$

$$10 + 2 \overset{?}{=} 22$$

$$12 \neq 22$$

Since **A** is too small, the answer must be **B**.

---

19. What is the greatest common factor of the numbers 18, 24, and 30?

    A.   2

    B.   3

    C.   4

    D.   6

    E.   12

The correct answer is **D**. The largest number which divides evenly into 18, 24, and 30 is 6. You could have worked from the answers. But here you should start with the largest answer choice, since you're looking for the *greatest* common factor.

Some questions will need to be completely worked out. If you don't see a fast method but do know that you could compute the answer, use your calculator.

Samples

20. What is the final cost of a watch that sells for $49.00 if the sales tax is 7%?

    A. $49.07

    B. $49.70

    C. $52.00

    D. $52.43

    E. $56.00

The correct answer is **D.** Since the sales tax is 7% of $49.00,

7% of $49.00 = (.07)($49.00) = $3.43

The total cost of the watch is therefore

$49.00 + $3.43 = $52.43

Your calculator might have helped with these calculations.

Price List	
Top sirloin	$2.99 per pound or 2 pounds for $5.00
Filet mignon	$4.00 per pound
London broil	$1.79 per pound or 3 pounds for $5.00

21. Randy owns and manages Randy's Steakhouse. He needs to buy the following meats in order to have enough for the weekend business: 9 pounds of top sirloin, 8 pounds of filet mignon, and 7 pounds of London broil. What is the least amount Randy can spend to buy the meat he needs for the weekend business?

A. $97.00

B. $71.44

C. $66.78

D. $54.99

E. $34.78

The correct answer is **C.**

top sirloin:
8 pounds + 1 pound
= (4 × $5.00) + $2.99 (note: 2 pounds for $5.00)
= $20.00 + $2.99
= $22.99

filet mignon:
8 pounds
= 8 × $4.00
= $32.00

London broil:
6 pounds + 1 pound
= (2 × $5.00) + $1.79 (note: 3 pounds for $5.00)
= $10.00 + $1.79
= $11.79

Add to find the total: $22.99 + $32.00 + $11.79 = $66.78

Some problems may ask you to identify a sequence of either numbers or figures. If numbers are given, look for an obvious pattern (odd numbers then even numbers, increasing, decreasing, etc.). You may wish to first check for a common difference between the numbers.

Sample

1, 3, 6, 10, 15 . . .

22. Which of the following is the next number in the series given above?

A. 20

B. 21

C. 25

D. 26

E. 30

Notice that the pattern here is based on the difference between the numbers:

Therefore, the answer is **B** 21.

Some questions will involve probability and possible combinations. If you don't know a formal method, try some possibilities. Set up what could happen. But set up only as much as you need to.

Samples

23. What is the probability of throwing two dice in one toss so that they total 11?

A. $\frac{1}{6}$

B. $\frac{1}{11}$

C. $\frac{1}{18}$

D. $\frac{1}{20}$

E. $\frac{1}{36}$

You should simply list all the possible combinations resulting in 11, $(5 + 6)$ and $(6 + 5)$, and realize that the total possibilities are 36 (6×6). Thus the probability equals

$$\frac{\text{possibilities totaling } 11}{\text{total possibilities}} = \frac{2}{36} = \frac{1}{18}$$

Answer **C** is correct.

---

24. What is the probability of tossing a penny twice so that both times it lands heads up?

   A. ⅛

   B. ¼

   C. ⅓

   D. ½

   E. ⅔

The correct answer is **B.** The probability of throwing a head in one throw is

$$\frac{\text{chances of a head}}{\text{total chances} \,(1 \text{ head} + 1 \text{ tail})} = \frac{1}{2}$$

Since you are trying to throw a head *twice*, multiply the probability for the first toss (½) times the probability for the second toss (again ½). Thus, $\frac{1}{2} \times \frac{1}{2} = \frac{1}{4}$, and ¼ is the probability of throwing heads twice in two tosses. Another way of approaching this problem is to look at the total number of possible outcomes:

	First Toss	Second Toss
1.	H	H
2.	H	T
3.	T	H
4.	T	T

Thus, there are four different possible outcomes. There is only one way to throw two heads in two tosses. Thus, the probability of tossing two heads in two tosses is 1 out of 4 total outcomes, or ¼.

---

25. How many combinations are possible if a person has 4 sports jackets, 5 shirts, and 3 pairs of slacks?

   A.   4

   B.   5

   C.   12

   D.   60

   E.   120

The correct answer is **D**. Since each of the 4 sports jackets may be worn with 5 different shirts, there are 20 possible combinations. These may be worn with each of the 3 pairs of slacks for a total of 60 possible combinations. Stated simply, $5 \times 4 \times 3 = 60$ possible combinations.

> **Some problems may not ask you to solve for a numerical answer or even an answer including variables. Rather, you may be asked to set up the equation or expression without doing any solving. A quick glance at the answer choices will help you know what is expected.**

Samples

---

26. Which equation can be used to find the perimeter, P, of a rectangle that has a length of 18 feet and a width of 15 feet?

    A. $P = (18)(15)$

    B. $P = 18 + 15$

    C. $P = 2(15)(18)$

    D. $P = (2)15 + 18$

    E. $P = 2(15 + 18)$

The correct answer is **E**. The perimeter of a rectangle can be found by adding the length to the width and doubling this sum: $P = 2(15 + 18)$.

Harold's age is 3 years less than half Sue's age.

If Harold is 9 years old, how old is Sue?

27. Suppose S represents Sue's age. Which of the following equations can be used to find Sue's age?

    A. $9 = \frac{1}{2}(S) - 3$

    B. $9 - 3 = \frac{1}{2}(S)$

    C. $9 = 3 - \frac{1}{2}(S)$

    D. $3 - 9 = \frac{1}{2}(S)$

    E. $\frac{1}{2}(9) = S - 3$

The correct answer is **A**. Changing the word sentence into a number sentence (equation):

28. Rick is three times as old as Maria, and Maria is four years older than Leah. If Leah is z years old, what is Rick's age in terms of z?

   A. $3z + 4$

   B. $3z - 12$

   C. $3z + 12$

   D. $\dfrac{(z + 4)}{3}$

   E. $\dfrac{(z - 4)}{3}$

The correct answer is **C**. Since

$$z = \text{Leah's age}$$

$$z + 4 = \text{Maria's age}$$

$$3(z + 4) = \text{Rick's age}$$

$$3z + 12 = \text{Rick's age}$$

In some problems, you may be given special symbols that you are unfamiliar with. Don't let these special symbols alarm you. They typically represent an operation or combination of operations that you are familiar with. Look for the definition of the special symbol or how it is used.

Sample

29. If $\odot$ is a binary operation such that $a \odot b$ is defined as $\dfrac{a^2 - b^2}{a^2 + b^2}$, then what is the value of $3 \odot 2$?

   A. $^{-5}/_{13}$

   B. $^{1}/_{13}$

   C. $^{1}/_{5}$

   D. $^{5}/_{13}$

   E. 1

The correct answer is **D**. The value of $a \odot b =$

$$\frac{a^2 - b^2}{a^2 + b^2}$$

Simply replacing a with 3 and b with 2 gives

$$\frac{3^2 - 2^2}{3^2 + 2^2} = \frac{9 - 4}{9 + 4} = \frac{5}{13}$$

A Summary of Strategies for Multiple-Choice Math Questions

- Underline or circle what you are looking for.

- Substitute in simple numbers.

- Use a reasonable approach.

- Pull out information.

- Draw or sketch diagrams and figures.

- Mark in or label diagrams.

- Approximate.

- Work from the answers.

- Use your calculator.

- Look for obvious patterns in a series.

- Try some possible outcomes.

- Check the answer choices for procedure-type problems.

- Look for definitions in special-symbol problems.

- Finally, don't get stuck on any one problem!

Quantitative Comparison

You should have a total of about 15 quantitative comparison questions. They will typically appear as the first 15 questions in a 30-minute section which also includes about 10 grid-in questions.

Ability Tested

Quantitative comparisons test your ability to use mathematical insight, approximation, simple calculations, or common sense to quickly compare two given quantities.

Basic Skills Necessary

This section requires twelfth-grade competence in high school arithmetic, algebra, and intuitive geometry. Skills in approximating, comparing, and evaluating are also necessary. No advanced mathematics is necessary.

Directions

In this section, you will be given two quantities, one in column A and one in column B. You are to determine a relationship between the two quantities and mark —

A. if the quantity in column A is greater than the quantity in column B.

B. if the quantity in column B is greater than the quantity in column A.

C. if the quantities are equal.

D. if the comparison cannot be determined from the information that is given.

AN **E** RESPONSE WILL NOT BE SCORED.

Notes

1. Sometimes information concerning one or both of the quantities to be compared is given. This information is not boxed and is centered above the two columns.

2. All numbers used are real numbers. Letters such as a, b, m, and x represent real numbers.

3. In a given question, if the same symbol is used in column A and column B, that symbol stands for the same value in each column.

Analysis of Directions

The purpose here is to make a comparison. Therefore, exact answers are not always necessary. (Remember that you can tell whether you are taller than someone in many cases without knowing that person's height. Comparisons such as this can be made with only partial information — just enough to compare.) **D** is not a possible answer if there are values in each column because you can always compare values.

If you get different relationships, depending on the values you choose for variables, then the answer is always **D**. Notice that there are only four possible choices here. *Never* mark **E** on your answer sheet for quantitative comparison.

Note that you can add, subtract, multiply, and divide both columns by the same value and the relationship between them will not change. **Exception** — You should not multiply or divide both columns by negative numbers because then the relationship reverses. Squaring both columns is permissible as long as each side is positive. *Memorize the directions to save time in answering the questions.*

Suggested Approach with Samples

This section emphasizes shortcuts, insight, and quick techniques. Long and/or involved mathematical computation is unnecessary and is contrary to the purpose of this section.

Sample

	Column A	Column B
1.	$\dfrac{1}{3} \times \dfrac{4}{7} \times \dfrac{8}{9}$	$\dfrac{4}{7} \times \dfrac{1}{3} \times \dfrac{5}{9}$

Cancel each side as follows:

This leaves $\dfrac{8}{9}$ $\dfrac{5}{9}$

Since ⅝ is greater than ⅝, the correct answer is **A**.

Always keep the columns in perspective before starting any calculations. Take a good look at the value in each column before starting to work on one column.

Samples

Column A	Column B
2. $\sqrt[3]{7^6}$	2^8

After looking at each column (note that the answer could not be **D** because there are values in each column), compute the value on the left. Since you are taking a cube root, simply divide the power of 7 by 3 leaving 7^2, or 49. There is no need to take 2 out to the 8th power; just do as little as necessary.

$$2^2 = 4$$

$$2^3 = 8$$

$$2^4 = 16$$

$$2^5 = 32$$

STOP

It is evident that 2^8 is much greater than 49; the correct answer is **B**. Approximating can also be valuable while remembering to keep the columns in perspective.

Column A	Column B
3. $(.18)^{100}$	$(1.8)^{10}$

In column A, a fractional value (a value less than one) is multiplied by itself many times. So its value becomes increasingly smaller. (For example, ½ × ½ = ¼; ¼ × ½ = ⅛, and so forth). In column B, a number greater than 1 is multiplied by itself; its value grows larger. So column B is greater. Even a calculator wouldn't have helped here.

As you keep the columns in perspective, notice if the signs (+, –) in each column are different. If they are, you don't need to work out the problem.

Column A	Column B
4. $(-3)^4$	-3^4

Since $(-3)^4$ is to an even power, column A has a positive answer. Column B really means $-(3^4)$, which will give you a negative answer. Therefore, column A is greater.

Column A   **Column B**

5.

| $x + y$ | $a + b$ |

Since coordinates (x, y) are in quadrant III, they are both negative, so their sum is negative. Since coordinates (a, b) are in quadrant I, they are both positive, so their sum is positive. Therefore, column B is greater than column A.

Often, simplifying one or both columns can make an answer evident.

Sample

Column A   **Column B**

6.

| $a(b + c)$ | $ab + ac$ |

Using the distributive property on column A to simplify gives ab and ac. Therefore, the columns are equal.

If a problem involves variables (without an equation), substitute in the numbers 0, 1, and −1. Then try 1/2 and 2 if necessary. Using 0, 1, and −1 will often tip off the answer.

Samples

Column A   **Column B**

7.

| $a + b$ | ab |

Substituting 0 for a and 0 for b gives:

$$0 + 0 \qquad\qquad 0(0)$$

Therefore, $\qquad\qquad 0 \quad = \quad 0$

Using these values for a and b gives the answer **C**. But anytime you multiply two numbers, it is not the same as when you add them, so try some other values. Substituting 1 for a and −1 for b gives

$$1 + (-1) \qquad 1(-1)$$

Therefore,
$$0 \quad > \quad -1$$

and the answer is now **A.**

Anytime you get more than one comparison (different relationships) depending on the values chosen, the correct answer must be **D,** the relationship cannot be determined. Notice that if you substituted the values $a = 4$, $b = 5$; or $a = 6$, $b = 7$; or $a = 7$, $b = 9$; and so on, you would repeatedly have gotten the answer **B** and might have chosen the incorrect answer.

	Column A	Column B
	$x > y > 0$	
8.	$\dfrac{(x+y)^x}{x}$	$\dfrac{(x+y)^y}{y}$

Plug in values for x and y such that $x > y > 0$. For example, let $y = 1$ and $x = 2$. This gives

$$\dfrac{(2+1)^2}{2} \qquad \dfrac{(1+2)^1}{1}$$

$$\dfrac{(3)^2}{2} \qquad \dfrac{(3)^1}{1}$$

$$\dfrac{9}{2} \qquad \dfrac{3}{1}$$

Using these values, $\frac{9}{2}$ or $4\frac{1}{2}$ is greater than 3, so column A is greater. Using other values such that $x > y > 0$ will always give the same relationship. Column A is greater.

The use of partial comparisons can be valuable in giving you insight into finding a comparison. If you cannot simply make a complete comparison, look at each column part by part.

Sample

	Column A	Column B
9.	$\dfrac{1}{57} - \dfrac{1}{65}$	$\dfrac{1}{58} - \dfrac{1}{63}$

Since finding a common denominator would be too time consuming, you should first compare the first fraction in each column (partial comparison). Notice that $\frac{1}{57}$ is greater than $\frac{1}{58}$. Now compare the second fractions and notice that $\frac{1}{65}$ is less than $\frac{1}{63}$. Using some common sense and insight, if you start with a larger number and subtract a smaller number, it must be greater than starting with a smaller number and subtracting a larger number, as pointed out below.

The correct answer is **A**.

> Sometimes you can solve for a column directly, in one step, without solving and substituting. If you have to solve an equation or equations to give the columns values, take a second and see if there is a very simple way to get an answer before going through all of the steps.

Sample

Column A	Column B
$4x + 2 = 10$	

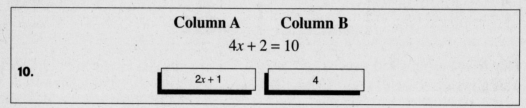

10.

Column A	Column B
$2x + 1$	4

Hopefully, you would spot that the easiest way to solve for $2x + 1$ is directly by dividing $4x + 2 = 10$ by 2, leaving $2x + 1 = 5$. Therefore,

$$5 \quad > \quad 4$$

Solving for x first in the equation and then substituting would also have worked out but would have been more time consuming. The correct answer is **A**.

> Marking diagrams can be very helpful for giving insight into a problem. Remember that figures and diagrams are drawn as accurately as possible, but just because something "looks" larger is not enough reason to choose an answer.

Sample

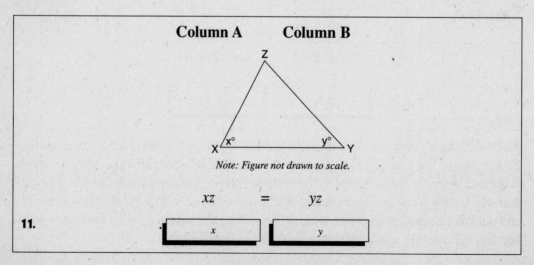

Column A   Column B

Note: Figure not drawn to scale.

$$xz \quad = \quad yz$$

11.

Column A	Column B
x	y

Even though x appears larger, this is not enough. Mark in the diagram as shown.

Notice that you should mark things of equal measure with the same markings, and since angles opposite equal sides in a triangle are equal, $x = y$. The correct answer is **C**.

> Drawing diagrams can be helpful in giving you insight into a problem or tipping off a simple solution. If you are given a description of a diagram or a geometry problem without a diagram, you may wish to make a sketch.

Sample

	Column A	Column B
12.	Perimeter of an equilateral triangle with side length $5x$	Perimeter of a square with side length $4x$

Simply sketch and label each geometric figure as follows:

Now it is evident that the perimeter of an equilateral triangle with side $5x$ is

$$3(5x) = 15x$$

The perimeter of a square with side $4x$ is

$$4(4x) = 16x$$

Since $4x$ and $5x$ represent lengths of sides, x must be a positive number. Therefore,

$$15x \quad < \quad 16x$$

The correct answer is **B**.

Check to see if you actually have enough information to make a comparison. Be aware of the information you are given and what you need.

Samples

13.

Column A	Column B
Distance traveled by an airplane going 200 miles per hour	Distance traveled by an airplane going 190 miles per hour

Since no information is given for the amount of time each of the airplanes was traveling, no determination can be made about their distances traveled. You cannot assume that each airplane traveled the same amount of time. The correct answer is **D.**

14.

Column A	Column B
Volume of right circular cylinder with diameter x	Volume of right circular cylinder with diameter $x + 1$

The correct answer is **D.** Since the height of each right circular cylinder is necessary to obtain the volume, no comparison can be made.

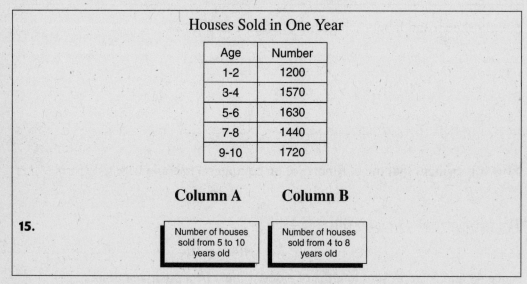

Houses Sold in One Year

Age	Number
1-2	1200
3-4	1570
5-6	1630
7-8	1440
9-10	1720

15.

Column A	Column B
Number of houses sold from 5 to 10 years old	Number of houses sold from 4 to 8 years old

The correct answer is **D.** Since the chart does not distinguish how many houses are 3 years old or 4 years old, the numbers cannot be determined, so no comparison can be made.

If you are given information that is unfamiliar to you and difficult to work with, change the number slightly (but remember what you've changed) to something easier to work with.

Sample

Since the 88° shown in the figure is unfamiliar to work with, change it to 90° for now so that you may use the Pythagorean theorem to solve for c.

$$a^2 + b^2 = c^2$$

Solve for c as follows:

$$(3)^2 + (4)^2 = c^2$$

$$9 + 16 = c^2$$

$$25 = c^2$$

Therefore, $$5 = c$$

But since you used 90° instead of 88°, you should realize that the side opposite the 88° will be slightly smaller, or less than 5. The correct answer is then **A, 5 > c.** (Some students may have noticed the 3:4:5 triangle relationship and not have needed the Pythagorean theorem.)

If you are given symbols that are unfamiliar to you, don't be alarmed. These new symbols typically represent an operation or some operations that you are familiar with. Look for the definition of the new symbol or how the symbol is used.

Sample

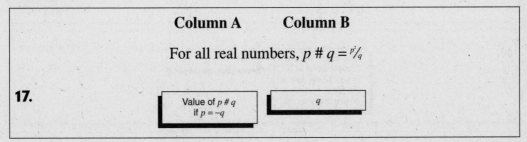

This new symbol # is defined as

$$p \# q = \frac{p^2}{q}$$

Now, since $p = -q$, simply plug in $-q$ in place of p.

$$p \# q = \frac{(-q)^2}{q} = \frac{q^2}{q} = q$$

Both columns are equal. The correct answer is **C**.

> On occasion, you will actually have to solve information centered between the columns or information in the columns. You should be able to work these quickly. *Remember, if it takes too long, you're probably doing it wrong.*

Samples

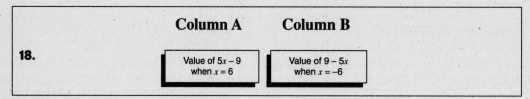

Column A	Column B
Value of $5x - 9$ when $x = 6$	Value of $9 - 5x$ when $x = -6$

18.

Quickly plug in the values given.

$5x - 9$	$9 - 5x$
$5(6) - 9$	$9 - 5(6)$
$30 - 9$	$9 + 30$
21 $<$	39

Therefore, **B** is the correct answer.

Column A	Column B
Number of ways to travel from A to B without going over a line more than once on any one attempt	7

19.

The following diagrams show eight ways of going from A to B, and there are more.

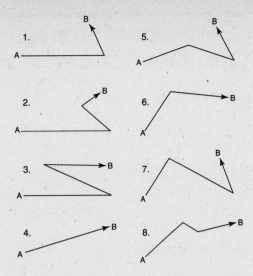

The correct answer is **A.**

Since quantitative comparison is designed for speed and shortcuts, long computation is normally not required, but if you don't see the fast method or if you need to do any involved calculations, remember that you can use a calculator on the test.

Samples

	Column A	Column B
20.	Number of seconds in two hours	Number of hours in 50 weeks

First set up the calculations as follows:

$$60 \text{ min} \times 60 \text{ sec} \times 2 \text{ hr} \qquad 24 \text{ hr} \times 7 \text{ days} \times 50 \text{ wk}$$

Using the calculator gives

$$7200 \quad < \quad 8400$$

The correct answer is **B.**

	Column A	Column B
21.	$(0.5)^4$	$(0.4)^5$

Using the calculator gives

$$.0625 \quad > \quad .01024$$

The correct answer is **A.**

A Summary of Strategies
for Quantitative Comparisons

- Use speed and shortcuts.

- Check each column before working.

- Watch the signs (+, −) in each column.

- Substitute in simple numbers (start with 0, 1, and −1).

- Simplify columns if possible.

- Compare part by part.

- Solve directly.

- Mark in or label diagrams.

- Draw or sketch diagrams or figures.

- Check the information given.

- Change the numbers slightly while working.

- Look for definitions in special-symbol problems.

- Do the work quickly.

- If no shortcut is evident, use a calculator if necessary.

- Don't get stuck on any one problem. If it takes too long, you're probably doing it wrong!

- **Remember:** Never choose **D** if there are values in each column.

- Always choose **D** if you get different comparisons depending on the values you use.

- When in doubt, plug in numbers.

Grid-In Questions

The SAT I has introduced a new and unfamiliar math question type — the grid-in question. This question type is very similar to the familiar multiple-choice question except that you will now solve the problem and enter your answer by carefully marking the circles on a special grid. You will not be selecting from a group of possible answers.

Since you will not be selecting from a group of possible answers, you should be extra careful in checking and double-checking your answer. Your calculator can be useful in checking answers. Also, keep in mind that answers to grid-in questions are given either full credit or no credit. There is no partial credit. No points are deducted for incorrect answers in this section. That is, there is no penalty for guessing or attempting a grid-in, so at least take a guess.

Ability Tested

The grid-in section tests your ability to solve mathematical problems involving arithmetic, algebra, geometry, and word problems by using problem-solving insight, logic, and application of basic skills.

Basic Skills Necessary

The basic skills necessary to do well on this section include high school algebra and intuitive geometry. No formal trigonometry or calculus is necessary. Skills in arithmetic and basic algebra, along with some logical insight into problem-solving situations, are also necessary. Understanding the rules and procedures for gridding in answers is important.

Before you begin working grid-in questions, it is important that you become familiar with the grid-in rules and procedures and learn to grid accurately. Let's start explaining the rules and procedures by analyzing the directions.

Directions with Analysis

The following questions require you to solve the problem and enter your answer by carefully marking the circles on the special grid. Examples of the appropriate way to mark the grid follow. (Comments in parentheses have been added to help you understand how to grid properly.)

Answer: 3.7

(Notice that the decimal point is located in the shaded row, just above the numbers. Also notice that the answer has been written in above the gridding. You should always write in your answer, but the filled-in circles are most important because they are the ones scored.)

Answer: ½

(Notice that the slash mark (/) indicates a fraction bar. This fraction bar is located in the shaded row and just above the decimal point in the two middle columns. Obviously, a fraction bar cannot be in the first or last column.)

Answer: 1½

Do not grid in mixed numbers in the form of mixed numbers. **Always** change mixed numbers to improper fractions or decimals.

Change to 1.5 or **Change to ³⁄₂**

(Either an improper fraction or a decimal is acceptable. Never grid in a mixed number because it will always be misread. For example, 1½ will be read by the computer doing the scoring as ¹¹⁄₂.)

Answer: 123

Space permitting, answers may start in any column. Each grid-answer below is correct.

(You should try to grid your answers from right to left, learning to be consistent as you practice. But space permitting, you may start in any column.)

Note: Circles must be filled in correctly to receive credit. Mark only one circle in each column. No credit will be given if more than one circle in a column is marked. Example:

Answer: 258

No credit!!!!

(Filling in more than one circle in a column is equivalent to selecting more than one answer in multiple choice. This type of answer fill-in will never receive any credit. Be careful to avoid this mistake.)

Answer: ⅞

Accuracy of decimals: Always enter the most accurate decimal value that the grid will accommodate. For example: An answer such as .8888 . . . can be gridded as .888 or .889. Gridding this value as .8, .88, or .89 is considered inaccurate and therefore **not acceptable.** The acceptable grid-ins of ⅞ are:

⅞   .888   .889

(Review "accuracy of decimals" a second time. Notice that you must be as accurate as the grid allows.)

Be sure to write your answers in the boxes at the top of the circles before doing your gridding. Although writing out the answers above the columns is not required, it is very important to insure accuracy. Even though some problems may have more than one correct answer, grid only **one answer.** Grid-in questions contain no negative answers.

(Fractions can be reduced to lowest terms, but it is not required as long as they will fit in the grid. You are not required to grid a zero before a fraction. For example, either .2 or 0.2 is acceptable. If your answer is zero, you are required only to grid a zero in one column. **Important:** If you decide to change an answer, be sure to erase the old gridded answer completely.)

Practice Grid-Ins

The following practice exercises will help you become familiar with the gridding process. Properly filled in grids are given following each exercise. Hand write and grid in the answers given.

Exercise 1

Answer: 4.5

Answer: .7

Answer: 22.7

Answer: ⅓

Answer: 4/7

Answer: ½

Answer: 3¼

Answer: 4½

Answer: 9¹/₇

Answers to Exercise 1

Answer: 4.5

or ½

Answer: .7

or ⁷⁄₁₀

Answer: 22.7

Answer: ⅓

or .333

Answer: ⁴⁄₇

or .571

Answer: ⁹⁄₂

or 4.5

Answer: 3¼

3¼ must be changed
to ¹³⁄₄ or 3.25

Answer: 4½

4½ must be changed
to ⁹⁄₂ or 4.5

Answer: 9¹⁄₇

9¹⁄₇ must be changed
to ⁶⁴⁄₇ or 9.14

Exercise 2

Answer: 0

Answer: 39

Answer: 1,542

Answer: 7⅓

Answer: 1

Answer: 685

Answer: .7272

Answer: .666 . . .

Answer: .222 . . .

Answers to Exercise 2

Answer: 0

Answer: 39

Answer: 1,542

Disregard the comma (,)

Answer: 7⅓

7⅓ must be changed
to ²²/₃ or 7.33

Answer: 1

Answer: 685

Answer: .7272

**.72 or .73 will
not be correct**

Answer: .666 …

**.666 will also be
correct or ⅔
(.66, .67, .7, or .6
will not be correct)**

Answer: .222 …

**⅔ will also be
correct (.2 or .22
will not be correct)**

Suggested Approaches with Samples

Most of the following strategies, described and suggested in the multiple-choice
section, will also work on grid-in questions.

- Circle or underline what you are looking for.

- Substitute numbers for variables to understand a problem.

- Try simple numbers to solve a problem.

- Pull information out of word problems.

- Draw/sketch diagrams or simple figures.

- Mark in diagrams.

- Use your calculator when appropriate to solve a problem.

You should also

- Make sure that your answer is reasonable.

- Jot down your scratch work or calculations in the space provided in your
  test booklet.

- Approximate or use your calculator to check your answers if time permits.

There are some specific items and strategies that should be noted for grid-in questions:

- There is no penalty for guessing on grid-in questions. Although it may be difficult to get an answer correct by simply writing in a wild guess, you should not be afraid to fill in your answer — even if you think it's wrong.

- Make sure to answer what is being asked. If the question asks for percent and you get an answer of 57%, grid in <u>57</u>, *not* .57. Or if a question asks for dollars and you get an answer of 75 cents, remember that 75 cents is .75 dollar. Grid in <u>.75</u> *not* 75.

- In some questions, more than one answer is possible. Grid-in only one answer. If you work out a question and get the answer $x > 5$, grid in 6, or 7, or 8 but *not more than one* of them.

- Some questions will have a note in parentheses ( ) that says, *Disregard the % sign when gridding your answer,* or *Disregard the $ sign when gridding your answer.* Follow the directions. If your answer is 68%, grid in <u>68</u>, or if it's $95, grid in <u>95</u>.

- Answers that are mixed numbers such as $3\frac{1}{2}$ or $7\frac{1}{4}$ must be changed to improper fractions ($3\frac{1}{2} = \frac{7}{2}$, $7\frac{1}{4} = \frac{29}{4}$) or decimals ($3\frac{1}{2} = 3.5$, $7\frac{1}{4} = 7.25$) before being gridded. Improper fractions or decimals can be gridded. Mixed numbers cannot. The scoring system cannot distinguish between $3\frac{1}{2}$ and $\frac{31}{2}$.

- Since you cannot work from answer choices that are given or eliminate given choices, you will have to actually work out each answer. The use of your calculator on some problems in this section could enhance the speed and accuracy of your work.

- Writing in your answer in the space provided at the top of the grid is for your benefit only. It's wise to always write in your answer, but remember, the grid-in answer is the only one scored. Be sure to grid accurately and properly.

Following are some sample grid-in questions. Consider for each how you would grid in the answer in the proper places on the answer sheet. Also consider when it would be appropriate to use a calculator to help you work out problems and to check the accuracy of your work.

Fraction and decimal forms are acceptable.

Sample

> **1.** If $\frac{1}{3}z - \frac{1}{4} = \frac{1}{2}$, then $z =$

The correct answer is $\frac{9}{4}$ or 2.25. (Either answer will receive full credit.) To solve for z you could multiply both sides of the equation by the lowest common denominator of 12 to get rid of the fractions as follows:

$$12(\tfrac{1}{3}z - \tfrac{1}{4}) = 12(\tfrac{1}{2})$$

$$4z - 3 = 6$$

$$4z = 9$$

$$z = \tfrac{9}{4} = 2.25$$

Your gridding is what counts. Your written-in answer is for your benefit. Be accurate.

Sample

> **2.** Acme Taxi lists the following rates on its door:
>
> $1.20 for the first ¼ mile
>
> $0.90 for each additional ¼ mile
>
> $6.00 per hour for waiting
>
> At these rates, if there was a 15-minute wait at the bank, how much will a 1.5-mile taxi trip cost? (Disregard the $ sign when gridding your answer.)

The correct answer is $7.20, gridded as 7.20. (You would **not** get credit for gridding 7.00, 7, 72, or 720, even if you had written the right answer above the grid circles.) You should solve the problem as follows:

At $6.00 per hour, a 15-minute (¼ hour) wait will cost $1.50. The first ¼ mile will cost $1.20. The remaining 1¼, or ⁵⁄₄ miles will cost 5(.90) = $4.50. The total bill will be the sum.

$$\$1.50 + \$1.20 + \$4.50 = \$7.20$$

Make sure that you answer the question. Your answer must be in the units asked for.

Sample

> **3.** If Gina completed ⅔ of her project in 12 days, how many days are needed to do the entire project?

The correct answer is 18. To solve, let n = number of days to complete the project. Then

$$\tfrac{2}{3} \cdot n = 12$$

$$n = 12 \div \tfrac{2}{3}$$

$$= \tfrac{12}{1} \cdot \tfrac{3}{2}$$

$$= \tfrac{36}{2}$$

$$= 18$$

The question asks for the number of *days* to complete the project. Therefore, 432 hours or 2⅔ weeks would *not* be correct.

> **Even if more than one answer is possible, grid in only one answer.**

Sample

> **4.** If $-4x + 12 > -16$ and $x > 0$, then what is one possible integer value for x?

The correct answer is 1, 2, 3, 4, 5, or 6. (Any of these answers would give you full credit. Do not grid more than one of them, however.) You could solve the problem as follows:

$$-4x + 12 > -16$$

Add -12 to each side

$$-4x + 12 + (-12) > -16 + (-12)$$

leaving $$-4x > -28$$

Dividing each side by (-4) gives

$$x < 7$$

(Note: The inequality sign is reversed.)

> **Fractions do not have to be reduced as long as they fit into the grid. (You probably should be in the habit of reducing them anyway, although that's not required here.)**

Sample

5. In the preceding parallelogram, if AB = BC = CD = DE, what is the ratio of the area of triangle ABF + triangle BCF to the area of triangle CDF + triangle DEF?

The correct answer is 1/1. (A 2/2 answer would also be acceptable because you don't have to reduce fractions.) You could mark the diagram and solve the problem as follows:

In parallelogram AEFG, if all the triangles marked have the same base and they all meet at F (giving them all the same height because the formula for the area of a triangle is ½ × base × height), then they all have equal areas. Therefore, the ratio of the area of triangle ABF + triangle BCF to the area of triangle CDF + triangle DEF is 2/2.

Follow directions when you're told to disregard the sign.

Sample

6. A basketball is fully inflated to 24 pounds per square inch. A football is fully inflated to 16 pounds per square inch. The air pressure in the basketball is what percentage of the air pressure in the football? (Disregard the % sign when gridding your answer.)

The correct answer is 150%, which is gridded as <u>150</u>. You could have worked the problem as follows:

To compute percentage, simply plug into the formula

$$\frac{\text{is number}}{\text{of number}} = \text{percentage}$$

Note that the question reads: The *air pressure in the basketball is* what percentage *of the air pressure in the football?* Therefore,

$$\frac{\text{air pressure in basketball}}{\text{air pressure in football}} = {}^{24}\!/_{16} = 1.50 = 150\%$$

Change your answer into a form to fit the grid if necessary.

Sample

> **7.** A collection of coins consists of 19 quarters, 21 dimes, and 16 nickels. What percentage of the coins is dimes? (Disregard the % sign when gridding your answer.)

The correct answer is 37.5. (Even though your answer could have been 37½, this answer could not have been placed in the grid.) You could solve the problem as follows: There is a total of 56 coins, of which 21 are dimes. The percentage of dimes (d) is

Set up a ratio: $\dfrac{d}{100} = \dfrac{21}{56}$

Reduce one side: $\dfrac{d}{100} = \dfrac{3}{8}$

Cross multiply: $8d = (3)(100)$

$$8d = 300$$

Divide by 8: $d = \dfrac{300}{8} = 37\frac{4}{8}$

$$d = 37\frac{1}{2} = 37.5$$

Use the calculator to your advantage.

Samples

> **8.** A speed of 75 miles per hour is approximately equivalent to how many feet per second?

The correct answer is 110. You could solve this problem as follows:

$$75 \text{ miles per hour} = \frac{75 \text{ miles}}{1 \text{ hour}}$$

Because 1 mile = 5280 feet and 1 hour = 60 minutes = 3600 seconds,

$$\frac{75 \text{ miles}}{1 \text{ hour}} = \frac{75 \times 5280 \text{ feet}}{1 \times 3600 \text{ seconds}}$$
$$= 110 \text{ feet per second}$$

9. What is ¾% of 540?

The correct answer is 4.05. You could solve this question as follows:

$$¾\% \text{ of } 540 = (¾\%)(540)$$
$$= (0.75\%)(540)$$
$$= (0.0075)(540)$$
$$= 4.05$$

Bowler	Score
1	148
2	163
3	157
4	148
5	181
6	164
7	157
8	131
9	182

10. The preceding chart shows how each of nine bowlers scored in the first game of a bowling tournament. Their average score was how much greater than their median score?

The correct answer is 2. To find the mean, simply total all scores and divide by 9. This step would give you $1431 \div 9 = 159$. To find the median, you must put the scores in order and count to the middle (the fifth spot).

$$131,148,148,157, \underline{157},163,164,181,182$$

The median is 157: $159 - 157 = 2$

A Summary of Strategies for Grid-In Questions

■ Realize that you receive no penalty for guessing.

■ Know the grid-in rules and procedures.

■ Change mixed numbers to improper fractions or decimals.

■ Understand that fractions and decimal forms are acceptable.

■ Write in your answer at the top, and remember that the grid-in part is scored.

■ Grid accurately and properly.

■ Be sure to answer the question being asked.

■ Grid in only one answer, even if more than one is possible.

■ Know that fractions do not have to be reduced if they fit.

■ Follow directions carefully.

■ Change your answer to fit the grid.

■ Use your calculator.

■ Draw figures.

■ Mark in diagrams.

■ Make sure that your answer is reasonable.

■ Jot down scratch work in the test booklet.

■ Check your answers.

■ Don't get stuck on any one problem!

Charts, Tables, and Graphs

The Mathematical Reasoning sections of the SAT I also include some questions about charts, tables, and graphs. You should know how to (1) read and understand information that is given (2) calculate, analyze, and apply the information given (3) spot trends and predict some future trends. When you encounter a chart, table, or graph, you should

- Focus on understanding the important information given.
- Not memorize the information, but rather refer to it when you need to.
- Review any additional information given with a graph (headings, scale factors, and legends, for example).
- Read the question and possible choices, noticing key words.
- Look for obvious large changes, high points, low points, and trends. Obvious information often leads to an answer.

Charts and Tables

Charts and tables are often used to give an organized picture of information, or data. Be sure that you understand what is given. Column headings and line items show important information. These titles give the numbers meaning.

Questions 1 and 2 are based on the following chart:

Burger Sales for the Week of August 8 to August 14		
Day	**Hamburgers**	**Cheeseburgers**
Sunday	120	92
Monday	85	80
Tuesday	77	70
Wednesday	74	71
Thursday	75	72
Friday	91	88
Saturday	111	112

1. On which day were the most burgers (hamburgers and cheeseburgers) sold?

   A. Saturday

   B. Monday

   C. Thursday

   D. Friday

   E. Sunday

The answer is **A.** Working from the answers is probably the easiest method of answering this question:

A.	Saturday	$111 + 112 = \underline{223}$
B.	Monday	$85 + 80 = 165$
C.	Thursday	$75 + 72 = 147$
D.	Friday	$91 + 88 = 179$
E.	Sunday	$120 + 92 = 212$

Another method is to *approximate* the answers.

---

2. On how many days were more hamburgers sold than cheeseburgers?

    A. 7

    B. 6

    C. 5

    D. 4

    E. 3

The correct answer is **B.** Hamburgers outsold cheeseburgers every day except Saturday.

Graphs

Information can be displayed in many ways. The three basic types of graphs you should know are *bar graphs, line graphs,* and *pie graphs* (or *pie charts*).

Bar Graphs

Bar graphs convert the information in a chart into separate bars or columns. Some graphs list numbers along one edge and list places, dates, people, or things (individual categories) along another edge. Always try to determine the *relationship* between the columns in a graph or chart.

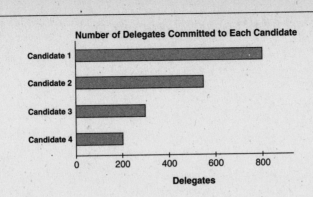

Number of Delegates Committed to Each Candidate

3. The preceding bar graph shows that Candidate 1 has how many more delegates committed than Candidate 2?

A. 150

B. 200

C. 250

D. 400

E. 550

The correct answer is **C**. Notice that the graph shows the *Number of Delegates Committed to Each Candidate,* with the numbers given along the bottom of the graph in increases of 200. The names are listed along the left side. Candidate 1 has approximately 800 delegates (possibly a few more). The bar graph for Candidate 2 stops about three quarters of the way between 400 and 600. Consider that halfway between 400 and 600 is 500, so Candidate 2 is at about 550:

$$800 - 550 = 250.$$

Line Graphs

Line graphs convert data into points on a grid. These points are then connected to show a relationship among the items, dates, and times, for example. Notice the slopes of the lines connecting the points. These lines show increases and decreases. The sharper the slope *upward,* the greater the *increase.* The sharper the slope *downward,* the greater the *decrease.* Line graphs can show trends, or changes, in data over a period of time.

Questions 4 and 5 are based on the following graph.

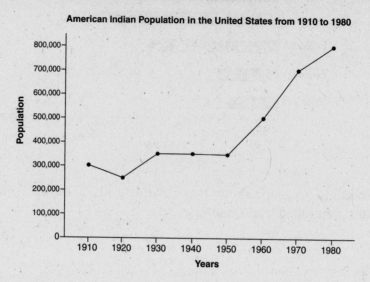

American Indian Population in the United States from 1910 to 1980

4. In which of the following years were there about 500,000 American Indians?

   A. 1930

   B. 1940

   C. 1950

   D. 1960

   E. 1970

The correct answer is **D.** The information along the left side of the graph shows the number of American Indians in increases of 100,000. The bottom of the graph shows the years from 1910 to 1980. Notice that in 1960 about 500,000 American Indians were in the United States. Using the edge of a sheet of paper as a ruler helps you see that the dot in the 1960 column lines up with 500,000 on the left.

5. During which of the following time periods was there a decrease in the American Indian population?

   A. 1910 to 1920

   B. 1920 to 1930

   C. 1930 to 1940

   D. 1960 to 1970

   E. 1970 to 1980

The correct answer is **A.** Because the slope of the line goes *down* from 1910 to 1920, there must have been a decrease. If you read the actual numbers, you will notice a decrease from 300,000 to 250,000.

Circle Graphs, or Pie Charts

A circle graph, or pie chart, shows the relationship between the whole circle
(100%) and the various slices that represent portions of that 100%. The larger the
slice, the higher the percentage.

Questions 6 and 7 are based on the following circle graph.

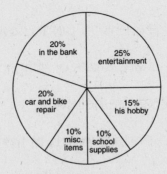

How John spends his monthly paycheck

6. If John receives $100 on this month's paycheck, how much will he put in
   the bank?

   A. $ 2

   B. $20

   C. $35

   D. $60

   E. $80

The correct answer is **B**. John puts 20% of his income in the bank, and 20% of
$100 is $20, so he will put $20 in the bank.

7. What is the ratio of the amount of money John spends on his hobby to the
   amount he puts in the bank?

   A. ⅙

   B. ½

   C. ⅝

   D. 5/7

   E. ¾

The correct answer is **E**. To answer this question, you must use the information in
the graph to make a ratio:

$$\frac{\text{his hobby}}{\text{in the bank}} = \frac{15\%}{20\%} = \frac{15}{20} = \frac{3}{4}$$

Notice that the ratio ¹⁵%/₂₀% reduces to ¾.

A Summary of Strategies for Charts, Tables, and Graphs

- Examine the entire graph, noticing labels and headings.

- Focus on the information given.

- Look for major changes — high points, low points, and trends.

- Don't memorize the chart, table, or graph; refer to it.

- Skimming questions can be helpful.

- Circle or underline important words in the question.

- Pay special attention to which part of the chart, table, or graph the question is referring to.

- If you don't understand the graph, reread the labels and headings.

- Don't get stuck on any one question!

PART II

PRACTICE-REVIEW-ANALYZE-PRACTICE

Three Full-Length Practice Tests

This section contains three full-length practice simulation SAT I tests. The practice tests are followed by complete answers, explanations, and analysis techniques. The format, levels of difficulty, question structure, and number of questions are similar to those on the actual SAT I. The SAT I is copyrighted and may not be duplicated, and these questions are not taken directly from the actual tests. The sections and question types in these practice exams are labeled by subject for your convenience in reviewing. They are not labeled on the actual SAT I.

When you take these exams, try to simulate the test conditions by following the time allotments carefully.

ANSWER SHEETS FOR PRACTICE TEST 1

(Remove This Sheet and Use It to Mark Your Answers)

SECTION 1

1 Ⓐ Ⓑ Ⓒ Ⓓ Ⓔ
2 Ⓐ Ⓑ Ⓒ Ⓓ Ⓔ
3 Ⓐ Ⓑ Ⓒ Ⓓ Ⓔ
4 Ⓐ Ⓑ Ⓒ Ⓓ Ⓔ
5 Ⓐ Ⓑ Ⓒ Ⓓ Ⓔ
6 Ⓐ Ⓑ Ⓒ Ⓓ Ⓔ
7 Ⓐ Ⓑ Ⓒ Ⓓ Ⓔ
8 Ⓐ Ⓑ Ⓒ Ⓓ Ⓔ
9 Ⓐ Ⓑ Ⓒ Ⓓ Ⓔ
10 Ⓐ Ⓑ Ⓒ Ⓓ Ⓔ
11 Ⓐ Ⓑ Ⓒ Ⓓ Ⓔ
12 Ⓐ Ⓑ Ⓒ Ⓓ Ⓔ
13 Ⓐ Ⓑ Ⓒ Ⓓ Ⓔ
14 Ⓐ Ⓑ Ⓒ Ⓓ Ⓔ
15 Ⓐ Ⓑ Ⓒ Ⓓ Ⓔ
16 Ⓐ Ⓑ Ⓒ Ⓓ Ⓔ
17 Ⓐ Ⓑ Ⓒ Ⓓ Ⓔ
18 Ⓐ Ⓑ Ⓒ Ⓓ Ⓔ
19 Ⓐ Ⓑ Ⓒ Ⓓ Ⓔ
20 Ⓐ Ⓑ Ⓒ Ⓓ Ⓔ
21 Ⓐ Ⓑ Ⓒ Ⓓ Ⓔ
22 Ⓐ Ⓑ Ⓒ Ⓓ Ⓔ
23 Ⓐ Ⓑ Ⓒ Ⓓ Ⓔ
24 Ⓐ Ⓑ Ⓒ Ⓓ Ⓔ
25 Ⓐ Ⓑ Ⓒ Ⓓ Ⓔ
26 Ⓐ Ⓑ Ⓒ Ⓓ Ⓔ
27 Ⓐ Ⓑ Ⓒ Ⓓ Ⓔ
28 Ⓐ Ⓑ Ⓒ Ⓓ Ⓔ
29 Ⓐ Ⓑ Ⓒ Ⓓ Ⓔ
30 Ⓐ Ⓑ Ⓒ Ⓓ Ⓔ

SECTION 2

1 Ⓐ Ⓑ Ⓒ Ⓓ Ⓔ
2 Ⓐ Ⓑ Ⓒ Ⓓ Ⓔ
3 Ⓐ Ⓑ Ⓒ Ⓓ Ⓔ
4 Ⓐ Ⓑ Ⓒ Ⓓ Ⓔ
5 Ⓐ Ⓑ Ⓒ Ⓓ Ⓔ
6 Ⓐ Ⓑ Ⓒ Ⓓ Ⓔ
7 Ⓐ Ⓑ Ⓒ Ⓓ Ⓔ
8 Ⓐ Ⓑ Ⓒ Ⓓ Ⓔ
9 Ⓐ Ⓑ Ⓒ Ⓓ Ⓔ
10 Ⓐ Ⓑ Ⓒ Ⓓ Ⓔ
11 Ⓐ Ⓑ Ⓒ Ⓓ Ⓔ
12 Ⓐ Ⓑ Ⓒ Ⓓ Ⓔ
13 Ⓐ Ⓑ Ⓒ Ⓓ Ⓔ
14 Ⓐ Ⓑ Ⓒ Ⓓ Ⓔ
15 Ⓐ Ⓑ Ⓒ Ⓓ Ⓔ
16 Ⓐ Ⓑ Ⓒ Ⓓ Ⓔ
17 Ⓐ Ⓑ Ⓒ Ⓓ Ⓔ
18 Ⓐ Ⓑ Ⓒ Ⓓ Ⓔ
19 Ⓐ Ⓑ Ⓒ Ⓓ Ⓔ
20 Ⓐ Ⓑ Ⓒ Ⓓ Ⓔ
21 Ⓐ Ⓑ Ⓒ Ⓓ Ⓔ
22 Ⓐ Ⓑ Ⓒ Ⓓ Ⓔ
23 Ⓐ Ⓑ Ⓒ Ⓓ Ⓔ
24 Ⓐ Ⓑ Ⓒ Ⓓ Ⓔ
25 Ⓐ Ⓑ Ⓒ Ⓓ Ⓔ

SECTION 3

1 Ⓐ Ⓑ Ⓒ Ⓓ Ⓔ
2 Ⓐ Ⓑ Ⓒ Ⓓ Ⓔ
3 Ⓐ Ⓑ Ⓒ Ⓓ Ⓔ
4 Ⓐ Ⓑ Ⓒ Ⓓ Ⓔ
5 Ⓐ Ⓑ Ⓒ Ⓓ Ⓔ
6 Ⓐ Ⓑ Ⓒ Ⓓ Ⓔ
7 Ⓐ Ⓑ Ⓒ Ⓓ Ⓔ
8 Ⓐ Ⓑ Ⓒ Ⓓ Ⓔ
9 Ⓐ Ⓑ Ⓒ Ⓓ Ⓔ
10 Ⓐ Ⓑ Ⓒ Ⓓ Ⓔ
11 Ⓐ Ⓑ Ⓒ Ⓓ Ⓔ
12 Ⓐ Ⓑ Ⓒ Ⓓ Ⓔ
13 Ⓐ Ⓑ Ⓒ Ⓓ Ⓔ
14 Ⓐ Ⓑ Ⓒ Ⓓ Ⓔ
15 Ⓐ Ⓑ Ⓒ Ⓓ Ⓔ
16 Ⓐ Ⓑ Ⓒ Ⓓ Ⓔ
17 Ⓐ Ⓑ Ⓒ Ⓓ Ⓔ
18 Ⓐ Ⓑ Ⓒ Ⓓ Ⓔ
19 Ⓐ Ⓑ Ⓒ Ⓓ Ⓔ
20 Ⓐ Ⓑ Ⓒ Ⓓ Ⓔ
21 Ⓐ Ⓑ Ⓒ Ⓓ Ⓔ
22 Ⓐ Ⓑ Ⓒ Ⓓ Ⓔ
23 Ⓐ Ⓑ Ⓒ Ⓓ Ⓔ
24 Ⓐ Ⓑ Ⓒ Ⓓ Ⓔ
25 Ⓐ Ⓑ Ⓒ Ⓓ Ⓔ
26 Ⓐ Ⓑ Ⓒ Ⓓ Ⓔ
27 Ⓐ Ⓑ Ⓒ Ⓓ Ⓔ
28 Ⓐ Ⓑ Ⓒ Ⓓ Ⓔ
29 Ⓐ Ⓑ Ⓒ Ⓓ Ⓔ
30 Ⓐ Ⓑ Ⓒ Ⓓ Ⓔ
31 Ⓐ Ⓑ Ⓒ Ⓓ Ⓔ
32 Ⓐ Ⓑ Ⓒ Ⓓ Ⓔ
33 Ⓐ Ⓑ Ⓒ Ⓓ Ⓔ
34 Ⓐ Ⓑ Ⓒ Ⓓ Ⓔ
35 Ⓐ Ⓑ Ⓒ Ⓓ Ⓔ

SECTION 4

1 Ⓐ Ⓑ Ⓒ Ⓓ Ⓔ
2 Ⓐ Ⓑ Ⓒ Ⓓ Ⓔ
3 Ⓐ Ⓑ Ⓒ Ⓓ Ⓔ
4 Ⓐ Ⓑ Ⓒ Ⓓ Ⓔ
5 Ⓐ Ⓑ Ⓒ Ⓓ Ⓔ
6 Ⓐ Ⓑ Ⓒ Ⓓ Ⓔ
7 Ⓐ Ⓑ Ⓒ Ⓓ Ⓔ
8 Ⓐ Ⓑ Ⓒ Ⓓ Ⓔ
9 Ⓐ Ⓑ Ⓒ Ⓓ Ⓔ
10 Ⓐ Ⓑ Ⓒ Ⓓ Ⓔ
11 Ⓐ Ⓑ Ⓒ Ⓓ Ⓔ
12 Ⓐ Ⓑ Ⓒ Ⓓ Ⓔ
13 Ⓐ Ⓑ Ⓒ Ⓓ Ⓔ
14 Ⓐ Ⓑ Ⓒ Ⓓ Ⓔ
15 Ⓐ Ⓑ Ⓒ Ⓓ Ⓔ

CUT HERE

(Remove This Sheet and Use It to Mark Your Answers)

CUT HERE

(Remove This Sheet and Use It to Mark Your Answers)

24

25

CUT HERE

SECTION 5

1 Ⓐ Ⓑ Ⓒ Ⓓ Ⓔ
2 Ⓐ Ⓑ Ⓒ Ⓓ Ⓔ
3 Ⓐ Ⓑ Ⓒ Ⓓ Ⓔ
4 Ⓐ Ⓑ Ⓒ Ⓓ Ⓔ
5 Ⓐ Ⓑ Ⓒ Ⓓ Ⓔ
6 Ⓐ Ⓑ Ⓒ Ⓓ Ⓔ
7 Ⓐ Ⓑ Ⓒ Ⓓ Ⓔ
8 Ⓐ Ⓑ Ⓒ Ⓓ Ⓔ
9 Ⓐ Ⓑ Ⓒ Ⓓ Ⓔ
10 Ⓐ Ⓑ Ⓒ Ⓓ Ⓔ
11 Ⓐ Ⓑ Ⓒ Ⓓ Ⓔ
12 Ⓐ Ⓑ Ⓒ Ⓓ Ⓔ
13 Ⓐ Ⓑ Ⓒ Ⓓ Ⓔ
14 Ⓐ Ⓑ Ⓒ Ⓓ Ⓔ
15 Ⓐ Ⓑ Ⓒ Ⓓ Ⓔ

SECTION 6

1 Ⓐ Ⓑ Ⓒ Ⓓ Ⓔ
2 Ⓐ Ⓑ Ⓒ Ⓓ Ⓔ
3 Ⓐ Ⓑ Ⓒ Ⓓ Ⓔ
4 Ⓐ Ⓑ Ⓒ Ⓓ Ⓔ
5 Ⓐ Ⓑ Ⓒ Ⓓ Ⓔ
6 Ⓐ Ⓑ Ⓒ Ⓓ Ⓔ
7 Ⓐ Ⓑ Ⓒ Ⓓ Ⓔ
8 Ⓐ Ⓑ Ⓒ Ⓓ Ⓔ
9 Ⓐ Ⓑ Ⓒ Ⓓ Ⓔ
10 Ⓐ Ⓑ Ⓒ Ⓓ Ⓔ

SECTION 7

1 Ⓐ Ⓑ Ⓒ Ⓓ Ⓔ
2 Ⓐ Ⓑ Ⓒ Ⓓ Ⓔ
3 Ⓐ Ⓑ Ⓒ Ⓓ Ⓔ
4 Ⓐ Ⓑ Ⓒ Ⓓ Ⓔ
5 Ⓐ Ⓑ Ⓒ Ⓓ Ⓔ
6 Ⓐ Ⓑ Ⓒ Ⓓ Ⓔ
7 Ⓐ Ⓑ Ⓒ Ⓓ Ⓔ
8 Ⓐ Ⓑ Ⓒ Ⓓ Ⓔ
9 Ⓐ Ⓑ Ⓒ Ⓓ Ⓔ
10 Ⓐ Ⓑ Ⓒ Ⓓ Ⓔ
11 Ⓐ Ⓑ Ⓒ Ⓓ Ⓔ
12 Ⓐ Ⓑ Ⓒ Ⓓ Ⓔ
13 Ⓐ Ⓑ Ⓒ Ⓓ Ⓔ
14 Ⓐ Ⓑ Ⓒ Ⓓ Ⓔ
15 Ⓐ Ⓑ Ⓒ Ⓓ Ⓔ
16 Ⓐ Ⓑ Ⓒ Ⓓ Ⓔ
17 Ⓐ Ⓑ Ⓒ Ⓓ Ⓔ
18 Ⓐ Ⓑ Ⓒ Ⓓ Ⓔ
19 Ⓐ Ⓑ Ⓒ Ⓓ Ⓔ
20 Ⓐ Ⓑ Ⓒ Ⓓ Ⓔ
21 Ⓐ Ⓑ Ⓒ Ⓓ Ⓔ
22 Ⓐ Ⓑ Ⓒ Ⓓ Ⓔ
23 Ⓐ Ⓑ Ⓒ Ⓓ Ⓔ
24 Ⓐ Ⓑ Ⓒ Ⓓ Ⓔ
25 Ⓐ Ⓑ Ⓒ Ⓓ Ⓔ

Section 1: Verbal Reasoning

Time: 30 Minutes

30 Questions

In this section, choose the best answer for each question and blacken the corresponding space on the answer sheet.

Sentence Completion

Directions: Each blank in the following sentences indicates that something has been omitted. Consider the lettered words beneath the sentence and choose the word or set of words that *best* fits the whole sentence.

1. Loved and hated by thousands, Dr. Lucy Bertram may well be the most _____ physician ever to become surgeon general.

   A. controversial

   B. popular

   C. successful

   D. well-trained

   E. professional

2. Over thousands of years, organisms have _____ many strategies to conserve water.

   A. administered

   B. evolved

   C. organized

   D. questioned

   E. considered

3. My cat is a creature of contradictions: _____ yet affectionate, _____ yet alert.

   A. aloof . . . dreamy

   B. cruel . . . shrewd

   C. quiet . . . lively

   D. selfish . . . nimble

   E. loving . . . sly

4. _____ for talking too much, the teacher _____ his reputation by keeping the class 30 minutes longer than the scheduled class time.

   A. Famous . . . evinced

   B. Renowned . . . overturned

   C. Notorious . . . verified

   D. Illustrious . . . rebutted

   E. Eminent . . . established

GO ON TO THE NEXT PAGE

5. If Senator Montana runs for reelection next year, she will have the money-raising advantage of the _____.

A. campaigner

B. favorite

C. underdog

D. incumbent

E. candidate

6. Using his own home as _____, Marlowe obtained a private loan that enabled him to _____ his financial obligations to the other partners and emerge free of debt.

A. pledge . . . increase

B. surety . . . augment

C. collateral . . . discharge

D. profit . . . eliminate

E. deposit . . . endorse

7. The absurdist as opposed to the heroic treatment of war reached maturity in *Catch-22,* and the Vietnam War made this approach, which seemed so _____ and shocking, the only way to write about that conflict.

A. banal

B. radical

C. plausible

D. cozy

E. familiar

8. Because the issue is so insignificant, it was surprising that the disagreement among city council members was so _____.

A. tepid

B. slovenly

C. trivial

D. acrimonious

E. genial

9. Many thought Billy Eckstine's band _____ because its musicians were young, avant-garde jazzmen, while its lead singer crooned _____ popular ballads.

A. progressive . . . romantic

B. old-fashioned . . . unique

C. inconsistent . . . conservative

D. unmusical . . . familiar

E. predictable . . . melodic

Analogies

Directions: In each question below, you are given a related pair of words or phrases. Select the lettered pair that *best* expresses a relationship similar to that in the original pair of words.

10. HORSE : BRIDLE ::

    A. canary : cage

    B. ox : plough

    C. dog : leash

    D. beaver : dam

    E. silver fox : trap

11. HUNTER : DECOY ::

    A. mouse : mousetrap

    B. angler : lure

    C. language : code

    D. treasure : map

    E. predator : prey

12. HERB : OREGANO ::

    A. poem : ballad

    B. drama : actor

    C. music : score

    D. grocer : vegetable

    E. automobile : truck

13. CHOREOGRAPHER : DANCE ::

    A. conductor : symphony

    B. artist : model

    C. director : actor

    D. ingredient : recipe

    E. playwright : play

14. FESTER : RANKLE ::

    A. dislike : tolerate

    B. approve : question

    C. adore : worship

    D. conjugate : spell

    E. inhibit : inhere

15. DISINTERESTED : PREJUDICE ::

    A. naïve : sophistication

    B. inattentive : tedium

    C. enthusiastic : alacrity

    D. secure : confidence

    E. narrow-minded : bias

GO ON TO THE NEXT PAGE

Critical Reading

Directions: Questions follow each of the passages below. Using only the stated or implied information in each passage and in its introduction, if any, answer the questions.

Questions 16–21 are based on the following passage.

The following passage is from a book about Paul Gauguin, the late 19th century artist who left France to live and paint on the Pacific island of Tahiti.

Gauguin decided to settle in Mataiea, some forty-five kilometres from Papeete, probably on the advice of a Tahitian chief whom he had befriended. There he rented a
(5) native-style oval bamboo hut, roofed with pandanu leaves. Once settled, he was in a position to begin work in earnest and to tackle serious figure studies. It was probably soon after this that he painted *Vahine*
(10) *no te tiare,* his first portrait of a Tahitian model.

By the late summer of 1892 the completed canvas was back in Paris, hanging in the Goupil gallery. From the many subsequent
(15) references to this image in his correspondence, it is clear that Gauguin set considerable store by his "Tahitienne" and, by sending her on ahead to Paris, wanted her to serve as an ambassadress for the further
(20) images of Tahitian women he would be bringing back with him on his return. He pressed his male friends for their reactions to the girl, rather than to the picture, anxious to know whether they, like him, would
(25) be responsive to the beauty of her face: "And her forehead," he later wrote, "with the majesty of upsweeping lines, reminded me of that saying of Poe's, 'There is no perfect beauty without a certain singularity
(30) in the proportions.'" No one, it seems, was quite attuned to his emotional perception:

while Aurier was enthusiastic, excited by the picture's rarity value, Schuffenecker was somewhat taken aback by the paint-
(35) ing's lack of Symbolist character. Indeed, apart from the imaginary floral background which harked back to Gauguin's 1888 *Self-Portrait,* the image is a relatively straightforward one. Recent anthropologi-
(40) cal work, backed by the use of photography, had scientifically characterized the physical distinctions between the different races, distinctions that in the past had been imperfectly understood. Generally speak-
(45) ing, artists before Gauguin's time had represented Tahitians as idealized types, adjusting their features and proportions to accord with European taste. This meant that hitherto the Tahitian in Western art
(50) could scarcely be distinguished from his African or Asian counterpart.

Unfortunately, Charles Giraud's paintings have disappeared, so we cannot compare them with Gauguin's, but this first image
(55) by Gauguin suggests a desire to portray the Tahitian physiognomy naturalistically, without the blinkers of preconceived rules of beauty laid down by a classical culture. Naturalism as an artistic creed, though,
(60) was anathema to Gauguin; it made the artist a lackey of science and knowledge rather than a god-like creator. He wanted to go beyond empirical observation of this kind, to find a way of painting Tahiti that
(65) would accord with his Symbolist aspirations, that would embody the feelings he had about the place and the poetic image he carried with him of the island's mysterious past.

16. In lines 15–16, the word "correspondence" means

    A. correlation.

    B. agreement.

    C. conformity.

    D. similarity.

    E. letters.

17. Gauguin found the faces of Tahitian women beautiful because of their

    A. elegant coloration.

    B. unusual proportions.

    C. refusal to wear makeup.

    D. dark hair covering the forehead.

    E. openness and innocence.

18. The passage suggests that a painter depicting a Tahitian in a period sometime before Gauguin would probably

    A. rely on photographs for models.

    B. make an image that was not in accord with European ideals of female beauty.

    C. paint a picture that employed a symbolic landscape as background.

    D. fail to differentiate a Tahitian from the inhabitants of Asian countries.

    E. paint only models who were fully clothed in Western-style costume.

19. It can be inferred that the author would like to see the lost paintings of Charles Giraud in order to

    A. determine whether they presented the Tahitians realistically.

    B. determine whether they were better paintings than Gauguin's.

    C. determine whether they deserve their high reputation.

    D. compare the symbolism of these paintings with that of Gauguin's.

    E. discover what subjects Giraud chose to paint.

20. Of the following phrases, which does the author use to refer to the aspect of Gauguin's art that attempts to depict the real world accurately?

    I. "the image is a relatively straightforward one" (lines 38–39)

    II. "desire to portray the Tahitian physiognomy naturalistically" (lines 55–56)

    III. "a way of painting Tahiti that would accord with his Symbolist aspirations" (lines 64–66)

    A. II only

    B. III only

    C. I and II only

    D. I and III only

    E. I, II, and III

GO ON TO THE NEXT PAGE

21. The passage suggests that an important problem Gauguin would have to deal with in his paintings of Tahiti was how to

   A. reconcile his naturalistic and symbolistic impulses.

   B. make Europeans understand the beauty of Tahiti.

   C. find the necessary supplies in a remote location.

   D. earn enough money to support himself by selling his paintings in Paris.

   E. make artistic use of the new advances in photography.

Questions 22 through 30 are based on the following passage:

Jim Hansen, a climatologist at NASA's Goddard Space Institute, is convinced that the earth's temperature is rising and places the blame on the buildup of greenhouse
(5) gases in the atmosphere. Unconvinced, John Sununu, former White House chief of staff, doubts that the warming will be great enough to produce a serious threat and fears that measures to reduce the emissions
(10) would throw a wrench into the gears that drive the United States' troubled economy. The stakes in this debate are extremely high, for it pits society's short-term well-being against the future of all the
(15) planet's inhabitants. Our past transgressions have altered major portions of the earth's surface, but the effects have been limited. Now we can foresee the possibility that to satisfy the energy needs of an ex-
(20) panding human population, we will rapidly change the climate of the entire planet, with consequences for even the most remote and unspoiled regions of the globe.

The notion that certain gases could warm
(25) the planet is not new. In 1896 Svante Arrhenius, a Swedish chemist, resolved the long-standing question of how the earth's atmosphere could maintain the planet's relatively warm temperature when the oxygen
(30) and nitrogen that make up 99 percent of the atmosphere do not absorb any of the heat escaping as infrared radiation from the earth's surface into space. He discovered that even the small amounts of carbon
(35) dioxide in the atmosphere could absorb large amounts of heat. Furthermore, he reasoned that the burning of coal, oil, and natural gas could eventually release enough carbon dioxide to warm the earth. Hansen
(40) and most other climatologists agree that enough greenhouse gases have accumulated in the atmosphere to make Arrhenius's prediction come true. Burning fossil fuels is not the only problem; a fifth
(45) of our emissions of carbon dioxide now come from clearing and burning forests. Scientists are also tracking a host of other greenhouse gases that emanate from a variety of human activities; the warming effect
(50) of methane, chlorofluorocarbons, and nitrous oxide combined equals that of carbon dioxide.

Although the current warming from these gases may be difficult to detect against the
(55) background noise of natural climate variation, most climatologists are certain that as the gases continue to accumulate, increases in the earth's temperature will become evident even to skeptics. The battle lines for
(60) this particular skirmish are surprisingly well balanced. Those with concerns about global warming point to the recent report from the United Nations Intergovernmental Plan on Climate Change, which suggests
(65) that with "business as usual," emissions of carbon dioxide by the year 2025 will be 25 percent greater than previously estimated. On the other side, the George C. Marshall Institute, a conservative think tank,

(70) published a report warning that without greenhouse gases to warm things up, the world would become cool in the next century. Stephen Schneider, a leading computer modeler of future climate change, accused
(75) Sununu of "brandishing the [Marshall] report as if he were holding a crucifix to repel a vampire."

If the reality of global warming were put on trial, each side would have trouble making
(80) its case. Jim Hansen's side could not prove beyond a reasonable doubt that carbon dioxide and the other greenhouse gases have warmed the planet. But neither could John Sununu's side prove beyond a reasonable
(85) doubt that the warming expected from greenhouse gases has not occurred.

22. The purpose of the first paragraph (lines 1–23) of the passage is to

   A. argue for the reduction of greenhouse gases in the atmosphere.

   B. defend on economic grounds the reduction of greenhouse gases.

   C. present two opposing positions on the subject of the earth's rising temperature.

   D. lessen the concern of the public about the alleged buildup of greenhouse gases.

   E. introduce the two most important spokesmen for and against ecological reforms.

23. In the first paragraph in line 13, the word "pits" means

   A. removes the core of.

   B. sets in competition.

   C. depresses.

   D. marks with small scars.

   E. hardens.

24. From the information in the second paragraph of the passage, you can infer that a planet

   A. whose atmosphere was made up entirely of oxygen would be warmer than a planet equally distant from the sun with an atmosphere made up entirely of nitrogen.

   B. whose atmosphere was made up entirely of nitrogen would be warmer than a planet equally distant from the sun with an atmosphere made up entirely of oxygen.

   C. with a larger amount of carbon dioxide in its atmosphere, other factors being equal, will be warmer than a planet with less carbon dioxide.

   D. with a small amount of carbon dioxide in its atmosphere cannot increase this amount.

   E. with little infrared radiation escaping from its surface is likely to be extremely cold.

25. The passage implies that a greenhouse gas is one that

   I. forms a large part of the earth's atmosphere.

   II. absorbs heat escaping from the earth's surface.

   III. can be formed by the clearing and burning of forests.

   A. III only

   B. I and II only

   C. I and III only

   D. II and III only

   E. I, II, and III

GO ON TO THE NEXT PAGE

26. From the passage, it can be inferred that all the following are greenhouse gases EXCEPT

   A. nitrogen.

   B. carbon dioxide.

   C. methane.

   D. chlorofluorocarbons.

   E. nitrous oxide.

27. Which of the following, if true, would call into question the argument of the Marshall report?

   I. Since the earth's climate did not grow colder in the five hundred years since 1400 when the amount of greenhouse gases released by humans was small, there is no reason to expect a decrease in temperature when the amounts of gas released are now much larger.

   II. The radical reduction of the emission of greenhouse gases will result in massive unemployment throughout the industrial world.

   III. Some scientific studies have shown that the temperature of the earth is unaffected by the presence of oxygen in the atmosphere.

   A. I only

   B. II only

   C. I and II only

   D. I and III only

   E. I, II, and III

28. The word "skeptics" in line 59 most nearly means

   A. scientists.

   B. ecologists.

   C. opponents.

   D. doubters.

   E. politicians.

29. Stephen Schneider probably referred to Sununu's "brandishing the [Marshall] report as if he were holding a crucifix to repel a vampire" in order to

   I. amuse his audience.

   II. suggest that Sununu's claims are melodramatic.

   III. imply that the idea that greenhouse gases are dangerous is as imaginary as a vampire.

   A. III only

   B. I and II only

   C. I and III only

   D. II and III only

   E. I, II, and III

30. The effect of the final paragraph of the passage is to

   A. stress the superiority of Jim Hansen's case.

   B. undermine Sununu's argument.

   C. support the conclusions of the Marshall report.

   D. call Arrhenius's theories into question.

   E. leave the debate about global warming unresolved.

IF YOU FINISH BEFORE TIME IS CALLED, CHECK YOUR WORK ON THIS SECTION ONLY. DO NOT WORK ON ANY OTHER SECTION IN THE TEST.

Section 2: Mathematical Reasoning

Time: 30 Minutes

25 Questions

Directions: Solve each problem in this section by using the information given and your own mathematical calculations, insights, and problem-solving skills. Then select the one correct answer of the five choices given and mark the corresponding circle on your answer sheet. Use the available space on the page for your scratch work.

Notes

1. All numbers used are real numbers.

2. Calculators may be used.

3. Some problems may be accompanied by figures or diagrams. These figures are drawn as accurately as possible EXCEPT when it is stated in a specific problem that a figure is not drawn to scale. The figures and diagrams are meant to provide information useful in solving the problem or problems. Unless otherwise stated, all figures and diagrams lie in a plane.

Data That Can Be Used for Reference

Area

rectangle
$A = lw$

triangle
$A = \frac{1}{2}bh$

circle
$A = \pi r^2$
$C = 2\pi r$

Pythagorean Relationship

$a^2 + b^2 = c^2$

Special Triangles

$30° - 60° - 90°$ $45° - 45° - 90°$

Volume

rectangular solid
$V = lwh$

right circular cylinder
$V = \pi r^2 h$

A circle is composed of 360°
A straight angle measures 180°
The sum of the angles of a triangle is 180°

GO ON TO THE NEXT PAGE

117

1. If ⅕ of a number is 2, what is ½ of the number?

   A. 10

   B. 5

   C. 3

   D. 2

   E. 1

8, 9, 12, 17, 24, . . .

2. In the preceding sequence, a certain pattern determines each of the subsequent numbers. What is the next number in the sequence?

   A. 41

   B. 35

   C. 33

   D. 30

   E. 29

---

3. If a store purchases several items for $1.80 per dozen and sells them at 3 for $0.85, what is the store's profit on 6 dozen of these items?

   A. $4.20

   B. $5.70

   C. $9.60

   D. $10.60

   E. $20.40

4. If $x = -1$, then $x^4 + x^3 + x^2 + x - 3 =$

   A. −13

   B. −7

   C. −3

   D. −2

   E. 1

---

5. Which of the following numbers is divisible by 15?

   A. 15,815

   B. 16,428

   C. 28,145

   D. 46,335

   E. 55,555

The product of two numbers is equal to twice the difference of the two numbers.

6. Which equation best represents the preceding situation?

   A. $x + y = 2(x - y)$

   B. $x + y = 2(x \div y)$

   C. $(x)(y) = 2(x \div y)$

   D. $(x)(y) = 2(x - y)$

   E. $(x)(y) = 2(x + y)$

7. Which of the following is equal to $(5x + 2)(3x - 4) - (2x - 3)(x + 2)$?

   A. $13x^2 - 14$

   B. $13x^2 + 2$

   C. $13x^2 - 13x - 14$

   D. $13x^2 - 13x - 2$

   E. $13x^2 - 15x - 2$

8. If D is between A and B on $\overleftrightarrow{AB}$, which of the following must be true?

   A. $AD = DB$

   B. $DB = AB - AD$

   C. $AD = AB + DB$

   D. $DB = AD + AB$

   E. $AB = AD - BD$

9. The symbol $\otimes$ represents a binary operation defined as $a \otimes b = a^3 + b^2$. What is the value of $(-2) \otimes (-3)$?

   A. 17

   B. 1

   C. 0

   D. −1

   E. −17

Note: Figure not drawn to scale.

10. In the preceding figure, $AB = AD$ and $BD = CD$. If $\angle C$ measures $19°$, what is the measure of $\angle A$ in degrees?

   A. 75

   B. 94

   C. 104

   D. 114

   E. 142

11. Angela has nickels and dimes in her pocket. She has twice as many dimes as nickels. What is the best expression of the amount of money she has in cents if x equals the number of nickels she has?

   A. $25x$

   B. $10x + 5(2x)$

   C. $x + 2x$

   D. $5(3x)$

   E. $20(x + 5)$

12. If $x - 4 = y$, what must $(y - x)^3$ equal?

   A. −64

   B. −12

   C. 12

   D. 64

   E. 128

GO ON TO THE NEXT PAGE

Section **2** Mathematical Reasoning

3x

13. The length of a rectangle is $3x$, and its perimeter is $10x + 8$. What is the width of the rectangle?

   A. $2x + 4$

   B. $2x + 8$

   C. $4x + 8$

   D. $4x + 4$

   E. $5x + 4$

---

14. If   , then x =

   A. $8\frac{2}{7}$

   B. 11

   C. $19\frac{1}{3}$

   D. $24\frac{2}{3}$

   E. $27\frac{1}{3}$

---

15. A car travels 140 miles in 4 hours, while the return trip takes $3\frac{1}{2}$ hours. What is the average speed in miles per hour for the entire trip?

   A. 35

   B. $37\frac{1}{3}$

   C. $37\frac{1}{2}$

   D. 40

   E. 75

16. If $a > b$, and $ab > 0$, which of the following must be true?

   I. $a > 0$

   II. $b > 0$

   III. $a/b > 0$

   A. I only

   B. II only

   C. III only

   D. I and II only

   E. I and III only

(0,0)

17. What is the slope of the line passing through the points $(-3c, 5c)$ and $(2c, 9c)$?

   A. -4

   B. $-\frac{5}{4}$

   C. $-\frac{4}{5}$

   D. $\frac{4}{5}$

   E. $\frac{5}{4}$

18. Today is Lucy's fourteenth birthday. Last year she was three years older than twice Charlie's age at that time. Using *C* for Charlie's age now, which of the following can be used to determined Charlie's age now?

   A. $13 - 3 = 2(C - 1)$

   B. $14 - 3 = 2C$

   C. $13 - 3 = 2C$

   D. $13 + 3 = 2C$

   E. $13 + 3 = 2(C - 1)$

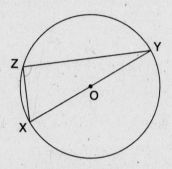

19. In circle O above, XY is a diameter, $OX = 8.5$, and $YZ = 15$. What is the area of　　　　in square units?

   A. 40

   B. 60

   C. 120

   D. 127.5

   E. 180

20. A bag contains 20 gumballs. If there are 8 red, 7 white, and 5 green, what is the minimum number of gumballs one must pick from the bag to be assured of one of each color?

   A. 16

   B. 9

   C. 8

   D. 6

   E. 3

21. If the five vowels are repeated continuously in the pattern *a, e, i, o, u, a, e, i, o, u,* and so on, what vowel will the 327th letter be?

   A. *a*

   B. *e*

   C. *i*

   D. *o*

   E. *u*

22. The base of an isosceles triangle exceeds each of the equal sides by 8 feet. If the perimeter is 89 feet, what is the length of the base in feet?

   A. 27

   B. 29⅔

   C. 35

   D. 54

   E. 70

GO ON TO THE NEXT PAGE

23. A random poll of 2,500 moviegoers throughout New York found that 1,500 preferred comedies, 500 preferred adventure films, and 500 preferred dramas. Of the 8,000,000 moviegoers in New York, which of the following is (are) the most reasonable estimate(s) drawn from the poll?

   I. 1,500,000 prefer comedies.

  II. 500,000 prefer dramas.

 III. 1,600,000 prefer dramas.

  A. I only

  B. II only

  C. III only

  D. I and II only

  E. I and Ill only

24. If the average of two numbers is y and one of the numbers is equal to z, then the other number is equal to

  A. $2z - y$

  B. $(y + z)/2$

  C. $z - y$

  D. $2y - z$

  E. $y - 2z$

25. What is the area of a rhombus with a perimeter of 40 and a diagonal of 10?

  A. $50\sqrt{3}$

  B. 100

  C. $100\sqrt{5}$

  D. 200

  E. 400

IF YOU FINISH BEFORE TIME IS CALLED, CHECK YOUR WORK ON THIS
SECTION ONLY. DO NOT WORK ON ANY OTHER SECTION IN THE TEST.

STOP

Section 3: Verbal Reasoning

Time: 30 Minutes

35 Questions

In this section, choose the best answer for each question and blacken the corresponding space on the answer sheet.

Sentence Completion

Directions: Each blank in the following sentences indicates that something has been omitted. Consider the lettered words beneath the sentence and choose the word or set of words that best fits the whole sentence.

1. It is _____ to assume that if aspirin can prevent second heart attacks, it can also _____ an attack in the first place.

   A. fanciful . . . eliminate

   B. logical . . . ward off

   C. sensible . . . encourage

   D. reasonable . . . foment

   E. idle . . . defend against

2. Cigars are not a safe _____ to cigarettes because, though cigar smokers do not inhale, they are still _____ higher rates of lung and mouth cancers than nonsmokers.

   A. answer . . . responsible for

   B. preference . . . free from

   C. alternative . . . subject to

   D. rejoinder . . . involved in

   E. accent . . . victimized by

3. Justices Marshall and Brennan opposed the death penalty on the grounds that it failed to _____ crimes, since all the available evidence made it clear that far more murders per capita were committed in states or countries with capital punishment than in those without it.

   A. explain

   B. augment

   C. foster

   D. deter

   E. exculpate

4. After the smoke and _____ of the city, Mr. Fitzgerald was glad to return to the _____ air and peace of the mountains.

   A. hubbub . . . turbid

   B. grime . . . murky

   C. tranquility . . . effulgent

   D. composure . . . brisk

   E. hustle-bustle . . . exhilarating

GO ON TO THE NEXT PAGE

5. A strike by Ford workers in Mexico poses a(n) _____ for the ruling party, which must choose between alienating its union ally or undermining its fight against inflation.

   A. enigma

   B. dilemma

   C. problem

   D. option

   E. riddle

6. By combining an American cartoon character with Japanese traditions, the popular comic by Stan Sakai presents as a hero a samurai rabbit, a unique _____ of East and West.

   A. fusion

   B. division

   C. rejection

   D. exclusion

   E. query

7. A _____ that allowed voters to decide on the legality of casino gambling was passed by a(n) _____ 9-to-1 margin.

   A. statute . . . meager

   B. referendum . . . overwhelming

   C. prohibition . . . huge

   D. bill . . . narrow

   E. ban . . . sizable

8. The _____ upon which this fine novel is developed with great _____ and intelligence is that no males live beyond the age of 18.

   A. theory . . . fatuity

   B. plot . . . understanding

   C. idea . . . recalcitrance

   D. premise . . . subtlety

   E. solution . . . cleverness

9. The _____ use of washing machines and automobiles in the Middle Ages is part of the comedy of this high-spirited film.

   A. untimely

   B. anachronistic

   C. unconvincing

   D. archaic

   E. supposed

10. Hoping to escape detection, Minnie _____ placed an ace in her sleeve while Rance shuffled the cards.

   A. brazenly

   B. overtly

   C. furtively

   D. hopefully

   E. eagerly

Analogies

Directions: In each question below, you are given a related pair of words or phrases. Select the lettered pair that *best* expresses a relationship similar to that in the original pair of words.

11. CLOTHES : LUGGAGE ::

    A. baggage car : train

    B. package : post office

    C. documents : briefcase

    D. airmail : mail carrier

    E. plant : flowerpot

12. CYMBAL : BRASS ::

    A. timpani : percussion

    B. conductor : baton

    C. viola : bow

    D. clarinet : woodwind

    E. violin : wood

13. DECADE : CENTURY ::

    A. month : year

    B. dime : dollar

    C. yard : mile

    D. gram : kilogram

    E. minute : hour

14. JURY : EVIDENCE ::

    A. lawyer : trial

    B. diner : table

    C. team : rules

    D. doctor : symptoms

    E. eyeglasses : reader

15. EARN : FILCH ::

    A. create : plagiarize

    B. injure : maim

    C. plant : bury

    D. lurk : sneak

    E. lie : perjure

16. DISLIKE : LOATHE ::

    A. praise : extol

    B. yearn : desire

    C. insure : rely

    D. stuff : cram

    E. hurry : run

17. CONSTELLATION : STAR ::

    A. quasar : comet

    B. sun : Milky Way

    C. asteroid : planet

    D. telescope : astronomer

    E. solar system : planet

18. FOLLOW : STALK ::

    A. dissipate : waste

    B. glower : scowl

    C. mature : ripen

    D. light : illuminate

    E. inquire : snoop

GO ON TO THE NEXT PAGE

19. BACTERIUM : AGAR ::

   A. plant : potting soil

   B. host : parasite

   C. meadow : mountainside

   D. trout : lake

   E. library : book

20. SLANDER : LIBEL ::

   A. magazine : book

   B. love : admiration

   C. dance : song

   D. speech : essay

   E. felony : misdemeanor

21. CREDULOUS : DOUBT ::

   A. naive : sorrow

   B. avaricious : money

   C. complacent : modesty

   D. arduous : task

   E. industrious : employment

22. SUPINE : PRONE ::

   A. lying : reclining

   B. dark : light

   C. straight : narrow

   D. open : overt

   E. pensive : thoughtful

23. SURFEIT : DEARTH ::

   A. reign : election

   B. flood : drought

   C. top : bottom

   D. teacher : pupil

   E. hand : finger

Critical Reading

Directions: Questions follow the passage below. Using only the stated or implied information in the passage and in its introduction, if any, answer the questions.

Questions 24 through 35 are based on the following passage:

Early in the day Dorothea had returned from the infant school which she had set going in the village, and was taking her usual place in the pretty sitting-room
(5) which divided the bedrooms of the sisters, bent on finishing a plan for some buildings (a kind of work which she delighted in), when Celia, who had been watching her with a hesitating desire to propose
(10) something, said — "Dorothea dear, if you don't mind — if you are not very busy — suppose we looked at mamma's jewels today, and divided them? It is exactly six months today since uncle gave them to
(15) you, and you have not looked at them yet."

Celia's face had the shadow of a pouting expression in it, the full presence of the pout being kept back by an habitual awe of Dorothea. To her relief, Dorothea's eyes
(20) were full of laughter as she looked up.

"What a wonderful little almanac you are, Celia! Is it six calendar or six lunar months?"

"It is the last day of September now, and it
(25) was the first of April when uncle gave them to you. You know, he said that he had forgotten them till then. I believe you have never thought of them since you locked them up in the cabinet here."

(30) "Well, dear, we should never wear them, you know." Dorothea spoke in a full cordial tone, half caressing, half explanatory. She had her pencil in her hand, and was making tiny side-plans on a margin.

(35) Celia coloured, and looked very grave. "I think, dear, we are wanting in respect to mamma's memory, to put them by and take no notice of them. And," she added, after hesitating a little, "necklaces are
(40) quite usual now; and Madame Poinçon, who was stricter in some things even than you are, used to wear ornaments. And Christians generally — surely there are women in heaven now who wore jewels."
(45) Celia was conscious of some mental strength when she really applied herself to argument.

"You would like to wear them?" exclaimed Dorothea, an air of astonished discovery
(50) animating her whole person. "Of course, then, let us have them out. Why did you not tell me before? But the keys, the keys!" She pressed her hands against the sides of her head and seemed to despair of
(55) her memory. "They are here," said Celia, with whom this explanation had been long meditated and prearranged.

The casket was soon open before them, and the various jewels spread out on the table. It
(60) was no great collection, but a few of the ornaments were really of remarkable beauty, the finest that was obvious at first being a necklace of purple amethysts set in exquisite gold work, and a pearl cross with five bril-
(65) liants in it. Dorothea immediately took up the necklace and fastened it round her sister's neck, where it fitted almost as closely as a bracelet; but the circle suited the style of Celia's head and neck, and she could see
(70) that it did, in the pier-glass opposite.

"There, Celia! You can wear that with your Indian muslin. But this cross you must wear with your dark dresses."

GO ON TO THE NEXT PAGE

Celia was trying not to smile with pleasure. (75) "O Dodo, you must keep the cross yourself."

"No, no, dear, no," said Dorothea, putting up her hand with careless deprecation.

"Yes, indeed you must; it would suit you — in your black dress, now," said Celia, insist- (80) ingly. "You *might* wear that."

"Not for the world, not for the world. A cross is the last thing I would wear as a trinket." Dorothea shuddered slightly.

"Then you will think it wicked in me to wear (85) it," said Celia, uneasily.

"No, dear, no," said Dorothea, stroking her sister's cheek. "Souls have complexions too: what will suit one will not suit another."

"But you might like to keep it for mamma's (90) sake."

"No, I have other things of mamma's — her sandal-wood box which I am so fond of — plenty of things. In fact, they are all yours, dear. We need discuss them no longer. (95) There — take away your property."

Celia felt a little hurt. There was a strong assumption of superiority in this Puritanic toleration, hardly less trying to the blond flesh of an unenthusiastic sister than a Puritanic (100) persecution.

24. From the details of the passage, it can be learned or inferred that

    I. Dorothea and Celia are sisters.

    II. Dorothea and Celia may be orphans.

    III. Dorothea and Celia are temperamentally very alike.

    A. III only

    B. I and II only

    C. I and III only

    D. II and III only

    E. I, II, and, III

25. The first paragraph of the passage refers to the "infant school" and "plan for some buildings" in order to suggest that Dorothea is

    A. prying and interfering.

    B. rich and idle.

    C. self-centered and ambitious.

    D. active and unselfish.

    E. philanthropic and ineffectual.

26. In lines 22–23, Dorothea asks Celia whether it is "six calendar or six lunar months" because she

    A. wants to know exactly how many days have passed.

    B. is good-humoredly teasing Celia.

    C. had hoped to keep the jewels from Celia.

    D. wants to demonstrate the scientific precision of her mind.

    E. has forgotten what the current month is.

27. In line 36, the phrase "wanting in respect" can be best understood to mean

    A. obliged to be more deferential.

    B. desirous to esteem.

    C. lewd in regard.

    D. deficient in regard.

    E. eager for consideration.

28. The "argument" to which Celia has "really applied herself" (line 46) is intended to convince Dorothea to

    A. show greater respect for their dead mother.

    B. give all the jewels to her.

    C. give the most valuable of the jewels to her.

    D. agree to sharing and wearing the jewels.

    E. examine the jewels and lock them up again.

29. Although in lines 30–31 Dorothea has said, "we should never wear them, you know," she changes her opinion because she

   A. is moved by Celia's appeal to the memory of their mother.
   B. is convinced by Celia's reference to Madame Poinçon.
   C. realizes that Celia wants to wear the jewels.
   D. sees how becoming the jewels are to Celia.
   E. can appear superior to Celia by refusing to wear them herself.

30. In line 77, the word "deprecation" means

   A. protest.
   B. lessening.
   C. indifference.
   D. removal.
   E. agreement.

31. The word "trying" in line 98 means

   A. irksome.
   B. attempting.
   C. effortful.
   D. experimental.
   E. determining.

32. In lines 97–98, "Puritanic toleration" is a reference to

   A. Celia's awe of Dorothea.
   B. Celia's acceptance of Dorothea's foibles.
   C. Celia's love of jewels and finery.
   D. Dorothea's hypocritical indifference to finery.
   E. Dorothea's self-denial and generosity.

33. In the last sentence of the passage, the word "unenthusiastic" refers to

   A. Dorothea's refusal to wear jewels.
   B. Dorothea's giving her permission for Celia to wear jewels.
   C. Celia's attitude toward self-denial.
   D. Celia's attitude toward wearing jewels.
   E. the author's attitude toward Dorothea.

34. The inconsistency in Dorothea's reasoning that the passage reveals is her

   A. forgetting about when the jewels were given to her.
   B. losing the keys to the cabinet holding the jewels.
   C. insistence that Christians cannot wear jewels.
   D. wanting Celia to wear jewels but refusing to wear them herself.
   E. deceitful claim that she honors the memory of her mother.

35. The purpose of the passage as a whole is to

   A. reveal the likeness of Celia and Dorothea.
   B. expose the submerged ill feelings between Celia and Dorothea.
   C. reveal the differences in the natures of Celia and Dorothea.
   D. demonstrate the dangers of materialism.
   E. satirize the hypocrisy of the two young women.

IF YOU FINISH BEFORE TIME IS CALLED, CHECK YOUR WORK ON THIS SECTION ONLY. DO NOT WORK ON ANY OTHER SECTION IN THE TEST.

Section **3** Verbal Reasoning

Section 4: Mathematical Reasoning

Time: 30 Minutes

25 Questions

Directions: This section is composed of two types of questions. Use the 30 minutes allotted to answer both question types. Your scratch work should be done on any available space in the section.

Notes

1. All numbers used are real numbers.

2. Calculators may be used.

3. Some problems may be accompanied by figures or diagrams. These figures are drawn as accurately as possible *except* when it is stated in a specific problem that a figure is not drawn to scale. The figures and diagrams are meant to provide information useful in solving the problem or problems. Unless otherwise stated, all figures and diagrams lie in a plane.

Data That Can Be Used for Reference

Quantitative Comparison

Directions: In this section, you will be given two quantities, one in column A and one in column B. You are to determine a relationship between the two quantities and mark —

   A. whether the quantity in column A is greater than the quantity in column B.

   B. whether the quantity in column B is greater than the quantity in column A.

   C. whether the quantities are equal.

   D. whether the comparison cannot be determined from the information that is given.

AN **E** RESPONSE WILL NOT BE SCORED.

Notes

1. Sometimes, information concerning one or both of the quantities to be compared is given. This information is not boxed and is centered above the two columns.

2. All numbers used are real numbers. Letters such as *a, b, m,* and *x* represent real numbers.

3. In a given question, if the same symbol is used in column A and column B, that symbol stands for the same value in each column.

Column A	**Column B**
1. $3^2 + 4 \times 10^2 - 4^2$	$3^2 - 4 \times 10^2 - 4^2$

2. x | y

$5y = 10$

$3x + 2y = 10$

3. x | y

Column A	**Column B**
4. $\dfrac{3}{7} \times \dfrac{2}{5} \times \dfrac{5}{8}$	$\dfrac{2}{5} \times \dfrac{4}{11} \times \dfrac{5}{8}$

$x > 0$

5. $3x^2$ | $2x^3$

6. $(2.3)^{10}$ | $(.23)^{100}$

$\dfrac{a}{6} = \dfrac{b}{4}$

7. $2a$ | $3b$

GO ON TO THE NEXT PAGE

Column A   **Column B**   **Column A**   **Column B**

Questions 8 and 9 refer to the diagram.

8.

| x | $3\sqrt{2}$ |

9.

| y | $43°$ |

$$0 < y < 1$$

10.

| $4y^2 - 4y + 1$ | $(2y + 1)^2$ |

Questions 11 and 12 refer to the diagram.

11.

| c | d |

12.

| $c + d$ | $e + f$ |

13.

| Number of degrees in the interior angles of a pentagon | $500°$ |

$$n \neq 0$$
$$n \neq -\tfrac{1}{2}$$
$$n \neq -1$$

14.

| $\dfrac{1}{1 + \dfrac{1}{1 + 1/n}}$ | $\dfrac{n + 1}{2n + 1}$ |

Equilateral $\triangle ABC$ is inscribed in Circle O
$$AB = AC = CB = 8\sqrt{3}$$

15.

| OA + OB + OC | 24 |

Grid-In Questions

Directions: Questions 16-25 require you to solve the problem and enter your answer by carefully marking the circles on the special grid. Examples of the appropriate way to mark the grid follow.

Answer: 3.7   **Answer: ½**

Answer: 1½

Do not grid in mixed numbers in the form of mixed numbers. Always change mixed numbers to improper fractions or decimals.

GO ON TO THE NEXT PAGE

Answer: 123

Space permitting, answers may start in any column. Each grid-in answer below is correct.

Note: Circles must be filled in correctly to receive credit. Mark only one circle in each column. No credit will be given if more than one circle in a column is marked. Example:

Answer: 258 (no credit)

Answer: $^8/_9$

Accuracy of decimals: Always enter the most accurate decimal value that the grid will accommodate. For example: An answer such as .8888. . . can be gridded as .888 or .889. Gridding this value as .8 , .88, or .89 is considered inaccurate and therefore **not acceptable**. The acceptable grid-ins of $^8/_9$ are:

Be sure to write your answers in the boxes at the top of the circles before doing your gridding. Although writing out the answers above the columns is not required, it is very important to insure accuracy. Even though some problems may have more than one correct answer, grid only **one answer**. Grid-in questions contain no negative answers.

---

16. What is the value of $5x^2 - 3x + 2$ when $x = -4$?

17. A long-distance telephone call costs $2.45 for the first 3 minutes and $.32 per minute for each additional minute. What is the cost in dollars and cents for a 25-minute call? (Disregard the $ sign when gridding your answer.)

18. A jacket sold for $56, which was 80% of the original price. What was the original price in dollars and cents? (Disregard the $ sign when gridding your answer.)

19. What is the length of the side of a cube whose volume is 64 cubic units?

BILL FOR PURCHASE	
Science Textbooks	$840
Lab Equipment	$460
Formaldehyde	$320
Teacher's Manuals	$120
TOTAL	$2220

20. Scholastic Supplies, Inc. sends the bill above to Zither Junior High School. Although the bill includes the cost of science lab workbooks, Scholastic Supplies forgot to list them on the bill. How much did the science lab workbooks cost Zither High School? (Disregard the $ sign when gridding your answer.)

GO ON TO THE NEXT PAGE

21. If the numerator of a fraction is tripled, and the denominator of a fraction is doubled, the resulting fraction will reflect an increase of what percent? (Disregard the % sign when gridding your answer.)

24. In the figure above, what is the ratio of the degree measure of _____ to the degree measure of _____ ?

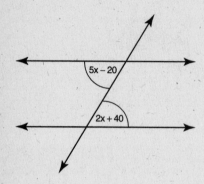

22. In the figure above, what is the value of x?

25. A bus leaves from Burbank at 9:00 a.m. traveling east at 50 miles per hour. At 1:00 p.m., a plane leaves Burbank traveling east at 300 miles per hour. How many minutes will it take the plane to overtake the bus?

23. Based on the chart above, how much more money was spent on clothing than on insurance?

IF YOU FINISH BEFORE TIME IS CALLED, CHECK YOUR WORK ON THIS SECTION ONLY. DO NOT WORK ON ANY OTHER SECTION IN THE TEST.

Section 5: Verbal Reasoning

Time: 15 Minutes

15 Questions

In this section, choose the best answer for each question and blacken the corresponding space on the answer sheet.

Critical Reading

Directions: Questions follow the two passages below. Using only the stated or implied information in each passage and in its introduction, if any, answer the questions.

Questions 1-15 are based on the following passages.

The two passages that follow are taken from recent historical studies of Christopher Columbus.

Passage 1

In his history published in 1552, Francisco Lopez de Gomara wrote: "The greatest event since the creation of the world (excluding the incarnation and death of Him who created it)
(5) is the discovery of the Indies." On the strength of this realization, Columbus emerged from the shadows, reincarnated not so much as a man and historical figure as he was as a myth and symbol. He came to epit-
(10) omize the explorer and discoverer, the man of vision and audacity, the hero who overcame opposition and adversity to change history. By the end of the sixteenth century, English explorers and writers acknowledged
(15) the primacy and inspiration of Columbus. He was celebrated in poetry and plays, especially by the Italians. Even Spain was coming around. In a popular play, Lope de Vega in 1614 portrayed Columbus as a dreamer up
(20) against the stolid forces of entrenched tradition, a man of singular purpose who triumphed, the embodiment of that spirit driving humans to explore and discover.

Historians cannot control the popularizers of
(25) history, mythmakers, or propagandists, and in post-Revolutionary America the few historians who studied Columbus were probably not disposed to try. Even if they had been, there was little information available
(30) on which to assess the real Columbus and distinguish the man from the myth. With the discovery and publication of new Columbus documents by Martin Fernandez de Navarrete in 1825, this was less of an ex-
(35) cuse, and yet the material only provided more ammunition to those who would embellish the symbolic Columbus through the nineteenth century.

Washington Irving mined the new docu-
(40) ments to create a hero in the romantic mold favored in the century's literature. Irving's Columbus was "a man of great and inventive genius" and his "ambition was lofty and noble, inspiring him with high thoughts, and
(45) an anxiety to distinguish himself by great achievements." Perhaps. But an effusive Irving got carried away. He said that Columbus's "conduct was characterized by the grandeur of his views and the magna-
(50) nimity of his spirit . . . . Instead of ravaging the newly found countries . . . he sought to colonize and cultivate them, to civilize the natives." Irving acknowledged that Columbus may have had some faults, such

GO ON TO THE NEXT PAGE

(55) as his part in enslaving and killing people, but offered the palliating explanation that these were "errors of the times."

William H. Prescott, a leading American historian of the conquest period, said of
(60) Columbus that "the finger of the historian will find it difficult to point to a single blemish in his moral character." Writers and orators of the nineteenth century ascribed to Columbus all the human virtues that were
(65) most prized in that time of geographic and industrial expansion, heady optimism, and an unquestioning belief in progress as the dynamic of history.

Most people living in America four cen-
(70) turies after the voyages of discovery had created the Columbus they wanted to be-lieve in and were quite satisfied with their creation. But scholars were already finding grounds for a major reassessment of
(75) Columbus's reputation in history.

Passage 2

Why should one suppose that a culture like Europe's, steeped as it was in the ardor of wealth, the habit of violence, and the pride of intolerance, dispirited and adrift after a
(80) century and more of disease and famine and death beyond experience, would be able to come upon new societies in a fer-tile world, innocent and defenseless, and not displace and subdue, if necessary de-
(85) stroy, them? Why should one suppose such a culture would pause there to observe, to learn, to borrow the wisdom and the ways of a foreign, heathen people, half naked and befeathered, ignorant of cities and
(90) kings and metal and laws, and unschooled in all that the Ancients held virtuous? Was not Europe in its groping era of discovery in the fifteenth century in fact in search of salvation, as its morbid sonnets said, or of
(95) that regeneration which new lands and

new peoples and of course new riches would be presumed to provide?

And there was salvation there, in the New World, though it was not of a kind the
(100) Europeans then understood. They thought first that exploitation was salvation, and they went at that with a vengeance, and found new foods and medicines and trea-sures, but that proved not to be; that colo-
(105) nization and settlement was salvation, and they peopled both continents with con-querors, and it was not that either. The sal-vation there, had the Europeans known where and how to look for it, was obvi-
(110) ously in the integrative tribal ways, the nurturant communitarian values, the rich interplay with nature that made up the Indian cultures — as it made up, for that matter, the cultures of ancient peoples
(115) everywhere, not excluding Europe. It was there especially in the Indian conscious-ness, in what Calvin Martin has termed "the biological outlook on life," in which patterns and concepts and the large teleo-
(120) logical constructs of culture are not human-centered but come from the sense of being at one with nature, biocentric, ecocentric.

However one may cast it, an opportunity
(125) there certainly was once, a chance for the people of Europe to find a new anchorage in a new country, in what they dimly real-ized was the land of Paradise, and thus find finally the way to redeem the world.
(130) But all they ever found was half a world of nature's treasures and nature's peoples that could be taken, and they took them, never knowing, never learning the true regenera-tive power there, and that opportunity was
(135) lost. Theirs was indeed a conquest of Paradise, but as is inevitable with any war against the world of nature, those who win will have lost — once again lost, and this time perhaps forever.

1. In lines 18–23 of the first paragraph, the reference to the play by Lope de Vega serves to

   I.   give an example of Columbus's reputation in Spain.

   II. demonstrate how widespread Columbus's reputation had become.

   III. exemplify how Columbus was already a myth and symbol of the discoverer.

   A. I only

   B. II only

   C. I and III only

   D. II and III only

   E. I, II, and III

2. In Passage 1 (line 28), the word "disposed" means

   A. arranged.

   B. employed.

   C. settled.

   D. inclined.

   E. given away.

3. In Passage 1 (line 40), the phrase "romantic mold" most nearly means

   A. pattern concerned with love.

   B. idealized manner.

   C. visionary model.

   D. fictitious shape.

   E. escapist style.

4. Of the following words used in the third paragraph of Passage 1, which most clearly reveals a judgment of the modern author as opposed to that of Washington Irving?

   A. "mined" (line 39)

   B. "ambition" (line 43)

   C. "Perhaps" (line 46)

   D. "magnanimity" (lines 49–50)

   E. "palliating" (line 56)

5. The major purpose of Passage 1 is to

   A. praise the daring and accomplishments of Columbus.

   B. survey the reputation of Columbus from the sixteenth through the nineteenth century.

   C. contrast the real Columbus of history with the mythic Columbus of the nineteenth century.

   D. describe the benefits and the damage of Columbus's voyages.

   E. reveal the unforeseen and harmful consequences of Columbus's voyages.

6. With which of the following generalizations would the author of Passage 1 be most likely to agree?

   I. The values of a historical period are usually reflected by the heroes people of that time choose to idolize.

   II. What people believe about historical figures is usually what they want to believe.

   III. Written history is usually a record of the truth as it is known at the time of writing.

   A. I only

   B. I and II only

   C. I and III only

   D. II and III only

   E. I, II, and III

GO ON TO THE NEXT PAGE

7. The questions of the first paragraph of Passage 2 (lines 76–97) serve chiefly to

    A. raise doubts about issues that cannot be explained.

    B. defend and justify the actions of Europeans in the age of discovery.

    C. suggest areas that future historians might profitably explore.

    D. show how much easier it is to understand issues of the distant past with the objectivity given by time.

    E. reveal the author's ideas about the nature of Europeans at the time of Columbus's voyages.

8. In Passage 2 (lines 90–91), the phrase "unschooled in all that the Ancients held virtuous" is used to

    I. reflect the European view of the American natives.

    II. reveal a significant foundation of European culture in the period.

    III. give a reason for the European contempt for the native Americans.

    A. III only

    B. I and II only

    C. I and III only

    D. II and III only

    E. I, II, and III

9. Which of the following does Passage 2 present as discovered and understood by the Europeans in America?

    A. Human-centered cultures

    B. New foods and medicines

    C. Communitarian values

    D. An Indian consciousness

    E. An ecocentric culture

10. According to Passage 2, a "biological outlook on life" would be best defined as one in which

    A. the interdependence of all life forms is understood.

    B. humans are the measure of all things.

    C. the needs of rich and poor are equally considered.

    D. the economic well-being of all races is emphasized.

    E. the primary motivation is survival of the species.

11. The major purpose of Passage 2 is to

    A. describe the benefits and damage of Columbus's discovery.

    B. present Columbus's discovery as a tragically missed opportunity to regenerate Europe.

    C. attack the greed and cruelty that inspired the European colonization of America.

    D. defend the European colonization of America as historically determined and unavoidable.

    E. evaluate as objectively as possible the meaning of the European incursion into the Americas.

12. Of the five paragraphs in Passage 1, which one best prepares the reader for the contents of Passage 2?

    A. The first (lines 1–23)

    B. The second (lines 24–38)

    C. The third (lines 39–57)

    D. The fourth (lines 58–68)

    E. The fifth (lines 69–75)

13. Compared to Passage 1, Passage 2 may be described by all the following EXCEPT

    A. more personal

    B. more philosophical

    C. more judgmental

    D. more historical

    E. more emotional

14. Compared to that of Passage 1, the prose of Passage 2 makes greater use of all the following EXCEPT

    A. words in series

    B. rhetorical questions

    C. understatements

    D. repetitions

    E. parallel phrases

15. Which of the following aptly describes a relationship between Passage 1 and Passage 2?

    I. Passage 1 predicts a reevaluation of Columbus's accomplishments, and Passage 2 makes that reevaluation.

    II. Passage 1 calls attention to the way the image of Columbus in each period reflects the values of that period, and Passage 2 presents an image that reflects late twentieth-century ideas.

    III. Passage 1 focuses on the reputation of Columbus, and Passage 2 emphasizes his unique character.

    A. III only

    B. I and II only

    C. I and III only

    D. II and III only

    E. I, II, and III

IF YOU FINISH BEFORE TIME IS CALLED, CHECK YOUR WORK ON THIS SECTION ONLY. DO NOT WORK ON ANY OTHER SECTION IN THE TEST.

Section 6: Mathematical Reasoning

Time: 15 Minutes

10 Questions

Directions: Solve each problem in this section by using the information given and your own mathematical calculations, insights, and problem-solving skills. Then select the one correct answer of the five choices given and mark the corresponding circle on your answer sheet. Use the available space on the page for your scratch work.

Notes

1. All numbers used are real numbers.

2. Calculators may be used.

3. Some problems may be accompanied by figures or diagrams. These figures are drawn as accurately as possible EXCEPT when it is stated in a specific problem that a figure is not drawn to scale. The figures and diagrams are meant to provide information useful in solving the problem or problems. Unless otherwise stated, all figures and diagrams lie in a plane.

Data That Can Be Used for Reference

Area

rectangle — $A = lw$

triangle — $A = \frac{1}{2}bh$

circle — $A = \pi r^2$, $C = 2\pi r$

Volume

rectangular solid — $V = lwh$

right circular cylinder — $V = \pi r^2 h$

Pythagorean Relationship

$a^2 + b^2 = c^2$

Special Triangles

$30° - 60° - 90°$

$45° - 45° - 90°$

A circle is composed of 360°

A straight angle measures 180°

The sum of the angles of a triangle is 180°

1. If $2x + 13$ represents an odd number, what must the next consecutive odd number be?

   A. $2x + 15$

   B. $2x + 14$

   C. $3x + 13$

   D. $3x + 15$

   E. $4x + 1$

2. A suit that originally sold for $120 was on sale for $90. What was the rate of discount?

   A. 75%

   B. 33⅓%

   C. 30%

   D. 25%

   E. 20%

3. If $\sqrt{\dfrac{81}{x}} = \dfrac{9}{5}$, then $x =$

   A. 5

   B. 9

   C. 25

   D. 50

   E. 53

Note: Figure not drawn to scale.

4. If, in the figure above, $\angle CFD = \angle AFB$, then what is the degree measure of $\angle AFE$?

   A. 40°

   B. 45°

   C. 150°

   D. 160°

   E. 180°

5. What is the value of x if the average of 93, 82, 79, and x is 87?

   A. 87

   B. 90

   C. 93

   D. 94

   E. 348

Section **6** Mathematical Reasoning

GO ON TO THE NEXT PAGE

SCHOOLWIDE EYE COLOR SURVEY

6. Annette does a schoolwide survey and publishes her results in the preceding circle graph. If 62 people at Annette's school have hazel eyes, how many have brown eyes?

    A.   20

    B.   40

    C.   62

    D.   124

    E.   248

---

7. How many degrees has the minute hand moved on a clock from 4:00 p.m. to 4:12 p.m.?

    A.   12

    B.   36

    C.   72

    D.   90

    E.   102

---

8. If $\dfrac{x^2 - 5x + 7}{x^2 - 4x + 10} = 1$, then $x =$

    A. −3

    B. $\frac{1}{3}$

    C. $\frac{7}{10}$

    D. $\frac{17}{9}$

    E.   3

---

9. One angle of a triangle is 68°. The other two angles are in the ratio of 3:4. Which of the following is the number of degrees in the smallest angle of the triangle?

    A.   16

    B.   34

    C.   48

    D.   64

    E.   68

Note: Figure not drawn to scale.

10. If, in the preceding graph, point E has coordinates (−3, 5) and point F has coordinates (6, −7), then the length of EF =

    A.   21

    B.   15

    C.   7

    D.   5

    E.   3

IF YOU FINISH BEFORE TIME IS CALLED, CHECK YOUR WORK ON THIS SECTION ONLY. DO NOT WORK ON ANY OTHER SECTION IN THE TEST.

Section 7: Mathematical Reasoning

Time: 30 Minutes

25 Questions

Directions: Solve each problem in this section by using the information given and your own mathematical calculations, insights, and problem-solving skills. Then select the one correct answer of the five choices given and mark the corresponding circle on your answer sheet. Use the available space on the page for your scratch work.

Notes

1. All numbers used are real numbers.

2. Calculators may be used.

3. Some problems may be accompanied by figures or diagrams. These figures are drawn as accurately as possible EXCEPT when it is stated in a specific problem that a figure is not drawn to scale. The figures and diagrams are meant to provide information useful in solving the problem or problems. Unless otherwise stated, all figures and diagrams lie in a plane.

Data That Can Be Used for Reference

GO ON TO THE NEXT PAGE

1. If $2x - 5 = 9$, then $3x + 2 =$

   A. 44

   B. 23

   C. 16

   D. 14

   E. 7

2. On the above number line, what is the point 15 units to the left of point Q?

   A. 10

   B. 5

   C. 0

   D. –9

   E. –10

3. If $x = 3$, $y = 4$, and $z = -1$, what is the value of $2x + 3y^2 - z$?

   A. 151

   B. 149

   C. 55

   D. 53

   E. 19

4. If cassette tapes cost $2.98 for a package of two tapes, how much change will Roy receive from a twenty-dollar bill if he purchases 12 tapes?

   A. $2.02

   B. $2.12

   C. $2.18

   D. $2.22

   E. $3.02

5. $\dfrac{6^4 + 6^5}{6^4} =$

   A. 36

   B. 31

   C. 30

   D. 7

   E. 6

6. Gasoline varies in cost from $0.96 to $1.12 per gallon. If a car's mileage varies from 16 to 24 miles per gallon, what is the difference between the most and the least that the gasoline for a 480-mile trip will cost?

   A. $ 5.12

   B. $ 7.04

   C. $11.52

   D. $14.40

   E. $52.80

7. Ernie cut a yardstick into two pieces, the larger piece being six inches more than the smaller. How could Ernie compute the size of the smaller piece, *x*?

  A. $x + 6 = 36$

  B. $2x = 36$

  C. $x + x + 6 = 36$

  D. $2x - 6 = 36$

  E. $2x + 6 = 30$

```
    □□4
  x   8
  539□
```

8. The sum of the digits in the three boxes equals

  A. 5

  B. 7

  C. 9

  D. 13

  E. 15

9. If the length and width of a rectangle are increased by *x* units, its perimeter is increased by how many units?

  A. $4x$

  B. $2x$

  C. x^2

  D. x

  E. $x + 4$

10. Which of the following ordered pairs (*a, b*) is NOT a member of the solution set of $2a - 3b = 6$?

  A. $(6, 2)$

  B. $(-3, -4)$

  C. $(3, 0)$

  D. $(4, \frac{2}{3})$

  E. $(0, 2)$

11. Harriet planned to complete a certain task on Wednesday, January 1, but because of illness, the completion date was postponed 48 days. On which day of the week in February was the task completed?

  A. Monday

  B. Tuesday

  C. Wednesday

  D. Thursday

  E. Friday

12. Which of the following expresses the perimeter of the preceding triangle?

  A. $(2s - 6)(s + 4)$

  B. $\frac{1}{2}(2s - 6)(s + 4)$

  C. $4s$

  D. $4s + 12$

  E. $4s - 12$

GO ON TO THE NEXT PAGE

13. What percent of ⅔ is ½?

   A. 300%

   B. 133⅓%

   C. 75%

   D. 50%

   E. 33⅓%

---

14. How many inches are in m yards and n feet?

   A. $m + n$

   B. $36m + 12n$

   C. $36(m + n)$

   D. $3m + n$

   E. $12(m + n)$

---

15. A house is on the market for a selling price of $64,000. The buyer made a $1,500 deposit, but fifteen percent of the selling price is needed for the down payment. How much more money does the buyer need for the down payment?

   A. $3,200

   B. $6,400

   C. $8,100

   D. $9,600

   E. $11,100

16. The average of 9 numbers is 7, and the average of 7 other numbers is 9. What is the average of all 16 numbers?

   A. 8

   B. 7⅞

   C. 7½

   D. 7¼

   E. 7⅛

---

17. If the volume and the total surface area of a cube are equal, how long must the edge of the cube be?

   A. 2 units

   B. 3 units

   C. 4 units

   D. 5 units

   E. 6 units

---

18. If $l_1 \| l_2$, $x = 60°$, and $w = 2z$, then $y + w =$

   A. 60°

   B. 90°

   C. 120°

   D. 150°

   E. 180°

19. If # is a binary operation such that $a \, \# \, b$ is defined as

$$\frac{a^2 + b^2}{a^2 - b^2}$$

and $(a^2 - b^2 \neq 0)$, then what is the value of $a \, \# \, b$ if $2a = b$ and $a \neq 0$?

A. $1\frac{1}{3}$

B. $\frac{3}{5}$

C. $-\frac{1}{2}$

D. $-\frac{3}{5}$

E. $-1\frac{2}{3}$

20. If a pipe can drain a tank in t hours, what part of the tank does it drain in 3 hours?

A. $3t$

B. $t/3$

C. $t + 3$

D. $3/t$

E. $t - 3$

Note: Figure not drawn to scale.

21. In the preceding figure, BD $\perp$ AC, AB = 34, BD = 30, and BC = 34. What is the length of AC?

A. 8

B. 18

C. 30

D. 32

E. 34

22. What is the area of a square inscribed in a circle whose circumference is 16π?

A. 512

B. 256

C. 128

D. 64

E. 32

GO ON TO THE NEXT PAGE

Figure 1   **Figure 2**   **Figure 3**

23. The horizontal length of each rectangle above is marked within. What is the total horizontal length of $x + y$?

A. 40

B. 50

C. 80

D. 90

E. cannot be determined

25. In Figure 1, a square piece of paper is folded along dotted line AB so that X is on top of Y and W is on top of Z (Figure 2). The paper is then folded again so that B is on top of A and WZ is on top of XY (Figure 3). A small triangle is cut out of the folded paper as shown in Figure 3. If the paper is unfolded, which of the following could be the result?

24. 750 times 45 equals P. Therefore, 750 times 44 equals

A. $P - 45$

B. $P - 750$

C. $P - 1$

D. $44P$

E. $750P$

A.

B.

C.

D.

E.

IF YOU FINISH BEFORE TIME IS CALLED, CHECK YOUR WORK ON THIS SECTION ONLY. DO NOT WORK ON ANY OTHER SECTION IN THE TEST.

SCORING PRACTICE TEST 1

Answer Key

Section 1: Verbal Reasoning	Section 2: Mathematical Reasoning	Section 3: Verbal Reasoning		Section 4: Mathematical Reasoning
1. A	1. B	1. B	31. A	1. A
2. B	2. C	2. C	32. E	2. C
3. A	3. C	3. D	33. C	3. C
4. C	4. C	4. E	34. D	4. A
5. D	5. D	5. B	35. C	5. D
6. C	6. D	6. A		6. A
7. B	7. E	7. B		7. C
8. D	8. B	8. D		8. A
9. C	9. B	9. B		9. A
10. C	10. C	10. C		10. B
11. B	11. A	11. C		11. B
12. A	12. A	12. E		12. A
13. E	13. A	13. B		13. A
14. C	14. E	14. D		14. C
15. A	15. B	15. A		15. C
16. E	16. C	16. A		16. 94
17. B	17. D	17. E		17. 9.49
18. D	18. A	18. E		18. 70
19. A	19. B	19. A		19. 4
20. C	20. A	20. D		20. 480
21. A	21. B	21. C		21. 50
22. C	22. A	22. B		22. 20
23. B	23. C	23. B		23. 640
24. C	24. D	24. B		24. 4/9
25. D	25. A	25. D		25. 48
26. A		26. B		
27. A		27. D		
28. D		28. D		
29. B		29. C		
30. E		30. A		

Answer Key

Section 5: Verbal Reasoning	Section 6: Mathematical Reasoning	Section 7: Mathematical Reasoning
1. E	1. A	1. B
2. D	2. D	2. E
3. B	3. C	3. C
4. C	4. C	4. B
5. B	5. D	5. D
6. B	6. D	6. D
7. E	7. C	7. C
8. E	8. A	8. E
9. B	9. C	9. A
10. A	10. B	10. E
11. B		11. B
12. E		12. C
13. D		13. C
14. C		14. B
15. B		15. C
		16. B
		17. E
		18. E
		19. E
		20. D
		21. D
		22. C
		23. E
		24. B
		25. D

Analyzing Your Test Results

The charts on the following pages should be used to carefully analyze your results and spot your strengths and weaknesses. The complete process of analyzing each subject area and each individual problem should be completed for each practice test. These results should then be re-examined for trends in types of errors (repeated errors) or poor results in specific subject areas. *This reexamination and analysis is of tremendous importance to you in assuring maximum test preparation benefit.*

Verbal Reasoning Analysis Sheet

Section 1	Possible	Completed	Right	Wrong
Sentence Completion	9			
Analogies	6			
Critical Reading	15			
Subtotal	30			
Section 3	**Possible**	**Completed**	**Right**	**Wrong**
Sentence Completion	10			
Analogies	13			
Critical Reading	12			
Subtotal	30			
Section 5	**Possible**	**Completed**	**Right**	**Wrong**
Critical Reading	15			
Subtotal	30			
Overall Verbal Totals	**80**			

Mathematical Reasoning Analysis Sheet

Section 2	Possible	Completed	Right	Wrong
Multiple Choice	25			
Subtotal	30			
Section 4	Possible	Completed	Right	Wrong
Quantitative Comparison	15			
Grid-Ins	10			
Subtotal	30			
Section 6	Possible	Completed	Right	Wrong
Multiple Choice	10			
Subtotal	10			
Section 7	Possible	Completed	Right	Wrong
Multiple Choice	25			
Subtotal	25			
Overall Math Totals	85			

You can now use the Score Range Approximator on page 345 to convert your raw scores to an *approximate* scaled score.

Analysis/Tally Sheet for Problems Missed

One of the most important parts of test preparation is analyzing why you missed a problem so that you can reduce the number of mistakes. Now that you have taken the practice test and checked your answers, carefully tally your mistakes by marking them in the proper column.

	Reason for Mistakes				
	Total Missed	Simple Mistake	Misread Problem	Lack of Knowledge	Lack of Time
Section 1: Verbal					
Section 3: Verbal					
Section 5: Verbal					
Subtotal					
Section 2: Math					
Section 4: Math					
Section 6: Math					
Section 7: Math					
Subtotal					
Total Math and Verbal					

Reviewing the preceding data should help you determine *why* you are missing certain problems. Now that you've pinpointed the type of error, compare it to other practice tests to spot other common mistakes.

Section 1: Verbal Reasoning

Sentence Completion

1. **A.** The adjective here should pick up the implications of "loved" and "hated," not just one or the other. The word "controversial" **A** accounts for both. The other choices are not specifically related in any way to the rest of the sentence.

2. **B.** You need a verb here describing the action of organisms with a meaning like "developed" or "discovered." The best choice is **B** "evolved," developed gradually, which also fits well with the detail of "thousands of years." The wrong answers describe too conscious an action.

3. **A.** Here you need words that are contradictory to the two givens: "affectionate" and "alert." "Aloof" **A**, "cruel" **B**, or "selfish" **D** are possible first words, but "shrewd" **B**, "lively" **C**, and "nimble" **D** are not contradictions of "alert," so the only possible right answer is **A**.

4. **C.** The first adjective offers a choice among five, any one of which would fit the first phrase. Because this fame is for an unfavorably regarded trait, however, the best choice is "notorious." A hero is "famous," "renowned," "illustrious," or "eminent," but a man who talks too much is "notorious." Because the action described confirms the reputation for long-windedness, "verified" is the only possible choice of the verbs.

5. **D.** You know that Montana already is a senator who may run for reelection. Therefore, she is the "incumbent," the holder of an office. The details of the sentence support this choice. Although the other nouns are not wholly unsuitable, none of them has any real connection with the details in the rest of the sentence.

6. **C.** The first noun must be a term that refers to what is pledged to obtain a loan, a word like "pledge," or "surety," or "collateral," or "deposit." Only "profit" **D** can be eliminated. The verb must mean liquidate or get rid of because he emerges "free of debt." Only "discharge" **C** is left when you eliminate **A**, **B**, and **E**. This confirms the sense of "collateral" being the best of the four available nouns.

7. **B.** The missing word describes "absurdist" fiction and is parallel to the word shocking. Clearly, "banal" **A**, "plausible" **C**, "cozy" **D**, and "familiar" **E** will not do. The adjective "radical" means favoring fundamental change or very leftist.

8. **D.** The sense of the sentence calls for an adjective expressing strong feelings because the writer is surprised by this response to an "insignificant" issue. The only choice **D** is logical.

9. **C.** The sentence describes a division in the band, avant-garde instrumental-ists and a popular-ballad crooner, so the first adjective should account for this split. The word "progressive" **A** fits only the band, and "old-fashioned" **B** and "predictable" **E** fit the singer. The word "inconsistent" is the best of the choices. The second adjective should describe "popular ballads," and all except **B** "unique" will do.

Analogies

10. **C.** The first noun here is an animal, the second a means of controlling it, as a "horse" is controlled by a "bridle." The parallel is a "dog" controlled by a "leash."

11. **B.** The second of the two nouns is what the first uses to entice its prey: A "hunter" uses a "decoy" to attract ducks. The parallel is an "angler" (one who fishes) who uses a "lure" to attract fish. It is the human, not the mouse, who sets the mousetrap.

12. **A.** The second of the two nouns is an example or type of the more general first word. One kind of "herb" is "oregano." One kind of "poem" is a "ballad."

13. **E.** The two nouns denote an artist and the work he or she creates. A "choreo-grapher" (the roots of the word are "dance" and "write" or "draw") designs the movements or contents of a *dance,* as the *playwright* is responsible for the contents of a "play." A better parallel for **A** would have "composer" in place of "conductor."

14. **C.** These words are synonyms, both meaning to grow embittered or to be-come painful or infected. Though totally unlike "fester" and "rankle" in meaning, the relationship of "worship" and "adore" is similar. Both mean to love or honor greatly.

15. **A.** The two words here are an adjective that could describe a person and a noun that would "not" be a quality of such a person. "Disinterested" (not "uninterested") means fair or impartial. A "disinterested" person would avoid or not be characterized by "prejudice." Similarly, a person who is "naive" (simple, artless) would not be characterized by "sophistication."

Critical Reading

16. **E.** Although "correspondence" can mean correlation, agreement, or similarity, here it means communication by letters. Gauguin's "correspondence" refers to the letters he wrote to France from the South Pacific.

17. **B.** Gauguin's letter refers to the quotation from Poe that finds "singularity" (oddness, uniqueness, strangeness) in perfect beauty, and he is reminded of these lines by the beauty of his first Tahitian model.

18. **D.** The passage points out that most of the artists before Gauguin had not painted Tahitians realistically, but as "idealized types," altered to fit European tastes, just the opposite of choice **B.** The passage goes on to point out that the Tahitian could "scarcely be distinguished from his African or Asian counterpart."

19. **A.** The reader can infer that Charles Giraud painted Tahitians before Gauguin did, but because the paintings have not survived, the author cannot know whether Giraud followed other artists and painted to suit European ideas of beauty or if, like Gauguin, he painted the Tahitians as they really were. It is for this reason the author would like to see Giraud's work.

20. **C.** The passage opposes the terms "Naturalism" and "Symbolism." The naturalistic or realistic in Gauguin is alluded to in lines 38–39 ("straightforward") and lines 55–56 ("naturalistically"), and lines 64–66 refer to the nonrealistic "Symbolist aspirations."

21. **A.** The two impulses in Gauguin that appear to be at odds are his wish to render the Tahitians as they really are and at the same time to reveal a "poetic image" of the "island's mysterious past." The problem is discussed in the last 40 lines of the passage.

22. **C.** The first paragraph is introductory and presents the opposing positions on global warming and greenhouse gases represented by the climatologist Jim Hansen and the politician John Sununu.

23. **B.** Although "pit" (the verb) can mean to scar or remove the core of, the meaning here is sets in opposition or sets in competition.

24. **C.** Because neither oxygen nor nitrogen absorbs heat, neither **A** nor **B** is likely. The amount of carbon dioxide in the atmosphere can be increased by burning of fossil fuels **D.** In choice **E,** the opposite is more likely to be true because heat escapes as infrared radiation. Because carbon dioxide absorbs heat, a planet with more in its atmosphere would be warmer.

25. **D.** Because oxygen and nitrogen, which are not greenhouse gases, form 99% of the atmosphere according to the second paragraph, the passage does not imply that greenhouse gases make up a large part of the atmosphere. The second paragraph also tells us that carbon dioxide absorbs large amounts of heat and that the release of carbon dioxide can lead to warming. The third paragraph adds that clearing and burning forests create carbon dioxide.

26. A. If greenhouse gases absorb heat and nitrogen does not absorb heat (paragraph 2), then nitrogen is not a greenhouse gas. The other four are mentioned in the second and third paragraphs of the passage.

27. A. The first statement makes a point that logically questions the Marshall report theory that "without greenhouse gases to warm things up, the world would become cool in the next century." If so, why was it not cool before there were greenhouse gases? The passage does not give us any information about economic predictions in the Marshall report, and in any case, because the report advocates the encouragement of greenhouse gases, this idea would not undermine its conclusions. Similarly, the third statement would not affect the arguments of the report because oxygen is not a greenhouse gas.

28. D. The word "skeptic" now usually means a person who habitually questions or doubts even matters generally accepted.

29. B. The image of Mr. Sununu as a character in a Dracula film was probably intended to amuse the audience and to make the opponent seem a bit ridiculous. It would also suggest that the claims are melodramatic. A believer in the danger of too much greenhouse gas in the atmosphere would not be likely to suggest that the danger is imaginary, so the third statement is very unlikely.

30. E. The final paragraph leaves the debate unresolved. Although a reader of the whole passage may feel a slight bias in favor of the climatologists, the final paragraph asserts that neither side can prove its case beyond a reasonable doubt.

Section 2: Mathematical Reasoning

1. **B.** Setting up an equation gives $\frac{1}{5}x = 2$. Multiplying both sides by 5,

$$(5)\tfrac{1}{5}x = 2(5)$$

Then $x = 10$

And $\frac{1}{2}$ of 10 is 5.

2. **C.** In the series 8, 9, 12, 17, 24. . . ,

$$9 - 8 = 1$$
$$12 - 9 = 3$$
$$17 - 12 = 5$$
$$24 - 17 = 7$$

Therefore, the difference between the next term and 24 must be 9, or

$$x - 24 = 9$$
$$x = 33$$

Therefore, the next term in the series must be 33.

3. **C.** The selling price for 1 dozen at 3 for $0.85 is

$$3 \times 4 = 12 = 1 \text{ dozen} = \$0.85 \times 4 = \$3.40$$

Therefore, 6 dozen will yield $3.40 \times 6 = \$20.40$.

The store's cost for 6 dozen at $1.80 per dozen is $1.80 \times 6 = \$10.80$.

Therefore, the profit on 6 dozen of these items will be $20.40 - \$10.80$, or $9.60.

4. **C.** If $x = -1$,

$$x^4 + x^3 + x^2 + x - 3$$
$$= (-1)^4 + (-1)^3 + (-1)^2 + (-1) - 3$$
$$= 1 + (-1) + 1 + (-1) - 3$$
$$= 0 + 1 + (-1) - 3$$
$$= 1 + (-1) - 3$$
$$= 0 - 3$$
$$= -3$$

5. D. Because $15 = 3 \times 5$, a number divisible by 15 must be divisible by both 3 and 5. A number is divisible by 3 if the sum of its digits is divisible by 3. A number is divisible by 5 if its last digit is 0 or 5. Because 46,335 is divisible by 3 and by 5, it is also divisible by 15.

6. D. You should have a working knowledge of these expressions:

Sum: The result of addition

Difference: The result of subtraction

Product: The result of multiplication

Quotient: The result of division

Therefore, the *product of two numbers* may be represented as $(x)(y)$. The *difference of the two numbers* may be either $x - y$ or $y - x$. The term twice indicates that the expression is to be multiplied by 2. Therefore, the entire expression breaks down as follows:

The product of two numbers is equal to twice the difference of the two numbers
$(x)(y)$ $=$ 2 $(x - y)$

Therefore, $(x)(y) = 2(x - y)$.

7. E. $(5x + 2)(3x - 4) - (2x - 3)(x + 2)$

$= (15x^2 + 6x - 20x - 8) - (2x^2 - 3x + 4x - 6)$

$= (15x^2 - 14x - 8) - (2x^2 + x - 6)$

$= 15x^2 - 14x - 8 - 2x^2 - x + 6$

$= 13x^2 - 15x - 2$

8. B. Because D is between A and B on $\overleftrightarrow{AB}$ you know that the sum of the lengths of the smaller segments AD and DB is equal to the length of the larger segment AB.

Therefore, $AB = AD + DB$

$AB - AD = AD + DB - AD$

$AB - AD = DB$

9. B. Since $a \otimes b = a^3 + b^2$,

$(-2) \otimes (-3) = (-2)^3 + (-3)^2$

$= (-8) + 9$

$= 1$

10. **C.** Since BD = CD, $\angle CBD = \angle C = 19°$

Therefore, $\angle BDC = 180° - (\angle CBD - \angle C)$

$$= 180° - (19° + 19°)$$

$$= 180° - 38°$$

$$= 142°$$

Then $\angle BDA = 180° - \angle BDC$

$$= 180° - 142°$$

$$= 38°$$

Since AB = AD, $\angle ABD = \angle BDA = 38°$

Therefore, $\angle A = 180° - (\angle BDA + \angle ABD)$

$$= 180° - (38° + 38°)$$

$$= 180° - 76°$$

$$= 104°$$

11. **A.** The number of nickels that Angela has is x. Therefore, the total value of those nickels (in cents) is $5x$. Angela also has twice as many dimes as nickels, or $2x$. The total value in cents of those dimes is $2x(10)$, or $20x$. Adding together the value of the nickels and dimes gives $5x + 20x$, or $25x$.

12. **A.** If $x - 4 = y$, then $y - x = -4$. Therefore, $(y - x)^3 = (-4)^3 = -64$.

13. **A.** The perimeter of a rectangle with length l and width w is $2l + 2w$. Because the perimeter of the rectangle is $10x + 8$ and its length is $3x$,

$$\text{perimeter} = 2l + 2w$$

$$10x + 8 = 2(3x) + 2w$$

$$10x + 8 = 6x + 2w$$

$$10x + 8 - 6x = 6x + 2w - 6x$$

$$4x + 8 = 2w$$

$$\frac{4x + 8}{2} = \frac{2w}{2}$$

$$2x + 4 = w$$

Therefore, the width of the rectangle is $2x + 4$.

14. **E.** If $\frac{3}{7} = \frac{10}{x - 4}$ then cross multiplying yields

$$3(x - 4) = (7)(10)$$

$$3x - 12 = 70$$

$$3x - 12 + 12 = 70 + 12$$

$$3x = 82$$

$$\frac{3x}{3} = \frac{82}{3}$$

$$x = {}^{82}\!/_{3}, \text{ or } 27\frac{1}{3}$$

15. **B.** The car travels a total distance of 280 miles 7½ hours for the round trip. Its average speed in miles per hour is

$$280 \div 7\tfrac{1}{2} = \frac{280}{1} \div \frac{15}{2}$$
$$= \frac{280}{1} \times \frac{2}{15} = \frac{560}{15} = \frac{112}{3}$$
$$= 37\tfrac{1}{3}$$

You could have used your calculator here and simply divided 280 by 7.5, getting 37.333, or 37⅓.

16. **C.** Because a and b must both be positive or both be negative, choice **C III** is the only answer that *must* be true.

17. **D.** The slope (m) of a line passing through the points (x_1, y_1) and (x_2, y_2) is

$$m = \frac{y_2 - y_1}{x_2 - x_1}$$

Because $c = 1$ (see diagram), the line passes through $(-3, 5)$ and $(2, 9)$, and

$$m = \frac{9 - 5}{2 - (-3)} = \frac{4}{5}$$

Note that you could eliminate choices **A, B,** and **C** because they are all negative slopes, and the diagram shows a positive slope.

18. **A.** If today Lucy is 14, then last year she was 13. Likewise, if Charlie's age now is C, then last year he was $C - 1$. Now, put these into an equation:

Lucy's age last year is three years older than twice Charlie's age last year.

| 13 | = | $2(C-1) + 3$ |

Transposing, $13 - 3 = 2(C - 1)$.

19. **B.** $\angle XYZ$ is inscribed in a semicircle and is therefore a right angle. Therefore, $\triangle XYZ$ is a right triangle and the Pythagorean theorem states

$$(XY)^2 = (XZ)^2 + (YZ)^2$$
$$(17)^2 = (XZ)^2 + (15)^2 \ (XY \text{ is a diameter})$$
$$289 = (XZ)^2 + 225$$
$$289 - 225 = (XZ)^2$$
$$(XZ)^2 = 64$$
$$XZ = \sqrt{64}$$
$$XZ = 8$$
$$\text{area of } \triangle XYZ = \tfrac{1}{2}bh$$
$$= \tfrac{1}{2}(XZ)(YZ)$$
$$= \tfrac{1}{2}(8)(15)$$
$$= (4)(15)$$
$$= 60$$

20. **A.** If 15 gumballs were picked from the bag, it is possible that 8 of them are red and 7 are green. On the next pick, however (the 16th), one is assured of having one gumball of each color.

21. **B.** Because each letter repeats after every five vowels, divide 327 by 5, and the remainder will determine the vowel in that place of the pattern. Since $327 \div 5 = 65$ with a remainder of 2, the remainder of 2 indicates that the second vowel (e) will be the 327th letter.

22. **A.** Let x = length of equal sides in feet and $x + 8$ = length of base in feet.

Since the perimeter is 89 feet,

$$x + x + x + 8 = 89$$

$$3x + 8 = 89$$

$$3x + 8 - 8 = 89 - 8$$

$$3x = 81$$

$$x = 27$$

Therefore, the length of the base is $x + 8$, or 35 feet.

23. **C.** III only. The random sample indicates that 1,500 out of 2,500 New York moviegoers prefer comedies, or 60% of those polled prefer comedies. Of those polled, 500 out of 2,500, or 20%, prefer dramas. Therefore, out of 8,000,000 total New York moviegoers, 60% should be found to prefer comedies (4,800,000), and 20% (1,600,000) should be found to prefer dramas. Only III reflects either of these estimates.

24. **D.** Let x = the missing number. Since the average of x and z is y,

$$\tfrac{1}{2}(x + z) = y$$

$$2 \times \tfrac{1}{2}(x + z) = 2y$$

$$x + z = 2y$$

$$x + z - z = 2y - z$$

$$x = 2y - z$$

25. A. Because the perimeter of the rhombus is 40, each side has length 10. Because the diagonals of a rhombus are perpendicular and bisect each other,

$$x^2 + 5^2 = 10^2$$
$$x^2 + 25 = 100$$
$$x^2 = 75$$
$$x = \sqrt{75}$$
$$x = 5\sqrt{3}$$

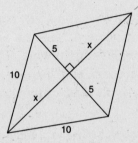

The area of a quadrilateral with perpendicular diagonals d_1 and d_2 is

$$\text{area} = \tfrac{1}{2}d_1 \cdot d_2$$
$$= \tfrac{1}{2}(10)(10\sqrt{3})$$
$$= 50\sqrt{3}$$

Section 3: Verbal Reasoning

Sentence Completion

1. **B.** The "also" in the second half of the sentence signals that the verb is parallel to "prevent" in the first half. You can eliminate **C** and **D**. The first adjective must mean something like reasonable or sensible, so **B** "logical" is a better choice than **A** "fanciful" or **E** "idle," which mean just the opposite.

2. **C.** The first noun must mean something like substitute but a word that will fit with the preposition "to." Choice **A** "answer" is possible, **C** "alternative" is a good answer, and **D** "rejoinder" might work. The phrase "responsible for" **A** makes little sense in this context, and "involved in" **D** is awkward. The phrase "subject to" is clearly the best of the three and **C** the best of the five choices.

3. **D.** The logic of the sentence suggests that the missing verb must mean something like prevent or decrease. Choices **B** "augment" (increase) and **C** "foster" are the opposite of what is needed. Neither "explain" **A** nor "exculpate" **E** (excuse) makes much sense, although "deter" (discourage, keep from doing) fits well.

4. **E.** The sentence opposes the unpleasant smoke,_____, and "city" with the _____ "air and peace of the mountains," so the first blank must be a noun similar in effect to "smoke," and the second blank requires an adjective with pleasant denotation. In **A** and **B** the nouns are possible, but the adjectives are not. In **C** and **D,** the noun choices cannot fit. Choice **E** correctly has the bad "hustle-bustle" and the good "exhilarating."

5. **B.** A situation requiring the choice between two unpleasant alternatives is the definition of the word "dilemma" and what this sentence describes. Some of the other choices are plausible, but because "dilemma" so exactly fits the situation, it is clearly the best.

6. **A.** The word "combining" should alert you to look for a noun here that denotes a coming together of East and West. Choices **B, C,** and **D** are clearly wrong. Choice **A** "fusion," the union of different things, fits well.

7. **B.** The noun referring to "what allowed voters to decide" on an issue could be "statute" **A**, "referendum" **B** (the most precise word), or "bill" **D**. The missing adverb that describes the nine-to-one win must denote a very resounding margin of victory. Neither "meager" **A** nor "narrow" **D** will do. Again, the best answer uses the most specific noun as well as the most suitable adverb.

8. **D.** The first blank requires a noun describing something a novel is based on. Choices **A, C,** and **D** are possible. **B** and **E** are eliminated by the use of "upon which." The second word must praise the book because it is parallel with "intelligence" and the novel has been called "fine." Choices **A** and **C** must be eliminated, and only **D** remains.

9. **B.** The adjective "anachronistic" means representing something as existing at other than its proper time, such as a washing machine in the Middle Ages or a knight in armor at a football game. Choice **A** is a possibility, although **B** is more exact.

10. **C.** Because she hoped to be undetected, she had to hide the card "furtively," that is, stealthily or surreptitiously. The words "brazenly" **A** and "overtly" **B** contradict the opening phrase.

Analogies

11. **C.** In this pair, the second noun is a carrier in which the first is carried. "Clothes" are carried in "luggage." The best answer is **C** because "documents" are carried in a "briefcase."

12. **E.** There are two nouns here, and the second denotes the material of which the first is made. A "cymbal" is made of brass. The parallel pair is **E;** a "violin" is made of "wood." Note that words have several meanings, and "brass" here does *not* refer to the section of the orchestra that contains such instruments as the trumpet. A "cymbal" is part of the percussion section. The test will usually call for knowledge of the more obvious meanings of a word when there are several.

13. **B.** The pair are related in length. A "decade" is ten years long; a "century" is one hundred years, or ten times longer. The related pair is "dime" and "dollar;" the first is one-tenth of the second, like "decade" to "century."

14. **D.** A "jury" must examine "evidence" in order to reach its verdict. Similarly, a "doctor" must examine "symptoms" to come to a diagnosis.

15. **A.** The two verbs here denote to receive as the result of service or "merit" (earn) and to obtain by stealth, to steal, to pilfer, or to "filch." The contrast is between verbs denoting a legitimate effort and a dishonest one. The best parallel is "create" as opposed to "plagiarize," which is to take ideas or words from someone else and pass them off as one's own.

16. **A.** Each of these verbs means to feel aversion to, but to "loathe" is a more intensive verb and means to "dislike" violently. The same relationship exists with to "praise" and to "extol," which means to praise very highly.

17. **E.** Though all these words are related to astronomy, the relation of the two nouns in the question is of whole to part. A "constellation" is made up of more than one "star." The best parallel is **E,** the "solar system," which contains more than one "planet."

18. **E.** The second of the two verbs here is like the first but with a suggestion of the sinister, not an exact synonym. Choices **A, B, C,** and **D** are pairs of very similar meaning, but **E** adds the suggestion of underhandedness; to "snoop" is to "inquire" in a sneaky or prying manner.

19. **A.** "Agar" (or agar-agar) is the medium in which a "bacterium" is grown. Choice **B** is a tempting answer because a parasite does grow on or within a host, but the terms are in the wrong order. The closest parallel is "potting soil," a substance specifically used to grow a "plant" in.

20. **D.** Both nouns describe falsehoods. "Slander" is a spoken false statement, and "libel" is written. The spoken-to-written difference is also used in a "speech as" opposed to an "essay."

21. **C.** The first adjective describes a person who would "not" be likely to demonstrate the quality denoted by the noun. A "credulous" (that is, gullible or very trusting) person would not be likely to harbor "doubt." A "complacent" (that is, smug or self-satisfied) person is also unlikely to have "modesty."

22. **B.** These adjectives are opposites. "Supine" means lying face up, and "prone" means lying face down. The other pair of opposites is "light" and "dark."

23. **B.** A "surfeit" is an excess or oversupply; a "dearth" is a lack or scarcity, so the two words are opposites. The best parallel is the contrast of "flood" (too much water) and "drought" (a severe water shortage).

Critical Reading

24. **B.** The passage explicitly refers to Celia and Dorothea as sisters. Although it does not mention their father's death, you know that the jewels belonged to their mother, and because an uncle, not her father, gave them to Dorothea, it may be that the father is dead and they are in the uncle's care.

25. **D.** That Dorothea has started an "infant school" in the village and is busy with plans for some buildings tells you at once that she is active and generous. No details in the passage suggest that she is prying, idle, ambitious, or ineffectual, although she may be rich or philanthropic.

26. **B.** The preceding sentence tells you that Dorothea's eyes are "full of laughter," and her tone when she speaks again is "full" and "cordial." She is teasing Celia good-naturedly, making fun of her sister's remark that it is exactly "six months today." In this dialogue, it is Celia who has planned what she will say, and Dorothea speaks spontaneously. Dorothea has probably forgotten all about the jewels, and Celia has probably been thinking about them for some time.

27. **D.** The phrase means disrespectful or lacking in respect. The reader must recognize that the verb "want" here means to lack, not the more common to wish for. Choice **C** confuses "wanting" and "wanton."

28. **D.** Celia does not wish to have all the jewels, although she does want a share, and she expects to wear them. Unlike Dorothea, she is not at all Puritanical. She correctly anticipates that Dorothea might object to wearing jewelry, so she has prepared this defense on the moral grounds that she thinks will best convince Dorothea.

29. C. Dorothea, who does not care about the jewels herself, has simply not realized that Celia really wants to wear them. In lines 48–50, the reader is told that this "discovery" is astonishing to her, and the moment she realizes Celia's true feeling, she rushes to open the cabinet. Celia's arguments would have been more effective if she had simply told Dorothea of her real wishes because Dorothea loves her sister and is eager to make her happy. Notice that Dorothea has said that the jewels would not be worn only before she realizes what Celia really wishes.

30. A. "Deprecation" is disapproval, or protest, as is suggested in this sentence by Dorothea's saying "no." A lessening is a "depreciation," and a removal is a "deprivation."

31. A. The adjective in this context comes from the verb meaning to annoy, to irk, as in to try one's patience. In some contexts, "trying" might mean attempting or determining, but here, irksome is the best definition.

32. E. The "Puritanic toleration" is Dorothea's. She has given up all the jewels to Celia and even encouraged her to wear them. Although this is in one way pleasing to Celia, it does put Dorothea in a position of moral superiority, which Celia finds annoying.

33. C. Dorothea is the Puritan, and Celia is the "unenthusiastic sister;" that is, one who has not adopted the religious extremes of self-denial, such as not wearing jewels.

34. D. Although some answers here describe Dorothea accurately, only **D** points to an inconsistency. Dorothea regards wearing jewelry as somehow immoral, and yet, because she sees that Celia really wants to wear the jewels, she encourages her to do so. What is right for her sister would not be right for her.

35. C. The passage is centrally concerned with delineating the two sisters. Although there is some mild comedy at the expense of both, the passage is not satiric, and it reveals as much love as friction between the sisters. They are not alike, and though Celia may take pleasure in jewels, the passage is not about the dangers of materialism. The author, the reader senses, is amused by and fond of both of these young women.

Section 4: Mathematical Reasoning

Quantitative Comparison

1. **A.** By inspection, both sides are exactly the same except that in column A you are adding $4 \cdot 10^2$ and in column B you are subtracting $4 \cdot 10^2$. Therefore, column A is greater. Solving for values would give

$3^2 + 4 \cdot 10^2 - 4^2$	$3^2 - 4 \cdot 10^2 - 4^2$
$9 + 4 \cdot 100 - 16$	$9 - 4 \cdot 100 - 16$
$9 + 400 - 6$	$9 - 400 - 16$
$409 - 16$	$-391 - 16$
393	$> \quad -407$

2. **C.** Angles x and y are vertical angles formed by two intersecting lines. Therefore, they are equal. Vertical angles are always equal.

3. **C.** Solving the top equation of $5y = 10$ gives $y = 2$. Substituting $y = 2$ into the second equation leaves

   $$3x + 2(2) = 10$$
   $$3x + 4 = 10$$
   $$3x = 6$$

   Therefore, $x = 2$, and columns A and B are equal.

4. **A.** Since both sides have the factors $\frac{2}{5}$ and $\frac{5}{8}$, you can eliminate them from each column. Now compare $\frac{3}{7}$ and $\frac{4}{11}$, by cross multiplying upward.

   $$33 \quad 28$$
   $$\frac{3}{7} \times \frac{4}{11}$$

   Since 33 is greater than 28, $\frac{3}{7}$ is greater than $\frac{4}{11}$.

5. **D.** Trying some small values is required here, keeping in mind that x must be greater than 0. Let $x = 1$. Then

$3(1)^2$	$2(1)^3$
$3(1)$	$2(1)$
3	$> \quad 2$

   In this case, column A is greater. Now try another value for x. Let $x = 2$. Then

$3(2)^2$	$2(2)^3$
$3(4)$	$2(8)$
12	$< \quad 16$

   In this case, column B is greater. Since there are different answers depending on the values chosen, the correct answer is **D,** cannot be determined.

6. **A.** In column A, a number greater than 1 is multiplied by itself 10 times. The answer will be greater than 1. In column B, however, a number less than 1(.23) is multiplied by itself 100 times. The answer in column B will be smaller than 1.

7. **C.** To solve $a/6 = b/4$, cross multiply, giving $4a = 6b$. Then divide by 2, leaving $2a = 3b$.

8. **A.** If the top angle were 90°, then x would be $3\sqrt{2}$. This could be calculated using the Pythagorean theorem.

$$a^2 + b^2 = c^2$$
$$3^2 + 3^2 = x^2$$
$$9 + 9 = x^2$$
$$18 = x^2$$

Therefore, $\sqrt{18} = x$

Simplified, this is $3\sqrt{2}$. But because the angle is larger than 90°, the side across from 92° must be larger than $3\sqrt{2}$. The correct answer is **A**.

9. **A.** Since there are 180° in a triangle and 92° in one angle, that leaves 88° to be split equally between two angles. Therefore, angle y is 44°. (The degrees must be split equally because angles across from equal sides are equal, and the triangle has two equal sides — isosceles.) The correct answer is **A**.

10. **B.** First, multiply out column B.

$4y^2 - 4y + 1 \qquad (2y + 1)^2$

$4y^2 - 4y + 1 \qquad 4y^2 + 4y + 1$

Now subtract out from both sides, getting

$-4y \qquad\qquad +4y$

Divide both sides by 4, getting

$-y \qquad\qquad +y$

Since y is a positive number between 0 and 1, column B is greater than column A.

11. **B.** Since d is above the x axis, it must be positive, and c, being to the left of the y axis, must be negative. Therefore, $c < d$ because all negatives are less than all positives.

12. **A.** Since point P is above the line containing points $(-2, 2)$, d (actual distance) is greater than $|c|$. Therefore, $c + d$ is a positive number. Point Q is on the line. Therefore, e and f are additive inverses of each other, totaling 0. Since all positive numbers are greater than 0, $c + d > e + f$.

13. **A.** To find the number of degrees in the interior angles of a pentagon, use the formula $180 \times (n - 2)$, where n is the number of sides. Therefore,

$$180 \times (5 - 2) = 180 \times 3 = 540$$

$$540° > 500°$$

Another method would be to draw the pentagon and break it into triangles connecting vertices (lines cannot cross), as shown here.

Multiplying the number of triangles (3) by 180 (degrees in a triangle) gives the same result, 540°.

14. **C.** Simplifying the complex fraction in column A,

$$\cfrac{1}{1 + \cfrac{1}{1 + 1/n}} = \cfrac{1}{1 + \cfrac{1}{n/n + 1/n}} = \cfrac{1}{1 + \cfrac{1}{(n + 1)/n}} = \cfrac{1}{1 + \cfrac{n}{n + 1}}$$

$$= \cfrac{1}{\cfrac{n + 1}{n + 1} + \cfrac{n}{n + 1}} = \cfrac{1}{\cfrac{n + 1 + n}{n + 1}} = \cfrac{1}{\cfrac{2n + 1}{n + 1}} = \cfrac{n + 1}{2n + 1}$$

15. **C.** Extend line CO as shown.

You now have triangle OBD, which is a 30°–60°–90 ° triangle. Since all 30° –60°–90° triangles are in proportion 1, $\sqrt{3}$, 2, and since side DB = half of $8\sqrt{3}$, or $4\sqrt{3}$, side OB = 8. Therefore, OA + OB + OC = 8 + 8 + 8 = 24.

Grid-In Questions

16. Answer: 94. Since $x = -4$,

$$5x^2 - 3x + 2 = 5(-4)^2 - 3(-4) + 2$$
$$= 5(16) + 12 + 2$$
$$= 80 + 12 + 2$$
$$= 94$$

17. Answer: 9.49. For a 25-minute call, the first 3 minutes will cost $2.45, and the additional 22 minutes will cost $.32 per minute. The cost (C) for the call will be

$$C = \$2.45 + (22)(\$.32)$$
$$= \$2.45 + \$7.04$$
$$= \$9.49$$

18. Answer: 70. Let $n =$ the original price of the jacket. 80% of n is $56.

$$(0.80) \cdot n = \$56$$
$$n = \$56 \cdot 0.8$$
$$n = \$70$$

19. Answer: 4. The volume of a cube with side of length x is x^3. Therefore,

$$x^3 = 64$$
$$x = \sqrt[3]{64}$$
$$x = 4$$

20. Answer: 480. You can quickly solve this problem by using your calculator. Total the four listed items: $840 + $460 + $320 + $120 = $1,740. Subtract $1,740 from the given total: $2,220 − $1,740 = $480. The lab workbooks cost $480.

21. Answer: 50. Begin by choosing a simple fraction, $^{100}/_{100}$, for example. If the numerator is tripled and the denominator is doubled, the resulting fraction is $^{300}/_{200,}$ or 1½. So the new fraction represents a 50% increase over the original fraction.

22. Answer: 20. Since $l_1 \| l_2$, the alternate interior angles have the same measure and

$$5x - 20 = 2x + 40$$

$$3x - 20 = 40$$

$$3x = 60$$

$$x = 20$$

23. Answer: 640. The phrase *how much more* indicates subtraction. Clothing was 13% of the total. Insurance was 5% of the total. So 13% − 5%, or 8%, more of the total of $8,000 was spent on clothing than on insurance.

$$.08 \times \$8,000 = \$640$$

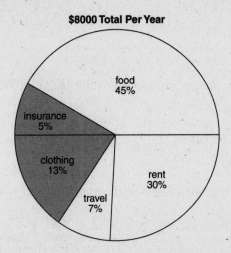

24. Answer: 4/9. In $\triangle MXN$, $\angle MNX = 50°$, $\angle MXN = 90°$, and $\angle NMQ = 30°$

$$\angle NMQ + \angle QMX = \angle NMX$$

So $\quad 50° + 90° + 30° + \angle QMX = 180°$

$$170° + \angle QMX = 180°$$

$$\angle QMX = 10°$$

In $\triangle MPQ$, $\angle QMP + \angle MPQ + \angle MQP = 180°$

$$10° + 130° + \angle MQP = 180°$$

$$140° + \angle MQP = 180°$$

$$\angle MQP = 40°$$

Angle PXN is 90°, so the ratio of $\angle MQP$ to $\angle PXN$ is 40/90, or 4/9.

25. Answer: 48. Set up the equations as follows: Let t be the length of time it will take the plane to overtake the bus. Then $t + 4$ is the time that the bus has traveled before the plane starts. The distance the bus has traveled by 1:00 p.m. is $50(t + 4)$ because distance equals rate times time ($d = rt$). The distance the plane will travel is $300t$. Now, equating these two (they will have to travel the same distance for one to overtake the other) gives $50(t + 4) = 300t$.

Solve the equation as follows.

$$50(t + 4) = 300t$$

$$50t + 200 = 300t$$

$$200 = 250t$$

Therefore, $\frac{4}{5} = t$

Four-fifths of an hour ($\frac{4}{5} \times 60$) is 48 minutes. Therefore, it will take 48 minutes for the plane to overtake the bus.

Section 5: Verbal Reasoning

Critical Reading

1. **E.** The sentence on Lope de Vega's play does all three. It gives an example of a play by a Spanish playwright using Columbus as a hero; it shows that Columbus's reputation had reached to the popular theater; and it gives an example of Columbus in his symbolic role as the "embodiment of that spirit driving humans to explore and discover."

2. **D.** The best of the five definitions here is "inclined." Although the verb "dispose" can mean to arrange or to give away, the context here makes clear that the meaning is something like not inclined to struggle against the myth of Columbus, and the next sentence, as well as the rest of the paragraph, confirms this meaning.

3. **B.** The nouns used for "mold" here — pattern, manner, model, shape, or style — are all adequate; "romantic" here is best defined by idealized. The word is explained further by the phrase "favored in the century's literature," and the quotations from Irving that follow depict an idealized rather than a visionary, fictitious, or escapist hero.

4. **C.** Since "ambition" and "magnanimity" are direct quotations from Irving, neither is possible. The word "mined" expresses no judgment, and "palliating" refers neutrally to Irving's inadequate explanation. The use of "Perhaps," the only word in its sentence, expresses the author's reluctance to accept Irving's assessment of Columbus.

5. **B.** The first paragraph surveys Columbus's reputation in the sixteenth and seventeenth centuries; the second, third, and fourth deal with the nineteenth century. Although the last paragraph predicts a reevaluation in the twentieth century, the passage does not deal with the hostile criticism of the explorer.

6. **B.** The fourth paragraph explains how the nineteenth-century Columbus reflected what that period most valued, and the last paragraph refers to people creating "the Columbus they want to believe in." The account of nineteenth-century historians' indifference to the Columbus documents discovered in 1825 contradicts the notion that history is truth as it is known at the time of writing.

7. **E.** Each of the questions reveals more of the author's ideas about the Europeans at the time of Columbus's voyages. The passage goes on to show how these limitations led to the exploitation of the New World. The paragraph does not defend or justify their actions.

8. **E.** All three are accurate descriptions of the effects of the phrase. The phrase "a foreign, heathen people, half naked and befeathered, ignorant of cities and kings and metal and laws, and unschooled in all that the Ancients held virtuous" is the European view of the native Americans as superior, contemptuous of their ignorance of Greece and Rome, which had become important to Europe in the age of discovery. The point of view of this phrase is that of the fifteenth-century European, not that of the twentieth-century author.

9. **B.** The second paragraph refers to new foods and medicines found in the New World.

10. **A.** The passage presents the biological outlook as one in which humans have a sense of being at one with nature, where humans' relation to earth and all its life forms is more important than their relation to other humans. Choices **B** and **E** are just what the biological outlook is not. Choices **C** and **D** are concerned with economic rather than ecological well-being.

11. **B.** The passage argues that, properly understood, the discovery might have brought regeneration to Europe, but the Europeans, tragically, could only exploit and destroy the new-found lands. The passage does criticize this European failure, but this criticism is not its real point. The passage does not describe the benefits of the discovery **A,** and it is by no means objective **E.**

12. **E.** The last paragraph of Passage 1 refers to "a major reassessment of Columbus's reputation," and Passage 2 presents a view of the consequences of Columbus's voyages totally unlike the heroic adulation of the first four paragraphs of the first passage.

13. **D.** Passage 2 presents a highly personal, highly emotional, judgmental, philosophical view of Columbus's discovery. But it is not more historical than Passage 1. In fact, it presents only the view of its twentieth-century author, and Passage 1 samples opinions from several periods.

14. **C.** The style of Passage 2 is characterized by its use of words in series, repetition, parallel phrases, and rhetorical questions. It does not use understatement. Some readers, no doubt, would argue that it depends on overstatement.

15. **B.** The first two statements are just, but although Passage 1 focuses on Columbus's reputation, Passage 2 does not even mention Columbus by name. The second passage does reevaluate the discovery of America. The second passage also presents an interpretation of the voyages of discovery that reflects the late twentieth-century concern for the wisdom of ancient cultures, for ecology, and for the dangers of warring against nature.

Section 6: Mathematical Reasoning

1. **A.** Since the difference between any two consecutive odd numbers is 2, the next odd number after $2x + 13$ would be

   $$2x + 13 + 2 = 2x + 15$$

2. **D.** The amount of discount was $120 - $90 = $30. The rate of discount is a percent, so

   $$\frac{\text{percent}}{100} = \frac{\text{is number}}{\text{of number}}$$

   $$\frac{x}{100} = \frac{30}{120}$$

   Cross multiplying

   $$120x = 3000$$

   $$\frac{120x}{120} = \frac{3000}{120}$$

   $$x = 25$$

   Therefore, the rate of discount was 25%.

3. **C.** $\sqrt{\frac{81}{x}} = \frac{9}{5}$

   Squaring both sides,

   $$\frac{81}{x} = \frac{81}{25}$$

   Therefore, $x = 25$.

4. **C.** Since $\angle CFD = \angle AFB$, then $\angle CFD = 45°$ and $\angle AFE = 45° + 40° + 45° + 20 = 150°$.

5. **D.** Average =

   $$\frac{93 + 82 + 79 + x}{4} = 87$$

   $$93 + 82 + 79 + x = 87 \cdot 4$$

   $$254 + x = 348$$

   $$x = 94$$

6. **D.** According to the graph, 20% have hazel eyes and 40% have brown eyes. This means that there are twice as many brown-eyed people as there are hazel-eyed people.

   $$62 = \text{people with hazel eyes}$$

   $$2 \times 62 = 124 \text{ people with brown eyes}$$

7. C. On a clock, 60 minutes $= 360°$

Therefore, $\dfrac{12 \text{ minutes}}{60 \text{ minutes}} = \dfrac{x°}{360°}$

$$\frac{1}{5} = \frac{x}{360}$$

$$5x = 360$$

$$\frac{5x}{5} = \frac{360}{5}$$

$$x = 72$$

Therefore, the minute hand has moved $72°$.

8. A. Since $\dfrac{x^2 - 5x + 7}{x^2 - 4x + 10} = 1 = \frac{1}{1}$, cross multiply to get

$$x^2 - 5x + 7 = x^2 - 4x + 10$$

$$x^2 - 5x + 7 - x^2 = x^2 - 4x + 10 - x^2$$

$$-5x + 7 = -4x + 10$$

$$-5x + 7 + 4x = -4x + 10 + 4x$$

$$-x + 7 = 10$$

$$-x + 7 - 7 = 10 - 7$$

$$-x = 3$$

$$x = -3$$

9. C. Let $3x =$ one angle and $4x =$ other angle.

$$3x + 4x + 68 = 180$$

$$7x + 68 = 180$$

$$7x = 112$$

$$x = 16$$

$$3x = 48$$

$$4x = 64$$

Therefore, the smallest angle of the triangle is $48°$.

10. B. If two points have coordinates (x_1, y_1) and (x_2, y_2), the distance, d, between these points is defined to be

$$d = \sqrt{(x_1 - x_2)^2 + (y_1 - y_2)^2}$$

Since E has coordinates $(-3, 5)$ and F has coordinates $(6, -7)$, the distance between E and F is

$$EF = \sqrt{(-3 - 6)^2 + \left[5 - (-7)\right]^2}$$

$$= \sqrt{(-9)^2 + (12)^2}$$

$$= \sqrt{81 + 144}$$

$$= \sqrt{225}$$

$$= 15$$

Section 7: Mathematical Reasoning

1. **B.** Solve for x.

   $$2x - 5 = 9$$
   $$2x = 14$$

   Then $x = 7$

   Now substitute 7 for x.

   $$3x + 2 = 3(7) + 2$$
   $$= 21 + 2$$
   $$= 23$$

2. **E.** Note that since there is a mark between +7 and +9, that mark must equal +8. Therefore, each mark equals 1. Counting back, point Q is at +5. Therefore, 15 units to the left of +5 would be $+5 - 15 = -10$.

3. **C.** $2x + 3y^2 - z = (2)(3) + 3(4)^2 - (-1)$

   $$= 6 + 3(16) + 1$$
   $$= 6 + 48 + 1$$
   $$= 55$$

4. **B.** To purchase twelve tapes, Roy must buy six packages. At $2.98 per package, he spends $17.88. His change from a twenty-dollar bill will be $20.00 - $17.88 = $2.12.

5. **D.** $\dfrac{6^4 + 6^5}{6^4} = \dfrac{6^4}{6^4} + \dfrac{6^5}{6^4}$

   $$= 1 + 6$$
   $$= 7$$

6. **D.** The most the trip would cost is when gas costs $1.12 and the mileage is 16 mpg. Therefore, $1.12 \times (480/16) = $33.60. The least would be $0.96 \times (480/24) = $19.20. The difference is therefore $14.40.

7. **C.** If we call the smaller piece x, then the larger piece (6 inches bigger) must be $x + 6$. Since the two pieces together equal a yardstick,

   $$x + (x + 6) = 36$$
   $$x + x + 6 = 36$$

8. **E.** For the multiplication problem to work correctly, the figures must be

   $$\boxed{6}\,\boxed{7}\,4$$
   $$\underline{\times\, 8}$$
   $$5\,3\,9\,\boxed{2}$$

   Therefore, the sum of the boxed digits is 15.

9. **A.** The perimeter of a rectangle equals $2l + 2w$, where l is the length and w is the width. If the length and width are increased by x, the perimeter will be

$$2(l + x) + 2(w + x)$$
$$= 2l + 2x + 2w + 2x$$
$$= 2l + 2w + 4x$$

which is an increase of $4x$ units.

10. **E.** In the ordered pair $(0, 2)$, $a = 0$ and $b = 2$. For $2a - 3b$,

$$2(0) - 3(2) = 0 - 6 = -6 \neq 6$$

Therefore, the ordered pair $(0, 2)$ is not a member of the solution sets of $2a - 3b = 6$.

11. **B.** Forty-eight days late is one day shy of exactly 7 weeks (7 weeks = $7 \times 7 =$ 49 days). If the job were finished in 49 days, then it would have been completed on the same day, Wednesday. Because 48 is one day less than 7 weeks, however, the job was completed one day earlier than Wednesday: Tuesday.

12. **C.** The perimeter is the sum of all sides. Therefore,

$$(2s - 6) + (s + 4) + (s + 2) = \text{perimeter}$$

$$\begin{array}{r} 2s - 6 \\ s + 4 \\ \underline{s + 2} \\ 4s + 0 = 4s \end{array}$$

13. **C.** $\dfrac{\text{is number}}{\text{of number}} = \dfrac{\text{percent}}{100}$

$$\frac{\frac{1}{2}}{\frac{2}{3}} = \frac{x}{100}$$

Cross multiplying,

$$\tfrac{2}{3}x = 50$$

$$x = \frac{150}{2} = 75\%$$

14. **B.** Since m yards = $36m$ inches and n feet = $12n$ inches, m yards and n feet = $(36m + 12n)$ inches.

15. **C.** Fifteen percent of the selling price is needed for a down payment. Since the selling price of the house is \$64,000, 15% of the selling price equals

$$(.15)(\$64,000) = \$9,600$$

The buyer has already paid \$1,500 toward the deposit. To figure how much more money is needed for the down payment, subtract \$1,500 from \$9,600.

$$\$9,600 - \$1,500 = \$8,100$$

16. **B.** If the average of 9 numbers is 7, then the sum of these numbers must be 9×7, or 63. If the average of 7 numbers is 9, then the sum of these numbers must be 7×9, or 63. The sum of all 16 numbers must be $63 + 63$, or 126. Therefore, the average of all 16 numbers must be

$$126 \div 16 = {}^{126}\!/_{16} = 7\ {}^{14}\!/_{16} = 7\ {}^{7}\!/_{8}$$

17. **E.** Let x equal the length of a side of the cube. The volume $V = x^3$, and the surface area $S = 6x^2$. Therefore, $x = 6$.

18. **E.** Since $l_1 \| l_2$, the corresponding angles formed on lines l_1 and l_2 are equal.

In any quadrilateral, the sum of interior degrees equals $360°$. Therefore, $\angle w + \angle z = 180°$. If $w = 2z$, $\angle w = 120°$, and $\angle z = 60°$. Therefore,

$\angle y = 60°$ (since there are $180°$ in a triangle). So the sum of $y + w = 60° + 120° = 180°$.

19. **E.** The value of $a\ \#\ b$

$$\frac{a^2 + b^2}{a^2 - b^2}$$

If $2a = b$, plug in $2a$ for b.

$$\frac{a^2 + (2a)^2}{a^2 - (2a)^2} = \frac{a^2 + 4a^2}{a^2 - 4a^2} = -\frac{5a^2}{3a^2} = -\frac{5}{3} = -1\frac{2}{3}$$

20. **D.** Since it takes the pipe t hours to drain the tank completely, it will drain $1/t$ part of the tank each hour. Therefore, in three hours, it will drain $3(1/t)$, or $3/t$, part of the tank.

21. **D.** Since $AB = BE = 34$, $\triangle ABC$ is an isosceles triangle and altitude BD will bisect AC. Since $\triangle BDC$ is a right triangle, use the Pythagorean theorem, which says

$$(BC)^2 = (BD)^2 + (CD)^2$$
$$(34)^2 = (30)^2 + x^2$$
$$1{,}156 = 900 + x^2$$
$$x^2 = 1{,}156 - 900$$
$$x^2 = 256$$
$$x = \sqrt{256} = 16$$

Therefore, $CD = 16 = AD$

$$AC = AD + DC$$
$$= 16 + 16$$
$$= 32$$

22. C. Circumference $= \pi d$.

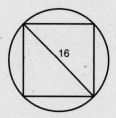

$$16\pi = \pi d$$
$$d = 16$$

diameter of circle = diagonal of square

area of square = ½(product of diagonals)

$$= \tfrac{1}{2} d_1 \times d_2$$
$$= \tfrac{1}{2}(16)(16) = 128$$

Therefore, the area of the square is 128.

Alternate method: Using the Pythagorean theorem for isosceles right triangles gives $x^2 + x^2 = 16^2$, $2x^2 = 256$, and $x^2 = 128$, which is the area of the square.

23. E. The horizontal length of x cannot be determined because there is no indication of the overlapping length of the rectangle to the left of x. If x cannot be determined, then $x + y$ cannot be determined.

24. B. Drawing a picture may be helpful. 750×45 equals P.

Note that 750 times 44 is the same as above but with one less circle. Therefore, it equals $P - 750$. If this concept is still difficult to understand, think in terms of dollars. You are paid $750 each week for 45 weeks. Therefore, your total pay (P) is $750 times 45. Suppose that you work only 44 weeks, however. Then your total pay will be P − one week's pay, or $P - \$750$.

25. D. Try it yourself with scissors and a square piece of paper.

ANSWER SHEET FOR PRACTICE TEST 2

(Remove This Sheet and Use It to Mark Your Answers)

SECTION 1

1 Ⓐ Ⓑ Ⓒ Ⓓ Ⓔ
2 Ⓐ Ⓑ Ⓒ Ⓓ Ⓔ
3 Ⓐ Ⓑ Ⓒ Ⓓ Ⓔ
4 Ⓐ Ⓑ Ⓒ Ⓓ Ⓔ
5 Ⓐ Ⓑ Ⓒ Ⓓ Ⓔ
6 Ⓐ Ⓑ Ⓒ Ⓓ Ⓔ
7 Ⓐ Ⓑ Ⓒ Ⓓ Ⓔ
8 Ⓐ Ⓑ Ⓒ Ⓓ Ⓔ
9 Ⓐ Ⓑ Ⓒ Ⓓ Ⓔ
10 Ⓐ Ⓑ Ⓒ Ⓓ Ⓔ
11 Ⓐ Ⓑ Ⓒ Ⓓ Ⓔ
12 Ⓐ Ⓑ Ⓒ Ⓓ Ⓔ
13 Ⓐ Ⓑ Ⓒ Ⓓ Ⓔ
14 Ⓐ Ⓑ Ⓒ Ⓓ Ⓔ
15 Ⓐ Ⓑ Ⓒ Ⓓ Ⓔ
16 Ⓐ Ⓑ Ⓒ Ⓓ Ⓔ
17 Ⓐ Ⓑ Ⓒ Ⓓ Ⓔ
18 Ⓐ Ⓑ Ⓒ Ⓓ Ⓔ
19 Ⓐ Ⓑ Ⓒ Ⓓ Ⓔ
20 Ⓐ Ⓑ Ⓒ Ⓓ Ⓔ
21 Ⓐ Ⓑ Ⓒ Ⓓ Ⓔ
22 Ⓐ Ⓑ Ⓒ Ⓓ Ⓔ
23 Ⓐ Ⓑ Ⓒ Ⓓ Ⓔ
24 Ⓐ Ⓑ Ⓒ Ⓓ Ⓔ
25 Ⓐ Ⓑ Ⓒ Ⓓ Ⓔ
26 Ⓐ Ⓑ Ⓒ Ⓓ Ⓔ
27 Ⓐ Ⓑ Ⓒ Ⓓ Ⓔ
28 Ⓐ Ⓑ Ⓒ Ⓓ Ⓔ
29 Ⓐ Ⓑ Ⓒ Ⓓ Ⓔ
30 Ⓐ Ⓑ Ⓒ Ⓓ Ⓔ

SECTION 2

1 Ⓐ Ⓑ Ⓒ Ⓓ Ⓔ
2 Ⓐ Ⓑ Ⓒ Ⓓ Ⓔ
3 Ⓐ Ⓑ Ⓒ Ⓓ Ⓔ
4 Ⓐ Ⓑ Ⓒ Ⓓ Ⓔ
5 Ⓐ Ⓑ Ⓒ Ⓓ Ⓔ
6 Ⓐ Ⓑ Ⓒ Ⓓ Ⓔ
7 Ⓐ Ⓑ Ⓒ Ⓓ Ⓔ
8 Ⓐ Ⓑ Ⓒ Ⓓ Ⓔ
9 Ⓐ Ⓑ Ⓒ Ⓓ Ⓔ
10 Ⓐ Ⓑ Ⓒ Ⓓ Ⓔ
11 Ⓐ Ⓑ Ⓒ Ⓓ Ⓔ
12 Ⓐ Ⓑ Ⓒ Ⓓ Ⓔ
13 Ⓐ Ⓑ Ⓒ Ⓓ Ⓔ
14 Ⓐ Ⓑ Ⓒ Ⓓ Ⓔ
15 Ⓐ Ⓑ Ⓒ Ⓓ Ⓔ
16 Ⓐ Ⓑ Ⓒ Ⓓ Ⓔ
17 Ⓐ Ⓑ Ⓒ Ⓓ Ⓔ
18 Ⓐ Ⓑ Ⓒ Ⓓ Ⓔ
19 Ⓐ Ⓑ Ⓒ Ⓓ Ⓔ
20 Ⓐ Ⓑ Ⓒ Ⓓ Ⓔ
21 Ⓐ Ⓑ Ⓒ Ⓓ Ⓔ
22 Ⓐ Ⓑ Ⓒ Ⓓ Ⓔ
23 Ⓐ Ⓑ Ⓒ Ⓓ Ⓔ
24 Ⓐ Ⓑ Ⓒ Ⓓ Ⓔ
25 Ⓐ Ⓑ Ⓒ Ⓓ Ⓔ

SECTION 3

1 Ⓐ Ⓑ Ⓒ Ⓓ Ⓔ
2 Ⓐ Ⓑ Ⓒ Ⓓ Ⓔ
3 Ⓐ Ⓑ Ⓒ Ⓓ Ⓔ
4 Ⓐ Ⓑ Ⓒ Ⓓ Ⓔ
5 Ⓐ Ⓑ Ⓒ Ⓓ Ⓔ
6 Ⓐ Ⓑ Ⓒ Ⓓ Ⓔ
7 Ⓐ Ⓑ Ⓒ Ⓓ Ⓔ
8 Ⓐ Ⓑ Ⓒ Ⓓ Ⓔ
9 Ⓐ Ⓑ Ⓒ Ⓓ Ⓔ
10 Ⓐ Ⓑ Ⓒ Ⓓ Ⓔ
11 Ⓐ Ⓑ Ⓒ Ⓓ Ⓔ
12 Ⓐ Ⓑ Ⓒ Ⓓ Ⓔ
13 Ⓐ Ⓑ Ⓒ Ⓓ Ⓔ
14 Ⓐ Ⓑ Ⓒ Ⓓ Ⓔ
15 Ⓐ Ⓑ Ⓒ Ⓓ Ⓔ
16 Ⓐ Ⓑ Ⓒ Ⓓ Ⓔ
17 Ⓐ Ⓑ Ⓒ Ⓓ Ⓔ
18 Ⓐ Ⓑ Ⓒ Ⓓ Ⓔ
19 Ⓐ Ⓑ Ⓒ Ⓓ Ⓔ
20 Ⓐ Ⓑ Ⓒ Ⓓ Ⓔ
21 Ⓐ Ⓑ Ⓒ Ⓓ Ⓔ
22 Ⓐ Ⓑ Ⓒ Ⓓ Ⓔ
23 Ⓐ Ⓑ Ⓒ Ⓓ Ⓔ
24 Ⓐ Ⓑ Ⓒ Ⓓ Ⓔ
25 Ⓐ Ⓑ Ⓒ Ⓓ Ⓔ
26 Ⓐ Ⓑ Ⓒ Ⓓ Ⓔ
27 Ⓐ Ⓑ Ⓒ Ⓓ Ⓔ
28 Ⓐ Ⓑ Ⓒ Ⓓ Ⓔ
29 Ⓐ Ⓑ Ⓒ Ⓓ Ⓔ
30 Ⓐ Ⓑ Ⓒ Ⓓ Ⓔ
31 Ⓐ Ⓑ Ⓒ Ⓓ Ⓔ
32 Ⓐ Ⓑ Ⓒ Ⓓ Ⓔ
33 Ⓐ Ⓑ Ⓒ Ⓓ Ⓔ
34 Ⓐ Ⓑ Ⓒ Ⓓ Ⓔ
35 Ⓐ Ⓑ Ⓒ Ⓓ Ⓔ

SECTION 4

1 Ⓐ Ⓑ Ⓒ Ⓓ Ⓔ
2 Ⓐ Ⓑ Ⓒ Ⓓ Ⓔ
3 Ⓐ Ⓑ Ⓒ Ⓓ Ⓔ
4 Ⓐ Ⓑ Ⓒ Ⓓ Ⓔ
5 Ⓐ Ⓑ Ⓒ Ⓓ Ⓔ
6 Ⓐ Ⓑ Ⓒ Ⓓ Ⓔ
7 Ⓐ Ⓑ Ⓒ Ⓓ Ⓔ
8 Ⓐ Ⓑ Ⓒ Ⓓ Ⓔ
9 Ⓐ Ⓑ Ⓒ Ⓓ Ⓔ
10 Ⓐ Ⓑ Ⓒ Ⓓ Ⓔ
11 Ⓐ Ⓑ Ⓒ Ⓓ Ⓔ
12 Ⓐ Ⓑ Ⓒ Ⓓ Ⓔ
13 Ⓐ Ⓑ Ⓒ Ⓓ Ⓔ
14 Ⓐ Ⓑ Ⓒ Ⓓ Ⓔ
15 Ⓐ Ⓑ Ⓒ Ⓓ Ⓔ

(Remove This Sheet and Use It to Mark Your Answers)

16

17

18

19

20

21

22

23

CUT HERE

(Remove This Sheet and Use It to Mark Your Answers)

24

25

SECTION 5

1 Ⓐ Ⓑ Ⓒ Ⓓ Ⓔ
2 Ⓐ Ⓑ Ⓒ Ⓓ Ⓔ
3 Ⓐ Ⓑ Ⓒ Ⓓ Ⓔ
4 Ⓐ Ⓑ Ⓒ Ⓓ Ⓔ
5 Ⓐ Ⓑ Ⓒ Ⓓ Ⓔ
6 Ⓐ Ⓑ Ⓒ Ⓓ Ⓔ
7 Ⓐ Ⓑ Ⓒ Ⓓ Ⓔ
8 Ⓐ Ⓑ Ⓒ Ⓓ Ⓔ
9 Ⓐ Ⓑ Ⓒ Ⓓ Ⓔ
10 Ⓐ Ⓑ Ⓒ Ⓓ Ⓔ
11 Ⓐ Ⓑ Ⓒ Ⓓ Ⓔ
12 Ⓐ Ⓑ Ⓒ Ⓓ Ⓔ
13 Ⓐ Ⓑ Ⓒ Ⓓ Ⓔ
14 Ⓐ Ⓑ Ⓒ Ⓓ Ⓔ

SECTION 6

1 Ⓐ Ⓑ Ⓒ Ⓓ Ⓔ
2 Ⓐ Ⓑ Ⓒ Ⓓ Ⓔ
3 Ⓐ Ⓑ Ⓒ Ⓓ Ⓔ
4 Ⓐ Ⓑ Ⓒ Ⓓ Ⓔ
5 Ⓐ Ⓑ Ⓒ Ⓓ Ⓔ
6 Ⓐ Ⓑ Ⓒ Ⓓ Ⓔ
7 Ⓐ Ⓑ Ⓒ Ⓓ Ⓔ
8 Ⓐ Ⓑ Ⓒ Ⓓ Ⓔ
9 Ⓐ Ⓑ Ⓒ Ⓓ Ⓔ
10 Ⓐ Ⓑ Ⓒ Ⓓ Ⓔ

SECTION 7

1 Ⓐ Ⓑ Ⓒ Ⓓ Ⓔ
2 Ⓐ Ⓑ Ⓒ Ⓓ Ⓔ
3 Ⓐ Ⓑ Ⓒ Ⓓ Ⓔ
4 Ⓐ Ⓑ Ⓒ Ⓓ Ⓔ
5 Ⓐ Ⓑ Ⓒ Ⓓ Ⓔ
6 Ⓐ Ⓑ Ⓒ Ⓓ Ⓔ
7 Ⓐ Ⓑ Ⓒ Ⓓ Ⓔ
8 Ⓐ Ⓑ Ⓒ Ⓓ Ⓔ
9 Ⓐ Ⓑ Ⓒ Ⓓ Ⓔ
10 Ⓐ Ⓑ Ⓒ Ⓓ Ⓔ
11 Ⓐ Ⓑ Ⓒ Ⓓ Ⓔ
12 Ⓐ Ⓑ Ⓒ Ⓓ Ⓔ
13 Ⓐ Ⓑ Ⓒ Ⓓ Ⓔ
14 Ⓐ Ⓑ Ⓒ Ⓓ Ⓔ
15 Ⓐ Ⓑ Ⓒ Ⓓ Ⓔ
16 Ⓐ Ⓑ Ⓒ Ⓓ Ⓔ
17 Ⓐ Ⓑ Ⓒ Ⓓ Ⓔ
18 Ⓐ Ⓑ Ⓒ Ⓓ Ⓔ
19 Ⓐ Ⓑ Ⓒ Ⓓ Ⓔ
20 Ⓐ Ⓑ Ⓒ Ⓓ Ⓔ
21 Ⓐ Ⓑ Ⓒ Ⓓ Ⓔ
22 Ⓐ Ⓑ Ⓒ Ⓓ Ⓔ
23 Ⓐ Ⓑ Ⓒ Ⓓ Ⓔ
24 Ⓐ Ⓑ Ⓒ Ⓓ Ⓔ
25 Ⓐ Ⓑ Ⓒ Ⓓ Ⓔ
26 Ⓐ Ⓑ Ⓒ Ⓓ Ⓔ
27 Ⓐ Ⓑ Ⓒ Ⓓ Ⓔ
28 Ⓐ Ⓑ Ⓒ Ⓓ Ⓔ
29 Ⓐ Ⓑ Ⓒ Ⓓ Ⓔ
30 Ⓐ Ⓑ Ⓒ Ⓓ Ⓔ
31 Ⓐ Ⓑ Ⓒ Ⓓ Ⓔ
32 Ⓐ Ⓑ Ⓒ Ⓓ Ⓔ
33 Ⓐ Ⓑ Ⓒ Ⓓ Ⓔ
34 Ⓐ Ⓑ Ⓒ Ⓓ Ⓔ
35 Ⓐ Ⓑ Ⓒ Ⓓ Ⓔ

CUT HERE

PRACTICE TEST 2

Section 1: Verbal Reasoning

Time: 30 Minutes

30 Questions

In this section, choose the best answer for each question and blacken the corresponding space on the answer sheet.

Sentence Completion

Directions: Each blank in the following sentences indicates that something has been omitted. Consider the lettered words beneath the sentence and choose the word or set of words that *best* fits the whole sentence.

1. Understanding the _____ that separate us from each other can also enable us to _____ the complex fabric of our society.

   A. differences . . . appreciate

   B. truths . . . combat

   C. traditions . . . resolve

   D. similarities . . . enrich

   E. fears . . . complete

2. What is most needed in a discussion of immigration are solid facts, not wishful thinking; realities, not _____.

   A. explanations

   B. reasons

   C. ideas

   D. fears

   E. myths

3. South Korea's industrial production fell 6 percent last year, the largest annual _____ since 1980, fueling fears that the _____ economy is slipping deeper into recession.

   A. figure . . . flourishing

   B. decrease . . . steady

   C. decline . . . sagging

   D. change . . . lethargic

   E. drop . . . booming

GO ON TO THE NEXT PAGE

4. By gradually winning the support of both liberals and conservatives, both rich and poor, the governor has demonstrated that her remarkable _____ skills go side by side with her willingness to speak openly and _____ on controversial issues.

   A. interpersonal . . . equivocally

   B. diplomatic . . . frankly

   C. organizational . . . covertly

   D. personal . . . deceptively

   E. intimidating . . . obscurely

5. Slander and libel laws stand as a protection of an individual's reputation against the _____ dissemination of falsehoods.

   A. unintentional

   B. inevitable

   C. inferential

   D. irresponsible

   E. incontestable

6. Presenting love as foolish, compromised, or dangerous, his love songs are frankly _____.

   A. lyrical

   B. antiromantic

   C. conventional

   D. melodic

   E. sentimental

7. By showing that the trainer's voice _____ gave commands to the horse, he was able to _____ the clever ruse which contended that an animal could add and subtract.

   A. ostensibly . . . confirm

   B. never . . . debunk

   C. covertly . . . unmask

   D. unwittingly . . . prove

   E. potentially . . . defend

8. For an actor so changeable and unpredictable, even the word _____ seems inadequate.

   A. immutable

   B. mercurial

   C. stoical

   D. placid

   E. obstinate

9. A _____ is distrustful of human goodness and sincerity, and a _____ has a hatred of people in general.

   A. pessimist . . . ingrate

   B. siren . . . tyrant

   C. altruist . . . anarchist

   D. cynic . . . misanthrope

   E. philanthropist . . . misogynist

Analogies

Directions: In each question below, you are given a related pair of words or phrases. Select the lettered pair that best expresses a relationship similar to that in the original pair of words.

---

10. TUNE : PIANO ::

    A. erase : pencil

    B. focus : camera

    C. transmit : plague

    D. ripen : fruit

    E. examine : biologist

11. ISLAND : OCEAN ::

    A. tree : forest

    B. automobile : highway

    C. radio : sound

    D. star : zodiac

    E. oasis : desert

12. SQUARE : CUBE ::

    A. triangle : hexagon

    B. trapezoid : quadrangle

    C. circle : sphere

    D. pentagon : pentagram

    E. addition : subtraction

13. ZIRCON : DIAMOND ::

    A. gold : silver

    B. garnet : ruby

    C. oyster : pearl

    D. necklace : bracelet

    E. emerald : sapphire

14. COMPLAISANT : COURTESY ::

    A. offensive : smile

    B. wise : riches

    C. eager : inaction

    D. vain : correctness

    E. greedy : gluttony

15. GAUCHE : GRACE ::

    A. impecunious : wealth

    B. ignorant : fool

    C. prejudiced : bigotry

    D. conservative : reserve

    E. proud : vanity

GO ON TO THE NEXT PAGE

Critical Reading

Directions: Questions follow each of the passages below. Using only the stated or implied information in each passage and in its introduction, if any, answer the questions.

Questions 16–21 are based on the following passage.

The following passage is from The Autobiography of Benjamin Franklin.

In 1732 I first publish'd my *Almanack,* under the name of *Richard Saunders;* it was continu'd by me about twenty-five years, commonly call'd *Poor Richard's*
(5) *Almanack.* I endeavor'd to make it both entertaining and useful, and it accordingly came to be in such demand, that I reap'd considerable profit from it, vending annually near ten thousand. And observing that
(10) it was generally read, scarce any neighborhood in the province being without it, I consider'd it as a proper vehicle for conveying instruction among the common people, who bought scarcely any
(15) other books; I therefore filled all the little spaces that occurr'd between the remarkable days in the calendar with proverbial sentences, chiefly such as inculcated industry and frugality, as the means of
(20) procuring wealth, and thereby securing virtue; it being more difficult for a man in want, to act always honestly, as, to use here one of those proverbs, *it is hard for an empty sack to stand upright.*

(25) These proverbs, which contained the wisdom of many ages and nations, I assembled and form'd into a connected discourse prefix'd to the Almanack of 1757, as the harangue of a wise old man to
(30) the people attending an auction. The bringing all these scattered counsels thus into a focus enabled them to make greater impression. The piece, being universally approved, was bought by the clergy and

(35) gentry, to distribute gratis among their poor parishioners and tenants. In Pennsylvania, as it discouraged useless expense in foreign superfluities, some thought it had its share of influence in
(40) producing that growing plenty of money which was observable for several years after its publication.

I considered my newspaper, also, as another means of communicating instruction,
(45) and in that view frequently reprinted in it extracts from the *Spectator,* and other moral writers; and sometimes publish'd little pieces of my own. Of these are a Socratic dialogue, tending to prove that,
(50) whatever might be his parts and abilities, a vicious man could not properly be called a man of sense; and a discourse on self-denial, showing that virtue was not secure till its practice became a
(55) habitude, and was free from the opposition of contrary inclinations.

In the conduct of my newspaper, I carefully excluded all libelling and personal abuse. Whenever I was solicited to insert
(60) any thing of that kind, and the writers pleaded, as they generally did, the liberty of the press, and that a newspaper was like a stage-coach, in which any one who would pay had a right to a place, my an-
(65) swer was, that I would print the piece separately if desired, but that I would not take upon me to spread his detraction; and that, having contracted with my subscribers to furnish them with what might be
(70) either useful or entertaining, I could not fill their papers with private altercation, in which they had no concern, without doing them manifest injustice.

16. In line 22, the word "want" means

    A. custom.

    B. captivity.

    C. covetousness.

    D. desire.

    E. need.

17. According to the passage, the best way to become virtuous is to first become

    A. wealthy.

    B. educated.

    C. self-knowing.

    D. reasonable.

    E. self-serving.

18. With which of the following ideas about the freedom of the press would Franklin be likely to disagree?

    I. A person who is willing to pay for printing in a newspaper should be allowed to publish whatever he or she chooses.

    II. The primary obligation of the free press is to its subscribers.

    III. Personal disputes do not belong in the public press.

    A. I only

    B. II only

    C. III only

    D. I and II only

    E. I and III only

19. Franklin's refusal to publish in his newspaper any personal abuse was based on his belief that

    A. the newspaper might be prosecuted for libel.

    B. personal abuse should not be printed for any price.

    C. false personal attacks are too difficult to distinguish from attacks that are based on fact.

    D. a newspaper's responsibility is to furnish its subscribers with worthy reading matter.

    E. anyone who has paid for an item has the right to have it printed.

20. The passage suggests that Franklin's principal profession was as a

    A. politician.

    B. inventor.

    C. printer.

    D. scientist.

    E. novelist.

21. According to the passage, in both his almanac and newspaper, Franklin hoped to combine

    A. profit and religion.

    B. wisdom and appeal to a large public.

    C. ideas of thrift and virtue.

    D. instruction and entertainment.

    E. comedy and tragedy.

GO ON TO THE NEXT PAGE

Questions 22–30 are based on the following passage.

Immediately after *Hubble*'s launch, operators at the National Aeronautics and Space Administration Goddard Space Flight Center and at the Space Telescope Science
(5) Institute began an extensive series of systems checks and calibrations. The first test images revealed an inherent focusing problem, technically known as spherical aberration. A close examination of the im-
(10) ages revealed that the telescope's main mirror had been ground to the wrong shape: it is two microns flatter at the edges than stipulated by design (a micron is one millionth of a meter). Small though the er-
(15) ror may seem, it is a gross mistake by the standards of modern precision optics. The shape of the mirror makes it impossible to focus all the light collected by *Hubble* to a single point. *Hubble*'s designers intended
(20) that the telescope should be able to concentrate 70 percent of the light of a point source—a distant star, for example—into a spot 0.1 arcsecond across (an arcsecond is a tiny angle, equal to 1/1,800 the apparent
(25) diameter of the moon). Actually, only 15 percent of the light falls into this central image; the other 85 percent spills over into an unwanted halo several arcseconds in diameter.

(30) Various other difficulties have surfaced. Twice each orbit, when *Hubble* passes in and out of the earth's shadow, the sudden temperature change causes the telescope's large solar cell panels to flap up and down
(35) about 30 centimeters every 10 seconds. The resulting jitter can disrupt the telescope's pointing system and cause additional blurring of astronomical images. Two of *Hubble*'s six gyroscopes have
(40) failed, and a third works only intermittently; the telescope needs at least three gyroscopes to perform its normal science operations. Faulty electrical contacts

threatened to shut down the
(45) High-Resolution Spectrograph.

NASA hopes to address some of these problems in 1994, when astronauts are scheduled to visit *Hubble*. They will attempt to replace the telescope's solar pan-
(50) els and two of the gyroscopes. The astronauts may also try to install a package of corrective optics and an upgraded Wide Field and Planetary Camera if the new devices are completed by then.

(55) In the meantime, scientists have quickly learned how to wring as much performance from the space telescope as possible. Because *Hubble*'s mirror was ground to fine precision and because its error is
(60) well understood, computer enhancement can restore many images to their intended sharpness. The resulting astronomical views have eloquently refuted some early pessimism about the telescope's scientific
(65) capabilities. Regrettably, attaining such resolution often involves discarding the smeared halos that appear around celestial targets, literally throwing away most of the light captured by *Hubble*.

(70) The greatest blow to *Hubble*'s scientific mission therefore has been not a loss of resolution but a loss of sensitivity. *Hubble* was designed to be able to detect objects a billion times fainter than those
(75) visible to the human eye. At present, the telescope is limited to observing objects roughly 20 times brighter than intended. *Hubble* cannot detect some particularly elusive targets, such as extremely distant
(80) galaxies and quasars or possible planets around nearby stars. Astronomers have had to postpone many of their potentially most significant observations until the telescope is fixed.

(85) Although designed to home in on some of the most remote cosmic objects, *Hubble*

has proved well suited to studying objects within the solar system. For example, it has captured stunning views of the giant planets,
(90)Jupiter and Saturn. NASA's two *Voyager* space probes closely scrutinized Jupiter in 1979 and Saturn in 1980 and 1981. The space telescope can routinely produce images of Jupiter and Saturn compara-
(95)ble in detail to those obtained by the *Voyagers* only a few days before their closest approaches to the two planets.

22. In line 7, the word "inherent" means

   A. correctable, insignificant

   B. theoretical, hypothetical

   C. serious, grave

   D. innate, basic

   E. suppressing, holding back

23. How much greater a percentage of the light of a point source would have been concentrated into an arcsecond spot if the mirror of the *Hubble Telescope* had been ground correctly?

   A. 15 percent

   B. 30 percent

   C. 55 percent

   D. 70 percent

   E. 80 percent

24. It can be inferred from the third paragraph that the telescope is subjected to sharp temperature changes because the temperature is

   A. affected by its proximity to the moon.

   B. affected by the presence of the earth's shadow.

   C. affected by the proximity of other planets to the earth.

   D. affected by the earth's atmosphere.

   E. much higher as the telescope moves away from the sun.

25. According to the passage, all of the following have been troubled or defective EXCEPT

   A. solar cell panels.

   B. gyroscopes.

   C. main mirror.

   D. High-Resolution Spectrograph.

   E. lens.

26. The word "address" as used in line 46 means

   A. write to.

   B. use a proper form.

   C. apply itself.

   D. take a stand.

   E. repair.

GO ON TO THE NEXT PAGE

27. Which of the following best describes the difference between a telescope's sensitivity and its resolution?

A. Sensitivity is response to light or sound waves; resolution is its ability to separate an image into parts.

B. Sensitivity is the condition of receiving accurately outside stimuli; resolution is the capability of making darker shades lighter.

C. Sensitivity is its ability to perceive light; resolution is its ability to make the parts of an image visible.

D. Sensitivity is the distance at which a telescope can pick up foreign objects; resolution is the image of these objects.

E. Sensitivity is what is always lost in an image when resolution is gained.

28. The last paragraph of the passage provides

A. a summary of the arguments of the whole passage.

B. an irrelevant comparison of the *Hubble Telescope* and the *Voyager* probes.

C. a personal anecdote of the author.

D. a contradiction of the assertions of the third paragraph (lines 30–45) of the passage.

E. a rebuttal of media claims that the *Hubble Telescope* is a failure.

29. In line 85, the phrase "home in on" is best paraphrased by

A. fall upon rapidly.

B. expose clearly.

C. fix upon.

D. be comfortable with.

E. photograph.

30. The purpose of the passage as a whole is to

A. assess the accomplishments and shortcomings of the *Hubble Telescope*.

B. compare the successes of the *Hubble Telescope* with those of other space telescopes.

C. explain why the media disappointment with the Hubble Space Telescope is unjustified.

D. remind readers of what the *Hubble Telescope* may accomplish after repairs are made.

E. explain why the loss of sensitivity in the *Hubble Telescope* is compensated by a gain in resolution.

IF YOU FINISH BEFORE TIME IS CALLED, CHECK YOUR WORK ON THIS SECTION ONLY. DO NOT WORK ON ANY OTHER SECTION IN THE TEST.

Section 2: Mathematical Reasoning

Time: 30 Minutes

25 Questions

Directions: Solve each problem in this section by using the information given and your own mathematical calculations, insights, and problem-solving skills. Then select the one correct answer of the five choices given and mark the corresponding circle on your answer sheet. Use the available space on the page for your scratch work.

Notes

1. All numbers used are real numbers.

2. Calculators may be used.

3. Some problems may be accompanied by figures or diagrams. These figures are drawn as accurately as possible EXCEPT when it is stated in a specific problem that a figure is not drawn to scale. The figures and diagrams are meant to provide information useful in solving the problem or problems. Unless otherwise stated, all figures and diagrams lie in a plane.

Data That Can Be Used for Reference

GO ON TO THE NEXT PAGE

1. A man purchased 4 pounds of steak priced at $3.89 per pound. How much change did he receive from a $20 bill?

   A. $44.66

   B. $15.56

   C. $ 4.46

   D. $ 4.44

   E. $ 4.34

2. If a number is divisible by 7 but is not divisible by 21, then the number cannot be divisible by

   A.   2

   B.   3

   C.   5

   D.   8

   E.   10

3. If .0039y = 39, then y =

   A.   10

   B.   100

   C.   1000

   D.   10,000

   E.   100,000

4. In △XYZ, XY = 10, YZ = 10, and ∠a = 84°. What is the degree measure of ∠Z?

   A.   96°

   B.   84°

   C.   48°

   D.   42°

   E.   24°

5. If $a = \sqrt{b}$ and $b = 81$, what is the value of $\sqrt{a}$?

   A.   ⅓

   B.   3

   C.   9

   D.   81

   E.   100

6. A plumber charges $45 for the first hour of work and $20 per hour for each additional hour of work after the first. What would be the total bill for labor if the plumber works for 6 consecutive hours?

   A. $ 65

   B. $120

   C. $145

   D. $165

   E. $180

| 6″ | 2″ | 10″ | 2″ | 5″ |

7. Above are the measures of rainfall for five consecutive days during the winter. For the measure of those five days, which of the following is true?

  I. The median equals the mode.

 II. The median equals the arithmetic mean.

III. The range equals the median.

A. I only

B. II only

C. III only

D. I and II only

E. I and III only

8. Three-fifths of a geometry class is made up of female students. What is the ratio of male students to female students?

A. ⅖

B. ⅗

C. ⅔

D. ⅚

E. ¾

9. If $a = p + prt$, then $r =$

A. $\dfrac{a-1}{t}$

B. $\dfrac{a-p}{pt}$

C. $a - p - pt$

D. $\dfrac{a}{t}$

E. $\dfrac{a+p}{pt}$

10. What is the slope of the line for the equation $6x + y = 3$?

A. 6

B. 3

C. −2

D. −6

E. −9

11. Maria plans to make sandwiches for a picnic. She has three types of bread from which to choose (rye, sourdough, and white), four types of meat from which to choose (salami, bologna, ham, and pastrami), and three types of cheese from which to choose (Swiss, cheddar, and jack). If Maria will use only one type of bread, one type of meat, and one type of cheese on each sandwich, how many different kinds of sandwiches can Maria make?

A. 3

B. 4

C. 10

D. 17

E. 36

Section **2** Mathematical Reasoning

GO ON TO THE NEXT PAGE

12. In the figure above, all line segments meet at right angles, and each segment has a length of x. What is the area of the figure in terms of x?

    A. $25x$

    B. $36x$

    C. $36x^2$

    D. $41x^2$

    E. $41x^3$

---

13. If $x - y = 15$ and $3x + y = 13$, then $y =$

    A. -8

    B. -7

    C. 7

    D. 8

    E. 15

14. WX and WZ are angle bisectors of the base angles of isosceles triangle XYZ above. If $Y = 80°$, what is the degree measure of $\angle XWZ$?

    A. $65°$

    B. $80°$

    C. $100°$

    D. $130°$

    E. $160°$

---

15. If $m^2 + n^2 = 12$ and $mn = 9$, then $(m + n)^2 =$

    A. 12

    B. 24

    C. 30

    D. 42

    E. 48

---

16. The perimeter of a rectangle is 42, and its length is 8 more than its width. What is the length of the rectangle?

    A. 25

    B. 17

    C. $16\frac{1}{2}$

    D. $14\frac{1}{2}$

    E. $6\frac{1}{2}$

17. If x, y, and z are consecutive positive integers greater than 1, not necessarily in that order, which of the following is (are) true?

   I. $x > z$

   II. $x + y > z$

   III. $yz < xz$

   IV. $xy < y + z$

  A. I only

  B. II only

  C. II and III only

  D. II and IV only

  E. III and IV only

18. Rajiv will be y years old x years from now. How old will he be z years from now?

  A. $y - x + z$

  B. $y + x + z$

  C. $y + x - z$

  D. $y - x - z$

  E. $x + z - y$

19. The average of three numbers is 55. The second is 1 more than twice the first, and the third is 4 less than three times the first. What is the largest number?

  A. 165

  B. 88

  C. 80

  D. 57

  E. 28

20. The area of a square is 72 square feet. What is the length of a diagonal of the square?

  A. 36 feet

  B. $18\sqrt{2}$ feet

  C. 12 feet

  D. $6\sqrt{2}$ feet

  E. 6 feet

21. In a triangle, the ratio of two angles is 5:2, and the third angle is equal to the difference between the other two. What is the number of degrees in the smallest angle?

  A. 36

  B. $25\frac{5}{7}$

  C. $25\frac{2}{7}$

  D. 18

  E. 9

22. If $(a, b) \oplus (c, d) = (ac - bd, ad)$, then $(-2, 3) \oplus (4, -1) =$

  A. $(-5, 2)$

  B. $(-5, -2)$

  C. $(-11, 2)$

  D. $(-11, -2)$

  E. $(-5, -3)$

Section 2 Mathematical Reasoning

GO ON TO THE NEXT PAGE

23. A collection of 25 coins consists of nickels, dimes, and quarters. There are three times as many dimes as nickels and three more dimes than quarters. What is the total value of the collection in dollars and cents?

    A. $3.65

    B. $3.25

    C. $2.25

    D. $1.65

    E. $1.25

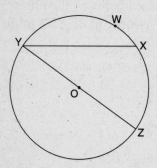

24. On the circle with center O above, arc YWX equals 100°. Which of the following is the degree measure of ∠XYZ?

    A. 130°

    B. 100°

    C. 80°

    D. 50°

    E. 40°

25. If m and n are integers and $\sqrt{mn} = 10$, which of the following CANNOT be a value of $m + n$?

    A. 25

    B. 29

    C. 50

    D. 52

    E. 101

IF YOU FINISH BEFORE TIME IS CALLED, CHECK YOUR WORK ON THIS SECTION ONLY. DO NOT WORK ON ANY OTHER SECTION IN THE TEST.

Section 3: Verbal Reasoning

Time: 30 Minutes

35 Questions

In this section, choose the best answer for each question and blacken the corresponding space on the answer sheet.

Sentence Completion

Directions: Each blank in the following sentences indicates that something has been omitted. Consider the lettered words beneath the sentence and choose the word or set of words that *best* fits the whole sentence.

1. With the benefit of _____, it is easy to see the mistakes we made last week or last year.

   A. hindsight

   B. prophecy

   C. insight

   D. tactfulness

   E. nostalgia

2. The pamphlet argues that imagination is not a gift _____ to poets, but something everyone possesses.

   A. relevant

   B. inimical

   C. unique

   D. unrestricted

   E. conducive

3. That "less is more" is a(n) _____ upon which all of the governor's conservation program is based.

   A. hope

   B. question

   C. enigma

   D. image

   E. paradox

4. Though McCarthy tried to provoke a _____, Eisenhower ignored all the senator's _____ as if he had not heard them.

   A. fight . . . avocations

   B. compromise . . . overtures

   C. confrontation . . . accusations

   D. condemnation . . . motives

   E. consensus . . . implications

GO ON TO THE NEXT PAGE

Section **3** Verbal Reasoning

5. Again and again, out of indifference or sheer stupidity, we have _____ our resources, assuming that there was no end to the earth's _____ to recover from our mistakes.

A. invested . . . resolve

B. expanded . . . ability

C. wasted . . . failure

D. husbanded . . . inability

E. squandered . . . capacity

6. Despite _____ reports of freewheeling spending on political candidates by large corporations, most business contributions are _____ divided between the two major parties.

A. lurid . . . equitably

B. shocking . . . unfairly

C. unfair . . . secretly

D. favorable . . . evenly

E. encouraging . . . carefully

7. With characteristic understatement, Webster called his client's embezzlement of 4 million dollars a regretted _____.

A. peccadillo

B. crime

C. atrocity

D. theft

E. enormity

8. Keynes's theory that unemployment is caused by a(n) _____ disposition to save cannot explain the high unemployment in _____ countries that have no savings at all.

A. simple . . . wealthy

B. bizarre . . . prosperous

C. orderly . . . rich

D. individualistic . . . successful

E. excessive . . . indigent

9. His biographer believed that Pierce's _____ was caused by his _____ to travel and his refusal to read about any position different from his own.

A. parochialism . . . reluctance

B. insularity . . . readiness

C. bigotry . . . zeal

D. narrow-mindedness . . . eagerness

E. magnanimity . . . failure

10. Though she was _____ by the medical establishment, Dr. Sandstrom bravely continued her work until other doctors could no longer deny the _____ of her theories.

A. ignored . . . conviction

B. vilified . . . probability

C. encouraged . . . originality

D. supported.. credibility

E. attacked . . . tenets

Analogies

Directions: In each question below, you are given a related pair of words or phrases. Select the lettered pair that *best* expresses a relationship similar to that in the original pair of words.

11. COWHAND : HERD ::

    A. wolf : fold

    B. chef : cuisine

    C. shepherd : flock

    D. snowmobile : snow

    E. newspaper : editor

12. MOTH : WOOL ::

    A. earthworm : potato

    B. termite : wood

    C. ant : aphid

    D. silkworm : silk

    E. lizard : scale

13. DOCUMENT : PASSPORT ::

    A. mirror : looking glass

    B. league : team

    C. pen : ball-point

    D. army : captain

    E. ice cream : dessert

14. PATTERN : DRESSMAKER ::

    A. rule : carpenter

    B. recipe : chef

    C. composer : musician

    D. canvas : sailmaker

    E. novel : novelist

15. LIABILITY : IMMUNITY ::

    A. pardon : amnesty

    B. debit : credit

    C. real estate : property

    D. equinox : winter

    E. fidelity : honesty

16. PLAN : INTRIGUE ::

    A. move : slink

    B. fear : doubt

    C. run : hasten

    D. eat : devour

    E. boil : seethe

17. REQUEST : REQUIREMENT ::

    A. solicitation : contribution

    B. hope : faith

    C. aspiration : inspiration

    D. inquiry : interrogation

    E. question : answer

18. SWEET : SACCHARINE ::

    A. loud : deafening

    B. quiet : still

    C. bright : dark

    D. initial : first

    E. delicious : tasty

Section **3** Verbal Reasoning

GO ON TO THE NEXT PAGE

19. ABBOT : MONASTERY ::

   A. nun : convent

   B. conductor : orchestra

   C. priest : bishop

   D. author : book

   E. runner : marathon

20. KNOT : BOWLINE ::

   A. atoll : lagoon

   B. state : senator

   C. musician : pianist

   D. volcano : lava

   E. book : index

21. LEARNING : PEDANT ::

   A. city : mayor

   B. music : violinist

   C. revenge : destroyer

   D. politics : candidate

   E. discipline : martinet

22. JINGO : CHAUVINIST ::

   A. pain : analgesic

   B. opera : oratorio

   C. toady : sycophant

   D. satirist : booster

   E. doctor : lawyer

23. ACCRETE : DIMINISH ::

   A. wax : wane

   B. divide : subtract

   C. decline : erode

   D. augment : increase

   E. tremble : waver

Critical Reading

Directions: Questions follow the passage below. Using only the stated or implied information in the passage and in its introduction, if any, answer the questions.

Questions 24–35 are based on the following passage.

Playfully, we call them "shrinks," acknowledging each time we do so that the psychiatrist's precursor was the head-shrinking witchdoctor, the original
(5) healer of souls. Often we use the name sardonically, implying that a certain residue of mumbo-jumbo still clings to our supposedly enlightened science of the mind. But by the same token might there not be
(10) something of at least marginal value to be found in the supposedly superstitious practice of witchdoctoring? Have traditional cultures anything to teach our industrial society about the meaning
(15) of sanity? The anthropologist Marshall Sahlins, assembling a composite picture of life among the hunters and gatherers, once undertook to reconstruct a "stone-age economics" from which he believed we might
(20) learn something about the meaning of wealth and poverty. Is there a "stone-age psychiatry" that can be mined for similarly heuristic insights?

Until well into this century, even
(25) trained anthropological observers tended to regard tribal healers as charlatans whose practices were mere quackery. Some scholars classified all shamans as psychotics whose practices were "witchcraft" in the

(30) most pejorative meaning of the word. The terms used ranged from the politely technical ("neurotic–epileptoid type") to the bluntly dismissive ("veritable idiots"), but all came down to regarding tribal therapy (35) as the mad treating the mad. Thanks largely to the work of Claude Levi–Strauss and subsequent studies in transcultural psychiatry, we have since come to see that tribal societies possess spiritual and psychothera-(40) peutic traditions that may be more effective in the treatment of their own people than Western medicine, especially when it comes to mental and emotional disorders. The anthropologist I. M. Lewis, standing (45) the question on its head, has gone so far as to suggest that our psychotherapy might be viewed as a scaled-down subspecies of traditional healing. "The more meaningful equivalence," he observes, "is that psychia-(50) try, and especially psychoanalysis, as Jung would perhaps have admitted much more freely than most Freudians would care to, represent limited and imperfect forms of shamanism." The remark is not entirely fair (55) to Freud, who readily acknowledged that tribal healers can be as adept as many psychiatrists at creating a "condition of expectant faith" that can have great therapeutic effect.

(60) Perhaps the most marked difference between psychotherapy old and new is the complexity and breadth of traditional healing. In tribal societies, the distinction between the physical and psychic is far less (65) rigid than we understand it to be. One might almost say that traditional medicine regards all disease as psychosomatic, in the sense that the psyche is implicated in its etiology. Even a frozen foot may be (70) treated by Eskimo shamans as a psychic disturbance.

Therefore, thoughts, dreams, memories, emotions must be mobilized in its cure.

The province of stone-age psychiatry is a (75) broad one.

E. Fuller Torrey, taking issue with the "psychiatric imperialism" of Western society, points out that healing has everything to do with the cultural bond that (80) unites therapist and client. A common worldview, a shared diagnostic vocabulary, mutually respected ideas and principles make for the trust and conviction without which healing may be impossible. But if (85) we have learned that tribal techniques can be more effective than modern psychiatry in treating native people, this knowledge may have little direct value for us — unless we can find some common ground (90) with tribal peoples that allows us to borrow a portion of their culture. That common ground may be the ground of desperation. If our relations with nature are as deeply failed as the environmental crisis suggests, (95) we may have to look for help wherever we can find it, including insights long absent from our own society. Where else are these to be found but in the experience of our fellow humans living different lives in a (100) different world?

Traditional therapy can be stub-bornly parochial; it is embedded in a place and a history, in the rhythms of climate, in the contours of a landscape where the birds and (105) beasts have been close companions for centuries. In local lore, a river, a mountain, a grove may take on the personality of a tribal elder, a presence named and known over the generations. Artifacts assume a pe-(110) culiarly evocative power. The *manangs* of Borneo come to their patients bearing a bundle filled with strange implements: the horns of the giant beetle, a quartz amulet that is "the stone of light," a wild (115) boar's tusk that can retrieve lost souls. What can these things mean to us? They seem like the proverbial "eye of newt and

GO ON TO THE NEXT PAGE

toe of frog" that make witchcraft appear so lu-
dicrous. Yet the effectiveness of the shaman's
(120)method largely lies in its emotional speci-
ficity. What we as modern observers achieve
by our efforts to universalize is, at last, something of our own, a new creation that may
lack the color and force of the original.

24. In the first paragraph, the author uses
the word "shrinks" (line 1) in order to

   I.   jokingly refer to the forerunners of
the contemporary psychiatrist.

  II. suggest a distrust of contemporary
psychiatry.

 III. remind readers of the potential
value in the traditional practices.

  A. I only

  B. I and II only

  C. I and III only

  D. II and III only

  E. I, II, and III

25. The first paragraph cites the work of
anthropologist Marshall Sahlins in order
to suggest that

  A. if the stone age can teach us about
economics, perhaps it can teach us
about psychiatry.

  B. the problems of poverty in our era
can be solved by consulting
stone-age economics.

  C. the stone-age notions of rich and
poor are irrelevant in today's
complex civilization.

  D. modern anthropologists need not
limit their studies to the lifestyles
of lost civilizations.

  E. modern psychiatry is dependent on
ancient ideas.

26. The passage argues that tribal medical
treatment may be

  A. more universally effective than
modern methods.

  B. more effective in treating people
living in civilized countries than
modern methods.

  C. about as effective as Western
methods in treating members of
tribal societies.

  D. more effective than Western
methods in treating mental
disorders of tribal members.

  E. more effective than Western
methods in treating mental
disorders of non-Western nations.

27. The passage implies that one reason for
the success within a tribe of tribal
medicine is that

  A. some tribal doctors may use
curative herbs.

  B. the patient expects to be cured.

  C. some tribal doctors have Western
training.

  D. the patients are not really sick.

  E. some tribal doctors refuse to use
amulets.

28. Which of the following would be likely
to be treated by ancient psychotherapy
but not by modern?

  A. Depression

  B. Broken arm

  C. Fear of crowds

  D. Schizophrenia

  E. Mental illness

29. The word "marked" in line 60 means

    A. signaled.

    B. indicated.

    C. scored.

    D. conspicuous.

    E. recorded.

30. Which of the following best expresses the meaning of the phrase "between the physical and psychic" in lines 63-64?

    A. Between body and mind

    B. Between the sensual and sensuous

    C. Between the real and supernatural

    D. Between logic and the uncanny

    E. Between sensory and extrasensory perception

31. In line 67, the word "psychosomatic" can be best defined as

    A. curable by herbal medicine or spells

    B. contagious

    C. originating in the mind

    D. imaginary

    E. subject to treatment by witchcraft

32. Freud and E. Fuller Torrey agree on the importance in healing of

    A. mutual trust between doctor and patient.

    B. a conviction of the superiority of shamanism to psychiatry.

    C. the patient's desire to be cured.

    D. a conviction of the superiority of psychiatry to shamanism.

    E. a genuine belief in the efficacy of witchcraft.

33. In line 76, the phrase "taking issue with" can be best defined as

    A. departing from.

    B. resulting from.

    C. disagreeing with.

    D. proceeding with.

    E. siding with.

34. Anticipating the skepticism that might arise from taking ancient medicine seriously, the author has deliberately used all the following words and phrases to mock ancient medicine or its practitioners EXCEPT

    A. "mumbo-jumbo" (line 7).

    B. "charlatans" (line 26).

    C. "psychotics" (line 28).

    D. "eye of newt and toe of frog" (lines 117-118).

    E. "shaman's method" (line 119-120).

Section **3** Verbal Reasoning

GO ON TO THE NEXT PAGE

35. The purpose of the passage as a whole is to

A. question the usefulness of modern psychotherapy as opposed to tribal healing methods.

B. assert the superiority of tribal methods to Western psychiatric procedures.

C. urge the study of tribal medicine and tribal ways to abet Western psychiatry.

D. criticize Western civilization's arrogant dismissal of tribal lore.

E. reconstruct as far as it is possible some principles of stone-age mental therapy.

IF YOU FINISH BEFORE TIME IS CALLED, CHECK YOUR WORK ON THIS SECTION ONLY. DO NOT WORK ON ANY OTHER SECTION IN THE TEST.

Section 4: Mathematical Reasoning

Time: 30 Minutes

25 Questions

Directions: This section is composed of two types of questions. Use the 30 minutes allotted to answer both question types. Your scratchwork should be done on any available space in the section.

Notes

1. All numbers used are real numbers.

2. Calculators can be used.

3. Some problems may be accompanied by figures or diagrams. These figures are drawn as accurately as possible EXCEPT when it is stated in a specific problem that a figure is not drawn to scale. The figures and diagrams are meant to provide information useful in solving the problem or problems. Unless otherwise stated, all figures and diagrams lie in a plane.

Data That Can Be Used for Reference

Area

rectangle
$A = lw$

triangle
$A = \frac{1}{2}bh$

circle
$A = \pi r^2$
$C = 2\pi r$

Volume

rectangular solid
$V = lwh$

right circular cylinder
$V = \pi r^2 h$

Pythagorean Relationship

$a^2 + b^2 = c^2$

Special Triangles

$30° - 60° - 90°$

$45° - 45° - 90°$

A circle is composed of 360°
A straight angle measures 180°
The sum of the angles of a triangle is 180°

GO ON TO THE NEXT PAGE

Quantitative Comparison

Directions: In this section, you are given two quantities, one in column A and one in column B. You are to determine a relationship between the two quantities and mark —

    A. if the quantity in column A is greater than the quantity in column B.

    B. if the quantity in column B is greater than the quantity in column A.

    C. if the quantities are equal.

    D. if the comparison cannot be determined from the information that is given.

AN **E** RESPONSE WILL NOT BE SCORED.

Notes

1. Sometimes, information concerning one or both of the quantities to be compared is given. This information is not boxed and is centered above the two columns.

2. All numbers used are real numbers. Letters such as a, b, m, and x represent real numbers.

3. In a given question, if the same symbol is used in Column A and Column B, that symbol stands for the same value in each column.

Column A	Column B

1. 35% of 50   50% of 35

$$x^2 = 36$$

2. 6 x

3. $3\sqrt{2}$ $\sqrt{17}$

Column A	Column B

Questions 4 and 5 refer to the diagram.

Note: Figure not drawn to scale.

$$AD = BD = 6, \angle ADB = 90°$$

4. AB   BC

5. $\angle DBC + \angle BCD$ 90°

Column A   **Column B**

$$a = b$$
$$a < c$$

6. 2a   b + c

---

x is 30% of 60
20% of y is 4

7. x   y

---

8. Number of integer multiples of 8, greater than 8, but less than 50   Number of integer multiples of 6, greater than 6, but less than 40

Circle with center P

9. AB   CD

---

10. Volume of cube with side 6   Volume of rectangular prism with two dimensions less than 6

---

11. The number of cents in 8n dimes   The number of cents in 3n quarters

Column A   **Column B**

$$5x + y = 2$$
$$x + 3y = 6$$

12. x   y

---

13. x + 30   2x

---

x < y

14. $(x - y)^2$ $x^2 - y^2$

---

15. $9^{19} - (8)9^{18}$ 9^{18}

GO ON TO THE NEXT PAGE

Grid-In Questions

Directions: Questions 16–25 require you to solve the problem and enter your answer by carefully marking the circles on the special grid. Examples of the appropriate way to mark the grid follow.

Answer: 3.7

Answer: ½

Decimal point   Fraction bar

Answer: 1½

Do not grid in mixed numbers in the form of mixed numbers. *Always* change mixed numbers to improper fractions or decimals.

Change to 1.5   or   Change to ³⁄₂

Answer: 123

Space permitting, answers can start in any column. Each grid-in answer that follows is correct.

Note: Circles must be filled in correctly to receive credit. Mark only one circle in each column. No credit will be given if more than one circle in a column is marked. Example:

Answer: 258

No credit!

GO ON TO THE NEXT PAGE

Answer: ⅛/₉

Accuracy of decimals: Always enter the most accurate decimal value that the grid will accommodate. For example: An answer such as .8888 . . . can be gridded as .888 or .889. Gridding this value as .8, .88, or .89 is considered inaccurate and therefore *not acceptable*. The acceptable grid-ins of ⅛/₉ are

⅛/₉   .888   .889

Be sure to write your answers in the boxes at the top of the circles before doing your gridding. Although writing out the answers above the columns is not required, it is very important to ensure accuracy. Even though some problems may have more than one correct answer, grid *only one answer*. Grid-in questions contain no negative answers.

16. If $x + \frac{3}{5}x = 1$, then $x =$

17. In a class of 35 students, 60% are girls. How many boys are in the class?

18. What is the average of ¼, ⅙, and 1/12?

19. If a car averages 317.9 miles on 17 gallons of gas, how many miles will it travel on 5 gallons of gas?

Springfield High School's average SAT scores over a five-year period were

	Math	Verbal
1989	520	540
1990	515	532
1991	518	528
1992	510	525
1993	507	510

20. What was the mean (average) of the verbal SAT scores for the five-year period 1989 through 1993?

21. The ratio of the measures of the angles of a quadrilateral is 3:5:7:9. What is the degree measure of the smallest angle?

22. If Jim takes 6 days to paint a house alone and Mike takes 8 days to paint the same house alone, what part of the job will be completed if both boys work for 2 days?

25. What is the measure in degrees of arc MQN in the circle above with center P?

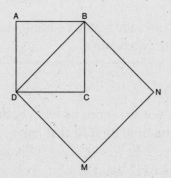

23. In square ABCD in the figure above, AB = 5. What is the area of square BDMN?

Car Sales

24. In the graph above, if each point aligns exactly with a grid mark or aligns halfway between two grid marks, what was the greatest percentage increase between two consecutive years? (Disregard the % sign when you are gridding your answer.)

IF YOU FINISH BEFORE TIME IS CALLED, CHECK YOUR WORK ON THIS SECTION ONLY. DO NOT WORK ON ANY OTHER SECTION IN THE TEST.

Section 5: Verbal Reasoning

Time: 15 Minutes

14 Questions

In this section, choose the best answer for each question and blacken the corresponding space on the answer sheet.

Critical Reading

Directions: Questions follow the two passages below. Using only the stated or implied information in each passage and in its introduction, if any, answer the questions.

Questions 1–14 are based on the following passages.

The two passages that follow are about the conductor of the modern symphony orchestra. The first was written in the 1950s by a well-known composer–conductor. The second was written in the 1960s by a well-known composer.

Passage 1

There was an era of the so-called violin–conductor, whose main duty was to start and stop the orchestra and generally keep the flow of the music going. This was
(5) all well and good as long as orchestras were small enough. But around Beethoven's time, orchestras began getting larger and larger, and it soon became apparent that somebody had to be up there to
(10) keep the players together. So conducting as we know it is actually less than 150 years old.

The first real conductor in our sense of the word was Mendelssohn, who founded a
(15) tradition of conducting based on the concept of precision, as symbolized in the wooden stick we call the baton.
Mendelssohn dedicated himself to an exact realization of the score he was conducting,
(20) through manipulation of that baton. There soon arrived, however, a great dissenter named Richard Wagner who declared that everything Mendelssohn was doing was wrong and that any conductor worth his
(25) salt should personalize the score he was conducting by coloring it with his own emotions and his own creative impulse. And so out of the clash of these two points of view the history of conducting was
(30) born; and there arose all those great names in conducting, as well as all the fights that go on about them right up to our own time. Mendelssohn fathered the "elegant" school, whereas Wagner inspired the "pas-
(35) sionate" school of conducting. Actually, both attitudes are necessary, the Apollonian and the Dionysian, and neither one is completely satisfactory without the other. Both of them can be badly abused,
(40) as we know from having heard performances that seemed clear but were dry as dust, and others in which passion became simple distortion.

The ideal modern conductor is a synthesis
(45) of the two attitudes, and this synthesis is rarely achieved. In fact, it's practically impossible. Almost any musician can be a conductor, even a pretty good one; but

only a rare musician can be a great one.
(50) This is not only because it is so hard to achieve the Mendelssohn–Wagner combination, but also because the conductor's work encompasses such a tremendous range. Unlike an instrumentalist or a
(55) singer, he has to play on an orchestra. His instrument is one hundred human instruments, each one a thorough musician, each with a will of his own; and he must cause them to play like one instrument with a
(60) single will. Therefore, he must have enormous authority, to say nothing of psychological insight in dealing with this large group and all this is just the beginning. He must be a master of the mechanics of con-
(65) ducting. He must have an inconceivable amount of knowledge. He must have a profound perception of the inner meanings of music, and he must have uncanny powers of communication. If he has all this, he
(70) is the ideal conductor.

Passage 2

Conducting, like politics, rarely attracts original minds, and the field is more for the making of careers and the exploitation of personalities — another resemblance to
(75) politics — than a profession for the application of exact and standardized disciplines. A conductor may actually be less well equipped for his work than his players, but no one except the players need
(80) know it, and his career is not dependent on them in any case, but on the society women (including critics) to whom his musical qualities are of secondary importance. The successful conductor can be an
(85) incomplete musician, but he must be a complete angler. His first skill *has* to be power politics.

In such people the incidence of ego disease is naturally high to begin with, and I
(90) hardly need add that the disease grows like

a tropical weed under the sun of a pandering public. The results are that the conductor is encouraged to impose a purely egotistical, false, and arbitrary authority,
(95) and that he is accorded a position out of all proportion to his real value in the musical, as opposed to the music-business, community. He soon becomes a "great" conductor, in fact, or as the press agent of one of
(100) them recently wrote me, a "titan of the podium," and as such is very nearly the worst obstacle to genuine music-making. "Great" conductors, like "great" actors, are unable to play anything but themselves;
(105) being unable to adapt themselves to the work, they adapt the work to themselves, to their "style," their mannerisms. The cult of the "great" conductor also tends to substitute looking for listening, so that to con-
(110) ductor and audience alike (and to reviewers who habitually fall into the trap of describing a conductor's appearance rather than the way he makes music sound, and of mistaking the conductor's gestures
(115) for the music's meanings), the important part of the performance becomes the gesture. If you are incapable of listening, the conductor will show you what to feel. Thus, the film-actor type of conductor will
(120) act out a life of Napoleon in "his" *Eroica*[1], wear an expression of noble suffering on the retreat from Moscow (TV having circumvented the comparatively merciful limitation to the dorsal view) and one of
(125) ultimate triumph in the last movement, during which he even dances the Victory Ball. If you are unable to listen to the music, you watch the corybantics[2], and if you *are* able, you had better not go to the
(130) concert.

[1]*Eroica* = a symphony by Beethoven originally dedicated to Napoleon

[2]corybantics = dancing

GO ON TO THE NEXT PAGE

1. From Passage 1, the reader can infer that in the seventeenth century

   I. orchestras did not employ a conductor.

   II. orchestras were smaller than they are today.

   III. orchestral players were better trained and more skillful.

   A. I only

   B. II only

   C. I and II only

   D. I and III only

   E. I, II, and III

2. From its use in Passage 1 (line 37) it can be inferred that the word "Apollonian" means

   A. sunny and optimistic.

   B. Wagnerian.

   C. emotionally intense.

   D. Bacchic.

   E. clear and elegant.

3. According to Passage 1, instrumentalists and singers have an advantage over a conductor because they

   A. have only to do what the conductor directs.

   B. need not master the mechanics of conducting.

   C. must cope with only one instrument, not a hundred.

   D. must be able to read music.

   E. need not understand the meaning of a score.

4. Of which of the following kinds of conductor described in Passage 1 would the author of that passage be most likely to approve?

   A. One "dedicated . . . to an exact realization of the score" (lines 18–19)

   B. One "coloring [the score] with his own emotions and his own creative impulse" (lines 26–27)

   C. One whose performances "seemed clear but were dry as dust" (lines 41–42)

   D. One in whose performances "passion became simple distortion" (lines 42–43)

   E. One who is both "elegant" and "passionate" and can "personalize the score" (lines 33, 34–35, and 25)

5. By adding the parenthetical phrase "including critics" (line 82) the author of Passage 2 suggests all of the following EXCEPT:

   A. Music critics and society women are alike.

   B. Music critics are more interested in orchestras than in orchestra conductors.

   C. Music critics are more important to a conductor's success than are the conductor's musical abilities.

   D. Music critics are less interested in musical ability than are orchestra players.

   E. Music critics are less able to judge musical qualities than are musicians.

6. The author of Passage 2 believes that politicians are

   A. original thinkers.

   B. career-minded.

   C. highly disciplined professionals.

   D. modest and self-effacing.

   E. indifferent to power.

7. By the phrase "the incidence of ego disease is naturally high" (lines 88–89), the author of the Passage 2 means

   A. there is a great deal of illness among musicians.

   B. conductors are rarely sick.

   C. conducting is a dangerous and demanding profession.

   D. conductors are very self centered.

   E. orchestras are likely to thrive in tropical countries.

8. In Passage 2, the distinction implied in lines 96–98 between the "music-business community" and the "musical community" is that

   A. in the music-business community, conductors are undervalued.

   B. in the music-business community, composers are overvalued.

   C. in the musical community, music is more important than personality.

   D. only the music-business community is concerned with money.

   E. the music-business community is concerned with popular music, and the musical community with classical music.

9. The phrase "TV having circumvented the comparatively merciful limitation to the dorsal view" (lines 122–124) in Passage 2 can be best understood to mean

   A. television has brought conductors to a much larger audience than ever before.

   B. television allows the viewer to see and hear details of a performance that are not clear in the concert hall.

   C. television distorts both the sound and the appearance of a symphony concert.

   D. television unfortunately allows the viewers to see the front of the conductor.

   E. television programs have the fortunate advantage of being easily turned off.

10. In the last paragraph of Passage 2, the phrase "if you *are* able" refers to

   I. visualize the "Victory Ball."

   II. "listen to the music."

   III. "watch the corybantics."

   A. II only

   B. III only

   C. I and III only

   D. II and III only

   E. I, II, and III

GO ON TO THE NEXT PAGE

Section **5** Verbal Reasoning

11. The author of Passage 2 either directly or obliquely makes fun of all the following EXCEPT

    A. conductors.

    B. politicians.

    C. the musical public.

    D. music critics.

    E. orchestral players.

12. Of the following kinds of conductor described in Passage 1, which would the author of Passage 2 be most likely to approve?

    A. One "dedicated . . . to an exact realization of the score" (lines 18–19)

    B. One "coloring [the score] with his own emotions and his own creative impulse" (lines 26–27)

    C. One whose performances "seemed clear but were dry as dust" (lines 41–42)

    D. One in whose performances "passion become simple distortion" (lines 42–43)

    E. One who is both "elegant" and "passionate" and can "personalize the score" (lines 33, 34–35, and 25)

13. Which of the following words is used in both passages but with totally different connotations?

    A. "conductor"

    B. "exact"

    C. "music"

    D. "great"

    E. "orchestra"

14. That both passages were written at mid-century rather than very recently is suggested by their

    I. assumption that an orchestra will be led by a conductor rather than by a concert-master.

    II. assumption that a conductor is a male.

    III. assumption that a performance may be reviewed by a music critic.

    A. I only

    B. II only

    C. III only

    D. I and II only

    E. I, II, and III

IF YOU FINISH BEFORE TIME IS CALLED, CHECK YOUR WORK ON THIS SECTION ONLY. DO NOT WORK ON ANY OTHER SECTION IN THE TEST.

STOP

Section 6: Mathematical Reasoning

Time: 15 Minutes

10 Questions

Directions: Solve each problem in this section by using the information given and your own mathematical calculations, insights, and problem-solving skills. Then select the one correct answer of the five choices given and mark the corresponding circle on your answer sheet. Use the available space on the page for your scratchwork.

Notes

1. All numbers used are real numbers.

2. Calculators can be used.

3. Some problems may be accompanied by figures or diagrams. These figures are drawn as accurately as possible EXCEPT when it is stated in a specific problem that a figure is not drawn to scale. The figures and diagrams are meant to provide information useful in solving the problem or problems. Unless otherwise stated, all figures and diagrams lie in a plane.

Data That Can Be Used for Reference

1. What is .25% of 12?

   A. ³/₁₀₀

   B. ³/₁₀

   C. ⅓

   D. 3

   E. 300

2. A square 4 inches on a side is cut up into smaller squares 1 inch on a side. What is the maximum number of such squares that can be formed?

   A. 4

   B. 8

   C. 16

   D. 36

   E. 64

3. If a book costs $5.70 after a 40% discount, what was its original price?

   A. $2.28

   B. $6.10

   C. $7.98

   D. $9.12

   E. $9.50

4. $\dfrac{\frac{2}{3} + \frac{1}{2}}{\frac{1}{6} + \frac{1}{4} + \frac{2}{3}}$

   A. ²/₁₃

   B. ²/₉

   C. ¹³/₂₀

   D. 1¹/₁₃

   E. 3¼

Number of Wild Bear Sightings Before and After Conservation Measures in Five Different Counties

5. According to the graph above, which county had the most bear sightings before the conservation measures?

   A. 1

   B. 2

   C. 3

   D. 4

   E. 5

6. If $(x + 1)$ times $(2x + 1)$ is an odd integer, then x must be

   A. an odd integer.

   B. an even integer.

   C. a prime number.

   D. a composite number.

   E. a negative number.

7. A certain geometry class has 36 students. If two-thirds of the students are boys and three-fourths of the boys are under six feet tall, how many boys in the class are under six feet tall?

   A.   6

   B. 12

   C. 18

   D. 24

   E. 27

8. What is the area of the preceding trapezoid in square inches?

   A. 108

   B. 234

   C. 368

   D. 468

   E. 585

9. Three factories of Conglomerate Corporation are capable of manufacturing hubcaps. Two of the factories can each produce 100,000 hubcaps in 15 days. The third factory can produce hubcaps 30% faster. Approximately how many days would it take to produce a million hubcaps with all three factories working simultaneously?

   A. 38

   B. 42

   C. 44

   D. 46

   E. 50

10. What is the area in square yards of an equilateral triangle if the length of one of its sides is 12 yards?

   A. $18\sqrt{3}$

   B. $36\sqrt{3}$

   C. 72

   D. $72\sqrt{3}$

   E. 216

IF YOU FINISH BEFORE TIME IS CALLED, CHECK YOUR WORK ON THIS SECTION ONLY. DO NOT WORK ON ANY OTHER SECTION IN THE TEST.

STOP

Section **6** Mathematical Reasoning

Section 7: Verbal Reasoning

Time: 30 Minutes

35 Questions

In this section, choose the best answer for each question and blacken the corresponding space on the answer sheet.

Sentence Completion

Directions: Each blank in the following sentences indicates that something has been omitted. Consider the lettered words beneath the sentence and choose the word or set of words that best fits the whole sentence.

1. In poor and politically unsettled countries, trucks are the only means of getting in or out, public transportation being virtually _____.

   A. indecipherable

   B. ubiquitous

   C. indifferent

   D. inadequate

   E. nonexistent

2. Parker is known for the _____ of her stories, many of them less than three pages long.

   A. wit

   B. sincerity

   C. cynicism

   D. economy

   E. development

3. Because most parents who watched *Sesame Street* as children are likely to regard the show as _____ viewing for their children, an advertiser can _____ a very large young audience.

   A. educational . . . alienate

   B. obligatory . . . rely on

   C. compulsory . . . avoid

   D. required . . . apprehend

   E. habitual . . . expect

4. A fiscal _____, Lloyd would sell shares when all the best economic advisors were recommending against doing so.

   A. conservative

   B. maverick

   C. investor

   D. Tory

   E. moderate

5. The clothes she designs for men are conservative, but her fashions for women are more _____.

   A. liberal

   B. flamboyant

   C. tasteful

   D. expensive

   E. conventional

6. His _____ protests against elephant poaching, an illegal but enormously _____ pursuit, put the warden at risk.

   A. vigorous . . . unpopular

   B. realistic . . . costly

   C. unregarded . . . profitable

   D. outspoken . . . lucrative

   E. tactful . . . popular

7. Although it is _____ that scientists will discover even smaller particles, we have theoretical reasons to believe that we _____ or are very close to a knowledge of nature's ultimate building blocks.

   A. unlikely . . . have misapprehended

   B. uncertain . . . have approached

   C. possible . . . have reached

   D. probable . . . have avoided

   E. moot . . . have acquired

8. Contrary to several sports writers' opinion, Valdez is neither _____ nor _____, but an affable and articulate young man.

   A. sullen . . . winsome

   B. genial . . . quiet

   C. morose. . . reticent

   D. gracious . . . impolite

   E. aggressive . . . well spoken

9. In 1900, Spanish operatic composers faced a problem of language, for if works were not written in Italian, singers of international stature _____ to sing them.

   A. refused

   B. hoped

   C. vocalized

   D. desired

   E. preferred

10. The reason for reduced spending on arms throughout the world is not _____, but _____, not a change in thinking, but a shortage of money.

   A. ideological . . . economic

   B. personal . . . political

   C. pacifist . . . practical

   D. local . . . universal

   E. liberal . . . conservative

GO ON TO THE NEXT PAGE

Analogies

Directions: In each of the following questions, you are given a related pair or words or phrases. Select the lettered pair that *best* expresses a relationship similar to that in the original pair of words.

11. CLIPPER SHIP : SAIL ::

    A. automobile : windshield

    B. train : baggage

    C. dirigible : helium

    D. submarine : propeller

    E. seaplane : pontoon

12. NURSERY : PLANTS ::

    A. classroom : teacher

    B. department store : charge account

    C. radio : news

    D. bakery : bread

    E. cobbler : shoes

13. WITCH : SORCERER ::

    A. surgeon : anesthetist

    B. playwright : dramatist

    C. contralto : baritone

    D. cook : waitress

    E. director : editor

14. JANITOR : BUILDING ::

    A. rider : horse

    B. fisherman : fire

    C. violinist : orchestra

    D. ranger : forest

    E. police officer : judge

15. BREAKFAST : DINNER ::

    A. lark : nightingale

    B. stone : wood

    C. tent : tepee

    D. radar : sonar

    E. realism : rationalism

16. RING : BRACELET ::

    A. log : pencil

    B. tennis ball : basketball

    C. trash barrel : wastebasket

    D. mile : yard

    E. square : cube

17. WALNUT : WOOD ::

    A. parsnip : vegetable

    B. bulb : tulip

    C. apple : seed

    D. chair : living room

    E. spice : recipe

18. CALORIE : HEAT ::

    A. weight : menu

    B. exercise : muscle

    C. personality : psychiatrist

    D. omen : bird

    E. acre : area

19. POPE : CARDINALS ::

    A.   supreme court : senate

    B.   abbess : abbots

    C.   bishop : dioceses

    D.   lama : temple

    E.   president : electoral college

20. TRIAL : SUMMATION ::

    A.   composition : coda

    B.   newspaper : editorial

    C.   drama : exposition

    D.   serial : episode

    E.   ballot : election

21. CAPRICIOUS : WHIM ::

    A.   indecisive : idea

    B.   optimistic : hope

    C.   parsimonious : poverty

    D.   garrulous : talk

    E.   philanthropic : cynicism

22. URBANITY : BUMPKIN ::

    A.   wit : comedian

    B.   egotism : show-off

    C.   tolerance : bigot

    D.   timidity : grammarian

    E.   literacy : librarian

GO ON TO THE NEXT PAGE

Critical Reading

Directions: Questions follow the passage below. Using only the stated or implied information in the passage and in its introduction, if any, answer the questions.

Questions 23–35 are based on the following passage.

Acid rain, in the past half decade, has been added to the technological world's litany of fears. Like carbon dioxide, it is an unintended by-product of the Industrial
(5) Revolution. Evidence strongly suggests that pollutants in the atmosphere are acidifying rains, lakes, and streams.

The problem is not well understood. It is not even well named. The words would
(10) sound less sinister if it were commonly known that all rains and snows are naturally acidic. A substance's acidity is measured on the pH scale, in which 7 is perfectly neutral, neither acidic nor alka-
(15) line. Speaking very roughly, the average pH of rain in nature — though it varies from place to place on the globe — is thought to be 5.6, which is slightly acidic.

In many parts of the industrial world, how-
(20) ever, and in forested country far downwind of factory country, the pH of rains and snows is much lower. Rainfall in the eastern United States is currently estimated by the Environmental Protection
(25) Agency to be about pH 4.5. The pH scale is logarithmic, which means that as one counts down the scale, each integer is 10 times more acidic than normal. And they often come worse. "One long rainfall in
(30) the autumn of 1978 holds a dubious national record," environmentalist and writer John Luoma reports in his book Troubled Skies, Troubled Waters. "Instruments registered values less than pH 2, a level six to
(35) eight times more acidic than vinegar and some five thousand times more acidic than normal rain." The pollutants responsible

for this increase are chiefly sulfur dioxide and the oxides of nitrogen. Swirled and
(40) cooked together with other gases and chemicals in the atmosphere, they can combine to form, among other things, sulfuric acid, which then falls on our country's soil and gathers in our lakes. Those
(45) lakes most at risk are in territory that was scraped clean of topsoil during the last advances and retreats of the ice age. In the great chain of wilderness lakes that extends from northern Minnesota into
(50) Canada; in the Appalachians; and in much of Scandinavia, the ice scoured right down to the bedrock, and the new soil that has collected there is still quite thin. These regions are poor in the kind of natural alka-
(55) line rock, like limestone, that elsewhere helps to neutralize acid rain. Many of their lakes have been greatly acidified, altering their chemistry in complex ways that are only beginning to be understood. Fish in
(60) these lakes have died off. The water is eerily clear and clean, because in it so little life survives.

Ironically, part of the problem is an engineering feat that was once seen as the
(65) problem's solution. Coal-burning plants such as Kyger Creek, and the General James M. Gavin plant, both in Cheshire, Ohio, have built huge smokestacks (Gavin's is over 1,000 feet high) to loft
(70) their emissions of sulfur dioxide and nitrogen oxides high into the atmosphere and keep these wastes from sickening their neighbors in Cheshire. The gases are borne extraordinary distances in the upper at-
(75) mosphere, where they have plenty of time and space to recombine into sulfuric acid, which then falls thousands of miles from

Kyger Creek and Gavin. Tall stacks help convert acid rain from a local to an environ-
(80) mental problem.

Environmentalists and industrialists agree that acid rain is poorly understood and must be studied further. But they disagree about what to do in the meanwhile. Some argue for
(85) several kinds of preventive action now. For instance, expensive "scrubbers" could be installed immediately by plants such as Kyger Creek and Gavin to clean sulfur dioxides from the stacks' emissions. But many other
(90) people — including most of those who would have to pay to install the scrubbers — think the expense premature. The issue has as many sides as any in climatology. Some of the chemical emissions in question even
(95) make good fertilizer. Notes climatologist Reid Bryson of the University of Wisconsin, "It may be the old saying about a silver lining to every cloud — but here in Wisconsin, when they cleaned up the sulfur emissions
(100) from one of our local power plants, the farmers in the area had to start adding sulfur to their fields."

Though the debate continues, Jon Luoma says, "the difficulties in the way of reducing
(105) acid rain are not so much scientific as political."

23. The second paragraph describes acid rain as "not even well named" because

    A. rain is naturally acid.

    B. no liquids are perfectly neutral.

    C. some rains are alkaline.

    D. the public cannot understand the meaning of the phrase.

    E. the phrase makes acid rain appear to be a serious problem.

24. The first sentence of the third paragraph refers to "forested country far downwind of factory country" as having rains and snows of low pH because

    A. industrial pollution travels upwind.

    B. the pH scale is logarithmic.

    C. rainfall is heavier in forested country.

    D. all rainfall is acidic.

    E. pollution from factories is blown here by winds.

25. From the information in the third paragraph, it can be inferred that the pH of vinegar is probably

    A. 2

    B. 4

    C. 6

    D. 7

    E. 8

26. In the third paragraph, the phrase "a dubious national record" is best taken to mean a

    A. record not scientifically confirmed.

    B. record not generally accepted as a record.

    C. record not expected to endure.

    D. local rather than an international record.

    E. record not worth achieving.

27. Of the following, which would be the most alkaline?

    A. A liquid with a pH of 3

    B. A liquid with a pH of 5

    C. A liquid with a pH of 7

    D. A liquid with a pH of 9

    E. A liquid with a pH of 11

GO ON TO THE NEXT PAGE

28. The passage suggests that an area with limestone may be harmed less by acid rain because

   A. no rain will run off into lakes and streams.

   B. streams will be more abundant and faster flowing.

   C. the limestone may neutralize the acid.

   D. the limestone will absorb less water than other rocks.

   E. limestone is a natural by-product of coal burning.

29. As it is used in line 61, the word "eerily" means

   A. scrupulously

   B. immaculately

   C. strangely

   D. partially

   E. ostensibly

30. In line 63, the adverb "ironically" is used because

   A. the smokestacks failed to protect Cheshire.

   B. the result is the opposite of what was expected.

   C. the builders of the smokestacks failed to consider the problems of acid rain.

   D. smokestacks cannot solve the problems of acid rain.

   E. engineers, rather than scientists, were responsible for the construction.

31. In line 64, the word "feat" means

   A. failure.

   B. foundation.

   C. attempt.

   D. achievement.

   E. sleight of hand.

32. Near the end of the fifth paragraph, the reference to "the old saying about a silver lining to every cloud" is used because

   A. some effects of acid rain are beneficial.

   B. there is hope that someday acid rain problems will be eliminated.

   C. acid rain falls far from the source of pollution.

   D. the solution to the problem of acid rain is political, not scientific.

   E. lakes in some regions are now clear and clean because of acid rain.

33. The chief antagonists in the debate about how to deal with causes of acid rain are most likely to be

   A. industrial polluters and farmers.

   B. industrialists and environmentalists.

   C. the federal government and private landowners.

   D. farmers whose soils benefit from acid rain and farmers whose soils do not.

   E. foresters and fishermen.

34. The passage implies that acid rain could be reduced by all of the following EXCEPT

    A. emission controls on smokestacks.

    B. reduction of coal burning in industry.

    C. reduction of sulfur dioxide in the atmosphere.

    D. reduction of the use of sulfur as fertilizer.

    E. reduction of oxides of nitrogen in the atmosphere.

35. That "the difficulties in the way of reducing acid rain are not so much scientific as political" is due chiefly to the fact that

    A. scientists do not yet fully understand acid rain.

    B. the side effects of acid rain can be beneficial as well as harmful.

    C. many scientists believe preventive measures should be undertaken immediately.

    D. acid rain falls on areas at great distances from the source of pollution.

    E. the cost of cleaning sulfur dioxides from smokestacks may be paid by the federal government.

IF YOU FINISH BEFORE TIME IS CALLED, CHECK YOUR WORK ON THIS SECTION ONLY. DO NOT WORK ON ANY OTHER SECTION IN THE TEST.

SCORING PRACTICE TEST 2

Answer Key

Section 1: Verbal Reasoning	Section 2: Mathematical Reasoning	Section 3: Verbal Reasoning	Section 4: Mathematical Reasoning
1. A	1. D	1. A	1. C
2. E	2. B	2. C	2. D
3. C	3. D	3. E	3. A
4. B	4. C	4. C	4. D
5. D	5. B	5. E	5. C
6. B	6. C	6. A	6. B
7. C	7. B	7. A	7. B
8. B	8. C	8. E	8. C
9. D	9. B	9. A	9. B
10. B	10. D	10. B	10. D
11. E	11. E	11. C	11. A
12. C	12. D	12. B	12. B
13. B	13. A	13. C	13. B
14. E	14. D	14. B	14. D
15. A	15. C	15. B	15. C
16. E	16. D	16. A	16. 5/8
17. A	17. B	17. D	17. 14
18. A	18. A	18. A	18. 1/6
19. D	19. C	19. B	19. 93.5
20. C	20. C	20. C	20. 527
21. D	21. A	21. E	21. 45
22. D	22. A	22. C	22. 7/12
23. C	23. A	23. A	23. 50
24. B	24. E	24. E	24. 100
25. E	25. C	25. A	25. 264
26. C		26. D	
27. C		27. B	
28. E		28. B	
29. C		29. D	
30. A		30. A	
		31. C	
		32. A	
		33. C	
		34. E	
		35. C	

**Section 5:
Verbal
Reasoning**

1. C
2. E
3. C
4. E
5. B
6. B
7. D
8. C
9. D
10. A
11. E
12. A
13. D
14. B

**Section 6:
Mathematical
Reasoning**

1. A
2. C
3. E
4. A
5. D
6. B
7. C
8. D
9. D
10. B

**Section 7:
Verbal
Reasoning**

1. E
2. D
3. B
4. B
5. B
6. D
7. C
8. C
9. A
10. A
11. D
12. D
13. C
14. D
15. A
16. B
17. A
18. E
19. E
20. A
21. B
22. C
23. A
24. E
25. A
26. E
27. E
28. C
29. C
30. B
31. D
32. A
33. B
34. D
35. D

Analyzing Your Test Results

The charts on the following pages should be used to carefully analyze your results and spot your strengths and weaknesses. The complete process of analyzing each subject area and each individual problem should be completed for each practice test. These results should then be re-examined for trends in types of errors (repeated errors) or poor results in specific subject areas. *This reexamination and analysis is of tremendous importance to you in ensuring maximum test preparation benefit.*

Verbal Reasoning Analysis Sheet

Section 1	*Possible*	*Completed*	*Right*	*Wrong*
Sentence Completion	9			
Analogies	6			
Critical Reading	15			
Subtotal	30			
Section 3	*Possible*	*Completed*	*Right*	*Wrong*
Sentence Completion	10			
Analogies	13			
Critical Reading	12			
Subtotal	35			
Section 5	*Possible*	*Completed*	*Right*	*Wrong*
Critical Reading	14			
Subtotal	14			
Section 7	*Possible*	*Completed*	*Right*	*Wrong*
Sentence Completion	10			
Analogies	12			
Critical Reading	13			
Subtotal	35			
Overall Verbal Totals	114			

Mathematical Reasoning Analysis Sheet

Section 1	Possible	Completed	Right	Wrong
Multiple Choice	25			
Subtotal	25			
Section 4	**Possible**	**Completed**	**Right**	**Wrong**
Quantitative Comparison	15			
Grid-Ins	10			
Subtotal	25			
Section 6	**Possible**	**Completed**	**Right**	**Wrong**
Multiple Choice	10			
Subtotal	10			
Overall Math Totals	60			

You can now use the Score Range Approximator on page 439 to convert your raw scores to an *approximate* scaled score.

Analysis/Tally Sheet for Problems Missed

One of the most important parts of test preparation is analyzing why you missed a problem so that you can reduce the number of mistakes. Now that you have taken the practice test and checked your answers, carefully tally your mistakes by marking them in the proper column.

	Reason for Mistakes				
	Total Missed	Simple Mistake	Misread Problem	Lack of Knowledge	Lack of Time
Section 1: Verbal					
Section 3: Verbal					
Section 5: Verbal					
Subtotal					
Section 2: Math					
Section 4: Math					
Section 6: Math					
Section 7: Math					
Subtotal					
Total Math and Verbal					

Reviewing the preceding data should help you determine *why* you are missing certain problems. Now that you have pinpointed the type of error, compare it to other practice tests to spot other common mistakes.

237

COMPLETE ANSWERS AND EXPLANATIONS FOR PRACTICE TEST 2

Section 1: Verbal Reasoning

Sentence Completion

1. **A.** The first noun could be any of the five except "similarities," although at first glance, **A** "differences" looks like the best. The second blank needs a verb that follows from "understanding," and **A** "appreciate" is the closest to the earlier word. Choices **B** and **C** make little sense with the fabric metaphor (how can one "resolve" or "combat" a "fabric"?).

2. **E.** The phrase "facts, not wishful thinking" is parallel to "realities, not _____," so you need a word that is opposite to "realities" and similar in effect to "wishful thinking." Only "myths" describes something that contrasts with "realities."

3. **C.** The verb "fell" tells you that the first noun must mean "decline" or fall. Choices **B** "decrease," **C** "decline," and **E** "drop" are all possibilities. The adjective describing this economy must also denote falling, so you can eliminate "steady" **B** and "booming" **E**, but **C** "sagging" is appropriate.

4. **B.** The first adjective must be consistent with the information that the skills have won over both liberals and conservatives. Choices **A**, **B**, and **D** would fit, and "organizational" **C** or "intimidating" **E** would not. The second blank requires an adverb that parallels or accords with "openly." Both "equivocally" (ambiguously) and "deceptively" are clearly the opposite of what is needed. The correct choice is **B** "frankly."

5. **D.** The missing adjective here should describe the actions of a slanderer. The noun "dissemination" means spreading abroad; the action of spreading a "libel" or "slander" is not well described by any of these choices except by **D** "irresponsible."

6. **B.** The final adjective must describe songs that satirize love as "foolish" or "compromised." The best choice is "antiromantic." The four other choices conflict with the assertion of the first half of the sentence.

7. **C.** If signaling the horse by the voice is part of a "clever ruse," the missing adverb must be something signifying "secretly" or "without being observed." Only **C** "covertly" has this meaning. The verb that fills the second blank must mean something like expose, and **C** "unmask" fits the requirement.

8. **B.** The needed word here is a strong way of saying "changeable" or "unpredictable." Of the five choices, "mercurial" (volatile, "changeable") is clearly the best.

9. **D.** The sentence presents two related definitions and is a straightforward test of vocabulary. A "cynic" distrusts "human goodness;" a "misanthrope" hates "people in general." A "pessimist" looks on the dark side of things and expects the worst; an "ingrate" is an ungrateful person. A "siren" is a temptress; a "tyrant" is an absolute ruler, usually a cruel or despotic one. An "altruist" is unselfishly concerned for the welfare of others; an "anarchist" opposes all forms of government. A "philanthropist" is a generous lover of humankind; a "misogynist" is a person who hates women.

Analogies

10. **B.** The words here are a verb ("tune") and a noun ("piano"), with the verb describing an action that must be performed before the noun can function properly. As a piano must be tuned, so a camera must be focused. This is a better choice than **D** ("ripen : fruit") because although "fruit" should "ripen" before it's eaten, both the "camera" and "piano" are mechanical objects, and the verbs require some manual action.

11. **E.** An "island" is land surrounded by "water;" an "oasis" is a place of water surrounded by the dry sands of a "desert."

12. **C.** A "square" is a four-sided figure of two dimensions. With three dimensions, it becomes a "cube." The parallel geometric figures are the two-dimensional "circle" that in three dimensions will be a "sphere."

13. **B.** A "zircon" is a mineral that can be cut to resemble a "diamond," but it is far cheaper. Similarly, a "garnet" is a red, semiprecious stone that is used in jewelry to replace the much more valuable "ruby."

14. **E.** The pairing here combines an adjective and a noun, and the noun is a quality that would characterize a person whom the adjective describes. A "complaisant" person—that is, someone who is polite or obliging—would be characterized by "courtesy." Similarly, a "greedy" person would be likely to be guilty of "gluttony." Choice **B** is possible but a less good choice because, although the "wise" may become "rich," it is less certain than that the "greedy" are "gluttonous."

15. **A.** This pair also links an adjective and a noun, except that in this case the noun denotes a characteristic a person described by the adjective would lack. The adjective "gauche" (the French for "left") means awkward or without "grace." Similarly, an "impecunious" (having no money) person would be without "wealth."

Critical Reading

16. **E.** As it is used here, "want" means need or poverty rather than a wish or desire for something.

17. **A.** Franklin's first paragraph makes the point that procuring wealth will secure virtue because it is much harder for a person in need to resist a temptation to act dishonestly than for one who has no worry about the next meal. Although Franklin would no doubt encourage self knowledge, education, and reason, the passage specifically cites wealth as security for virtue.

18. **A.** Although Franklin was willing to print personal abuse for a fee, he insisted on doing so separately from his newspaper. He did so because he believed in his obligation to the subscribers of his newspaper, who had no concern with private altercations. He would "disagree" only with the first of these three statements.

19. **D.** Franklin believed that his obligation to his subscribers required him to print material that was useful or entertaining, materials worth their subscription fees.

20. **C.** Although Franklin is remembered as a statesman, scientist, and inventor, his chief means of support, as this passage implies, was as a printer.

21. **D.** The first and last paragraphs refer to Franklin's wish to make his publications "entertaining and useful" (line 6) and "useful or entertaining" (line 70).

22. **D.** The word "inherent" means innate, inborn, existing in something as a basic characteristic. The problem is "inherent" because the mirror had been ground to the wrong shape.

23. **C.** If the mirror had been ground correctly, it would have concentrated 70 percent rather than 15 percent of the light—that is, 55 percent more than the present 15 percent.

24. **B.** The passage refers to sudden temperature changes when the telescope passes in and out of the earth's shadow.

25. **E.** The passage makes no mention of defects in the lens of the telescope.

26. **C.** As it is used here, the verb means to apply (oneself) to, to deal with, to encounter.

27. **C.** A telescope's sensitivity is its ability to respond to light (rather than to sound), and the resolution, which can be computer-enhanced, is the ability to make the image that it detects visible and clear. Of the five choices, **C** offers the best definitions.

28. **E.** The last paragraph deals chiefly with the telescope's success with objects within the solar system. This success is sufficient to rebut media claims of failure because *Hubble* makes it possible for astronomers to see the planets well whenever they want to do so.

29. **C.** The phrase to "home in on" (also used for automatic weapons) means to fix upon, to track, to pick out and follow home. It refers here to the distant objects that *Hubble* is unable to "home in on."

30. **A.** The passage as a whole gives a balanced view of the "Hubble Space Telescope." It admits the disappointments and specifies several tasks that the instrument is not yet able to handle. But it also points out the areas in which the telescope has been successful—not "revolutionary," but useful to astronomers.

Section 2: Mathematical Reasoning

1. **D.** The 4 pounds of steak would cost

    $4 \times \$3.89 = \$15.56$

    The change from a $20 bill would be

    $$
    \begin{array}{r}
    \$20.00 \\
    -15.56 \\
    \hline
    \$\ 4.44
    \end{array}
    $$

2. **B.** For a number to be divisible by 21, it must be divisible by 3 and by 7 because $21 = 3 \times 7$. Therefore, if a number is divisible by 7 but not by 21, it cannot be divisible by 3.

3. **D.** $.0039y = \dfrac{39}{10,000}\,y = 39$

    $$
    y = \frac{10,000}{39} \times 39
    $$
    $$
    y = 10,000
    $$

    Or, using your calculator, divide 39 by .0039.

4. **C.** Since XY = YZ = 10, $\triangle$XYZ is an isoceles triangle and $\angle$X = $\angle$Z. $\angle$Y = 84° because it forms a vertical angle with the given angle.

    $$
    \angle X + \angle Y + \angle Z = 180°
    $$
    $$
    \angle X + 84° + \angle Z = 180°
    $$
    $$
    2(\angle Z) + 84° = 180°
    $$
    $$
    2(\angle Z) = 96°
    $$
    $$
    \angle Z = 48°
    $$

    Therefore, the measure of $\angle Z = 48°$.

5. **B.** If $a = \sqrt{b}$ and $b = 81$, then $a = \sqrt{81}$, or $a = 9$. So the value of $\sqrt{a}$ is $\sqrt{9} = 3$.

6. **C.** If the plumber works for 6 consecutive hours, the charge is $45 for the first hour plus $20 for each of the five additional hours:

    $\$45 + 5(\$20) = \$45 + \$100 = \$145$

7. **B.** II only. The arithmetic mean is the average (sum divided by number of items), or $6 + 2 + 10 + 2 + 5 = 25$ divided by $5 = 5$.

The median is the middle number after the numbers have been ordered: 2, 2, 5, 6, 10. The median is 5.

The mode is the most frequently appearing number: 2.

The range is the highest minus the lowest, or $10 - 2 = 8$.

Therefore, only II is true: The median (5) equals the mean (5).

8. **C.** Since three-fifths of the class are females, two-fifths of the class are males. Therefore, the ratio of males to females is

$$\frac{2}{5} \text{ to } \frac{3}{5} = \frac{\frac{2}{5}}{\frac{3}{5}}$$

$$= \frac{2}{5} \div \frac{3}{5}$$

$$= \frac{2}{5} \cdot \frac{5}{3}$$

$$= \frac{2}{3}$$

9. **B.** Since $a = p + prt$,

$$a - p = p + prt - p$$

$$a - p = prt$$

$$\frac{a - p}{pt} = \frac{prt}{pt}$$

$$\frac{a - p}{pt} = r$$

Therefore, $r = \dfrac{a - p}{pt}$

10. **D.** First change the equation to slope-intercept form $y = mx + b$, where m is the slope and b is the y intercept.

$$\begin{array}{r} 6x + y = 3 \\ -6x \qquad - 6x \\ \hline y = 3 - 6x \quad \text{or} \quad -6x + 3 \end{array}$$

Next, you can see that in the equation $y = -6x + 3$, -6 is in the m position and is therefore the slope.

11. **E.** Total number of different combinations ("how many different kinds") is found by multiplying the number of ways for each item. Therefore, three different breads times four different meats times three different cheeses = $3 \times 4 \times 3 = 36$.

12. **D.** Breaking the figure into squares of side x by adding lines gives

Remember that each square has area x^2. Then the total area is $41x^2$. Choices **A**, **B**, and **E** are not possible because area must be in square units.

13. **A.** Adding the two equations,

$$x - y = 15$$
$$\underline{3x + y = 13}$$
$$4x \quad = 28$$

$$\frac{4x}{4} = \frac{28}{4}$$

$$x = 7$$

Since $x = 7$	or	Since $x = 7$

Since $x = 7$ and $x - y = 15$

$$7 - y = 15$$
$$7 - 7 - y = 15 - 7$$
$$-y = 8$$
$$y = -8$$

Since $x = 7$ and $3x + y = 13$

$$3(7) + y = 13$$
$$21 + y = 13$$
$$21 - 21 + y = 13 - 21$$
$$y = -8$$

Therefore, $x = y$ and $y = -8$.

14. **D.** In isosceles $\triangle XYZ$, $\angle X = \angle Z$.

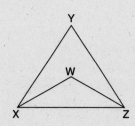

$$\angle X + \angle Y + \angle Z = 180°$$
$$\angle X + 80° + \angle Z = 180°$$
$$\angle X + \angle Z = 100°$$
$$\angle X = \angle Z = 50°$$

Since WX bisects $\angle YXZ$ and WZ bisects $\angle YZX$,

$$\angle YXW = \angle WXZ = \angle YZW = \angle WZX = 25°$$

Therefore, on $\triangle XWZ$,

$$\angle XWZ + \angle WXZ + \angle WZX = 180°$$
$$\angle XWZ + 25° + 25° = 180°$$
$$\angle XWZ + 50° = 180°$$
$$\angle XWZ = 130°$$

15. C. $(m + n)^2 = (m + n)(m + n)$

$$= m^2 + mn + mn + n^2$$

$$= m^2 + 2mn + n^2$$

$$= (m^2 + n^2) + (2mn)$$

Since $m^2 + n^2 = 12$ and $mn = 9$,

$$(m^2 + n^2) + (2mn) = 12 + 2(9)$$

$$= 12 + 18$$

$$= 30$$

16. D. Let x = width and $x + 8$ = length.

Since the perimeter of the rectangle is 42,

$$2x + 2(x + 8) = 42$$

$$2x + 2x + 16 = 42$$

$$4x + 16 = 42$$

$$4x = 26$$

$$x = \frac{26}{4} = 6\frac{1}{2}$$

$$x + 8 = 14\frac{1}{2}$$

Therefore, the length of the rectangle is $14\frac{1}{2}$.

17. B. Adding any two of three consecutive positive integers greater than 1 will always be greater than the other integer. Therefore, II is true. The others cannot be determined because they depend on values and/or the order of x, y, and z.

18. A. Since Rajiv will be y years old x years from now, he is $y - x$ years old now. Therefore, z years from now he will be $y - x + z$ years old.

19. C. Let x = first number, $2x + 1$ = second number, and $3x - 4$ = third number. Since the average of the three numbers is 55,

$$\frac{x + (2x + 1) + (3x - 4)}{3} = 55$$

Multiplying both sides of the equation by 3,

$$x + (2x + 1) + (3x - 4) = 165$$

$$6x - 3 = 165$$

$$6x - 3 + 3 = 165 + 3$$

$$6x = 168$$

$$\frac{6x}{6} = \frac{168}{6}$$

$$x = \frac{168}{6}$$

245

$$x = 28 = \text{first number}$$
$$2x + 1 = 57 = \text{second number}$$
$$3x - 4 = 80 = \text{third number}$$

Therefore, the largest number is 80.

20. C. Area of the square = ½ × product of diagonals

$$= \tfrac{1}{2}d_1 d_2$$
$$= \tfrac{1}{2}d^2 \text{ (because } d_1 = d_2 \text{ in a square)}$$

Therefore, $\tfrac{1}{2}d^2 = 72$

$$d^2 = 144$$
$$d = 12 \text{ feet}$$

21. A. Let $5x$ = first angle, $2x$ = second angle, and $5x - 2x = 3x$ = third angle. Since the sum of the angles in any triangle is 180°,

$$5x + 2x + 3x = 180°$$
$$10x = 180°$$
$$\frac{10x}{10} = \frac{180°}{10}$$
$$x = 18°$$

Therefore, $5x = 90°$

$$2x = 36°$$
$$3x = 54°$$

The smallest angle will have a measure of 36°.

22. A. $(-2, 3) \oplus (4, -1) = [(-2)(4) - (3)(-1), (-2)(-1)]$
$$= [(-8) - (-3), (2)]$$
$$= (-5, 2)$$

23. A. Let n = number of nickels, $3n$ = number of dimes, and $3n - 3$ = number of quarters. Since 25 coins are in the collection,

$$n + 3n + (3n - 3) = 25$$
$$7n - 3 = 25$$
$$7n = 28$$
$$n = 4 \text{ nickels} = \$0.20$$
$$3n = 12 \text{ dimes} = \$1.20$$
$$3n - 3 = 9 \text{ quarters} = \$2.25$$

Therefore, the total value of the collection is $\$0.20 + \$1.20 + \$2.25 = \$3.65$

24. E. Since arc YXZ is a semicircle, its measure is 180°.

$$\text{arc XZ} = \text{arc YXZ} - \text{arc YWX}$$

$$= 180° - 100°$$

$$= 80°$$

Since an inscribed angle = ½ (intercepted arc),

$$\angle XYZ = \tfrac{1}{2} \,(\text{arc XZ})$$

$$= \tfrac{1}{2}(80°)$$

$$= 40°$$

Therefore, $\angle XYZ$ has a measure of 40°.

25. C. Since $\sqrt{mn} = 10$, $mn = 100$, and the possible values for m and n would be

1 and 100

2 and 50

4 and 25

5 and 20

10 and 10

Since none of these combinations yields $m + n = 50$, choice **C** is correct.

Section 3: Verbal Reasoning

Sentence Completion

1. **A.** The informative phrase here is "mistakes we made last week or last year." These mistakes we understand by looking back, by "hindsight." None of the other choices fits the rest of the sentence so well.

2. **C.** The parallel phrases here are "something everyone possesses" and "imagination is not a gift _____ to poets." The right word must be the opposite of universal, since the word "not" precedes it. The best choice is "unique," different from all others. With "not," this is equivalent to "something everyone possesses."

3. **E.** The phrase "less is more" is not a "hope," a "question" (that would be "is less more?"), an "enigma" (riddle), or an "image." It is a "paradox," an apparent self-contradiction, since less *should* be less, not more.

4. **C.** Choices **A, C,** and **D** would seem to fit the first blank, but the second noun, which describes something the senator did that the president ignored, could be only **B** or **C,** and **B** has already been eliminated. Both of the nouns in **C** make very good sense in this context.

5. **E.** Since the action is described as stupid and indifferent, it cannot be something that has helped our resources, so we are left with two possible answers: "wasted" **C** or "squandered" **E.** The second blank must be a word meaning "ability; capacity" **E** makes good sense, but "failure" **C** does not.

6. **A.** Reports of "freewheeling" corporate spending are unlikely to be "favorable" or "encouraging," but choices **A** and **B** fit well, and **C** is a possibility. The "despite" at the beginning of the sentence tells us that the reports are not true, and the missing adverb should be very different from "freewheeling." Both **B** "unfairly" and **C** "secretly" contradict the "despite," but **A** makes good sense. The reports must be "lurid," that is, sensational or startling, and the adverb is "equitably," that is, fairly or even-handedly.

7. **A.** The first phrase tells us the crime will be described by an "understatement." Choices **B, C, D,** and **E** all call a crime a crime, but "peccadillo" suggests that stealing four million dollars is insignificant, a minor fault, a petty crime. This is "understatement."

8. **E.** The second adjective modifies "countries that have no savings at all," so it cannot be any of the words meaning rich (**A, B, C,** and **D**). The correct choice is "indigent," that is, poor. Although **A, C,** or **E** might have fit the first blank, choice **E** also makes the most sense.

9. **A.** The sentence tells us that Pierce refused to read about positions different from his own. You need first a noun to describe a quality of a man like this, and all of the answers except **E** are possibilities. The second blank calls for a word to go with "to travel" that will also fit this parochial, insular, bigoted, or narrow-minded man. The right answer must mean something like "failure" or refusal. Either **A** or **E** will do, but only **A** has the first word right.

10. **B.** If the doctor must be brave to continue her work, the missing verb must describe something to be resisted. The best choices are "vilified" **B** and "attacked" **E.** The result of the brave work is acceptance by other doctors of the "probability" or the "tenets" of her theories. "Tenets" usually refers to doctrines or principles of a school of thought and is not quite right in this context. But both "vilified" (reviled, defamed) and "probability" fit well.

Analogies

11. **C.** The two nouns here describe a caretaker and the group for which that person is responsible. Here the clear parallel is the "cowhand," who oversees a "herd" of cattle, and the "shepherd," who oversees a "flock" of sheep.

12. **B.** A clothes "moth" is an insect which feeds upon "wool" or fur. The closest parallel is another insect, the "termite," which feeds upon "wood." The first term of the other choices does not actually feed upon the second term, although they may have some connection.

13. **C.** A "passport" is a type of "document." If the order of choice **E** were reversed, the parallel would be a good one, but the question puts the specific example ("passport") as the second term. Choice **C** is the correct answer because a "ball-point" is a type of "pen."

14. **B.** A "dressmaker" uses a "pattern" to guide the making of an article of clothing just as a "chef" uses a "recipe" to make food. The first term is a plan or guide rather than a tool, material, or product.

15. **B.** The nouns are opposites. An "immunity" is an exemption or release from an obligation such as taxes or prosecution, while "liability" is an obligation or responsibility for something. The only pair of antonyms among the answer choices is **B,** where "debit," an entry of money owed, is the opposite of "credit," an entry of money received or to be received.

16. **A.** Both words here are verbs, although in another context they might be nouns. To "intrigue" is to *plan* or scheme in a secret or underhanded way. The parallel is "move" and "slink" (to move in a sneaking manner).

17. **D.** "Request" and "requirement" here are nouns; the difference between them is the element of force or compulsion in "requirement" as opposed to the voluntary "request." A similar difference is approximated in the pairing of "inquiry" (a question or a questioning) and "interrogation" (a questioning in a formal examination, especially of a witness). The correspondence is not exact, but it is clearly the closest of the five choices.

18. **A.** The second of these two adjectives is an intensive form of the first. "Saccharine" means very "sweet," even too "sweet." Choices **B, C, D,** and **E** are either synonyms or antonyms **C,** but "deafening" is intensely "loud."

19. **B.** An "abbot" is a monk who is the head, not merely a member, of a "monastery," so the two nouns present a person in charge and what he or she is in charge of. The best choice here is the "conductor" of an "orchestra."

20. **C.** A "bowline" is a kind of "knot" as a "pianist" is a kind of "musician." None of the other options is close.

21. **E.** A "pedant" is a person who is narrow-minded, stressing details of "learning" which he or she professes rigorously. Similarly, a "martinet" is a strict disciplinarian, who enforces "discipline" with equal concern. The second term here is a person and the first that which the person is narrowly interested in.

22. **C.** A "chauvinist" is not, as is often assumed, simply a male who blindly champions maleness. The word originally denoted any militant, unreasoning supporter of a country, that is, a "jingo." The word is now also used to describe mindless supporters of a gender or a race. The terms here are synonyms, as are "toady" (a flatterer) and "sycophant" (also a flatterer).

23. **A.** To "accrete" is to grow by being added to, while to "diminish" is to grow smaller, its antonym. The verbs "wax" and "wane" are also opposites and, in fact, are synonyms for "accrete" and "diminish."

Critical Reading

24. **E.** The first paragraph cites our using the words "shrinks playfully" and, in the second sentence, as a means of suggesting a criticism of modern psychotherapy. The third sentence asks (and suggests an affirmative answer) whether "witchdoctoring" might have "at least marginal value."

25. **A.** The allusion to Sahlin's "stone-age economics" is intended to suggest the possibility of a stone-age psychiatry that may have some relevance to the modern world. The idea is advanced tentatively, in the form of a question that concludes the paragraph.

26. **D.** The passage never makes outrageous claims for tribal therapy, but it does assert that it "may be more effective in the treatment of their own people," with the added qualification "especially when it comes to mental and emotional disorders."

27. **B.** The second paragraph concludes with a reference to the "condition of expectant faith," Freud's words of praise for tribal healers who create this feeling that can have a "great therapeutic effect." That is, a patient who expects to be healed is more likely to recover.

28. **B.** The third paragraph describes the much greater range of ills that traditional shamans would treat, including a frozen foot. Modern psychotherapists can be expected to deal with the mental afflictions of choices **A, C, D,** and **E** but not with the broken arm.

29. **D.** The word "marked" is an adjective here meaning conspicuous or obvious.

30. **A.** The phrase is best paraphrased by between body and mind. Although "psychic" as a noun can mean a person sensitive to forces beyond the physical world, here it means that which is of the mind.

31. **C.** As it is used in this context, "psychosomatic" means originating in the mind and carries no suggestion of imaginary or unreal.

32. **A.** Freud, the second paragraph says, believed in the importance of the "condition of expectant faith" based on the patient's trust in the therapist's skill. Torrey, in the fourth paragraph, insists upon the importance of the "cultural bond" uniting the therapist and the client. The best answer here is choice **A.**

33. **C.** "To take issue with" is to argue, disagree, contest with. Torrey is disagreeing with assumed superiority of the Western scientist.

34. **E.** The author deliberately uses the words "mumbo-jumbo, charlatans, psychotics," and "eye of newt" not because he agrees with them but because he realizes that many of his readers approach this subject with these prejudices. The phrase "shaman's method" does not have the pejorative denotation or connotations of the four other choices.

35. **C.** The passage is suggesting that we study tribal lore before we dismiss it because it may have uses even in modern Western society. The passage is not so unrealistic as to assert that tribal medicine is superior to Western, and its chief purpose is not to criticize the West.

Section 4: Mathematical Reasoning

Quantitative Comparison

1. C. This comparison should be made without any actual computation as follows:

$$35\% \text{ of } 50 \qquad 50\% \text{ of } 35$$

$$.35 \times 50 \qquad .50 \times 35$$

Since 35×50 is on each side and each column's answer has no decimal places, the quantities are equal. Or

$$^{35}\!/_{100} \times 50 \qquad ^{50}\!/_{100} \times 35$$

$$^{1}\!/_{100} \times 35 \times 50 = ^{1}\!/_{100} \times 50 \times 35$$

2. D. Solving $x^2 = 36$ gives +6 and −6. Therefore, x can be equal to 6 or −6, making no comparison possible.

3. A. Changing the form of column A by squaring 3 and then multiplying it by 2 to get everything under the radical sign leaves the simple comparison $\sqrt{18} > \sqrt{17}$.

4. D. The length of side AB is determinable by using the Pythagorean theorem, but since DC is not known, BC cannot be determined. Note that you cannot make a determination by measuring.

5. C. Since there are 180° in a triangle and ∠BDC is 90°, the remaining two angles, ∠DBC and ∠BCD, must total 90°.

6. B. If $a = b$ and $a < c$, then the following substitutes make the comparison simpler.

$$2a \qquad\qquad b + c$$

$$a + a \qquad\qquad b + c$$

Since $a = b$, then,

$$a + b \qquad\qquad b + c$$

Now, canceling b's from each column leaves

$$a \qquad < \qquad c$$

7. B. Solve the first problem as follows:

$$x \text{ is } 30\% \text{ of } 60$$

Substituting "=" for "is" and "÷" for "of" ($30\% = ^{3}\!/_{10}$)

Then $x = (^{3}\!/_{10} \cdot 60)$

$$x = 18$$

Solve the second problem as follows:

20% of y is 4 (20% = ⅕)

$⅕y = 4$

Multiplying by 5/1 gives

$(5/1) \cdot (⅕)y = 4 \cdot (5/1)$

Then $y = 20$

8. C. The integer multiples of 8 greater than 8 but less than 50 are 16, 24, 32, 40, and 48. Column A is therefore 5. The integer multiples of 6 greater than 6 but less than 40 are 12, 18, 24, 30, and 36. Therefore, column B is also 5. The correct answer is **C.**

9. B. The chord that is closer to the center of the circle will be longer than the chord that is farther from the center. Hence CD > AB.

10. D. Volume of a cube with side 6 is $6 \times 6 \times 6 = 216$. Volume of a rectangular prism with two dimensions less than 6 is not determinable because the third dimension is needed. Therefore, no comparison can be made.

11. A. Since there are 10 cents in each dime, the number of cents in $8n$ dimes is

$10(8n) = 80n$

Since there are 25 cents in each quarter, the number of cents in $3n$ quarters is

$25(3n) = 75n$

Hence, the number of cents in $8n$ dimes is greater than the number of cents in $3n$ quarters. Or you can disregard the n, since it is the same positive number on each side. Thus you are actually comparing 80¢ in column A and 75¢ in column B.

12. B. Solving the systems of equations as follows by first multiplying the bottom equation by [−5] gives

$5x + y = 2$

$-5x + -15y = -30$

Now, adding equations leaves

$-14y = -28$

Therefore, $y = 2$

Substituting $y = 2$ into the original second equations gives

$x + 3(2) = 6$

Then $x + 6 = 6$

and $x = 0$

Therefore $x < y$.

13. B. Since the three angles whose measures are given as x, $2x$, and $x + 30$ form a straight line,

$$x + 2x + (x + 30) = 180$$
$$4x + 30 = 180$$
$$4x = 150$$
$$x = 150 \div 4$$
$$x = 37.5$$
$$2x = 75$$
$$x + 30 = 67.5$$

Hence, $2x > x + 30$

14. D. Substituting $x = 0$ and $y = 1$,

$$(x - y)^2 \qquad\qquad x^2 - y^2$$
$$(0 - 1)^2 \qquad\qquad (0)^2 - (1)^2$$

Then $1 > -1$

Now, substituting $x = -1$ and $y = 0$,

$$(-1 - 0)^2 \qquad\qquad (-1)^2 - (0)^2$$
$$(-1)^2 \qquad\qquad (-1)^2$$

Then $1 = 1$

Since different values give different comparisons, no comparison can be made.

15. C. It would be much too time consuming to multiply out 9^{19} or 9^{18}. Therefore, the quick way to solve this problem is to factor out column A as follows:

$$9^{19} - (8)9^{18}$$
$$(9^1)\,(9^{18}) - (8)9^{18}$$
$$(9^1 - 8)(9^{18})$$
$$(1)(9^{18})$$

Thus, they are equal.

Grid-In Questions

16. Answer: $\frac{5}{8}$. Multiplying both sides of the equation by the LCD of 5,

$$5(x + \tfrac{3}{5}x) = 5(1)$$
$$5x + 3x = 5$$
$$8x = 5$$
$$x = \tfrac{5}{8}$$

17. Answer: 14. Since 60% of the students are girls, 40% of the students are boys. Hence,

$$40\% \text{ of } 35 = (.40)(35)$$
$$= 14 \text{ boys}$$

18. Answer: $\frac{1}{6}$. The average of any three numbers is equal to the sum of the numbers divided by 3.

$$\frac{1}{4} + \frac{1}{6} + \frac{1}{12} = \frac{3}{12} + \frac{2}{12} + \frac{1}{12}$$

The sum $= \frac{6}{12}$

$$= \tfrac{1}{2}$$

The average of the numbers is

$$\frac{1}{2} \div 3 = \frac{1}{2} \cdot \frac{1}{3} = \frac{1}{6}$$

19. Answer: 93.5.

$$\frac{317.9 \text{ miles}}{17 \text{ gallons}} = \frac{x \text{ miles}}{5 \text{ gallons}}$$
$$17x = (317.9)(5)$$
$$17x = 1589.5$$
$$x = 1589.5 \div 17$$
$$x = 93.5 \text{ miles}$$

20. Answer: 527. The total of the five verbal SAT scores is 2,635. Dividing that total by 5 (the number of scores) gives 527 as the average.

21. Answer: 45. Since the sum of the measures of the angles of a quadrilateral is 360 and the ratio of the angle measures is 3:5:7:9,

$$3x + 5x + 7x + 9x = 360$$
$$24x = 360$$
$$x = 360 \div 24$$
$$x = 15$$

The smallest angle is $3x = (3)(15) = 45$.

22. Answer: $\frac{7}{12}$. If Jim works for 2 days, he will complete $\frac{2}{6}$, or $\frac{1}{3}$, of the job. If Mike works for 2 days, he will complete $\frac{2}{8}$, or $\frac{1}{4}$, of the job. Together they will complete

$$\frac{1}{3} + \frac{1}{4} = \frac{4}{12} + \frac{3}{12} = \frac{7}{12} \text{ of the job.}$$

23. Answer: 50. Since BD is a diagonal of square ABCD,

$$BD = 5\sqrt{2}$$

The area of square BDMN

$$= (BD)^2$$
$$= \left(5\sqrt{2}\right)^2$$
$$= 25 \times 2$$
$$= 50$$

24. Answer: 100. The greatest increase is indicated by the steepest rise in the graph lines, between 1991 and 1992. But you are looking for the greatest *percentage* increase, which means the increase as compared to the starting point. To find percentage increase:

$$\frac{\text{amount of increase}}{\text{starting point}} = \text{percentage increase}$$

1989-1990	20 to 25	$\frac{5}{20} = 25\%$ increase
1990-1991	25 to 50	$\frac{25}{25} = 100\%$ increase
1991-1992	50 to 90	$\frac{40}{50} = 80\%$ increase
1992-1993	decrease	

25. Answer: 264. In $\triangle$MNP, PM = PN and $\angle$PMN = $\angle$PNM = 42°. Also, in $\triangle$MNP,

$$\angle PMN + \angle PNM + \angle MNP = 180°$$
$$42° + 42° + \angle MPN = 180°$$
$$84° + \angle MPN = 180°$$
$$\angle MPN = 96°$$

Since $\angle$MPN is a central angle,

$$\text{arc } MN = 96°$$

Also, arc MN + arc MQN = 360°

$$96° + \text{arc } MQN = 360°$$
$$\text{arc } MQN = 264°$$

Section 5: Verbal Reasoning

Critical Reading

1. **C.** The passage makes no comment on the skills of the players in the earlier period as opposed to today. The first paragraph tells us that orchestra conducting is "less than 150 years old" and that it became necessary because orchestras began to increase in size in the late 1700s.

2. **E.** The sentence structure suggests that "Apollonian" and "Dionysian" are parallel to "Mendelssohn" and "Wagner," to "elegant" and "passionate," and to *clear* and *emotional*. Although Apollo is the sun god, the best choice here is "clear" and "elegant."

3. **C.** The third paragraph discusses the difficulties of conducting, citing the conductor's having to "play" upon an instrument of one hundred musicians, while the singer or orchestral player must deal with only one.

4. **E.** The author of Passage 1 presents the "ideal modern conductor" as a synthesis of the "elegant" and the "passionate" schools (lines 44, 33-35).

5. **B.** The snide parenthesis manages to suggest that music critics are society ladies who are less interested in and less able to judge musical abilities than are musicians. Like the society women, the critics are more important to a conductor's success than are a conductor's real musical abilities. The sentence does not imply that critics are more interested in the players than in the conductor.

6. **B.** The author compares conductors and politicians, suggesting that both are careerists. They are, like conductors, conspicuously *not* original, disciplined, modest, or indifferent to power.

7. **D.** The phrase is in fact saying that conductors are self-centered, are egoists.

8. **C.** The passage suggests that in the "musical community" — that is, the community of musicians and music lovers — music is paramount. In the "music-business community," however, with its cult of personality, music is not the main concern. Although choices **D** and **E** may well be true, the passage does not deal with these issues.

9. **D.** What the sentence in its roundabout way is really saying is that television, unfortunately, makes it possible for viewers to see the front of the conductor. In the concert hall, the conductor's back is to the audience, but television has made it possible for viewers to see every grimace of the conductor. To circumvent is to go around or to avoid, and "dorsal" means back.

10. **A.** The phrase refers to "listen to the music." The author implies that it will be so bad you had much better have stayed at home.

11. **E.** At one time or another, the passage mocks or directly attacks conductors, politicians, the public, and the critics, but it spares the instrumentalists who play in the orchestras.

12. **A.** Unlike the author of Passage 1, the author of Passage 2 wants no part of the conductor's personality or feelings to interfere with what the composer has written. The ideal performance would be "an exact realization of the score." Since the second author is a composer, whereas the first is a conductor, these preferences are understandable.

13. **D.** Both passages use the word "great," but Passage 2 always puts quotation marks around the word. The author is quoting the word from people like the author of the first passage (and may, in fact, have the first passage specifically in mind), but "great" in the second passage is said with a sneer. It refers to so-called "great" conductors whose qualifications have too little to do with music.

14. **B.** Both passages assume that a conductor will be male. Since that time, an increasing number of female conductors have appeared before the public. In addition, a gender-neutral style of writing has become more common.

Section 6: Mathematical Reasoning

1. A. $\dfrac{\text{percent}}{100} = \dfrac{\text{is number}}{\text{of number}}$

$\dfrac{.25}{100} = \dfrac{x}{12}$

Cross multiplying,

$100x = 3.00$

$\dfrac{100x}{100} = \dfrac{3.00}{100}$

$x = .03 \text{ or } \sfrac{3}{100}$

2. C. The maximum number of squares 1 inch by 1 inch will be 16.

3. E. Let x = original price. Then

$x - .40x = 5.70$

$.60x = 5.70$

$x = 9.50$

Hence, the book originally cost $9.50.

4. A. Multiply the numerator and denominator by 12 (LCD).

$$\dfrac{12\,(\sfrac{2}{3} - \sfrac{1}{2})}{12\,(\sfrac{1}{6} + \sfrac{1}{4} + \sfrac{2}{3})} = \dfrac{8 - 6}{2 + 3 + 8} = \sfrac{2}{3}$$

5. D. According to the graph, the tallest "B" (before) bar is county 4.

6. B. Solve this problem by plugging in simple numbers. Start with 1, an odd integer.

$(1 + 1) \text{ times } (2 \cdot 1 + 1)$

$= (2) \text{ times } (2 + 1)$

$= 2 \cdot 3$

$= 6 \text{ (not odd)}$

Now, try 2, an even integer.

$(2 + 1) \text{ times } (2 \cdot 2 + 1)$

$= (3) \text{ times } (4 + 1)$

$= 3 \cdot 5$

$= 15 \text{ (an odd integer)}$

7. C. Since two-thirds of the students are boys, ⅔ (36) = 24 boys in the class. Out of the 24 boys in the class, three-fourths of them are under six feet tall, or ¾ (24) = 18 boys under six feet tall.

8. D. Since the area of a trapezoid = ½ · h · ($b_1 + b_2$), we need to find the altitude, h. Draw altitudes in the figure as follows:

Since the triangles formed are right triangles, use the Pythagorean theorem, which says

$$c^2 = a^2 + b^2$$

$$15^2 = 9^2 + h^2$$

$$225 = 81 + h^2$$

$$h^2 = 225 - 81$$

$$h^2 = 144$$

$$h = \sqrt{144} = 12 \text{ inches}$$

Hence, the area of the trapezoid will be

$$½ · h · (b_1 + b_2) = ½ · 12 · (30 + 48)$$

$$= (6)(78)$$

$$= 468 \text{ square inches}$$

9. D. First, calculate the rates of production per day. Two of the factories each make $100,000/15 \cong 6667$ hubcaps per day. The third plant makes $1.3 \times 6667 \cong 8667$ hubcaps per day. The total production rate is 8667 + 2(6667) = 22,001 hubcaps per day. At that rate, it would take 45.5 days to produce a million hubcaps.

10. B. Area = ½ × base × height

Since △BCD is a 30-60-90 triangle,

$$h = \frac{\sqrt{3}}{2}(BC)$$
$$= \frac{\sqrt{3}}{2}(12)$$
$$= 6\sqrt{3}$$

Hence, area of △ABC = ½(AC)(BD)

$$= \frac{1}{2}(12)(6\sqrt{3})$$
$$= (6)(6\sqrt{3})$$
$$= 36\sqrt{3} \text{ square yards}$$

Section 7: Verbal Reasoning

Sentence Completion

1. **E.** If trucks are the "only" means of transport, then there can be no public transportation, and a word that denotes this is needed. The best choice is "nonexistent," that is, not in existence.

2. **D.** The clue in the second part of the sentence describes the stories as often "less than three pages long." Although any one of the answers could make sense, only "economy" is specifically related to the short length of the stories.

3. **B.** For the first blank, each of the first four choices would be suitable, but the second blank requires a verb that follows from the paternal sympathy with the program. Either **B** or **E** is appropriate, but "obligatory" is a better adjective choice than "habitual."

4. **B.** The missing word must describe someone who acts in opposition to the "best economic advisors." Choices **A, D,** and **E** all denote a conservative, and choice **C** is neutral. A "maverick" is a person who acts independently, deriving from the term for an unbranded, lost calf that any rancher could claim.

5. **B.** The "but" signals a word that is very different from "conservative" in meaning. Although "liberal" in some contexts is the opposite of "conservative," that use refers to politics, not clothing, and the best choice here is **B** "flamboyant," which means ornate or showy.

6. **D.** If the protests put the warden at risk, they were probably "vigorous" or "outspoken" and not "tactful," "realistic," or "unregarded," although "realistic" might work. "Poaching" is "illegal" but also very "something" that makes people risk breaking the law. The possibilities here are "profitable" or its synonym "lucrative." The best choice, then, is **D,** which has "outspoken protests" and "lucrative pursuit."

7. **C.** The "Although" signals the possibility of smaller particles being found, so **B** and **C** are the best first words. With the phrase "or are very close to" in the sentence, "have approached" is redundant, whereas "have reached" makes good sense.

8. **C.** The blanks must be the opposites or contradictions of "affable" and "articulate," given the "neither" and "nor." Of the choices, not "morose" and not "reticent" would be the closest to "affable" and "articulate." The adjectives "sullen," "quiet," or "aggressive" could work but not paired with the words given here.

9. **A.** If there is a "problem" for Spanish composers, the missing word must be "refused." With **B, D,** or **E,** there would be no problem, and **C** makes no sense.

10. **A.** The two missing adjectives modify "reason" and are defined by "not a change in thinking" and "but a shortage of money." The choices that most clearly refer to belief and money are "ideological" and "economic."

Analogies

11. **D.** The motion of the "clipper ship" depends upon the "sail" as the motion of the "submarine" depends upon the "propeller." Although helium may hold the dirigible up, it is not the force that moves the airship.

12. **D.** A "nursery" is a place where "plants" are sold. A "bakery" is a place where "bread" is sold.

13. **C.** "Witch" refers to a female with supernatural powers, a sorceress. The male is called a "sorcerer." Similarly, a female singer in a lower register is a "contralto," while a male is a "baritone."

14. **D.** The "janitor" is the person in charge of the maintenance of "building" property. The parallel here is a "ranger," who is responsible for the "forest."

15. **A.** The nouns describe meals, one of the morning, one of the evening. The "lark" is conventionally presented as a dawn singer, while the "nightingale" is associated with evening or night. While it is true that "dinner" can also describe a midday meal, no answer choice provides a morning/midday option.

16. **B.** A "ring" and a "bracelet" have the same shape, but the bracelet is larger. A "tennis ball" and a "basketball" are both spheres, with the larger second.

17. **A.** "Walnut" is a kind of "wood" as a "parsnip" is a kind of "vegetable."

18. **E.** A "calorie" is a unit that measures "heat" as an "acre" is a unit of measurement for an "area."

19. **E.** The "pope" is elected by the college of "cardinals" as a president is chosen by the "electoral college."

20. **A.** The "summation" is the final summing up of arguments in a "trial." In a musical "composition," the passage that brings it to an end is the "coda."

21. **B.** The adjective "capricious" describes a person who is governed by "whim" as "optimistic" describes a person who is governed by "hope."

22. **C.** A "bumpkin," a loutish person, would be especially deficient in "urbanity," suave and polished manners. Similarly, a "bigot" would lack "tolerance."

Critical Reading

23. **A.** Since all rain is naturally acidic, the passage suggests that the name is inadequate. Although the paragraph says that the name may sound "sinister," it does not suggest that acid rain is not a serious problem. Acid rain with a low pH is a serious problem.

24. **E.** Areas downwind of industrial polluters are likely to be affected by acid rain.

25. **A.** It can be inferred that an acidic reading of less than pH 2, which is "six to eight times more acidic than vinegar," is less than one point lower than the pH of vinegar, since "each integer is 10 times more acidic" than the one before it. So the vinegar pH would be approximately 2.

26. **E.** The record itself is not in doubt. What is questionable is if this record for intense pollution is a record anyone would want to set.

27. **E.** The pH scale is neutral at 7, more acidic below, and more alkaline above. So pH 11 would be the most alkaline.

28. **C.** In the fifth paragraph, the passage points to "natural alkaline rock, like limestone," that "helps to neutralize acid rain."

29. **C.** The word "eerily" means strangely or weirdly.

30. **B.** Irony is a set of circumstances or result that is just the opposite of what might be expected. Here the expected result was the solution to a pollution problem (the smokestacks), and the result was increased pollution somewhere else.

31. **D.** A "feat" is an exploit, a remarkable achievement.

32. **A.** The "silver lining" here was the beneficial effect of the sulfur emissions in fertilizing the soil. The reference to "cloud" is especially apt in this case.

33. **B.** The seventh paragraph suggests that the chief opponents in the acid rain debate are the environmentalists who want the pollution reduced and the industrialists who would probably have to pay the cost of reducing emissions.

34. **D.** The passage implies that choices **A, B, C,** and **E** would reduce acid rain but does not present reduction of the use of sulfur fertilizer as an opportunity to stem pollution.

35. **D.** Because the rain falls on places far from the source of the pollutants, crossing international boundaries into Canada.

ANSWER SHEET FOR PRACTICE TEST 3

(Remove This Sheet and Use It to Mark Your Answers)

Section 1

1 Ⓐ Ⓑ Ⓒ Ⓓ Ⓔ
2 Ⓐ Ⓑ Ⓒ Ⓓ Ⓔ
3 Ⓐ Ⓑ Ⓒ Ⓓ Ⓔ
4 Ⓐ Ⓑ Ⓒ Ⓓ Ⓔ
5 Ⓐ Ⓑ Ⓒ Ⓓ Ⓔ
6 Ⓐ Ⓑ Ⓒ Ⓓ Ⓔ
7 Ⓐ Ⓑ Ⓒ Ⓓ Ⓔ
8 Ⓐ Ⓑ Ⓒ Ⓓ Ⓔ
9 Ⓐ Ⓑ Ⓒ Ⓓ Ⓔ
10 Ⓐ Ⓑ Ⓒ Ⓓ Ⓔ
11 Ⓐ Ⓑ Ⓒ Ⓓ Ⓔ
12 Ⓐ Ⓑ Ⓒ Ⓓ Ⓔ
13 Ⓐ Ⓑ Ⓒ Ⓓ Ⓔ
14 Ⓐ Ⓑ Ⓒ Ⓓ Ⓔ
15 Ⓐ Ⓑ Ⓒ Ⓓ Ⓔ
16 Ⓐ Ⓑ Ⓒ Ⓓ Ⓔ
17 Ⓐ Ⓑ Ⓒ Ⓓ Ⓔ
18 Ⓐ Ⓑ Ⓒ Ⓓ Ⓔ
19 Ⓐ Ⓑ Ⓒ Ⓓ Ⓔ
20 Ⓐ Ⓑ Ⓒ Ⓓ Ⓔ
21 Ⓐ Ⓑ Ⓒ Ⓓ Ⓔ
22 Ⓐ Ⓑ Ⓒ Ⓓ Ⓔ
23 Ⓐ Ⓑ Ⓒ Ⓓ Ⓔ
24 Ⓐ Ⓑ Ⓒ Ⓓ Ⓔ
25 Ⓐ Ⓑ Ⓒ Ⓓ Ⓔ

Section 2

1 Ⓐ Ⓑ Ⓒ Ⓓ Ⓔ
2 Ⓐ Ⓑ Ⓒ Ⓓ Ⓔ
3 Ⓐ Ⓑ Ⓒ Ⓓ Ⓔ
4 Ⓐ Ⓑ Ⓒ Ⓓ Ⓔ
5 Ⓐ Ⓑ Ⓒ Ⓓ Ⓔ
6 Ⓐ Ⓑ Ⓒ Ⓓ Ⓔ
7 Ⓐ Ⓑ Ⓒ Ⓓ Ⓔ
8 Ⓐ Ⓑ Ⓒ Ⓓ Ⓔ
9 Ⓐ Ⓑ Ⓒ Ⓓ Ⓔ
10 Ⓐ Ⓑ Ⓒ Ⓓ Ⓔ
11 Ⓐ Ⓑ Ⓒ Ⓓ Ⓔ
12 Ⓐ Ⓑ Ⓒ Ⓓ Ⓔ
13 Ⓐ Ⓑ Ⓒ Ⓓ Ⓔ
14 Ⓐ Ⓑ Ⓒ Ⓓ Ⓔ
15 Ⓐ Ⓑ Ⓒ Ⓓ Ⓔ
16 Ⓐ Ⓑ Ⓒ Ⓓ Ⓔ
17 Ⓐ Ⓑ Ⓒ Ⓓ Ⓔ
18 Ⓐ Ⓑ Ⓒ Ⓓ Ⓔ
19 Ⓐ Ⓑ Ⓒ Ⓓ Ⓔ
20 Ⓐ Ⓑ Ⓒ Ⓓ Ⓔ
21 Ⓐ Ⓑ Ⓒ Ⓓ Ⓔ
22 Ⓐ Ⓑ Ⓒ Ⓓ Ⓔ
23 Ⓐ Ⓑ Ⓒ Ⓓ Ⓔ
24 Ⓐ Ⓑ Ⓒ Ⓓ Ⓔ
25 Ⓐ Ⓑ Ⓒ Ⓓ Ⓔ
26 Ⓐ Ⓑ Ⓒ Ⓓ Ⓔ
27 Ⓐ Ⓑ Ⓒ Ⓓ Ⓔ
28 Ⓐ Ⓑ Ⓒ Ⓓ Ⓔ
29 Ⓐ Ⓑ Ⓒ Ⓓ Ⓔ
30 Ⓐ Ⓑ Ⓒ Ⓓ Ⓔ

(Remove This Sheet and Use It to Mark Your Answers)

Section 3

1 Ⓐ Ⓑ Ⓒ Ⓓ Ⓔ   6 Ⓐ Ⓑ Ⓒ Ⓓ Ⓔ   11 Ⓐ Ⓑ Ⓒ Ⓓ Ⓔ
2 Ⓐ Ⓑ Ⓒ Ⓓ Ⓔ   7 Ⓐ Ⓑ Ⓒ Ⓓ Ⓔ   12 Ⓐ Ⓑ Ⓒ Ⓓ Ⓔ
3 Ⓐ Ⓑ Ⓒ Ⓓ Ⓔ   8 Ⓐ Ⓑ Ⓒ Ⓓ Ⓔ   13 Ⓐ Ⓑ Ⓒ Ⓓ Ⓔ
4 Ⓐ Ⓑ Ⓒ Ⓓ Ⓔ   9 Ⓐ Ⓑ Ⓒ Ⓓ Ⓔ   14 Ⓐ Ⓑ Ⓒ Ⓓ Ⓔ
5 Ⓐ Ⓑ Ⓒ Ⓓ Ⓔ   10 Ⓐ Ⓑ Ⓒ Ⓓ Ⓔ   15 Ⓐ Ⓑ Ⓒ Ⓓ Ⓔ

16

17

18

19

20

21

CUT HERE

(Remove This Sheet and Use It to Mark Your Answers)

22

23

24

25

(Remove This Sheet and Use It to Mark Your Answers)

Section 4

1 Ⓐ Ⓑ Ⓒ Ⓓ Ⓔ	26 Ⓐ Ⓑ Ⓒ Ⓓ Ⓔ
2 Ⓐ Ⓑ Ⓒ Ⓓ Ⓔ	27 Ⓐ Ⓑ Ⓒ Ⓓ Ⓔ
3 Ⓐ Ⓑ Ⓒ Ⓓ Ⓔ	28 Ⓐ Ⓑ Ⓒ Ⓓ Ⓔ
4 Ⓐ Ⓑ Ⓒ Ⓓ Ⓔ	29 Ⓐ Ⓑ Ⓒ Ⓓ Ⓔ
5 Ⓐ Ⓑ Ⓒ Ⓓ Ⓔ	30 Ⓐ Ⓑ Ⓒ Ⓓ Ⓔ
6 Ⓐ Ⓑ Ⓒ Ⓓ Ⓔ	31 Ⓐ Ⓑ Ⓒ Ⓓ Ⓔ
7 Ⓐ Ⓑ Ⓒ Ⓓ Ⓔ	32 Ⓐ Ⓑ Ⓒ Ⓓ Ⓔ
8 Ⓐ Ⓑ Ⓒ Ⓓ Ⓔ	33 Ⓐ Ⓑ Ⓒ Ⓓ Ⓔ
9 Ⓐ Ⓑ Ⓒ Ⓓ Ⓔ	34 Ⓐ Ⓑ Ⓒ Ⓓ Ⓔ
10 Ⓐ Ⓑ Ⓒ Ⓓ Ⓔ	35 Ⓐ Ⓑ Ⓒ Ⓓ Ⓔ
11 Ⓐ Ⓑ Ⓒ Ⓓ Ⓔ	
12 Ⓐ Ⓑ Ⓒ Ⓓ Ⓔ	
13 Ⓐ Ⓑ Ⓒ Ⓓ Ⓔ	
14 Ⓐ Ⓑ Ⓒ Ⓓ Ⓔ	
15 Ⓐ Ⓑ Ⓒ Ⓓ Ⓔ	
16 Ⓐ Ⓑ Ⓒ Ⓓ Ⓔ	
17 Ⓐ Ⓑ Ⓒ Ⓓ Ⓔ	
18 Ⓐ Ⓑ Ⓒ Ⓓ Ⓔ	
19 Ⓐ Ⓑ Ⓒ Ⓓ Ⓔ	
20 Ⓐ Ⓑ Ⓒ Ⓓ Ⓔ	
21 Ⓐ Ⓑ Ⓒ Ⓓ Ⓔ	
22 Ⓐ Ⓑ Ⓒ Ⓓ Ⓔ	
23 Ⓐ Ⓑ Ⓒ Ⓓ Ⓔ	
24 Ⓐ Ⓑ Ⓒ Ⓓ Ⓔ	
25 Ⓐ Ⓑ Ⓒ Ⓓ Ⓔ	

Section 5

1 Ⓐ Ⓑ Ⓒ Ⓓ Ⓔ
2 Ⓐ Ⓑ Ⓒ Ⓓ Ⓔ
3 Ⓐ Ⓑ Ⓒ Ⓓ Ⓔ
4 Ⓐ Ⓑ Ⓒ Ⓓ Ⓔ
5 Ⓐ Ⓑ Ⓒ Ⓓ Ⓔ
6 Ⓐ Ⓑ Ⓒ Ⓓ Ⓔ
7 Ⓐ Ⓑ Ⓒ Ⓓ Ⓔ
8 Ⓐ Ⓑ Ⓒ Ⓓ Ⓔ
9 Ⓐ Ⓑ Ⓒ Ⓓ Ⓔ
10 Ⓐ Ⓑ Ⓒ Ⓓ Ⓔ

Section 6

1 Ⓐ Ⓑ Ⓒ Ⓓ Ⓔ
2 Ⓐ Ⓑ Ⓒ Ⓓ Ⓔ
3 Ⓐ Ⓑ Ⓒ Ⓓ Ⓔ
4 Ⓐ Ⓑ Ⓒ Ⓓ Ⓔ
5 Ⓐ Ⓑ Ⓒ Ⓓ Ⓔ
6 Ⓐ Ⓑ Ⓒ Ⓓ Ⓔ
7 Ⓐ Ⓑ Ⓒ Ⓓ Ⓔ
8 Ⓐ Ⓑ Ⓒ Ⓓ Ⓔ
9 Ⓐ Ⓑ Ⓒ Ⓓ Ⓔ
10 Ⓐ Ⓑ Ⓒ Ⓓ Ⓔ
11 Ⓐ Ⓑ Ⓒ Ⓓ Ⓔ
12 Ⓐ Ⓑ Ⓒ Ⓓ Ⓔ
13 Ⓐ Ⓑ Ⓒ Ⓓ Ⓔ

Section 7

1 Ⓐ Ⓑ Ⓒ Ⓓ Ⓔ	6 Ⓐ Ⓑ Ⓒ Ⓓ Ⓔ	11 Ⓐ Ⓑ Ⓒ Ⓓ Ⓔ
2 Ⓐ Ⓑ Ⓒ Ⓓ Ⓔ	7 Ⓐ Ⓑ Ⓒ Ⓓ Ⓔ	12 Ⓐ Ⓑ Ⓒ Ⓓ Ⓔ
3 Ⓐ Ⓑ Ⓒ Ⓓ Ⓔ	8 Ⓐ Ⓑ Ⓒ Ⓓ Ⓔ	13 Ⓐ Ⓑ Ⓒ Ⓓ Ⓔ
4 Ⓐ Ⓑ Ⓒ Ⓓ Ⓔ	9 Ⓐ Ⓑ Ⓒ Ⓓ Ⓔ	14 Ⓐ Ⓑ Ⓒ Ⓓ Ⓔ
5 Ⓐ Ⓑ Ⓒ Ⓓ Ⓔ	10 Ⓐ Ⓑ Ⓒ Ⓓ Ⓔ	15 Ⓐ Ⓑ Ⓒ Ⓓ Ⓔ

16

17

18

CUT HERE

(Remove This Sheet and Use It to Mark Your Answers)

19

20

21

22

23

24

25

Section 1: Mathematical Reasoning

Time: 30 Minutes

25 Questions

Directions: Solve each problem in this section by using the information given and your own mathematical calculations, insights, and problem-solving skills. Then select the one correct answer of the five choices given and mark the corresponding circle on your answer sheet. Use the available space on the page for your scratch work.

Notes

1. All numbers used are real numbers.

2. Calculators can be used.

3. Some problems may be accompanied by figures or diagrams. These figures are drawn as accurately as possible EXCEPT when it is stated in a specific problem that a figure is not drawn to scale. The figures and diagrams are meant to provide information useful in solving the problem or problems. Unless otherwise stated, all figures and diagrams lie in a plane.

Data That Can Be Used for Reference

Area

rectangle
$A = lw$

triangle
$A = \frac{1}{2} bh$

circle
$A = \pi r^2$
$C = 2\pi r$

Volume

rectangular solid
$V = lwh$

right circular cylinder
$V = \pi r^2 h$

Pythagorean Relationship

$a^2 + b^2 = c^2$

Special Triangles

$30° - 60° - 90°$

$45° - 45° - 90°$

A circle is composed of 360°
A straight angle measures 180°
The sum of the angles of a triangle is 180°

1. If $3m + n = 7$, then $9m + 3n =$

    A. $\frac{7}{9}$

    B. $\frac{7}{3}$

    C. 10

    D. 21

    E. 63

2. If it takes 18 minutes to fill $\frac{2}{3}$ of a container, how long will it take to fill the rest of the container at the same rate?

    A. 6 minutes

    B. 9 minutes

    C. 12 minutes

    D. 27 minutes

    E. 36 minutes

3. What is the sales tax on $132.95 if the tax rate is 7%?

    A. $0.93

    B. $9.30

    C. $9.31

    D. $63.06

    E. $93.07

4. In the figure above, what is the number of degrees in the sum of $m + n$?

    A. 103

    B. 97

C.   93

D.   83

E.   72

5. The length of a rectangle is $6l$, and the width is $4w$. What is the perimeter?

    A. $24lw$

    B. $20lw$

    C. $10lw$

    D. $12l + 8w$

    E. $6l + 4w$

6. If x is between 0 and 1, which of the following statements must be true?

    I. $x^2 > 1$

    II. $x^2 > 0$

    III. $x^2 > x$

    A. I only

    B. II only

    C. III only

    D. I and II only

    E. II and III only

7. Tom is just 4 years older than Fran. The total of their ages is 24. What is the equation for finding Fran's age?

    A. $x + 4x = 24$

    B. $x + 4 = 24$

    C. $4x + x = 24$

    D. $x + (x + 4) = 24$

    E. $4x + 1 = 24$

8. If a plane travels 840 miles in 1½ hours, how many hours will it take for the plane to travel 3,500 miles at the same speed?

A. 2⅞

B. 4¹⁄₁₆

C. 5⅚

D. 6¼

E. 6½

9. What is 30% of ²⁵⁄₁₈?

A. ⁵⁄₁₀₈

B. ⁵⁄₁₂

C. ²⁵⁄₅₄

D. ²⁵⁄₆

E. ¹²⁵⁄₃

10. The seventh row in the diagram above could not have any

A. even numbers.

B. odd numbers.

C. perfect numbers.

D. prime numbers.

E. perfect cube numbers.

11. If $x = \frac{3}{4}$ and $y = \frac{1}{7}$, then $\frac{y-x}{y+x} =$

A. −1

B. −⁵⁄₇

C. ⁵⁄₃₇

D. ½

E. ¹¹⁄₂₁

12. In a class of 40 students, there are 24 girls. What percent of the class are boys?

A. 16%

B. 24%

C. 40%

D. 50%

E. 60%

13. Bob is older than Jane, but he is younger than Jim. If Bob's age is b, Jane's age is c, and Jim's age is d, then which of the following is true?

A. $c < b < d$

B. $b < c < d$

C. $b < d < c$

D. $c < d < b$

E. $d < c < b$

14. In ΔXYZ above, points M, N, and P are midpoints. If XY = 10, YZ = 15, and XZ = 17, what is the perimeter of ΔMNP?

A. 10⅔

B. 14

C. 16

D. 21

E. 42

GO ON TO THE NEXT PAGE

Note: Figure not drawn to scale.

15. On the circle above with center C,
CD ⊥ AB, AB = 24, and CD = 5.
What is the radius of the circle?

A. 19

B. 17

C. 13

D. 12

E. 7

---

16. George scored an average of 80% on
three tests. What score must he get on
the fourth test to bring his average to
85%?

A. 85%

B. 88%

C. 90%

D. 95%

E. 100%

---

17. The angles of a quadrilateral are in the
ratio of 2:3:4:6. What is the degree
measure of its largest angle?

A. 72°

B. 120°

C. 144°

D. 150°

E. 180°

18. If $x(y - z) = t$, then $y =$

A. $(\frac{1}{x}) + z$

B. $\dfrac{tz}{x}$

C. $t + x - z$

D. $\dfrac{(t + z)}{x}$

E. $t - x + z$

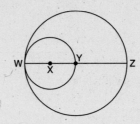

19. In the figure above, X and Y are the
centers of the two circles. If the area of
the larger circle is 144π, what is the
area of the smaller circle?

A. 72π

B. 36π

C. 24π

D. 12π

E. cannot be determined

---

20. If $m * n = \dfrac{m + n - 1}{n^2} =$, then $2 * 3 =$

A. ⁴⁄₉

B. ⅔

C. 1

D. 1⅓

E. 2

21. If $\frac{a}{b} = \frac{c}{d}$ and a, b, c, and d are positive integers, then which of the following is true?

A. $\frac{a}{b} = \frac{d}{c}$

B. $ac = bd$

C. $a + d = b + c$

D. $\frac{d}{b} = \frac{c}{a}$

E. $\frac{a}{d} = \frac{c}{b}$

$$6x - 12 = -6y$$
$$5y + 5x = 15$$

22. Which of the following is the number of solutions in the system of equations shown above?

A. More than three

B. Exactly three

C. Exactly two

D. Exactly one

E. None

23. If y varies directly as x and if $x = 18$ when $y = 12$, what is y when $x = 20$?

A. $11\frac{1}{5}$

B. $13\frac{1}{3}$

C. 14

D. 16

E. 30

24. If the diameter of circle R is 30% of the diameter of circle S, the area of circle R is what percent of the area of circle S?

A. 9%

B. 15%

C. 30%

D. 60%

E. 90%

25. The midpoint of xy is B. The coordinates of x are $(-4, 3)$, and the coordinates of B are $(5, -2)$. What are the coordinates of y?

A. $(\frac{1}{2}, \frac{1}{2})$

B. $(1, 1)$

C. $(6, -7)$

D. $(14, -3)$

E. $(14, -7)$

IF YOU FINISH BEFORE TIME IS CALLED, CHECK YOUR WORK ON THIS SECTION ONLY. DO NOT WORK ON ANY OTHER SECTION IN THE TEST.

STOP

Section 2: Verbal Reasoning

Time: 30 Minutes

30 Questions

In this section, choose the best answer for each question and blacken the corresponding space on the answer sheet.

Sentence Completion

Directions: Each blank in the following sentences indicates that something has been omitted. Consider the lettered words beneath the sentence and choose the word or set of words that best fits the whole sentence.

1. As the boat drifted closer and closer to the rocks, the people on the beach became increasingly _____ about its safety.

   A. cowardly

   B. intrepid

   C. apprehensive

   D. eager

   E. receptive

2. If only a native can understand the dialect of this region, even the best foreign linguist will be _____ by the indigenous speakers.

   A. mistaken

   B. baffled

   C. misrepresented

   D. addressed

   E. translated

3. Carlson described the changes he had made in the story as merely _____, not censorship, because the alterations were made with the writer's prior knowledge and _____.

   A. editing . . . permission

   B. revising . . . prohibition

   C. expurgation . . . warrant

   D. corrections . . . disapproval

   E. decimation . . . connivance

4. The thousand-mile trek across the wilderness was a severe test of the children's _____ and their capacity to adapt.

   A. proportion

   B. immaturity

   C. openness

   D. weakness

   E. resilience

5. A change in fashion to a very thin look is not just an innocent _____ or trend; it is a serious _____ for many women who may suffer from dangerous eating disorders.

   A. victim . . . peril

   B. prank . . . challenge

   C. whim . . . undertaking

   D. fad . . . hazard

   E. idea . . . response

6. The public was _____ by the use of human bones and teeth in the jewelry and made their disapproval clear by refusing to buy any of the _____ items.

   A. enthralled . . . unusual

   B. fascinated . . . remarkable

   C. horrified . . . ghoulish

   D. repulsed . . . amiable

   E. hypnotized . . . grisly

7. In the unsuccessful conference, none of the speakers _____ much response from the audience, but Dr. Schultz's address reached the _____ in tediousness.

   A. aggrandized . . . pinnacle

   B. elicited . . . nadir

   C. attributed . . . record

   D. raised . . . ebb

   E. induced . . . medley

8. In a landscape so calm and beautiful, it was hard to believe that anything _____ could occur.

   A. untoward

   B. temperate

   C. halcyon

   D. seemly

   E. refined

9. The land lying at even a slight distance from the river is not _____, so the farming tribes _____ only the fields near its banks.

   A. arable . . . cultivated

   B. barren . . . settled

   C. fallow . . . colonized

   D. fertile . . . shunned

   E. fertilizable . . . eschewed

Section **2** Verbal Reasoning

GO ON TO THE NEXT PAGE

Analogies

Directions: In each of the following questions, you are given a related pair of words or phrases. Select the lettered pair that best expresses a relationship similar to that in the original pair of words.

10. BOW : VIOLIN ::

A. brass : tuba

B. pedal : piano

C. percussion : drum

D. stop : clarinet

E. drumstick : drum

11. SPEAR : SHIELD ::

A. bomb : torpedo

B. mace : trident

C. fighter : aircraft carrier

D. gun : bulletproof vest

E. moat : portcullis

12. SKILLET : BACON ::

A. palette : paints

B. napkin : grease

C. grass : lawnmower

D. skeptic : doubt

E. cocoon : twig

13. ARIA : OPERA ::

A. song : music

B. waltz : dance

C. chapter : novel

D. artist : painting

E. poem : epic

14. LOVER : ELOPE ::

A. thief : burglarize

B. army : retreat

C. convict : escape

D. coward : flee

E. embezzler : abscond

15. CALLOUS : TACT ::

A. certain : carelessness

B. dark : mourning

C. lethargic : speed

D. cheerful : joy

E. mature : growth

Critical Reading

Directions: Questions follow each of the passages below. Using only the stated or implied information in each passage and in its introduction, if any, answer the questions.

Questions 16–22 are based on the following passage.

The rabies virus, which can cause disease in any mammal, is spread by the bite of an infected animal. It is lethal once symptoms develop but can be blocked by timely ad-
(5) ministration of a series of vaccine injections soon after an attack. The vaccine, which today may be given in an arm rather than the abdomen, is derived from a killed rabies virus. The inactivated virus prods the
(10) immune system to destroy active virus, especially when the injections are combined with application of rabies-specific antibodies to the wound area [see "Rabies" by Martin M. Kaplan and Hilary Koprowski;
(15) *Scientific American,* January 1980].

Unfortunately, in any year thousands of people who are probably uninfected undergo treatment because they do not know whether the animal that bit them had ra-
(20) bies. These high numbers are disturbing because therapy is costly and because vaccination of any kind carries a risk of side effects. (The expense is a major reason veterinarians and others who are very likely to
(25) encounter rabid animals are generally the only people immunized prophylactically.)

Even more distressing, most people who die of rabies are lost simply because they live in impoverished nations. Those
(30) who are attacked by infected animals often lack access to therapy or cannot pay for it.

Routine immunization of the animal species most likely to transmit the virus to humans would be a more efficient, health-
(35) conscious way to save human lives and, not incidentally, to spare animals from

suffering. To an extent, such inoculation is already a reality. In many wealthy nations, including the U.S., periodic injection
(40) of pet dogs with vaccine has all but stopped canine transmission to humans. Disease caused by cats can be limited in the same way.

In developing countries, however, obtain-
(45) ing veterinary care can be extremely difficult, which is one reason why dogs continue to account for at least 90 percent of all human deaths from rabies. Another problem is that even where pet rabies is un-
(50) der good control, wild animals — not being very amenable to collection and carting to the local veterinarian — pose a threat.

For these unattended groups, distribution of vaccine-laced baits for animals to eat in
(55) the field is showing particular promise. This approach is already halting the spread of rabies by foxes in many parts of western Europe and Canada. More preliminary work suggests rabies in other species
(60) can be controlled as well.

Indeed, a vaccine-filled bait for raccoons is now being tested in the U.S. If the results are good, the bait method might finally check an epidemic of raccoon rabies
(65) that has been spreading up the East Coast from Florida since the 1950s. If baiting can be perfected for distribution to dogs in developing countries, then the goal of sharply curtailing human cases worldwide
(70) would finally seem feasible.

This encouraging state of affairs stands in marked contrast to the situation in the 1960s, when research into vaccinating wild animals started in earnest. By then

GO ON TO THE NEXT PAGE

(75) immunization had already reduced the incidence of dog rabies in the U.S. But infection by foxes, skunks, raccoons, and bats — the other significant rabies reservoirs in this country — was a continuing concern.
(80) Compared with dogs, those groups have less direct contact with humans, but collectively they are more abundant.

To control rabies in free-ranging animals, health officials in the 1950s had depended on
(85) thinning populations that harbored the offending virus. They tried gassing of dens, poisoning, trapping, and shooting, among other tactics. The workers reasoned that destruction of enough animals would so reduce a
(90) population that any infected individuals would die without tangling with another animal. When diseased creatures disappeared, only healthy ones would remain. Yet the strategy halted the spread of the malady in target
(95) groups only some of the time.

16. All of the following could be infected with rabies EXCEPT:

   A. raccoons.

   B. cats.

   C. humans.

   D. skunks.

   E. carrion birds.

17. The passage suggests that a human infected with rabies by a dog bite who did nothing for a long period of time would

   A. be unable to spread the disease to another human.

   B. probably never be aware of having been infected.

   C. die.

   D. be cured by a vaccine injection.

   E. be cured by applying rabies-specific antibodies in the area of the bite.

18. The passage suggests that throughout the world the largest cause of human exposure to the rabies virus is from

   A. dogs that have not been immunized.

   B. dogs that have been immunized.

   C. cats that have not been immunized.

   D. cats that have been immunized.

   E. wild animals such as raccoons, foxes, or skunks.

19. It can be inferred that the number of fatalities from rabies in the United States is small because

   I. most dogs have been immunized by injections.

   II. people exposed to the virus have access to immediate treatment.

   III. the rabies virus is rare in the wild-animal populations of the United States.

   A. I only

   B. I and II only

   C. I and III only

   D. II and III only

   E. I, II, and III

20. As it is used in line 70, the word "feasible" means

   A. unpredictable.

   B. inexpensive.

   C. hygienic.

   D. practicable.

   E. endurable.

21. At present, humans infected with rabies virus can be treated by

   I. a vaccine injection in the abdomen.

   II. a vaccine injection in the arm.

   III. an oral recombinant vaccine.

   A. I only

   B. II only

   C. I and II only

   D. II and III only

   E. I, II, and III

22. Vaccine-laced baits would be most effective in preventing rabies among

   I. wild-animal populations susceptible to rabies.

   II. domestic animals in areas where injections are impossible.

   III. wild or domestic animals already infected with disease.

   A. III only

   B. I and II only

   C. I and III only

   D. II and III only

   E. I, II, and III

Questions 23–30 are based on the following passage.

The following passage is from the autobiography of a young black woman who was among the first women to attend the New England prep school St. Paul's.

Outside my personal circle, the school that term seemed to buzz, buzz. Class officers, it seemed, were often called upon to talk. We talked day and evening, in club activi-
(5) ties and rehearsals, in the houses, in the hallways, in our rooms, in the bathrooms, and in meetings after meetings. We gossiped. We criticized. We whined. We analyzed. We talked trash. We talked race
(10) relations, spiritual life, mate–female relations, teacher-student trust. We talked confidentially. We broke confidences and talked about the results. We talked discipline and community. We talked Watergate
(15) and social-fabric stuff.

I did not follow the Watergate hearings. I did not rush to the third floor of the Schoolhouse for the ten-thirty New York Times delivery to read about it; nor did I
(20) crowd around the common-room TV to watch the proceedings. I could not bother to worry about which rich and powerful white people had hoodwinked which other rich and powerful white people. It seemed
(25) of a piece with their obsession with fairness.

I was unprepared, therefore, to dine at the Rectory with Mr. Archibald Cox, the St. Paul's alumnus whom President Nixon had fired when, as U.S. Special Prosecutor, Mr.
(30) Cox began to reveal the Watergate break-in and cover-up. Seated around him were the Rector and a handful of faculty members and student leaders. I said as little as possible in order to conceal my ignorance. Mr.
(35) Cox was acute. He referred to the Watergate players and the major events in witty shorthand. I couldn't quite follow, so I ate and smiled and made periodic conversation noises.

Section **2** Verbal Reasoning

(40) Then he wanted to hear about St. Paul's School. There had been so many changes since his time. I found myself saying, in answer to his question, or the Rector's signal, that I was more aware of being black at St.
(45) Paul's than I was of being a girl. I used a clever phrase that I stole from somewhere and hoped he hadn't already heard: "Actually, we're still more like . . . a boys' school with girls in it. But black people's
(50) concerns — diversifying the curriculum and that sort of thing — the truth is that that's more important to me than whether the boys have the better locker room."

Pompous it was, and I knew it, but better to
(55) be pompous in the company of educated and well-off white folk, better even to be stone wrong, than to have no opinion at all.

Mr. Cox thought a moment. God forbid he should go for the cross-examination. I
(60) added more. "Black concerns here at school may look different, but are not really, from the concerns that my parents have taught me all my life at home." I put that one in just so he'd know that I had a family. "And
(65) believe me, Sir, my mama and daddy did not put President Nixon into the White House. *We* didn't do that!"

Mr. Cox wrinkled his lean, Yankee face into a mischievous smile. His voice whispered
(70) mock conspiracy. He leaned toward me. "Do you know who Nixon hates worst of all?"

I shook my head no. I had no idea.

"Our kind of people."

My ears felt hot. I wanted to jump on the
(75) table. I wanted go back home and forget that I'd ever come. I wanted to take him to West Philly, and drop him off at the corner of Fifty-second and Locust, outside Foo-Foo's steak emporium, right by the drug dealers,
(80) and leave him there without a map or a bow tie. Then tell me about our kind of people.

The Rector gave me a look that urged caution. I fixed my face. "What kind of people are those?" I asked.

(85) "Why, the educated Northeastern establishment," he said. The Rector smiled as if relieved.

23. The speaker's lack of interest in the Watergate hearings is chiefly due to her

   A. feeling alienated from the others at her school.

   B. concern with issues of gender rather than politics.

   C. belief that it was just another rich white person's problem.

   D. eagerness to be accepted by her peers at school.

   E. fear that it would separate her from her family's values.

24. In line 25, the phrase "of a piece" means

   A. consistent with.

   B. a small part of.

   C. indifferent to.

   D. partly to blame for.

   E. inconsistent with.

25. The word "acute" in line 35 means

   A. sharp-pointed.

   B. shrewd.

   C. critical.

   D angular.

   E. severe.

26. The speaker in line 59 uses the phrase "cross-examination" because

    A. she wishes to amuse the others in the discussion.

    B. she feels she has committed a serious crime.

    C. she prefers to be wrong than to have no opinion at all.

    D. Archibald Cox is a lawyer.

    E. she has misunderstood Cox's questions.

27. The speaker chooses which of the following words or phrases to deflate the seriousness or self-importance of what she has said?

    I. "social-fabric stuff" (line 15)

    II. "conversation noises" (lines 38–39)

    III. "that one" (line 63)

    A. I only

    B. II only

    C. I and II only

    D. I and III only

    E. I, II, and III

28. When the speaker responds with the thoughts expressed in lines 74–81 ("My ears felt hot . . . people"), she is responding especially to what single word in the dialogue before?

    A. "Nixon" (line 71)

    B. "hates" (line 71)

    C. "worst" (line 71)

    D. "Our" (line 73)

    E. "people" (line 73)

29. It can be inferred from the passage that the "Rector smiled as if relieved" (lines 86–87) because he

    A. has been afraid the speaker would say something shocking.

    B. disapproves of political arguments.

    C. has not understood what the speaker has been thinking.

    D. is too conventional to imagine a violent difference in opinion or in background.

    E. is amused by Archibald Cox's witty remark.

30. The passage as a whole is characterized by the speaker's

    A. lack of feeling and self-discipline.

    B. candor and self-awareness.

    C. bitterness and sense of unfairness.

    D. hypocrisy and self-deception.

    E. naivete and charm.

Section **2** Verbal Reasoning

IF YOU FINISH BEFORE TIME IS CALLED, CHECK YOUR WORK ON THIS SECTION ONLY. DO NOT WORK ON ANY OTHER SECTION IN THE TEST.

STOP

Section 3: Mathematical Reasoning

Time: 30 Minutes

25 Questions

Directions: This section is composed of two types of questions. Use the 30 minutes allotted to answer both question types. Your scratch work should be done on any available space in the section.

Notes

1. All numbers used are real numbers.

2. Calculators can be used.

3. Some problems may be accompanied by figures or diagrams. These figures are drawn as accurately as possible EXCEPT when it is stated in a specific problem that a figure is not drawn to scale. The figures and diagrams are meant to provide information useful in solving the problem or problems. Unless otherwise stated, all figures and diagrams lie in a plane.

Data That Can Be Used for Reference

Quantitative Comparison

Directions: In this section, you are given two quantities, one in column A and one in column B. You are to determine a relationship between the two quantities and mark —

    A. if the quantity in column A is greater than the quantity in column B.

    B. if the quantity in column B is greater than the quantity in column A.

    C. if the quantities are equal.

    D. if the comparison cannot be determined from the information that is given.

AN **E** RESPONSE WILL NOT BE SCORED.

Notes

1. Sometimes, information concerning one or both of the quantities to be compared is given. This information is not boxed and is centered above the two columns.

2. All numbers used are real numbers. Letters such as a, b, m, and x represent real numbers.

3. In a given question, if the same symbol is used in column A and column B, that symbol stands for the same value in each column.

	Column A	Column B
1.	$\dfrac{.89 \times 57}{.919}$	58
2.	$(x^2y^3)^8$	$(x^4y^6)^4$

$$2x + 5y > 4$$

	Column A	Column B
3.	x	y

	Column A	Column B
4.	x	y

$$x < 0$$

	Column A	Column B
5.	$x^3 - 1$	0

GO ON TO THE NEXT PAGE

Column A   **Column B**   **Column A**   **Column B**

6. $\frac{1}{3} \times \frac{2}{5} \times \frac{1}{8}$ $.33 \times .4 \times .125$

$$a = 3b$$
$$b = -2$$

7. $\dfrac{a^2 + b}{ab}$ $\dfrac{a + b^2}{ab}$

Questions 8–10 refer to the diagram.

Note: Figure not drawn to scale.

8. $\angle X + \angle Z$ $\angle Y$

9.   XY   YZ

10.   XY $3\sqrt{2}$

a, b, and *c* are positive integers
$$(b + c)^a = 81$$
$$a \neq b \neq c$$

11. a $b + c$

Questions 12 and 13 refer to the diagram.

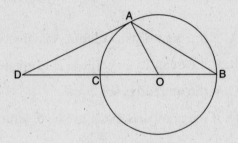

O is the center.

12. $\overset{\frown}{AC}$ $2(\angle B)$

13. $\angle AOB$ $\angle ADB$

14.   Total distance traveled in 3 hours at an average rate of 30 miles per hour   Total distance traveled in 3 hours at an average rate of 45 feet per second

Note: Figure not drawn to scale.

Each dimension of the rectangular solid above is an even number.

The area of face TUWY is 20, and the area of face WXZY is 8.

15.   Total surface area of the rectangular solid   Volume of the rectangular solid

Grid-In Questions

Directions: Questions 16–25 require you to solve the problem and enter your answer by carefully marking the circles on the special grid. Examples of the appropriate way to mark the grid follow.

Answer: 3.7   Answer: 1/2

Decimal point

Fraction bar

Answer: 1½

Do not grid in mixed numbers in the form of mixed numbers. *Always* change mixed numbers to improper fractions or decimals.

Change to 1.5   or   Change to ⅜

Answer: 123

Space permitting, answers can start in any column. Each grid-in answer below is correct.

Note: Circles must be filled in correctly to receive credit. Mark only one circle in each column. No credit will be given if more than one circle in a column is marked. Example:

Answer: 258

No credit!

GO ON TO THE NEXT PAGE

Answer: ⅞

Accuracy of decimals: Always enter the most accurate decimal value that the grid will accommodate. For example: An answer such as .8888 . . . can be gridded as .888 or .889. Gridding this value as .8, .88, or .89 is considered inaccurate and therefore *not acceptable*. The acceptable grid-ins of ⅞ are:

⅞   .888

.889

Be sure to write your answers in the boxes at the top of the circles before doing your gridding. Although writing out the answers above the columns is not required, it is very important to ensure accuracy. Even though some problems may have more than one correct answer, grid only *one answer*. Grid-in questions contain no negative answers.

16. If $12a = 5b$, then $\frac{a}{b} =$

17. At a particular university, the ratio of males to females is 5 to 3. What percent of the students are female? (Disregard the % sign when gridding your answer.)

18. How many different outfits can be obtained from 5 shirts, 3 pairs of slacks, and 3 sports jackets?

19. If $\sqrt{m-3} = 6$ then m =

Friendly Fruit Stand Price List	
apples	60¢ each
bananas	20¢ each
cantaloupes	59¢ each or 2 for $1
oranges	39¢ each or 3 for $1

20. Mr. and Mrs. Adams are planning to attend a company picnic and need to make a fruit salad for the occasion. Their recipe calls for 5 apples, 10 bananas, 4 cantaloupes, and 5 oranges. Based on the prices given above, what is the least amount they could spend at the fruit stand to buy all the fruit they need for their salad? (Disregard the $ sign when gridding your answer.)

21. Ben's average for seven math exams is 89%. What percent must he score on the next exam to raise his average to 90%? (Disregard the % sign when gridding your answer.)

22. What is the area of a square whose diagonal has a length of 12?

Products	1980	1982	1984	1986	1988	1990
A	$4.20	$4.60	$5.00	$5.40	$5.80	$6.20
B	$6.30	$6.45	$6.60	$6.75	$6.90	$7.05

23. The chart above shows the prices of products A and B from 1980 to 1990. Using the chart, in what year will product A cost 40¢ more than product B?

24. What is the height (*h*) of the trapezoid if its area is 98?

25. What is the length in centimeters of a chord that is 12 centimeters from the center of a circle whose radius is 20 centimeters?

IF YOU FINISH BEFORE TIME IS CALLED, CHECK YOUR WORK ON THIS SECTION ONLY. DO NOT WORK ON ANY OTHER SECTION IN THE TEST.

Section **3** Mathematical Reasoning

Section 4: Verbal Reasoning

Time: 30 Minutes

35 Questions

In this section, choose the best answer for each question and blacken the corresponding space on the answer sheet.

Sentence Correction

Directions: Each blank in the following sentences indicates that something has been omitted. Consider the lettered words beneath the sentence and choose the word or set of words that best fits the whole sentence.

1. By banning cameras from the courtroom, the judge has _____ the public access to the most important civil-rights trial.

   A. belied

   B. denied

   C. defied

   D. afforded

   E. disowned

2. The grocer reluctantly admitted that, despite his care, shoplifting was still _____.

   A. exceptional

   B. sporadic

   C. commonplace

   D. redundant

   E. hackneyed

3. The work that once takes two men one week might well, one year later, take the same two men three weeks, since as Parkinson's law _____, "Work _____ so as to fill the time for its completion."

   A. urges . . . grows easier

   B. plains . . . becomes familiar

   C. states . . . decreases

   D. forbids . . . increases

   E. asserts . . . expands

4. Although they loudly cheered the news of the renewed contract, the _____ of many workers was _____ by a fear that this would be the last year of government support.

   A. sorrow . . . tempered

   B. happiness . . . augmented

   C. gladness . . . enervated

   D. euphoria . . . moderated

   E. buoyancy . . . debilitated

5. The local conversation was nothing if not _____ for no sentence was ever more than four words long.

   A. ambiguous

   B. timely

   C. vague

   D. terse

   E. cordial

6. If both political parties can abandon _____ positions in the face of economic realities, a _____ may be achieved that will permit the government to function.

   A. sensible . . . compromise

   B. dogmatic . . . consensus

   C. incisive . . . schism

   D. irrational . . . dichotomy

   E. reasoned . . . division

7. The universal Victorian preference of the more conventional morality of Charlotte Brontë to that of her sister is indicative of the nineteenth century reader's _____ conformity.

   A. impolitic

   B. genteel

   C. discordant

   D. iconoclastic

   E. individualistic

8. Though the first thirty pages are interesting and lively, chapter after chapter about obscure musicians grows _____, and the book never recovers the _____ of its opening chapter.

   A. unmanageable . . . pace

   B. tedious . . . verve

   C. repetitive . . . torpor

   D. dull . . . lethargy

   E. boring . . . challenge

9. Some of the dangerous dishes on the menu are _____, but most are made without peppers or other spices and are as mild as most American restaurant food.

   A. bland

   B. palatable

   C. torrid

   D. insipid

   E. piquant

10. As a young man, he regarded France as _____, but in his malcontent maturity, he considered visiting any place outside of Ireland to be _____.

   A. hostile . . . irritating

   B. perfect . . . jocund

   C. irksome . . . drab

   D. Edenic . . . perplexing

   E. ideal . . . painful

GO ON TO THE NEXT PAGE

Analogies

Directions: In each of the following questions, you are given a related pair of words or phrases. Select the lettered pair that best expresses a relationship similar to that in the original pair of words.

11. SURFING : SKATEBOARDING ::

    A. baseball : tennis
    B. golf : football
    C. bicycling : basketball
    D. water-skiing : roller-skating
    E. field hockey : ice hockey

12. VEGETARIAN : MEAT ::

    A. dieter : food
    B. teetotaler : alcohol
    C. herbivore : grass
    D. athlete : protein
    E. dairy farmer : cheese

13. HONEYCOMB : WAX ::

    A. worker : drone
    B. beet : sugar
    C. dress : designer
    D. starch : shirt
    E. kimono : fabric

14. TYPEWRITER : PENCIL ::

    A. calculator : slide rule
    B. paper clip : rubber band
    C. mixer : refrigerator
    D. rolling pin : ice tray
    E. loaf pan : slotted spoon

15. QUIVER : ARCHER ::

    A. pocket : wallet
    B. holster : gun
    C. forceps : surgeon
    D. crossbow : arrow
    E. dart : blowgun

16. DISINFECTANT : IODINE ::

    A. gauze : adhesive tape
    B. shampoo : styling gel
    C. analgesic : aspirin
    D. suture : surgeon
    E. puncture : wound

17. DIGITAL : FINGER ::

    A. aural : eye
    B. orbital : planet
    C. manual : hand
    D. solar : star
    E. radial : communication

18. SLOTH : RAIN FOREST ::

    A. cow : barn
    B. pride : ocean
    C. Gila monster : desert
    D. elephant : zoo
    E. porpoise : water park

19. FOLLOW : ENSUE ::

A. request : litigate

B. inter : bury

C. ridicule : revere

D. propose : dispose

E. invoke : testify

20. DUCHY : DUKE ::

A. monarchy : queen

B. county : count

C. knighthood : knight

D. marchioness : marquis

E. estate : earl

21. QUILL : MANUSCRIPT ::

A. scalpel : operation

B. monk : prayer

C. brush : fresco

D. gearshift : automobile

E. editor : newspaper

22. DORSAL : VENTRAL ::

A. snowy : windy

B. dexterous : ambidextrous

C. red : crimson

D. retreating : advancing

E. oblique : indirect

23. VICTIM : MARTYR ::

A. trade : barter

B. action : crusade

C. zealot : fanatic

D. intention : purpose

E. liberty : freedom

Critical Reading

Directions: Questions follow the passage below. Using only the stated or implied information in the passage and in its introduction, if any, answer the questions.

Questions 24–35 are based on the following passage.

Bilingual ballots have never enjoyed much public support because the public has never known much about their origin and rationale. For instance, it is often assumed
(5) that any non-English speaker is entitled to vote in his or her native tongue. The reality is that this right applies only to linguistic minorities who have historically faced discrimination at the polls — Hispanics,
(10) Asians, and Native Americans — and only in areas where they meet strict requirements. A language group must represent more than 5 percent of the local population and have below-average rates
(15) of voter turnout and English literacy. Moreover, the cost of assisting non-English-speaking voters is quite modest. San Francisco officials have estimated that the annual expense of trilingual
(20) English–Spanish–Chinese ballots comes to less than three cents per household. In 1984, a federal survey of eighty-three "covered" jurisdictions found that it cost them a grand total of $388,000, or 7.6 per-
(25) cent of election expenses, to provide bilingual ballots. Hardly an exorbitant price to safeguard what the Supreme Court has called a "fundamental right because it is preservative of all rights."

GO ON TO THE NEXT PAGE

(30) The trend toward bilingual ballots originated in the Voting Rights Act of 1965. This law suspended literacy requirements for voting in southern states where they had been systematically used to disfran-
(35) chise African-Americans. A related provision, sponsored by Senator Robert F. Kennedy, prohibited such tests elsewhere for voters who had completed the sixth grade on U.S. soil in a school whose "pre-
(40) dominant classroom language was other than English." In other words, native-born U.S. citizens could no longer be prevented from voting simply because they had grown up in a non-English-speaking
(45) environment. Puerto Ricans were the main beneficiaries of this section, particularly in New York, where a 1921 amendment to the state constitution (aimed principally at Yiddish-speaking Jews) had denied the
(50) franchise to anyone unable to read English.

Federal courts soon went further. Banning English literacy tests was a hollow gesture, they reasoned, if formerly excluded voters still faced a language barrier at the polls.
(55) Accordingly, they mandated bilingual election materials for Puerto Rican voters in Philadelphia, Chicago, and New York. "It is simply fundamental," wrote one judge, "that voting instructions and ballots, in ad-
(60) dition to any other material which forms part of the official communication to registered voters prior to an election, must be in Spanish as well as in English, if the vote of Spanish-speaking citizens is not to be seri-
(65) ously impaired."

Bilingual voting, like bilingual education, was designed to compensate for decades of inequality, a goal that could not be achieved through strictly "equal" treatment.
(70) Simply prohibiting the English literacy test, or ending the segregation of Mexican and Chinese American students, was insufficient

to restore rights that linguistic minorities had lost through no fault of their own. For
(75) such groups, affirmative measures were needed to guarantee equalopportunity. Clearly, this approach can lead to anomalies, as when naturalized citizens of "Spanish origin" are entitled to bilingual
(80) ballots but their Portuguese- or French-speaking neighbors are not. Congressional critics of the expanded Voting Rights Act have argued that its effect is "to mandate an 'unequal protection of the laws,'" privi-
(85) leging some minority voters over others from non-English-speaking backgrounds — namely, that it favors nonwhite immigrants and indigenous minorities over white Euro-ethnics.

(90) Under current law an individual's need for a bilingual ballot does not enter into the equation. Perhaps it should. Why encourage immigrants to become U.S. citizens and then limit their ability to participate in
(95) our political system? Why not make every effort to eliminate language barriers to voting? It is true that most applicants for naturalization must pass an English literacy test (except for those aged fifty or older who
(100) have been legal U.S. residents for at least twenty years). But the level of proficiency required is quite low. In 1982, an average year, the Immigration and Naturalization Service turned down only twenty-nine out
(105) of 201,507 petitions for citizenship because of inability to speak, read, or write the English language. The literacy skills required to decipher voter registration notices or complex ballot propositions are
(110) normally the last to be acquired in a second language.

24. It can be inferred from the passage that objections have been made to the use of bilingual ballots on the grounds that

   I. they cost too much taxpayer money.

   II. any non-English speaker can demand a bilingual ballot.

   III. any Spanish-speaking voter can demand a bilingual ballot.

   A. I only

   B. I and II only

   C. I and III only

   D. II and III only

   E. I, II, and III

25. Which of the following non-English-speaking groups could qualify for a bilingual ballot in an American election at the present time?

   A. an Italian-speaking group making up 6 percent of the local population

   B. a Samoan-speaking group making up 2 percent of the local population

   C. a Portuguese-speaking group with above-average rates of English literacy

   D. a Korean-speaking group making up 12 percent of the local population

   E. a Spanish-speaking group with above-average rates of voter turnout

26. In the first paragraph, the concluding phrase, "fundamental right because it is preservative of all rights," refers to the fact that

   A. laws are necessary to preserve order and justice in any society.

   B. the courts must be the final arbiter of what is and what is not permitted.

   C. by voting, citizens can guarantee that all their other rights are not lost.

   D. the rights of one class or group must be preserved for all classes or groups.

   E. the freedom of the citizenry is more important than the expenditure of a small sum of money.

27. Under the Voting Rights Act of 1965, a native-born, Spanish-speaking American citizen who did not read English would

   A. not be permitted to vote under any circumstances.

   B. not be permitted to vote if he or she had completed six grades in any school.

   C. be permitted to vote under any circumstances.

   D. be permitted to vote if he or she had completed six grades in a Spanish-speaking school in the United States.

   E. be permitted to vote if he or she passed a literacy test.

GO ON TO THE NEXT PAGE

28. The second paragraph suggests that, before 1965, there were laws designed to keep all of the following from voting EXCEPT

  A. native-born Hispanics.

  B. Irish Catholics.

  C. African-Americans.

  D. Yiddish-speaking Jews.

  E. foreign-language speakers unable to speak English.

29. The word "franchise" in line 50 means

  A. ownership.

  B. marketing privilege.

  C. the right to vote.

  D. corporate rights.

  E. a team that represents a city.

30. In line 52, the phrase "a hollow gesture" can be best interpreted to mean

  A. a useless action.

  B. a resounding success.

  C. an empty boast.

  D. a sacred motion.

  E. a foolish joke.

31. Which of the following statements could reasonably be used to argue against the belief that all the laws supporting bilingual voting should be repealed because they discriminate against white immigrants from Europe?

  I. Since many native English speakers have trouble understanding the complex language of ballots, non-English speakers are not at a serious disadvantage.

  II. Though the laws may be imperfect, it is better to spare a large number of other voters from discrimination.

  III. Elimination of bilingual voting would decrease the incidence of election fraud.

  A. I only

  B. II only

  C. III only

  D. I and II only

  E. I, II, and III

32. Bilingual voting equality could not be achieved by strictly equal treatment of all foreign-language speakers because

  A. some minorities had been subject to unequal treatment for many years.

  B. the complexity of Asian languages is greater than that of European languages.

  C. the costs of printing languages such as Korean or Chinese are higher than those for printing Spanish.

  D. some minorities control more of the wealth than others.

  E. under any circumstances, equal treatment is impossible because all minorities are different.

33. Which of the following citizens would probably have the most difficulty in obtaining a bilingual ballot in his or her native language?

    A. a Hispanic immigrant from Argentina

    B. a white immigrant from Spain

    C. a white immigrant from Greece

    D. a non-white immigrant from Taiwan

    E. a Hispanic immigrant from El Salvador

34. The effect of the final paragraph of the passage is to suggest that

    I. the literacy test required of naturalized citizens is an inadequate test of the literacy required of a voter.

    II. the Voting Rights Act of 1965 is inadequate and additional laws should be enacted to enable all voters to vote.

    III. the availability of a bilingual ballot should be determined chiefly by the voters' need for language assistance.

    A. III only

    B. I and II only

    C. I and III only

    D. II and III only

    E. I, II, and III

35. From this passage, the reader can infer that the author's attitude toward the "English Only" movement, a group urging the elimination of bilingual schools and ballots, is one of

    A. enthusiastic approval.

    B. guarded approval.

    C. approval in theory, but not in practice.

    D. guarded disapproval.

    E. strong disapproval.

IF YOU FINISH BEFORE TIME IS CALLED, CHECK YOUR WORK ON THIS SECTION ONLY. DO NOT WORK ON ANY OTHER SECTION IN THE TEST.

Section 5: Mathematical Reasoning

Time: 15 Minutes

10 Questions

Directions: Solve each problem in this section by using the information given and your own mathematical calculations, insights, and problem-solving skills. Then select the one correct answer of the five choices given and mark the corresponding circle on your answer sheet. Use the available space on the page for your scratchwork.

Notes

1. All numbers used are real numbers.

2. Calculators can be used.

3. Some problems may be accompanied by figures or diagrams. These figures are drawn as accurately as possible EXCEPT when it is stated in a specific problem that a figure is not drawn to scale. The figures and diagrams are meant to provide information useful in solving the problem or problems. Unless otherwise stated, all figures and diagrams lie in a plane.

Data That Can Be Used for Reference

Area

rectangle
$A = lw$

triangle
$A = \frac{1}{2}bh$

circle
$A = \pi r^2$
$C = 2\pi r$

Pythagorean Relationship

$a^2 + b^2 = c^2$

Special Triangles

$30° - 60° - 90°$

$45° - 45° - 90°$

Volume

rectangular solid
$V = lwh$

right circular cylinder
$V = \pi r^2 h$

A circle is composed of 360°
A straight angle measures 180°
The sum of the angles of a triangle is 180°

1. If $3/x = 6$, then $x - 1 =$

   A. 1

   B. ½

   C. −½

   D. −⅔

   E. −1½

2. What is the reciprocal of $\dfrac{.25 \times \frac{2}{3}}{.06 \times 15}$?

   A. ³⁄₂₀

   B. ⁵⁄₂₇

   C. ⅔

   D. ²⁷⁄₅

   E. ²⁰⁄₃

3. Harmon's new sports car averages 35 miles per each gallon of gasoline. Assuming that Harmon is able to maintain his average miles per gallon, how far can he drive on 12 gallons of gas?

   A. Almost 3 miles

   B. 42 miles

   C. 350 miles

   D. 420 miles

   E. 700 miles

4. Given △ABC with ∠BCD = 84° and ∠B = 63°, what is the measure of ∠A?

   A. 21°

   B. 27°

   C. 84°

   D. 96°

   E. 116°

5. Teachers will be assigned special camp duty one day of the week during a seven-day camping trip. If all the days of the week (Monday through Sunday) are tossed into a cap and each teacher chooses one day of the week, what is the probability that the first teacher will randomly select a weekday (Monday through Friday)?

   A. ⅐

   B. ²⁄₇

   C. ⅕

   D. ⁵⁄₇

   E. ⁵⁄₂

Section **5** Mathematical Reasoning

GO ON TO THE NEXT PAGE

WOMEN'S BASKETBALL
Scoring Leader's Averages

6. According to the bar graph above, Reynolds's average score exceeds Doe's average score by how many points?

   A. 13.4
   B. 11.1
   C. 8.3
   D. 7.4
   E. 2.3

7. Given positive integer y, which of the following *cannot* be evenly divisible by y?

   A. $y + 1$
   B. $y + 2$
   C. $2y + 1$
   D. $y - 1$
   E. $y + \frac{1}{2}$

8. What is the total surface area in square meters of a rectangular solid whose length is 7 meters, width is 6 meters, and depth is 3 meters?

   A. $32m^2$
   B. $81m^2$
   C. $126m^2$
   D. $162m^2$
   E. $252m^2$

9. A girl runs k miles in n hours. How many miles will she run in x hours at the same rate?

   A. knx
   B. $\frac{k}{n}$
   C. $\frac{kx}{n}$
   D. kx
   E. $\frac{kn}{x}$

Note: Figure not drawn to scale.

10. If the diagonal of a rectangle is 16, then what is its area in square units?

    A. 32
    B. 64
    C. 160
    D. 256
    E. cannot be determined

IF YOU FINISH BEFORE TIME IS CALLED, CHECK YOUR WORK ON THIS SECTION ONLY. DO NOT WORK ON ANY OTHER SECTION IN THE TEST.

STOP

Section 6: Verbal Reasoning

Time: 15 Minutes

13 Questions

In this section, choose the best answer for each question and blacken the corresponding space on the answer sheet.

Critical Reading

Directions: Questions follow the two passages below. Using only the stated or implied information in each passage and in its introduction, if any, answer the questions.

Questions 1–13 are based on the following passages.

The following are critical commentaries by two well-known American film reviewers on the 1960s film The Graduate.

Passage 1

The Graduate is a director's picture because even its mistakes are the proofs of a personal style. Style is more an attitude toward things than the things themselves. It
(5) can be a raised eyebrow or a nervous smile or a pair of shrugged shoulders. It can even be an averted glance. By playing down some of the more offensive qualities of the book, Nichols expresses his own attitude
(10) toward the material. The main trouble with the book is its reduction of the world to the ridiculous scale of an overgrown and outdated Holden Caulfield. Charles Webb's Benjamin Braddock expresses himself with
(15) a monosyllabic smugness that becomes maddeningly self indulgent as the book unravels into slapstick passion. He is superior to his pathetic parents and adults generally. He is kind to the wife of his father's law
(20) partner even though she seduces him with cold-bloodedly calculating carnality.

Ben then falls in love with Elaine, his mistress's daughter, and makes her marry him through the sheer persistence of his pursuit.

(25) The screenplay has been improved by a series of little changes and omissions constituting a pattern of discretion and abstraction. The hero is made less bumptious, the predatory wife less calculating,the sensitive
(30) daughter less passive, and the recurring parental admonitions are reduced in number and intensity. The very end of the movie is apparently the result of an anti-cliche improvisation. In the book, Ben
(35) interrupts Elaine's wedding (to another) before the troths have been plighted. In the movie, the bride kisses the groom before Ben can disrupt the proceeding, but the bride runs off just the same. And this little
(40) change makes all the difference in dramatizing the triumph of people over proceedings. An entire genre of Hollywood movies had been constructed upon the suspenseful chase-to-the-altar proposition that what God
(45) hath joined together no studio scriptwriter can put asunder. *The Graduate* not only shatters this monogamous mythology; it does so in the name of a truer love. . . . I was with *The Graduate* all the way
(50) because I responded fully to its romantic

feelings. Some people have complained
that the Bancroft-Hoffman relationship is
more compelling than the subsequent
Ross-Hoffman relationship. I don't agree.
(55) It is easier to be interesting with an uncon-
ventional sexual relationship than with a
conventional love pairing. *The Graduate* is
moving precisely because its hero passes
from a premature maturity to an innocence
(60) regained, an idealism reconfirmed. That he
is so much out of his time and place makes
him more of an individual and less of a
type. Even the overdone caricatures that
surround the three principals cannot dimin-
(65) ish the cruel beauty of this love story.

Passage 2

Part of the fun of movies is in seeing
"what everybody's talking about," and if
people are flocking to a movie, or if the
press can con us into thinking that they
(70) are, then ironically, there is a sense in
which we want to see it, even if we suspect
we won't enjoy it, because we want to
know what's going on. Even if it's
the worst inflated pompous trash that is the
(75) most talked about (and it usually is) and
even if that talk is manufactured, we want
to see the movies because so many people
fall for whatever is talked about that they
make the advertisers' lies true.

(80) An analyst tells me that when his patients
are not talking about their personal
hang-ups and their immediate problems
they talk about the situations and charac-
ters in movies like *The Graduate,* and they
(85) talk about them with as much personal in-
volvement as about their immediate problems. The high-school and college students
identifying with Dustin Hoffman's
Benjamin are not that different from the
(90) stenographer who used to live and breathe
with the Joan Crawford-working girl and
worry about whether that rich boy would

really make her happy — and considered
her pictures "great." They don't see the
(95) movie as a movie but as part of the soap
opera of their lives. The person who responds this way does not respond more
freely but less freely and less fully than the
person who is aware of what is well done
(100) and what is badly done in a movie,
who can accept some things in it and reject
others, who uses all his senses in reacting,
not just his emotional vulnerabilities. The
small triumph of *The Graduate* was to
(105) have domesticated alienation and the difficulty of communication, by making what
Benjamin is alienated from a middle-class
comic strip and making it absurdly evident
that he has nothing to communicate —
(110) which is just what makes him an acceptable hero for the large movie audience.
The Graduate isn't a *bad* movie, it's entertaining, though in a fairly slick way.
What's surprising is that so many people
(115) take it so seriously.

What's funny about the movie are the
laughs on that dumb sincere boy who
wants to talk about art in bed. But then the
movie begins to pander to youthful narcis-
(120) sism, glorifying his innocence, and making
the predatory (and now crazy) woman the
villainess. Commercially this works: the
inarticulate dull boy becomes a romantic
hero for the audience to project into with
(125) all those squishy and now conventional
feelings of look, his parents don't communicate with him; look, he wants truth not
sham, and so on. But the movie betrays itself and its own expertise, sells out its
(130) comic moments that click along with the
rhythm of a hit Broadway show, to make
the oldest movie pitch of them all — asking the audience to identify with the sim-
pleton who is the latest version of the
(135) misunderstood teen-ager and the
pure-in-heart boy next door. It's almost
painful to tell kids who have gone to see

The Graduate eight times that once was enough for you because you've already (140) seen it [in other versions]. How could you convince them that a movie that sells innocence is a very commercial piece of work when they're so clearly in the market to buy innocence? *The Graduate* only wants (145) to succeed and that's fundamentally what's the matter with it. This kind of moviemaking shifts values, shifts focus, shifts emphasis, shifts everything for a sure-fire response. Mike Nichols's "gift" is that he (150) lets the audience direct him; this is demagoguery in the arts.

The success of *The Graduate* is sociological: the revelation of how emotionally accessible modern youth is to the same old (155) manipulation. The recurrence of certain themes in movies suggests that each generation wants romance restated in slightly new terms, mooning away in fixation on themselves and thinking this fixation meant (160) movies had suddenly become an art, and *their* art.

1. It can be inferred from the first paragraph of Passage 1 that Charles Webb is

   A. the director of the film *The Graduate*.

   B. the author of the novel on which the film *The Graduate* is based.

   C. the author of the screenplay of *The Graduate*.

   D. the actor playing Benjamin Braddock in the film *The Graduate*.

   E. a character in *The Catcher in the Rye*.

2. In Passage 1, line 7, the phrase "playing down" means

   A. concluding.

   B. minimizing.

   C. making unscrupulous use of.

   D. excluding.

   E. participating in.

3. By referring to the novel *The Graduate*'s "reduction of the world to the ridiculous scale of an overgrown and outdated Holden Caulfield" (the hero of Salinger's *The Catcher in the Rye*), the author of Passage 1 suggests that

   I. the characterization of Benjamin Braddock in the novel is inferior to that in the film.

   II. the Salinger novel is overgrown and outdated.

   III. the film is superior to the novel *The Graduate*.

   A. III only

   B. I and II only

   C. I and III only

   D. II and III only

   E. I, II, and III

GO ON TO THE NEXT PAGE

Section **6** Verbal Reasoning

4. As it is used in Passage 1, the word "bumptious" (line 28) means

   A. passive.

   B. slovenly.

   C. yokel-like.

   D. arrogant.

   E. jolting.

5. According to the critic of Passage 1, the most original event in the plot of the film is having

   A. Benjamin fall in love with Elaine, the daughter of his mistress.

   B. the older woman the seducer of the younger man.

   C. Benjamin pursue Elaine despite her engagement to another man.

   D. Benjamin interrupt Elaine's wedding after vows are exchanged.

   E. the young lovers united at the end.

6. According to Passage 1, the theme of the film *The Graduate* is the

   A. recovery of idealism through love.

   B. self-indulgent narcissism of youth.

   C. older generation's failure to nurture the younger.

   D. myth of the monogamous marriage.

   E. superiority of institutions to people.

7. The argument of the first paragraph of Passage 2 (lines 66–79) is that

   A. the advertising for films is often false.

   B. too many people believe advertisers and go to bad movies as a result.

   C. people go to movies partly to discover what has made a film popular or talked about.

   D. people waste time and money at trashy movies because they cannot see the falsity of advertising.

   E. more people would go to better films if advertising were more honest.

8. According to the critic of Passage 2, the popular success of *The Graduate* is due to the fact that Benjamin

   A. is empty-headed.

   B. is alienated.

   C. is unable to communicate with his parents.

   D. matures in the course of the film.

   E. is sincere.

9. In Passage 2, the meaning of the word "gift" in line 149 is

   A. present.

   B. talent.

   C. secret.

   D. idea.

   E. blessing.

10. When Passage 2 says that Mike Nichols "lets the audience direct him" (line 150), it is saying that

A. a good director has a firm hold on all the details of a film.

B. Nichols's films are badly directed because they are too difficult for many audiences to follow.

C. Nichols does not pay enough attention to the needs of his actors.

D. Nichols gives the audience what he knows it likes.

E. Nichols is indifferent to commercial success.

11. According to Passage 2, *The Graduate* is sociologically valuable because it

A. exposes the sentimentality of a generation.

B. expresses the universality of alienation in the modern world.

C. teaches mutual respect between the sexes.

D. expresses the nature of the difficulties generations that cannot communicate must face.

E. reveals how different the generation of the late 1960s is from older generations.

12. Of the following phrases from Passage 2, all might be applied by their author to the author of the first passage EXCEPT

A. a critic who is "not that different from the stenographer who used to live and breathe with the Joan Crawford-working girl" (lines 89–91)

B. a critic who sees a movie as "part of the soap opera of" his life (lines 95–96)

C. a critic who "uses all his senses in reacting, not just his emotional vulnerabilities" (lines 102–103)

D. a critic "clearly in the market to buy innocence" (lines 143–144)

E. a critic "emotionally accessible . . . to the same old manipulation" (lines 153–155)

13. With which of the following comments on the film would the authors of both Passage 1 and Passage 2 agree?

I. The presentation of Ben's parents is a caricature.

II. The older woman who seduces Ben is presented as predatory.

III. The latter part of the movie attempts to present Ben as an exemplar of innocence.

A. II only

B. I and II only

C. I and III only

D. II and III only

E. I, II, and III

IF YOU FINISH BEFORE TIME IS CALLED, CHECK YOUR WORK ON THIS SECTION ONLY. DO NOT WORK ON ANY OTHER SECTION IN THE TEST.

Section 6 Verbal Reasoning

Section 7: Mathematical Reasoning

Time: 30 Minutes

25 Questions

Directions: This section is composed of two types of questions. Use the 30 minutes allotted to answer both question types. Your scratch work should be done on any available space in the section.

Notes

1. All numbers used are real numbers.

2. Calculators can be used.

3. Some problems may be accompanied by figures or diagrams. These figures are drawn as accurately as possible EXCEPT when it is stated in a specific problem that a figure is not drawn to scale. The figures and diagrams are meant to provide information useful in solving the problem or problems. Unless otherwise stated, all figures and diagrams lie in a plane.

Data That Can Be Used for Reference

Quantitative Comparison

Directions: In this section, you are given two quantities, one in column A and one in column B. You are to determine a relationship between the two quantities and mark —

A. if the quantity in column A is greater than the quantity in column B.

B. if the quantity in column B is greater than the quantity in column A.

C. if the quantities are equal.

D. if the comparison cannot be determined from the information that is given.

AN **E** RESPONSE WILL NOT BE SCORED.

Notes

1. Sometimes, information concerning one or both of the quantities to be compared is given. This information is not boxed and is centered above the two columns.

2. All numbers used are real numbers. Letters such as a, b, m, and x represent real numbers.

3. In a given question, if the same symbol is used in column A and column B, that symbol stands for the same value in each column.

	Column A	Column B
1.	85%	$\dfrac{7}{8}$

Square with side 8; Rectangle with sides 7 and 9

| **2.** | Area of the square | Area of the rectangle |

| **3.** | $\dfrac{4+9}{12+18}$ | $\dfrac{4}{12}+\dfrac{9}{18}$ |

	Column A	Column B
	$x = y + z$	
4.	x	y
5.	$ac + bc + a + b$	$(a + b)(c + 1)$
6.	Diameter of circle with area $x + 1$	Circumference of circle with diameter y
7.	$1 + \frac{1}{2} + \frac{1}{4} + \frac{1}{16} + \frac{1}{32} + \frac{1}{64}$	2
8.	Number of ways to arrange four books on a shelf	12

GO ON TO THE NEXT PAGE

Column A   **Column B**

$$x > y > 0$$

9. | $\sqrt{x} - \sqrt{y}$ | $\sqrt{x - y}$ |

$$p > 0, q > 0$$

10. | $p^2 + q^2$ | $(p + q)^2$ |

11. | Number of inches in one mile | Number of minutes in one year |

$$a > b > c$$

12. | $a - b - c$ | $a + b - c$ |

Circle with center C

13. | CP | PQ |

14. | $\sqrt{3^{18}}$ | $(\sqrt{27^3})^2$ |

15. | The length of a diagonal of a square with side of length 10 | The length of a diagonal of a rectangle with sides of lengths 9 and 12 |

Grid-In Questions

Directions: Questions 16–25 require you to solve the problem and enter your answer by carefully marking the circles on the special grid. Examples of the appropriate way to mark the grid follow.

Answer: 3.7   **Answer: 1/2**

Decimal point   Fraction bar

Answer: 1½

Do not grid in mixed numbers in the form of mixed numbers. *Always* change mixed numbers to improper fractions or decimals.

Change to 1.5   or   Change to 3/2

Answer: 123

Space permitting, answers can start in any column. Each grid-in answer below is correct.

Note: Circles must be filled in correctly to receive credit. Mark only one circle in each column. No credit will be given if more than one circle in a column is marked. Example:

Answer: 258

No credit!

Answer: ⅛

Accuracy of decimals: Always enter the most accurate decimal value that the grid will

accommodate. For example: An answer such as .8888 . . . can be gridded as .888 or .889. Gridding this value as .8, .88, or .89 is considered inaccurate and therefore *not acceptable*. The acceptable grid-ins of ⅛ are:

Be sure to write your answers in the boxes at the top of the circles before doing your gridding. Although writing out the answers above the columns is not required, it is very important to ensure accuracy. Even though some problems may have more than one correct answer, grid only *one answer*. Grid-in questions contain no negative answers.

GO ON TO THE NEXT PAGE

16. If $F = \frac{9}{5}C + 32$, what is F when $C = 19$?

___

17. Red, green, and white jellybeans are combined in a ratio of 5:4:3, respectively. What is the ratio of green jelly beans to the total number of jelly beans?

___

18. A picture 8 inches by 10 inches is bordered by a frame that is 1½ inches wide. What is the total area of the picture and the frame in square inches?

___

Review Test Areas

- 30% measurement
- 10% statistics
- 10% numeration
- 20% geometry
- 30% algebra

19. According to the graph above, if the test contains 5 numeration problems, then how many algebra problems would be expected?

___

$y°$ $x°$

Note: Figure not drawn to scale.

20. If, in the figure above, $y = 3x$, then $x =$

21. If 150% of y is equal to 60% of z, and y and z are not zero, then $\frac{y}{z} =$

___

22. Three-fourths of a circle is divided into six equal parts. What fractional part of the whole circle does each piece represent?

___

Maximum Temperature Readings
Los Angeles: July 10-16, 1993

50 year average 1940-1990

23. Of the seven days shown in the graph above, what percent of the days did the maximum temperature exceed the average temperature? (Disregard the % sign when gridding your answer.)

___

24. How many days would it take for two people working together to complete a job if it takes one person 6 days working alone and it takes the other person 10 days working alone to complete the same job?

___

25. A fraction is equivalent to ⅔. If its numerator is decreased by 2 and its denominator is increased by 3, the new fraction is equivalent to ⅕. What is the original fraction?

IF YOU FINISH BEFORE TIME IS CALLED, CHECK YOUR WORK ON THIS SECTION ONLY. DO NOT WORK ON ANY OTHER SECTION IN THE TEST.

STOP

Answer Key

Section 1:
Mathematical
Reasoning

1. D
2. B
3. C
4. D
5. D
6. B
7. D
8. D
9. B
10. D
11. B
12. C
13. A
14. D
15. C
16. E
17. C
18. A
19. B
20. A
21. D
22. E
23. B
24. A
25. E

Section 2:
Verbal
Reasoning

1. C
2. B
3. A
4. E
5. D
6. C
7. B
8. A
9. A
10. E
11. D
12. A
13. C
14. E
15. C
16. E
17. C
18. A
19. B
20. D
21. C
22. B
23. C
24. A
25. B
26. D
27. E
28. D
29. A
30. B

Section 3:
Mathematical
Reasoning

1. B
2. C
3. D
4. B
5. B
6. A
7. A
8. C
9. A
10. B
11. D
12. C
13. A
14. B
15. A
16. 5/12
17. 37.5
18. 45
19. 39
20. 8.78
21. 97
22. 72
23. 2000
24. 7
25. 32

Section 4:
Verbal
Reasoning

1. B
2. C
3. E
4. D
5. D
6. B
7. B
8. B
9. C
10. E
11. D
12. B
13. E
14. A
15. C
16. C
17. C
18. C
19. B
20. A
21. C
22. D
23. B
24. E
25. D
26. C
27. D
28. B
29. C
30. A
31. B
32. A
33. C
34. E
35. E

Section 5: Mathematical Reasoning

1. C
2. D
3. D
4. A
5. D
6. B
7. E
8. D
9. C
10. E

Section 6: Verbal Reasoning

1. B
2. B
3. C
4. D
5. D
6. A
7. C
8. A
9. B
10. D
11. A
12. C
13. E

Section 7: Mathematical Reasoning

1. B
2. A
3. B
4. D
5. C
6. D
7. B
8. A
9. B
10. B
11. B
12. D
13. B
14. C
15. B
16. 66.2
17. 1/3
18. 143
19. 15
20. 45
21. 2/5
22. 1/8
23. 57.1
24. 3.75
25. 6/9

Analyzing Your Test Results

The charts on the following pages should be used to carefully analyze your results and spot your strengths and weaknesses. The complete process of analyzing each subject area and each individual problem should be completed for each practice test. These results should then be re-examined for trends in types of errors (repeated errors) or poor results in specific subject areas. *This reexamination and analysis is of tremendous importance to you in ensuring maximum test preparation benefit.*

Verbal Reasoning Analysis Sheet

Section 2	Possible	Completed	Right	Wrong
Sentence Completion	9			
Analogies	6			
Critical Reading	15			
Subtotal	30			
Section 4	Possible	Completed	Right	Wrong
Sentence Completion	10			
Analogies	13			
Critical Reading	12			
Subtotal	35			
Section 6	Possible	Completed	Right	Wrong
Critical Reading	13			
Subtotal	13			
Overall Verbal Totals	78			

Mathematical Reasoning Analysis Sheet

Section 1	Possible	Completed	Right	Wrong
Multiple Choice	25			
Subtotal	25			

Section 3	Possible	Completed	Right	Wrong
Quantitative Comparison	15			
Grid-Ins	10			
Subtotal	25			

Section 5	Possible	Completed	Right	Wrong
Multiple Choice	10			
Subtotal	10			

Section 7	Possible	Completed	Right	Wrong
Quantitative Comparison	15			
Grid-Ins	10			
Subtotal	25			
Overall Math Totals	85			

You can now use the Score Range Approximator on page 346–347 to convert your raw scores to an *approximate* scaled score.

Analysis/Tally Sheet for Problems Missed

One of the most important parts of test preparation is analyzing **why** you missed a problem so that you can reduce the number of mistakes. Now that you have taken the practice test and checked your answers, carefully tally your mistakes by marking them in the proper column.

	Reason for Mistakes				
	Total Missed	*Simple Mistake*	*Misread Problem*	*Lack of Knowledge*	*Lack of Time*
Section 1: Verbal					
Section 3: Verbal					
Section 5: Verbal					
Subtotal					
Section 2: Math					
Section 4: Math					
Section 6: Math					
Section 7: Math					
Subtotal					
Total Math and Verbal					

Reviewing the preceding data should help you determine **why** you are missing certain problems. Now that you've pinpointed the type of error, compare it to other practice tests to spot other common mistakes.

Section 1: Mathematical Reasoning

1. **D.** Multiplying each side by 3

$$3m + n = 7$$
$$3(3m + n) = 3(7)$$

Therefore, $9m + 3n = 21$

2. **B.** If ⅔ of the container is full, there remains ⅓ of the container to fill. The time to fill ⅓ of the container will be half as long as the time needed to fill ⅔ of the container. Hence, ½ (18 minutes) = 9 minutes.

3. **C.** To find the tax at 7% on $132.95, simply round off and multiply (the rule for rounding off is "5 or above rounds up"): 7% times $133.

$$.07 \times \$133 = \$9.31$$

Use a calculator without rounding off,

$$.07 \times \$132.95 = \$9.306 \text{ or } \$9.31$$

4. **D.** Since the sum of the angles is 180°,

$$m + n + 72 + 25 = 180$$
$$m + n + 97 = 180$$
$$m + n = 180 - 97$$
$$m + n = 83$$

Hence, the sum of $m + n$ is 83°.

5. **D.** The perimeter of a rectangle is equal to the sum of the dimensions of its sides. For this rectangle,

$$\text{perimeter} = 6l + 4w + 6l + 4w$$
$$= 6l + 6l + 4w + 4w$$
$$= 12l + 8w$$

6. **B.** Since the square of a positive number is a positive number, choice **B** is the correct answer.

7. D. If Tom is 4 years older than Fran, if we call Fran's age x, Tom's age must be 4 years more, or $x + 4$. Therefore, since the total of their ages is 24, Fran's age + Tom's age = 24.

$$x + (x + 4) = 24$$

8. D. $\dfrac{840 \text{ miles}}{1\frac{1}{2} \text{ hours}} = \dfrac{3,500 \text{ miles}}{x \text{ hours}}$

Cross multiplying yields $840x = 3500 \cdot 1\frac{1}{2}$

$$840x = 5250$$
$$x = 5250 \div 840$$
$$x = 6\frac{1}{4} \text{ hours}$$

9. B. $\dfrac{\text{percent}}{100} = \dfrac{\text{is number}}{\text{of number}}$ $\quad \dfrac{30}{100} = \dfrac{x}{25/18}$

$$100x = \frac{{}^{5}\cancel{30}}{1} \times \frac{25}{\cancel{18}_{3}}$$

Cross multiplying $\qquad 100x = \dfrac{125}{3}$

$$x = \frac{{}^{5}\cancel{125}}{3} \times \frac{1}{\cancel{100}_{4}}$$

$$x = \frac{5}{12}$$

10. D. The seventh row will be 1-6-15-20-15-6-1, which contains no prime numbers.

11. B. $\dfrac{y-x}{y+x} = \dfrac{\dfrac{4}{7} - \dfrac{3}{4}}{\dfrac{4}{7} + \dfrac{3}{4}}$

Multiplying by the lowest common denominator, which is 28,

$$= \frac{28\left(\dfrac{4}{7} - \dfrac{3}{4}\right)}{28\left(\dfrac{4}{7} + \dfrac{3}{4}\right)}$$

$$= \frac{16 - 21}{16 + 21}$$

$$= \frac{-5}{37}$$

12. **C.** There are $40 - 24 = 16$ boys in the class.

$$\frac{\text{is number}}{\text{of number}} = \frac{\text{percent}}{100}$$

$$\frac{16}{40} = \frac{x}{100}$$

$$40x = 1600$$

$$x = 40$$

Hence, 40% of the class are boys.

13. **A.** b = Bob's age, c = Jane's age, d = Jim's age.

Since Bob is older than Jane, $c < b$.

Since Bob is younger than Jim, $b < d$.

Hence, $c < b$, and $b < d$, or $c < b < d$.

14. **D.** Perimeter of $\triangle MNP$ = ½(perimeter of $\triangle XYZ$)

$$= ½(XY + YZ + XZ)$$

$$= ½(10 + 15 + 17)$$

$$= ½(42)$$

$$= 21$$

15. **C.** Using the Pythagorean theorem, $a^2 + b^2 = c^2$

$$(BC)^2 = (CD)^2 + (DB)^2$$

$$= 5^2 + 12^2$$

$$= 25 + 144$$

$$= 169$$

$$(BC) = \sqrt{169} = 13$$

Hence, the radius of the circle is 13.

16. **E.** So far, George has averaged 80% on each of three tests. Therefore, his *total* points scored equals three times 80, or 240 points. In order to average 85% of four tests, George needs a total point score of four times 85, or 340 points. Since George presently is 100 points short of 340, he needs to get 100 points, or 100%, on the fourth test.

17. C. Let $2x$ = first angle, $3x$ = second angle, $4x$ = third angle, and $6x$ = fourth angle. Since the sum of the measures of the angles in a quadrilateral must be $360°$,

$$2x + 3x + 4x + 6x = 360°$$

$$15x = 360$$

$$\frac{15x}{15} = \frac{360}{15}$$

$$x = 24°$$

$$2x = 48° = \text{first angle}$$

$$3x = 72° = \text{second angle}$$

$$4x = 96° = \text{third angle}$$

$$6x = 144° = \text{fourth angle}$$

Hence, the largest angle of the quadrilateral has a measure of $144°$.

18. A. If $x(y - z) = t$

$$\frac{\overset{1}{\cancel{x}}(y - z)}{\underset{1}{\cancel{x}}} = \frac{t}{x}$$

$$y - z = \frac{t}{x}$$

$$y - z + z = \left(\frac{t}{x}\right) + z$$

$$y = \left(\frac{t}{x}\right) + z$$

19. B. Area of larger circle = 144π. Since area = πr^2, then

$$\pi r^2 = 144\pi$$

$$r^2 = 144$$

$$r = 12$$

$$\text{radius of a larger circle} = 12$$

$$\text{diameter of a smaller circle} = 12$$

$$\text{radius of a smaller circle} = 6$$

$$\text{area of a smaller circle} = \pi r^2$$

$$= \pi(6)^2$$

$$= 36\pi$$

20. A. Substituting 2 for m and 3 for n gives

$$2 * 3 = \frac{2 + 3 - 1}{3^2}$$

$$= \frac{5 - 1}{9}$$

$$= \frac{4}{9}$$

21. **D.** If $\frac{a}{b} = \frac{c}{d}$, then, by cross multiplying, $ad = bc$.

    If $\frac{a}{b} = \frac{c}{d}$, then cross multiplying gives the same result, $ad = bc$.

    Hence, if $\frac{a}{b} = \frac{c}{d}$, then $\frac{a}{b} = \frac{c}{d}$.

22. **E.** First, rearrange and simplify the first equation as follows. Add $+12$ and $+6y$ to both sides of the equation $6x - 12 = -6y$, and you get

$$6x - 12 \qquad = -6y$$
$$\underline{+12 + 6y = +6y + 12}$$
$$6x \qquad +6y = \qquad 12$$

Now, dividing through by 6 leaves

$$x + y = 2$$

Next, rearrange and simplify the second equation as follows.

$$5y + 5x = 15 \text{ is the same as } 5x + 5y = 15$$

Now, dividing through by 5 leaves

$$x + y = 3$$

The equations $x + y = 2$ and $x + y = 3$ have no solutions in common because you can't add the same two numbers and get two different answers.

23. **B.** Since y varies directly as $xy = kx$ for some constant k. Since $x = 18$ when $y = 12$,

$$12 = k \cdot 18$$

$$k = \frac{12}{18} = \frac{2}{3}$$

and $y = \left(\frac{2}{3}\right) x$

Hence, when $x = 20$, $y = \left(\frac{2}{3}\right)(20)$

$$= \frac{40}{3}$$

$$= 13\frac{1}{3}$$

24. **A.** Ratio of diameters = ratio of radii.

$$\frac{d_1}{d_2} = \frac{r_1}{r_2} = \frac{30}{100} = \frac{3}{10}$$

Ratio of area = (ratio of radii)^2.

$$\frac{A_1}{A_2} = \left(\frac{r_1}{r_2}\right)^2$$

$$\frac{A_1}{A_2} = \frac{9}{100}$$

Hence the area of circle R is $\frac{9}{100}$, or 9%, of the area of circle S.

25. E. If the coordinates of two points x and y are (x_1, y_1) and (x_2, y_2), respectively, then the coordinates of the midpoint B (m_1, m_2) of xy are

$$\left(\frac{x_1 + x_2}{2}, \frac{y_1 + y_2}{2}\right) = (m_1, m_2)$$

Hence $\qquad m_1 = \dfrac{x_1 + x_2}{2} \qquad$ and $\qquad m_2 = \dfrac{y_1 + y_2}{2}$

$$5 = \frac{(-4 + x_2)}{2} \qquad \text{and} \qquad -2 = \frac{(3 + y_2)}{2}$$

$$(2)(5) = (2)\left(\frac{-4 + x_2}{2}\right) \qquad \text{and} \qquad (2)(-2) = 2\left(\frac{3 + y_2}{2}\right)$$

$$10 = -4 + x_2 \qquad\qquad\qquad -4 = 3 + y_2$$

$$10 + 4 = -4 + x_2 + 4 \qquad\qquad -4 - 3 = 3 + y_2 - 3$$

$$14 = x_2 \qquad\qquad\qquad\qquad -7 = y_2$$

Hence, the coordinates of y are $(x_2, y_2) = (14, -7)$.

Section 2: Verbal Reasoning

Sentence Completion

1. **C.** The adjective needed here will describe the growing fear of the watchers of the endangered boat. Choice **B** "intrepid" means fearless, and "cowardly" **A,** although it describes a fearful person, is for those who fear for themselves, not others. The best choice is "apprehensive," meaning uneasy, anxious, or troubled by fears.

2. **B.** "Native" and "indigenous" here mean the same thing. Since even the best language students who are foreign will not understand the native speaker, the missing word must mean something like puzzled or bewildered. The best choice, then, is "baffled."

3. **A.** With the use of "merely" and "not censorship," the sentence implies that the missing first word describes some minor changes in a test, something like "editing," or "revising," or "corrections" but not so serious as "expurgation" or "decimation." The phrase "with the writer's prior knowledge and" suggests that the last word must mean something like approval. In **B** the use of "prohibition" and in **C** the use of "disapproval" won't work, so the correct choice must be **A** "permission."

4. **E.** The missing noun probably describes a strength, since it is being tested and is parallel to the phrase "capacity to adapt." The best choice is "resilience," that is, the capacity to bounce back, to recover strength or good spirits.

5. **D.** The first noun is probably a synonym for "trend," but although **D** "fad" looks like the best choice, "prank" or "whim" might work. The second noun describes a serious threat (*not* an "innocent" or harmless "trend"). Either "peril" **A** (danger) or "hazard" **D** (risk) will do, but since **D** has the better first answer, it is the better choice.

6. **C.** Since the second half of the sentence tells us of the public's "disapproval," the missing participle must reflect this attitude. Either "horrified" **C** or "repulsed" **D** will fit. Only "ghoulish" continues the expression of condemnation. A "repulsed" public would not find the jewelry "amiable."

7. **B.** The first term, a verb, has "response" as its object; choices **A** and **C** do not fit this context. The second term, a noun, describes a point that can be reached. Only choices **A, B,** and **C** might fit here. Thus, the correct choice is **B.** "Elicited" means evoked or drew, while "nadir" means the lowest point.

8. **A.** Since the missing word must be surprising in an atmosphere of "calm" and beauty, choices **B, C, D,** and **E** are all unsuitable. But "untoward," that is, perverse, unseemly, unexpected, fits well.

9. **A.** The two blanks must be filled together, and you can solve this question only by looking at both answers. Choice **A** makes sense, since the first blank describes lands that are *not* something, in this case, not "arable," or capable of cultivation, and the second missing term, the verb, is logically one that means planted. **B** looks bad because, if the fields far from the river are *not* barren, why settle elsewhere? The adjectives in **D** and **E** would work, but the verbs are wholly inappropriate. A field is not "shunned," "eschewed," or "colonized" **C.**

Analogies

10. **E.** In this question, "bow" is a noun referring to the part that is drawn across the strings of the "violin" to produce sound. The analogy here is the "drumstick" which is used to produce sound from a "drum." The "pedal" of a "piano" controls the volume, but does not produce the sound.

11. **D.** A "spear" is an offensive weapon; a "shield" is protective armor, a defensive device. The parallel pair is **D**; the "gun" is an offensive weapon, while the "bulletproof vest" is a defensive item. None of the other pairs uses the offensive-defensive difference.

12. **A.** A "skillet" is a round, flat pan, a frying pan, the utensil in which "bacon" is usually prepared. A "palette" is the oval board on which an artist prepares "paints."

13. **C.** An "aria" is a melody or song in an "opera," a part of the whole. Similarly, a "chapter" is a section of a "novel," a part of the whole.

14. **E.** To "elope" is to run away secretly, a verb used of "lovers" who run away to get married. To "abscond" is to run away secretly, especially in order to escape the law. The verb is used of "embezzlers" (thieves who take money by fraud). When a "convict escapes," it may or may not be secret, and the verb itself has no suggestion of the surreptitious.

15. **C.** The first term here is an adjective; the second is a noun describing a quality which a person described by this adjective would *not* have. A "callous," unfeeling, insensitive person would lack "tact." Similarly, a "lethargic," sluggish person would lack "speed."

Critical Reading

16. **E.** The passage mentions raccoons, cats, humans, and skunks as rabies victims. Since the first paragraph explicitly limits the disease to any "mammal," carrion birds are not susceptible to the virus.

17. **C.** Unless rabies is treated by "timely" injections of vaccine, it is a fatal disease (lines 3-6).

18. **A.** Although dogs are no longer the major carriers in countries with good veterinary services and laws requiring inoculation, they still account for "90 percent of all human deaths from rabies," chiefly in developing nations.

19. **B.** The number of fatalities from the disease is small in the United States because most dogs have been immunized, people are aware of the danger of the disease, and those at risk of having been infected are treated before the symptoms of the disease can develop. The virus is not rare in wild-animal populations. In line 64, the passage refers to an epidemic among raccoons in America.

20. **D.** The word "feasible" means practicable or possible.

21. **C.** The treatment of humans can now include vaccine injections (in the abdomen or arm) and application of rabies-specific antibodies in the wound area. The passage makes no mention of an oral recombinant vaccine.

22. **B.** The vaccine-laced bait should be useful in dealing with wild populations and with dogs in countries where large-scale inoculation is impossible. The vaccine would not be useful in animals already infected, since once the symptoms of the disease develop, it is too late to save the victim.

23. **C.** In lines 21–24, the speaker says she did not follow the Watergate proceedings because it was just a case of one set of rich white people hoodwinking another set.

24. **A.** "Of a piece" means part of, consistent with, or in keeping with.

25. **B.** In this context, the word "acute" means shrewd or clever. Although some of the other meanings can apply in other contexts, the word here is opposed to "ignorance" and associated with wit.

26. **D.** The words here are the thoughts of the speaker, not what she says. Throughout the passage, the reader knows both what she says and also what she thinks but does not say. Aware here of the "pompous" remarks she had just made, she is not eager to elaborate on these second-hand ideas, and remembering that Cox is a lawyer, she hopes to herself that he will not cross-examine her further.

27. **E.** All three are deliberately used to undercut any pretentiousness of the passage. The phrases are conversational, even slangy in tone, and are characteristic of the writing in the passage, which is at pains to appear natural.

28. **D.** The comic scene she imagines — Cox left in West Philly "without a map or a bow tie" — is her response to his inclusive "Our." The speaker does not feel of a piece with the white New England establishment, and it is the pronoun which inspires her thoughts.

29. A. The Rector, a shrewd observer throughout the passage, has some idea of what is going on in the speaker's mind. For a moment, he is afraid she will blurt out something that will embarrass the school. He is relieved that the moment has passed without incident.

30. B. Because the passage was written some time after the events and allows the reader to know the thoughts of the speaker, the selection as a whole is very frank, even self-critical. The author understands herself and reveals this understanding very candidly. None of the other choices is appropriate.

Section 3: Mathematical Reasoning

Quantitative Comparison

1. **B.** By inspection, if you multiply $(^{89}/_{919}) \times 57$, this must be less than 57 (as you are multiplying 57 by a fraction less than 1). Therefore, it must be less than 58. The correct answer is **B.**

2. **C.** Simplifying columns A and B leaves $x^{16} y^{24} = x^{16} y^{24}$. Note that when you have a number with an exponent to a power, you simply multiply the exponents together.

3. **D.** This problem is best solved by inspection or insight. Since there are two variables in this single inequality, there are many possible values for x and y. Therefore, a comparison cannot be made.

4. **B.** Since the given point lies in quadrant II, $x < 0$ and $y > 0$. Hence, $y > x$.

5. **B.** Substituting -1 for x gives

   $$(-1)^3 - 1 = -1 - 1 = -2$$

   Now, trying -2 for x gives

   $$(-2)^3 - 1 = -8 - 1 = -9$$

   It is evident that this phrase will always generate negative values if $x < 0$. Therefore, the correct answer is **B.** The cube of a negative is a negative. One less than a negative is negative. Any negative is less than 0.

6. **A.** Change column A to decimals.

   $$\frac{1}{3} \times \frac{2}{5} \times \frac{1}{8}$$

   gives $.33\frac{1}{3} \times .4 \times .125$, which, by inspection, is greater than column B. Another method would be to change column B to all fractions and then compare.

7. **A.** Since $a = 3b$ and $b = -2$, then $a = 3(-2) = -6$, substituting into the numerator of each expression (since the denominators are positive and alike, they can be eliminated),

   $$\frac{a^2 + b}{9b} \qquad\qquad \frac{a + b^2}{9b}$$
   $$(-6)^2 + -2 \qquad\quad -6 + (-2)^2$$
   $$36 + -2 \qquad\qquad -6 + 4$$

   Therefore,

   $$34 > -2$$

8. **C.** Since a triangle has 180° in the interior angles, if one angle is 90°, then the other two must total 90°.

9. **A.** In the triangle, $\angle Z$ must be 60° and $\angle X$ is given as 30°. Since the side across from the larger angle in a triangle is the longer side, then $XY > YZ$.

10. **B.** The ratio of the sides of a 30°-60°-90° triangle is 1, 2, $\sqrt{3}$, and since the side across from 30° is 2, the side across from 90° is $2\sqrt{3}$. Compare each column by squaring the number outside and multiply by the numbers under the radical.

$$2\sqrt{3} \qquad 3\sqrt{2}$$
$$\sqrt{3\cdot 4} \qquad \sqrt{2\cdot 9}$$
$$\sqrt{12} \quad > \quad \sqrt{18}$$

11. **D.** There are only two ways for a positive integer to a positive power to equal 81: 9^2 or 3^4. Thus, $(b+c)^a$ could be, say, $(3+6)^2$. Or it could be $(1+2)^4$. In the first case $b+c$ is greater than a. But in the second instance, $b+c$ is less than a. Therefore, the answer is **D**.

12. **C.** $\overparen{AC} = 2(\angle B)$ because an inscribed angle is half of the arc it subtends (connects to).

13. **A.** Since $\angle AOB$ is a central angle, it equals the measure of $\overparen{AB}$, and since $\angle ADC$ is outside the circle but connects to $\overparen{AB}$, it is less than half of $\overparen{AB}$. Therefore,

$$\angle AOB > \angle ADC$$

Alternate method: The external angle AOB must be larger than either of the remote interior angles.

14. **B.** Converting the rate of 30 miles per hour to its equivalent rate in feet per second,

$$30 \text{ miles per hour} = \frac{30 \times 5,280 \text{ feet}}{3,600 \text{ seconds}}$$

$$= \frac{158,400 \text{ feet}}{3,600 \text{ seconds}}$$

$$= 44 \text{ feet per second}$$

Since the time is the same in both problems, the distance traveled would be greater at a rate of 45 feet per second.

15. **A.** Since the area of face TUWY is 20, the dimensions must be 2×10. Remember, each dimension must be an even number. The dimensions of face WXZY must therefore be 2×4. Since edge WY is common to both faces, the dimensions of face UVXW are 10×4.

The surface of the rectangular solid is

$$2 \times 20 = 20 \text{ (doubled)} = 40$$
$$2 \times 4 = 8 \text{ (doubled)} = 16$$
$$10 \times 4 = 40 \text{ (doubled)} = 80$$
$$= 136$$

Volume equals $2 \times 10 \times 4 = 80$

Therefore, the surface area is greater.

Grid-In Questions

16. Answer: $\frac{5}{12}$. Dividing both sides of the equation $12a = 5b$ by $12b$,

$$\frac{12a}{12b} = \frac{5b}{12b}$$
$$\frac{a}{b} = \frac{5}{12}$$

17. Answer: 37.5. Since the female students make up 3 parts out of the total 8 parts, the percent of students that are female is

$$\frac{3}{8} = \frac{x}{100}$$

$$8x = 300$$

$$x = \frac{300}{8}$$

$$x = 37\frac{4}{8}$$

$$x = 37\frac{1}{2} = 37.5$$

18. Answer: 45. Since each of the 5 shirts may be matched with each of the 3 pair of slacks, and these combinations may in turn be matched with each of the 3 sports jackets, the total number of combinations possible is

$$5 \cdot 3 \cdot 3 = 45$$

19. Answer: 39. Squaring both sides of the original equation yields

$$\left(\sqrt{m-3}\right)^2 = 6^2$$
$$m - 3 = 36$$
$$m = 39$$

Checking the answer in the original equation for extraneous solutions,

$$\sqrt{m-3} = \sqrt{39-3}$$
$$= \sqrt{36}$$
$$= 6$$

Hence, $m = 6$ is the solution for the given equation.

20. Answer: 8.78.

5 apples:	$5 \times .60 = \$3.00$
10 bananas:	$10 \times .20 = \$2.00$
4 cantaloupes:	$2 \times 1.00 = \$2.00$ ($4 = 2 \times 2$ for \$1)
5 oranges:	$\$1.00 + 2 \times .39 = \$1.78$ (3 for \$1 and 39 cents each for the other two)

To find the total, add

$$\$3.00 + \$2.00 + \$2.00 + \$1.78 = \$8.78$$

21. Answer: 97. To average 89% for seven exams, Ben must have a total of (89)(7), or 623 points. To average 90% for eight exams, Ben must have a total of (90)(8), or 720 points. Therefore, his score on the eighth exam must be

$$720 - 623 = 97\%$$

22. Answer: 72. The length of the side of a square with diagonal 12 is

$$12 \div \sqrt{2} = \frac{12}{\sqrt{2}}$$

The area of a square with side length x is

$$A = x^2$$
$$= \left(\frac{12}{\sqrt{2}}\right)^2$$
$$= {}^{144}\!\!/\!{}_2$$
$$= 72$$

23. Answer: 2000. Simply continue the chart as follows, adding 40 cents for each two years to Product A and 15 cents for each two years to Product B.

Products	1992	1994	1996	1998	2000
A	$6.60	$7.00	$7.40	$7.80	$8.20
B	$7.20	$7.35	$7.50	$7.65	$7.80

It is evident that the correct answer is 2000.

24. Answer: 7. The area of a trapezoid is

$$A = \tfrac{1}{2} h(b_1 + b_2)$$
$$98 = \tfrac{1}{2} h(12 + 16)$$
$$98 = \tfrac{1}{2} h(28)$$
$$98 = 14h$$
$$7 = h$$

25. Answer: 32. By the Pythagorean theorem,

$$x^2 + 12^2 = 20^2$$
$$x^2 + 144 = 400$$
$$x^2 = 256$$
$$x = 16$$

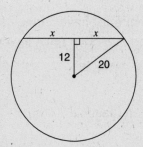

Therefore, the length of the chord is

$$2x = 32 \text{ centimeters}$$

Section 4: Verbal Reasoning

Sentence Completion

1. **B.** The clue in the sentence is "banning." If cameras have been banned, the public will not see the whole story, so their "access," right to approach, has been curtailed. The best word here is "denied" **B.** "Belied" means lied about.

2. **C.** The adverb "reluctantly" and the phrase "despite his care" suggest that the adjective that modifies "shoplifting" here is one that distresses the grocer and, so you can infer, one that means frequent. The only word that is close is "commonplace"; that is, common or ordinary.

3. **E.** The sentence presents the example of the same number of workers taking more time for the same job as an example of Parkinson's law. The missing word in the law must explain this phenomenon. If work does something to fill the time for its completion, and the time for its completion has increased, then work must grow larger to fill the longer time. The missing word cannot be "decreases" or "grows easier." The right answer must be **D** or **E**, and "expands" **E** goes better with "fill." The missing verb must be a synonym for "states" or "says." Choices **B, C,** and **E** would work, but **E** also has the best second answer.

4. **D.** The noun must reflect the mood of loud cheering or something happy, such as "happiness" **B**, "gladness" **C**, "euphoria" **D**, or "buoyancy" **E**. The second word must qualify this mood, however, because the first clause begins with "although." A proper word here could be "tempered" **A** or "moderated" **D**. The words "enervated" and "debilitated," although they can mean weaken, cannot be used in this context. They refer to physical weakness. Only **D** has two good choices; "euphoria" is a feeling of well-being.

5. **D.** The clues in the sentence tell you that the missing word must describe a conversation with no sentence longer than four words. The correct answer is "terse"; that is, brief or to the point. None of the other choices is plausible.

6. **B.** The second term, a noun, must be a word that accords with a functioning government, so you can eliminate "schism," "dichotomy," and "division." Either "compromise" or "consensus" (agreement) will fit. The first term, an adjective, describes a position that should be abandoned. Therefore, "dogmatic" is a much better choice than "sensible."

7. **B.** The words "conventional," "morality," and "conformity" suggest that the missing adjective to modify "conformity" will express the correctness of the Victorian reader. Choice **B** "genteel" means polite, refined, well bred — just what would be expected. The incorrect answers are all adjectives describing the opposite of what is suggested by "conventional morality."

8. **B.** The opening clause with its "though" at the beginning suggests that the missing adjective will be the opposite of "lively" and "interesting." The second missing word refers to the "lively" first chapter, so it must be a noun synonym for liveliness. The choice of "tedious" **B,** "repetitive" **C,** "dull" **D,** or "boring" **E** would do for the first blank, but only "pace" **A** or "verve" **B** are possible for the second. The right response must be **B.** Words like "torpor" and "lethargy" are the opposite of what is needed for the second noun, and "verve" means vigor or energy.

9. **C.** The useful clues here are "dangerous," "without peppers or other spices," and "mild," with the latter two set in opposition to the missing adjective by the word "but." Choices **A, B,** and **D** are just what you don't want. Both **C** "torrid" (that is, fiery or very hot) or **E** "piquant" are possible, but because "piquant" suggests an agreeable tartness and these dishes are dangerous, "torrid" is better.

10. **E.** The second adjective, expressing the response of a malcontent (a dissatisfied or rebellious person), must be disparaging, and the first adjective, coming before the "but," must be opposite in effect. The favorable first adjectives are **B** "perfect," **D** "Edenic," and **E** "ideal," and the pejorative second words are **A** "irritating," **C** "drab," and **E** "painful." The correct choice must be **E.**

Analogies

11. **D.** "Surfing" and "skateboarding" are individual (as opposed to team) sports, the one on water and the other on land. Similarly, "water-skiing" and "roller-skating" are sports for individuals, the one on water, the second on land. The other choices include at least one team sport and sometimes two.

12. **B.** A "vegetarian" is a person who does not consume "meat." A "teetotaler" is a person who does not consume alcohol. A "dieter" may restrict the "food" he or she eats, but a "dieter" does eat some food.

13. **E.** A "honeycomb" is the part of the beehive where the honey is stored. It is made of "wax." The parallel here is "kimono," which is made of "fabric."

14. **A.** A "typewriter" is a mechanism used for writing; a "pencil" is an instrument used for writing by hand. A "calculator" is a mechanism for making mathematical computations; a "slide rule" is an instrument used for making mathematical computations by hand.

15. **C.** A "quiver" is used by an "archer" to hold arrows. The first noun refers to an object and the second to a person who uses or is associated with that object. Only **C** has as its second term a word referring to a person. A "forceps" is an object used by a "surgeon."

16. **C.** An example of a "disinfectant" is "iodine." An example of an "analgesic" (something that allays pain) is "aspirin."

Complete Answers and Explanations for Practice Test 3

17. **C.** A "digit" is a numeral from zero to nine, but it also means "finger" or toe; the adjective form is "digital," of, or constituting, or like a "finger." The adjective "manual" means of a "hand." The adjective "aural" means of the ear, not the "eye." The root of *solar* is "sun," not "star."

18. **C.** A "sloth" is a South American animal whose natural habitat is the "rain forest." Although a "cow" can be found in a "barn," it is not the natural habitat. The same applies to "porpoise" and "water park." The *Gila monster* is a poisonous lizard whose natural habitat is the "desert."

19. **B.** To "follow" and to "ensue" are synonyms. A second pair of synonyms is "inter" and "bury."

20. **A.** A "duchy" is the area that is ruled by a "duke" or by a "duchess." A "count" does not rule a "county," but a "queen" is a monarch, and she rules a "monarchy."

21. **C.** A "quill," a feather from a bird, was at an earlier time used as a pen with which to write. A "manuscript" was at that time a document written by hand. A writer used a "quill" to produce a "manuscript." The parallel pair here is "brush" and "fresco." A "fresco" is a painting on a plaster surface which the artist makes by using a "brush."

22. **D.** The adjectives "dorsal" and "ventral" refer to the back and front of a human. They are, then, adjectives denoting opposite sides. The best parallel is "retreating" (going away from) and "advancing" (coming toward), actions that are also opposed and which, coincidentally, would reveal the "dorsal" and the "ventral" sides of a person.

23. **B.** A "victim" is someone or something killed or injured. A "martyr" is a victim who suffers for principles or beliefs. An "action" is the doing of something. A "crusade" is an action undertaken on behalf of some cause or idea, so in both cases, the second term adds a moral or religious motive to the idea of the first.

Critical Reading

24. **E.** Most of the first paragraph deals with what has been "often assumed" about bilingual ballots but which is untrue. The author attempts to respond to objections about the high costs and bilingual ballots on demand by pointing out what the costs are and what rules govern the qualifications for bilingual ballots.

25. **D.** Because the rules specify that a language group must make up "more than 5 percent of the local population," choice **B** would not qualify. The minorities who might qualify are Hispanic, Asian, and Native Americans, so choices **A** and **C** will not qualify. Choice **E** is disqualified because the group does not have a "below average" rate of "voter turnout." An Asian minority of 12 percent would qualify if it had a below-average voter turnout and English literacy.

26. **C.** The phrase refers to voting, a "fundamental right" of all citizens, which is the means the people have to preserve all their other rights. A watchful public seeing that a candidate or a law may limit its rights can vote against that candidate or law. Some of the other answers may be true, but they are not the point of the phrase in the passage.

27. **D.** In lines 32 – 41, the passage explains that a condition of the Voting Rights Act was the suspension of literacy tests for foreign-language speakers whose "predominant classroom language was other than English" who had completed six grades in an American school.

28. **B.** The second paragraph refers to laws intended to exclude voters who were Hispanic (line 45), African American (line 35), Yiddish speakers (line 49), and nonspeakers of English (lines 41 – 45) but makes no reference to Irish Catholics, who would presumably be English-speaking whites.

29. **C.** As it is used in line 50, the word "franchise" means the right to vote, the central issue in the passage.

30. **A.** The phrase "a hollow gesture" means an action with no consequence, a useless motion, an empty gesture. Choice **A** is the best of the five definitions.

31. **B.** The second statement is a responsible reply to the argument that all bilingual voting materials should be abolished. Granting that some discrimination may now exist, it argues that by repeal of the laws, those who are injured now would not be helped and those who are now enfranchised would lose their votes. The first statement, even if true, is not an argument against bilingual voting. The third statement, if true, would support the argument against bilingual voting.

32. **A.** If everyone starts from the same position, equal treatment should be the fairest way. If some groups start with a serious disadvantage, however, equal treatment will simply preserve the disadvantage. Therefore, to achieve equality, those groups who have not had a head start need to be helped more to catch up.

33. **C.** The fourth paragraph deals with the disadvantage of non-English-speaking white Europeans (save Hispanics). The only example of the white non-Hispanic European on this list is **C**, the Greek.

34. **E.** The final paragraph suggests all three. If only one in nearly seven thousand fails the literacy-in-English test, the test must be seriously flawed. Questions like "Why not make every effort to eliminate language barriers to voting?" call for the reader's assent, and "Perhaps it should" suggests that "need" should be taken into account in determining who should have a bilingual ballot.

35. **E.** As the last paragraph makes clear, the author of this passage favors liberalizing the laws to make bilingual ballots more available. The author would, you can be sure, strongly disapprove of a movement that attempted to restrict or abolish the use of bilingual ballots in American elections.

Section 5: Mathematical Reasoning

1. **C.** Because $\frac{3}{x} = \frac{6}{1}$, cross multiplying gives

$$6 \cdot x = 3$$

$$x = \tfrac{1}{2}$$

Therefore, $x - 1 = (\tfrac{1}{2}) - 1 = -\tfrac{1}{2}$

2. **D.** $\dfrac{.25 \times \dfrac{2}{3}}{.06 \times 15} = \dfrac{\dfrac{25}{100} \times \dfrac{2}{3}}{\dfrac{6}{100} \times \dfrac{15}{1}}$

$$= \dfrac{\dfrac{1}{4} \times \dfrac{2}{3}}{\dfrac{3}{50} \times \dfrac{15}{1}} = \dfrac{\dfrac{1}{6}}{\dfrac{9}{10}} = \dfrac{1}{6} \times \dfrac{10}{9} = \dfrac{5}{27}$$

Therefore, the reciprocal of $\dfrac{.25 \times \dfrac{2}{3}}{.06 \times 15}$ is the reciprocal of $\frac{5}{27}$, or $\frac{27}{5}$.

3. **D.** Since Harmon's sports car averages 35 miles for each gallon of gas, on 12 gallons, he'll be able to drive 12×35, or 420 miles.

4. **A.** $\angle BCD = \angle A + \angle B$ (exterior angle of a triangle equals the sum of the opposite two).

Then $84° = \angle A + 63°$

and $\angle A = 21°$

5. **D.** Using the probability formula

$$\text{probability} = \frac{\text{number of lucky chances}}{\text{total number of chances}}$$

The chance of choosing a weekday = 5 weekdays/7 total days = $\frac{5}{7}$.

6. **B.** Reynold's average score was 24.8, and Doe's average score was 13.7. Therefore, $24.8 - 13.7 = 11.1$.

7. **E.** If y is a positive integer, y could be 1. Choices **A, B, C,** and **D** are all evenly divisible by 1. Only choice **E**, $1\frac{1}{2}$, is not evenly divisible by 1.

8. **D.** A rectangular solid consists of six rectangular faces. This one in particular has two 7×6, two 6×3, and two 7×3 rectangles with areas of 42, 18, and 21, respectively. Therefore, the total surface area will be

$$2(42) + 2(18) + 2(21) = 84 + 36 + 42 = 162 \text{ square meters}$$

9. C. Distance = rate × time.

$$d = rt$$

$$k = rn$$

$$r = (^k/_n) \text{ miles per hour}$$

Therefore, $d = rt$

$$d = (^k/_n)(x) = {}^{kx}/_n$$

10. E. Because there are many different rectangles with a diagonal of 16, the lengths of the sides cannot be determined, and therefore the area of the rectangle cannot be determined.

Section 6: Verbal Reasoning

Critical Reading

1. **B.** Mike Nichols is the director of the film based on the novel *The Graduate,* by Charles Webb. The critic prefers Nichols's film to Webb's novel.

2. **B.** To "play down" is to minimize, to reduce the importance of. To exclude goes one step further.

3. **C.** The critic suggests that there are several limitations in the characterization of Ben Braddock in the novel; it is, in fact, its "main trouble." Since Nichols's film avoids or mitigates these faults, the film is better than the book. Though the phrase criticizes Webb's hero, it does not accuse Salinger's novel of being overgrown and outdated.

4. **D.** The word "bumptious" means arrogant, offensively conceited. It is not related to the word "bumpkin," which means yokel.

5. **D.** The critic says Ben's arriving at the wedding too late to prevent the final vows and then running away with the bride "shatters . . . a monogamous mythology" of an "entire genre of Hollywood movies."

6. **A.** *The Graduate,* according to Passage 1, is the story of a passage from a premature maturity to an innocence regained, an idealism reconfirmed, a passage made possible by love.

7. **C.** Although the author of the passage would probably agree with **A, B,** and **D,** the first paragraph is about why people go to movies that are talked about, even though they may expect them to be bad. They go not to see a good movie but to find out what everyone is talking about.

8. **A.** The critic in an unflattering remark about the taste of the mass audience says (lines 109 – 111) that Benjamin "has nothing to communicate, which is just what makes him an acceptable hero for the large movie audience." Brains, the passage implies, are not box-office.

9. **B.** Nichols's "gift" (which the critic puts in ironic quotation marks) is his talent, his singular ability.

10. **D.** The line is a denigration of the director. Nichols has no point of view of his own, the passage suggests; he anticipates just what an audience wants and gives that to them. His object is the "surefire response "and nothing more.

11. **A.** The last paragraph of Passage 2 finds sociological interest in the success of the film because it reveals that an educated generation is just as sentimental and self-satisfied as older generations who doted on romance in film.

12. **C.** Choices **A, B, D,** and **E** are essentially the same; they are complaining of moviegoers who identify too intensely with the heroes or heroines of film and see films only as emotional reflections of their own lives, not as works of art, or craft, or fiction. Choice **C** describes a critic who sees a film objectively, who does not became so emotionally involved that he cannot separate reality from cinema.

13. **E.** Both critics imply that Ben's parents are caricatures. The first refers to the "overdone caricatures that surround the three principals" (lines 63–64) and the second to the "middle-class comic strip" (lines 107–108). Both critics use the word "predatory" to describe the older woman (lines 29 and 121). Both see Ben as an exemplar of innocence (lines 59, 120, 141–142), although the first praises this aspect of the film, and the second regards it as trite.

Section 7: Mathematical Reasoning

Quantitative Comparison

1. **B.** $85\% = {}^{85}\!/_{100} = 0.85$ $\frac{7}{8} = 7 \div 8 = 0.875$

   Since 0.85 $<$ 0.875

   85% $<$ $\frac{7}{8}$

2. **A.** The area of a square is equal to the length of its side squared. The area of the given square is

   $$s^2 = 8^2 = 64$$

   The area of a rectangle is the product of its base times its height. The area of the given rectangle is

   $$bh = (9)(7) = 63$$

   Therefore, the area of the square is greater than the area of the rectangle.

3. **B.** $\dfrac{4+9}{12+18} = \dfrac{13}{30}$ $\dfrac{4}{12} + \dfrac{9}{18} = \dfrac{1}{3} + \dfrac{1}{2}$

   $$= \frac{2}{6} + \frac{3}{6}$$

   $$= \frac{5}{6} = \frac{25}{30}$$

   Hence, $\dfrac{13}{30}$ $<$ $\dfrac{25}{30}$

   And $\dfrac{4+9}{12+18}$ $<$ $\dfrac{4}{12} + \dfrac{9}{18}$

4. **D.** The relationship between the values of x and y cannot be determined without knowing what kind of number z is:

   If $z = 0$, then $x = y$.

   If $z > 0$, then $x > y$.

   If $z < 0$, then $x < y$.

5. **C.** Solve by factoring column A into $c\,(a + b) + (a + b)$. Using the distributive property gives $(c + 1)(a + b)$, which is the same as column B. Or substitute in numbers and you will notice that both columns consistently come out equal. Try $a = 0$, $b = 1$, $c = 2$:

   $0(2) + 1(2) + 0 + 1$ $(0 + 1)(2 + 1)$

   $2 + 1$ $1(3)$

   3 $=$ 3

6. **D.** Because the values of x and y are not known and no relationship exists between x and y, no comparison can be made.

7. B. The easiest method is by inspection (and/or addition). Column A is approaching 2 but will not get there. Mathematically, getting a common denominator and adding gives

$1 + \frac{1}{2} + \frac{1}{4} + \frac{1}{16} + \frac{1}{32} + \frac{1}{64}$ 2

$1 + \frac{32}{64} + \frac{16}{64} + \frac{4}{64} + \frac{2}{64} + \frac{1}{64}$

$1 + \frac{55}{64}$

$1\frac{55}{64}$ <   2

8. A. To find the number of ways four books can be arranged on a shelf, multiply $4 \times 3 \times 2 \times 1$, getting 24, which is greater than column B.

9. B. Substitute $x = 9$ and $y = 4$. (Note that these are square numbers and that they can make solving easier when you are dealing with square roots.)

$\sqrt{x} - \sqrt{y}$ $\sqrt{x-y}$

$\sqrt{9} - \sqrt{4}$ $\sqrt{9-4}$

$3 - 2$ $\sqrt{5}$

1   <   2.23

Now try $x = 16$ and $y = 1$.

$\sqrt{16} - \sqrt{1}$ $\sqrt{16-1}$

$4 - 1$ $\sqrt{15}$

3   <   3.87

Column B will always be greater.

10. B. $(p + q)^2 = p^2 + 2pq + q^2$

Since $p > 0$ and $q > 0$, $2pq > 0$, and

$p^2 + q^2$ < $p^2 + 2pq + q^2$

Hence, $p^2 + q^2$ < $(p + q)^2$

11. B. First, set up the numbers for each side:

Number of inches in one mile	Number of minutes in one year
(12" = 1 ft) × (5280 ft in 1 mi)	(60 min in 1 hr) × (24 hr in 1 day) × (365 days in 1 yr)
12 × 5280	60 × 24 × 365

Now, dividing out a 10 and 12 leaves

1 × 528	6 × 2 × 365
528	12 × 365

Column B is obviously greater.

12. **D.** You should substitute small numbers following the condition $a > b > c$. Let $a = 2$, $b = 1$, and $c = 0$. Then

$$(2) - (1) - 0 \qquad\qquad (2) + (1) - 0$$

$$1 \qquad\qquad < \qquad\qquad 3$$

Now try different values. Let $a = 1$, $b = 0$, and $c = -1$.

$$(1) - (0) - (-1) \qquad\qquad (1) + (0) - (-1)$$

$$2 \qquad\qquad = \qquad\qquad 2$$

Because different answers occur depending on the values chosen, the correct answer is **D.** You could have worked this problem by first eliminating a and $-c$ from each side and comparing b and $-b$ with different values.

13. **B.** In the given circle, CP = CQ because they are radii of the same circle. $\triangle$CPQ is an isosceles triangle, and $\angle P = \angle Q = 58°$. Because the sum of the measures of the angles of a triangle is $180°$:

$$\angle C + \angle P + \angle Q = 180°$$

$$\angle C + 58° + 58° = 180°$$

$$\angle C + 116° = 180°$$

$$\angle C = 64°$$

Because $\angle Q < \angle C$,

$$\text{CP} \qquad < \qquad \text{PQ}$$

14. **C.** Simplifying columns A and B gives

$$\sqrt{3^{18}} \qquad \left(\sqrt{27^3}\right)^2$$

$$27^3$$

$$(3 \cdot 3 \cdot 3)^3$$

$$3^9 \qquad = \qquad (3^3)^3$$

The correct answer is **C.**

15. B. By the Pythagorean theorem, the diagonal of a square with a side of length 10 is

$$x^2 = 10^2 + 10^2$$
$$x^2 = 100 + 100$$
$$x^2 = 200$$
$$x = \sqrt{200}$$
$$= 10\sqrt{2}$$
$$\cong 10(1.41)$$
$$\cong 14.1$$

$$y^2 = 9^2 + 12^2$$
$$y^2 = 81 + 144$$
$$y^2 = 225$$
$$y = \sqrt{225}$$
$$= 15$$

$$14.1 \quad < \quad 15$$

Therefore, the length of the diagonal of the square is less than the length of the diagonal of the rectangle.

Grid-In Questions

16. Answer: 66.2. Because $F = \frac{9}{5}C + 32$ and $C = 19$,

$$F = (\tfrac{9}{5}) \times (\tfrac{19}{1}) + 32$$

$$= (\tfrac{171}{5}) + 32$$

$$= 34.2 + 32$$

$$= 66.2$$

17. Answer: $\frac{1}{3}$. The total combination of red, green, and white jelly beans is made up of $5 + 4 + 3 = 12$ parts. Because the green jelly beans make up 4 parts of the total 12 parts, the portion of green jelly beans in the combination is $\frac{4}{12} = \frac{1}{3}$.

18. Answer: 143. Because the width of the frame is $1\frac{1}{2}$ inches, the dimensions of the rectangle containing both the frame and the picture are

width $= 8 + 1\frac{1}{2} + 1\frac{1}{2} = 11$ inches

length $= 10 + 1\frac{1}{2} + 1\frac{1}{2} = 13$ inches

The area of this rectangle is the product of its base times its height. So

$$\text{area} = bh = (11)(13) = 143 \text{ square inches}$$

19. Answer: 15. Numeration is 10%, and algebra is 30%, which means that there should be three times as many algebra problems. If there are 5 numeration problems, therefore, there should be

$$5 \times 3 = 15 \text{ algebra problems}$$

20. Answer: 45. $x + y = 180°$ (x plus y forms a straight line, or straight angle). Because $y = 3x$, substituting gives

$$3x + x = 180°$$
$$4x = 180°$$
$$x = 45°$$

21. Answer: $\frac{2}{5}$. Because 150% of y is equal to 60% of z,

$$\frac{150}{100} y = \frac{60}{100} z$$

Multiplying both sides of the equation by the LCD of 100 yields

$$100\left(\frac{150}{100} y\right) = 100\left(\frac{60}{100} z\right)$$
$$150y = 60z$$
$$\frac{150y}{150z} = \frac{60z}{150z}$$
$$\frac{y}{z} = \frac{60}{150}$$
$$\frac{y}{z} = \frac{2}{5}$$

22. Answer: $\frac{1}{8}$. Let n = whole circle. Three-fourths of the circle divided by 6 is

$$\frac{3}{4}n \div 6 = \frac{3}{4}n \cdot \frac{1}{6}$$
$$= \frac{3}{24}n$$
$$= \frac{1}{8}n$$

Therefore, each piece will be $\frac{1}{8}$ of the whole circle.

23. Answer: 57.1. There were 4 days (July 10, 11, 14, and 15) on which the maximum temperature exceeded the average. Therefore, $\frac{4}{7}$ is 57.1%.

24. Answer: 3.75. Let x = number of days to complete the job working together. The first person will complete $\frac{x}{6}$ part of the job in x days, and the other person will complete $\frac{x}{10}$ part of the job in x days. Because they complete the job in x days working together,

$$\frac{x}{6} + \frac{x}{10} = 1$$

Multiplying both sides of the equation by 30 yields

$$30\left(\frac{x}{6}+\frac{x}{10}\right)=(30)(1)$$
$$5x+3x=30$$
$$8x=30$$
$$x={}^{30}\!/_{8}$$
$$x=3\tfrac{3}{4}=3.75$$

Therefore, it will take the two people 3.75 days to complete the job working together.

25. Answer: $^6\!/_9$. Let x = numerator of original fraction and y = denominator of original fraction.

Therefore, $^x\!/_y = \frac{2}{3}$ and $x = \frac{2}{3}y$.

The new fraction is
$$\frac{x-2}{y+3}=\frac{1}{3}$$
Because $x = \frac{2}{3}y$,

$$3(x-2)=1\,(y+3)$$
$$3x-6=y+3$$
$$3(\tfrac{2}{3}y)-6=y+3$$
$$2y-6=y+3$$
$$y-6=3$$
$$y=9$$

Therefore, $x = \frac{2}{3}y = (\frac{2}{3})(9) = 6$

and the original fraction is $^x\!/_y = {}^6\!/_9$

The following charts are designed to give you only an approximate score range, not an exact score. When you take the actual SAT I, you will see questions similar to those in this book; however, some questions may be slightly easier or more difficult. Needless to say, this may affect your scoring range.

Because one section of the SAT I is experimental (it doesn't count toward your score), *for the purposes of this approximation, do not count Section 7.* Remember: On the actual test, the experimental section could appear anywhere on your test.

How to Approximate Your Score in Verbal Reasoning

1. Add the total number of correct responses for the three verbal sections. *Remember, for the purposes of this approximation, do not count Section 7.*

2. Add the total number of incorrect responses (only those attempted or marked in) for those sections.

3. The total number of incorrect responses for the verbal sections should be divided by 4, giving you an adjustment factor (round off to the nearest whole number, if necessary).

4. Subtract this adjustment factor from the total number of correct responses to obtain a raw score.

5. This raw score is then scaled to a range from 200 to 800.

   Example:

   If the total number of correct answers is 40 of a possible 78

   and 20 problems were attempted but missed,

   dividing 20 by 4 gives an adjustment factor of 5.

   Subtracting this adjustment factor of 5 from the original 40 correct gives a raw score of 35.

   This raw score is then scaled to a range from 200 to 800.

6. Use the following table to match your raw score for Verbal Reasoning and the corresponding approximate score range:

Raw Score	Approximate Score Range
75-78	720-800
61-74	580-720
46-60	480-580
31-45	390-480
16-30	290-390
0-15	200-290

Keep in mind that this is only an *approximate score range*.

How to Approximate Your Score in Mathematical Reasoning

1. Add the total number of correct responses for the three math sections. **Remember,** *for the purposes of this approximation, do not count Section 7.*

2. Add the total number of incorrect responses for the multiple-choice questions.

3. The total number of incorrect responses for these questions should be divided by 4, giving you an adjustment factor for multiple choice (round off to the nearest whole number).

4. Total the incorrect responses for the quantitative comparison questions and divide this total by 3, giving you an adjustment factor for quantitative comparison (round off to the nearest whole number).

5. Add the adjustment factors for multiple choice and quantitative comparison, giving you a single adjustment factor.

6. Subtract this adjustment factor from the total number of correct responses to obtain a raw score.

7. This raw score is then scaled to a range from 200 to 800.

   Example:

   If the total number of correct answers is 30 of a possible 60

   and 16 multiple-choice problems were attempted but missed,

   dividing 16 by 4 gives an adjustment factor of 4 for multiple choice.

   Now suppose that 6 quantitative comparison problems were attempted but missed.

   Dividing these 6 problems by 3 gives an adjustment factor of 2 for quantitative comparison.

Add the adjustment factors for multiple choice and quantitative comparison (4 + 2), giving you a single adjustment factor of 6.

Subtracting this adjustment factor of 6 from the original 30 correct gives a raw score of 24.

This raw score is then scaled to a range from 200 to 800.

Note: The reason for this unusual calculation is that ¼ point is deducted for each incorrect multiple-choice question and ⅓ point is deducted for each incorrect quantitative comparison question. No deduction is made for incorrect grid-in responses.

8. Use the following table to match your raw score for Mathematical Reasoning and the corresponding approximate score range:

Raw Score	*Approximate Score Range*
56-60	730-800
41-55	570-720
26-40	440-560
11-25	310-430
5-10	200-300

PART III

ABOUT THE PSAT/NMSQT

INTRODUCTION TO THE PSAT/NMSQT

Format of a Recent PSAT/NMSQT		
Section 1	**Verbal Reasoning**	**25 Questions**
25 Minutes	Sentence Completions	6 Questions
	Analogies	6 Questions
	Critical Reading	13 Questions
Section 2	**Mathematical Reasoning**	**20 Questions**
25 Minutes	Multiple Choice	20 Questions
Section 3	**Verbal Reasoning**	**27 Questions**
25 Minutes	Sentence Completions	10 Questions
	Analogies	6 Questions
	Critical Reading	11 Questions
Section 4	**Mathematical Reasoning**	**20 Questions**
25 Minutes	Quantitative Comparison	12 Questions
	Grid-ins	8 Questions
Section 5	**Writing Skills**	**39 Questions**
30 Minutes	Identifying Sentence Errors	19 Questions
	Improving Sentences	14 Questions
	Improving Paragraphs	6 Questions
Total Time 2 hours and 10 minutes		**Approximately 116 Questions**

Note: The order of the sections and the number of questions per section may vary.

General Description

The Preliminary Scholastic Assessment Test/National Merit Scholarship Qualifying Test (PSAT/NMSQT) is outstanding practice for taking the SAT I. By taking the PSAT/NMSQT, students also compete for national scholarships, get a good sense of their strengths and weaknesses in preparing for the SAT, and get mail from colleges. The PSAT/NMSQT is given in October and is usually taken by high school juniors. To get information about registering for this exam, contact your high school counselor.

The test lasts 2 hours and 10 minutes and consists of two verbal ability sections (containing sentence completions, analogies, and critical reading questions), two math ability sections (containing multiple-choice, quantitative comparisons, and grid-in questions) and one writing skills section (containing sentence-error identification, sentence improvement, and paragraph improvement).

The verbal sections test your ability to read critically, to understand word relationships, and to understand words in context.

The math sections test your mathematical reasoning ability by asking you to solve problems and word problems in arithmetic, algebra, and geometry.

The writing skills section tests your ability to use standard written English to find errors in usage and structure and to choose effective revisions in sentences and paragraphs.

The verbal, math, and writing questions each generate scores of 20 through 80. When you receive your score reports, you will get the three separate scores and two estimates of what your scores may have been on the SAT I: Reasoning Test (Verbal and Math) and SAT II: Writing Test.

The problems are slightly graduated in difficulty within each question type, except for critical reading, which is not in order of difficulty. You receive a penalty for incorrect answers, so don't guess unless you can eliminate at least one choice. On math grid-ins, you receive no penalty for guessing.

Additional information and sample problems are available on the Internet, at www.psat.org.

Verbal and Math Sections

The SAT I strategies, techniques, and sample problems given in the introductory sections of this guide also apply to the PSAT/NMSQT. The analogy, sentence completion, and critical reading approaches should be reviewed carefully as the basis for your verbal review (review pages 11–42). In the math sections, reviewing the approaches for SAT I multiple-choice math, quantitative comparisons, and grid-ins will be very helpful (review pages 48–96).

Writing Skills Section

The writing skills section is similar to the SAT II: Writing Test. This section is not included on the SAT I. Because this section is fairly new on the PSAT/NMSQT, the directions with a sample question and some strategies are included to help you become familiar with this question type.

Identifying Sentence Errors

Directions: The following sentences may contain one error of grammar, usage, diction, or idiom. No sentence contains more than one error, and some have no error. If the sentence does have an error, it is underlined and has a letter beneath it. Sections of the sentence that are not underlined cannot be changed. In selecting your answer, observe the requirements of standard written English.

If there is an error, choose the one underlined part that must be changed to correct the sentence. If there is no error, choose **E.**

Sample

1. The violinist and <u>her</u> <u>will audition</u> for the conductor <u>as soon as</u> they have
   A   B   C

   <u>completed</u> their studies. <u>No error</u>
   D   E

Answer: **A.** The subjects of the sentence are "the violinist" and "she." The "her" is an error.

Improving Sentences

Directions: The following questions test correctness and effective expression. In selecting the answer, pay attention to grammar, diction, sentence structure, and punctuation.

In the following questions, part or all of each sentence is underlined. The **A** *answer repeats the underlined portion of the original sentence, and the next four offer alternatives. Choose the answer that best expresses the meaning of the original sentence and at the same time is grammatically correct and stylistically superior. The correct choice should be clear, unambiguous, and concise.*

Sample

> **2.** In her performance, Eartha Kitt sang songs <u>in English, in French, and she sang in Arabic</u>.
>
> A. in English, in French, and she sang in Arabic.
>
> B. in English and French, and she also sang in Arabic.
>
> C. in English and French, singing also in Arabic.
>
> D. in English, French, and Arabic.
>
> E. in English, in French, and Arabic.

Answer: **D.** Answer choice **D** avoids a parallelism error with this series of three terms, and it is also the clearest and shortest version of the sentence.

Improving Paragraphs

Directions: Read the selection carefully and answer the questions that follow. These questions are about sentence structure, diction, and usage in individual sentences or parts of sentences. Other questions deal with the whole essay or paragraphs and ask you to decide about organization, development, and appropriate language. Choose the answer that follows the requirements of standard written English and most effectively expresses the intended meanings.

The following passage is an early draft of an essay. Some parts need to be revised.

After you have chosen your answer, fill in the corresponding space on your answer sheet.

(1) Is a man or a woman more likely to ask questions? (2) I think it depends on what the circumstances are and on who is around when a time to ask questions comes along. (3) In my family, my mother and I ask more questions than my brother or my father when all our family is together. (4) My father would never ask for directions when we're in the car, and this is when he is not sure of the way. (5) My mother would stop right away to ask, unless she was in an unsafe neighborhood.

(6) My brother tells me that he asks questions in school, and when he is at work after school, he doesn't. (7) It is because he thinks his boss will think he doesn't know his job. (8) He won't ask any questions at all. (9) At work he will ask questions only to his friend Eddie. (10) Based on the action of my brother and my father, men are more likely to not ask when they don't know something because they think it will hurt their image as able to do things well. (11) Women are more practical and will not drive around not knowing where you are.

> **3.** Which of the following is the best version of the underlined portion of sentence 2 (reproduced below)?
>
> I think it depends <u>on what the circumstances are and on who is around when a time to ask questions comes along.</u>
>
> **A.** (As it is now)
>
> **B.** on the circumstances
>
> **C.** on what the circumstances are and who is around at the time
>
> **D.** on the circumstances and who is around when a time to ask questions comes along
>
> **E.** on what the circumstances and the situation are for asking questions

Because the word "circumstances" really includes "who is around" or "situation," there is no need to say more than what is said in **B.** All the other choices are, by comparison, wordy.

Approaching the Writing Skills Section

The test has many question types. For example, some questions may ask about "the best way to revise and combine sentences" or "which phrase or sentences should be moved."

Here are a few strategies and hints for answering these question types:

- The most common grammatical errors in these exams are errors of agreement: For example, a plural subject with a singular verb (they . . . is) or a singular noun with a plural pronoun (Alice, she . . . their). Be especially careful when several words come between the two ("the *conductor* of the hundred-piece orchestra with a large chorus and three tenors . . . *is*," not *are*) despite all the plurals between the subject and the verb.

- Make sure that the elements of a sentence are consistent and logical. If a sentence begins with two similar phrases (I like to swim, to sail, and . . .) make sure that a third has the same form (to sail, and to lie on the beach, *not* and also *lying* on the beach). Keep the structures parallel after correlatives like *either . . . or, not only . . . but also, not . . . but.*

- If two versions of the same sentence have the same meaning and are grammatically correct, the shorter of the two is usually the better choice.

- If you cannot find a clear error in a sentence in the Identifying Sentence Errors section, do not hesitate to choose **E** (No error). In a test with 19 questions, you should expect 3 to 5 sentences that have no errors.

- If possible, choose the active voice *(I throw the ball)* over the passive *(The ball is thrown by me.)*

- Avoid wordy phrases. *(Say because,* not *due to the fact that.)*

- Listen carefully to be sure that the idioms of a sentence seem natural. Watch especially the choice of prepositions *(watch for,* not *watch to).*

Section 1: Verbal Reasoning

Time: 25 Minutes

25 Questions

(1–25)

Sentence Completions

Directions: In this section, choose the best answer for each question and blacken the corresponding space on the answer sheet.

Each blank in the following sentences indicates that something has been omitted. Consider the lettered words beneath the sentence and choose the word or set of words that best fits the whole sentence.

Example

> With a million more people than any other African nation, Nigeria is the most _____ country on the continent.
>
> A. impoverished
>
> B. successful
>
> C. populous
>
> D. developed
>
> E. militant
>
>

1. She preferred _____ objects to people, a bed or a chair to a man or a woman.

   A. sacred

   B. expensive

   C. inanimate

   D. impractical

   E. effete

GO ON TO THE NEXT PAGE

2. By equating dog owners who violate leash laws with smokers, the city hopes to persuade dog owners that it is inconsiderate, unhealthy, and even _____ to let dogs run free.

A. salubrious

B. shameful

C. ambiguous

D. edifying

E. mordant

3. For their patients who could not sleep, Victorian doctors commonly prescribed drugs made chiefly from opium with little or no concern for the _____ nature of these _____.

A. tonic . . . opiates

B. addictive . . . narcotics

C. perilous . . . placebos

D. soporific . . . remedies

E. somnolent . . . prescriptions

4. Though Europe has merged its currencies, there is no sign of _____ unity, since 11 different official languages are now used to operate the European Union.

A. linguistic

B. financial

C. commercial

D. political

E. religious

5. The _____ amounts of rain this winter have caused a record number of floods, and the losses are _____ by the increased number of homes built too close to the rivers.

A. minimal . . . increased

B. scant . . . maximized

C. massive . . . diminished

D. average . . . intensified

E. unprecedented . . . augmented

6. The designer's most _____ idea, one that shocked the visitors to the museum, was to _____ in a single small room famous Renaissance paintings and abstract 20th-century sculpture.

A. conventional . . . confine

B. unusual . . . exclude

C. conservative . . . combine

D. audacious . . . juxtapose

E. gauche . . . conceal

Analogies

Directions: In each of the following questions, you are given a related pair of words or phrases. Select the lettered pair that *best* expresses a relationship similar to that in the original pair of words.

Example:

HORSE : JOCKEY ::

A. pool : swimmer

B. race car : driver

C. pilot : helicopter

D. slope : skier

E. mountain : climber

---

7. HOSPITAL : SURGEON ::

A. airport : helicopter

B. bank : teller

C. garden : carnation

D. dishwasher : kitchen

E. skyscraper : elevator

8. MARATHON : RUNNER ::

A. vegetable : cauliflower

B. executive : corporation

C. lawyer : client

D. student : schoolboy

E. trial : juror

9. BRITTLE : SHATTER ::

A. tasty : eat

B. solid : separate

C. verdant : grow

D. porous : leak

E. ductile : swim

10. EMBARRASS : MORTIFY ::

A. inter : bury

B. please : delight

C. defer : delay

D. block : stymie

E. plagiarize : borrow

11. CHEF : COOK ::

A. newspaper : advertise

B. idol : worship

C. idler : dawdle

D. miser : spend

E. puppet : handle

12. SOLITARY : HERMIT ::

A. judicious : lawyer

B. eloquent : candidate

C. aged : grandparent

D. intrepid : daredevil

E. quixotic : explorer

GO ON TO THE NEXT PAGE

Critical Reading

Directions: Questions follow the passage below. Using only the stated or implied information in the passage and in its introduction, if any, answer the questions.

Questions 13–18 are based on the following passage:

In the early 1980s, as scientists were perfecting techniques for splicing foreign genes into bacteria, some investigators began suggesting ways to use the technology
(5) to benefit the environment. For instance, they proposed that genetically engineered bacteria might be deployed for such tasks as cleaning oil spills or protecting crops from predation and disease. But the enter-
(10) prise, known as *environmental biotechnology,* soon came under fire.

Then, as now, the proposals elicited concern that the altered microbes might run amok or that their genes would hop unpre-
(15) dictably to other organisms — a phenomenon termed "horizontal" gene transfer (to distinguish it from the "vertical" transfer occurring between a parent and its offspring). Such activities, it was feared, might
(20) somehow irreparably harm the environment, animals, or people. Some observers even issued dire warnings that the unnatural organisms would destroy the earth. No longer were tabloids worried about attacks
(25) by "killer tomatoes" from outer space; now the danger was homegrown — genetically altered microorganisms that would eat the environment.

Unfortunately, at the time, biologists had
(30) little solid information on which to base responses. They knew almost nothing about the fate of genetically engineered microbes in nature and about the propensity of innate or introduced bacterial genes to migrate to
(35) new hosts. That paucity of data is now being remedied, thanks to unprecedented cooperation between genetic researchers and microbial ecologists, who study microorganisms in their normal habitats.

(40) Today at least two strains of genetically engineered bacteria have gained approval (for agricultural use) by the U.S. Environmental Protection Agency, and dozens of field trials have been conducted. Those trials and
(45) more general investigations of gene transfer between bacteria in their natural habitats indicate that genetically manipulated bacteria themselves are unlikely to proliferate out of control. They tend to be fragile and to die
(50) out relatively quickly instead of persisting indefinitely; for that reason, their genes probably do not have much opportunity to spread.

Yet under certain circumstances, the genes
(55) can potentially find their way into other bacteria or even into other types of organisms. A key to the safe release of the microbes, then, is to identify the conditions that will encourage or deter specific bacte-
(60) ria from transferring their genes to other organisms. With such information in hand, biologists can select bacteria that will be least likely to exchange genes with organisms in the particular site being "treated."
(65) As an example, for release into a lake, biotechnologists might be able to choose a bacterial species that does not readily exchange its genes in water.

13. The author's purpose in this passage is to

   A. advise a moratorium on research in the field of environmental biotechnology.

   B. show that fears of gene swapping are groundless and that critics have reacted hysterically.

   C. explain the difference between "horizontal" and "vertical" gene swapping.

   D. show that research indicates that genetically altered bacteria may be safely used in nature under certain conditions.

   E. describe the types of research being conducted in the field of environmental technology.

14. According to the passage, critics of environmental biotechnology have been most concerned that introducing altered microbes into the environment will

   A. lead to uncontrolled gene transfer.

   B. interfere with normal vertical transfer.

   C. create new species.

   D. eliminate endangered species.

   E. transfer human disease to other animals.

15. In line 33, "propensity" most nearly means

   A. propriety.

   B. inclination.

   C. desire.

   D. ability.

   E. reliability.

16. Which of the following is the most promising safeguard against proliferation of altered bacteria in the environment?

   A. the reluctance of the U.S. Environmental Protection Agency to approve their use

   B. the tendency of altered bacteria to be short-lived

   C. the ability of normal micro-organisms to resist gene transfer

   D. the exclusive use of bacterial species that don't exchange genes in water

   E. the greater strength of "vertical" gene transfer

17. According to the passage, genetically manipulated bacteria might be useful in preserving the environment by

   A. attacking plant diseases.

   B. altering unstable ecosystems.

   C. preventing oil spills.

   D. eliminating the weakest members of a species.

   E. producing larger fruits and vegetables.

18. The author of the passage implies all of the following EXCEPT

   A. People often react fearfully to new technologies.

   B. The possible benefits of using manipulated bacteria for ecological purposes are not worth the risks.

   C. Research is needed to identify conditions that will discourage gene transfer in various environments.

   D. Genetic researchers have been willing to participate in finding safe applications for their research.

   E. The fragility of genetically manipulated bacteria reduces the possibility of their spreading unpredictably to other organisms.

GO ON TO THE NEXT PAGE

Directions: Questions follow the two passages below. Using only the stated or implied information in each passage and in its introduction, if any, answer the questions.

Questions 19–25 are based on the following passages.

The following passages concern women in science, the first in the 19th century, the second in the latter half of the 20th century.

The first passage follows a description of the lack of opportunities for African Americans in science during the 19th century.

Passage 1

Less oppressive, but in some ways analogous, was the lot of American women. As in the case of whites over blacks, men rationalized the denial of opportunity by
(5) stereotyping the victims as inherently unfit for it. God and nature made women to raise families and adorn society (or "man" the factories), most men liked to believe. Intellectual pursuits were manifestly out-
(10) side women's sphere. For a woman to aspire to serious scientific work was deemed especially grotesque, unseemly, hopeless, and impermissible.

Yet there were rents in the crinoline[1] cur-
(15) tain. Mothers, after all, raised sons, who might benefit from a home atmosphere of polite learning and informed reverence for God's work in nature. So no outcry arose when, in the second quarter of the nine-
(20) teenth century, genteel girls and women took up science as a polite study rather than as preparation for a career. Female academies and seminaries, like their male counterparts in those years, added a variety of
(25) science courses and even invested in expensive telescopes, physical and chemical apparatus, and natural history collections. Many sought to equal the quality of courses

at men's schools, though no women's
(30) school achieved a full range of college-level science courses until 1865. A few such schools could draw on nearby male professional scientists of some eminence for occasional lectures.

(35) Science reached women outside the classroom also. Many women attended the public lectures on science that were especially popular in the 1830s and 1840s. Both men and women wrote popular books and maga-
(40) zine articles on science for the growing women's market. Women wrote ten such books on botany alone from 1819–1859. From the late 1820s to the early 1870s, Mrs. Almira Phelps sold more than a quar-
(45) ter-million copies of her *Familiar Lectures on Botany,* the most popular of her books on science for children, drawing mostly on a few serious books by others. Several women, notwithstanding stereotypes, liked
(50) insects well enough to write popular yet knowledgeable articles on entomology.

[1] A woman's petticoat made from a stiff fabric.

Passage 2

Science has a vested interest in the idea of the intellectual meritocracy. It is important to scientists to believe that they act ratio-
(55) nally, that they do not distort or ignore evidence, that neither their work nor their profession is seriously influenced by politics, ambition, or prejudice.

Such, clearly, cannot be the case. Scientists,
(60) like all other people, make decisions on the basis of a shared social reality, are pulled about by convictions rooted in emotional prejudice, act on inherited ideas of what is

natural, and are certainly influenced by poli-
(65) tics, ambition, and issues of class, sex, and
race. But, as they have a strong need to
believe they are guided by intellectual objec-
tivity, they have a more difficult time than
other kinds of workers do in perceiving
(70) themselves as discriminatory.

Thus, the atmosphere in which women in
science have been held back, put off, discouraged and demoralized, and frozen in position is particularly disturbing because of its
(75) defensive denial that what is happening is
happening. In business, a woman looks into
the eyes of a corporation executive who says
openly to her, "We know what you're all
about, we've held you off as long as we
(80) could, and now you'll have to take us to
court to get what you want." In science, a
woman looks into the eyes of a man who
thinks of himself as decent, fair-minded,
above all reasonable, and who says to her, "I
(85) really don't know what you're talking about.
Surely you're not saying we've discrimi-
nated against you."

Although one knows that life for women in
science will not be the same in the next 40
(90) years as it has been in the last, right now the
statistics on women in science bears out the
claim that they are half in, half out. Yes,
there is change and growth recorded in the
statistics, but that growth in real numbers is
(95) small and painfully disproportionate.
Between 1978 and 1980, employment of
women in science and engineering increased
over five times faster than employment of
men. Despite this growth, women repre-
(100) sented about 13 percent of all employed scientists and engineers, and in real numbers
the total employment for men in scientific
and engineering fields was computed at
2,245,300 while for women it was 314,800.
The statistical picture for women in science
is graphic and sobering.

19. In line 14, "rents" most nearly means

A. holes.

B. payments.

C. disputes.

D. exceptions.

E. fissures.

20. According to the author of Passage 1, women became involved in science initially because

A. their husbands and fathers wanted them to improve their minds.

B. they wanted to give deeper meaning to their lives.

C. they wanted to help provide an atmosphere of learning at home.

D. they sensed future career possibilities in an increasingly important field.

E. the prejudice against their participation in scientific research was rapidly decreasing.

21. In Passage 2, line 53, "intellectual meritocracy" most nearly means

A. government managed by intellectuals.

B. a system without discrimination.

C. a system based on intellectual achievement and ability.

D. government by the best people available.

E. a system that is open to change and improvement.

GO ON TO THE NEXT PAGE

22. According to the author of Passage 2, science is

    A. a good field for women because of opportunities to advance.

    B. dominated by men who stereotype women as too emotional to be objective.

    C. less rewarding than business because of the attitudes toward women.

    D. influenced by the society's prejudices and convictions.

    E. guided by men whose primary concern is maintaining the status quo.

23. What would be the likely response by the author of Passage 2 to the information presented in Passage 1?

    A. Prejudice against women in science has in fact grown stronger in the past 100 years.

    B. Because of their achievements, women have overcome most of the prejudice against them.

    C. Attitudes similar to those in the 19th century continue to influence behavior, even in a field that is supposed to be immune from prejudices.

    D. Women have made progress in science, but only because of changes in discrimination laws.

    E. The negative attitude toward women scientists today is very different from the negative attitude described in Passage 1.

24. Which of the following best describes the difference between Passage 1 and Passage 2?

    A. In Passage 1, women are described as enjoying their social roles, whereas in Passage 2 they are shown to be angry and rebellious.

    B. The women described in Passage 1 are anti-intellectual, whereas the women described in Passage 2 are serious and determined.

    C. The author of Passage 1 presents facts with no opinions, and the author of Passage 2 presents opinions with no facts.

    D. Passage 1 presents an optimistic view of the future, and Passage 2 presents a pessimistic view.

    E. The author of Passage 1 presents his subject historically, whereas the author of Passage 2 is arguing a position.

25. Passage 2 is more concerned than Passage 1 with

    A. the social stereotyping of women.

    B. male scientists' denial that female scientists are the objects of discrimination.

    C. salary differences between men and women scientists.

    D. the types of scientific work that women must perform because of discrimination.

    E. the difficulties of women scientists torn between their profession and their families.

IF YOU FINISH BEFORE TIME IS CALLED, CHECK YOUR WORK ON THIS SECTION ONLY. DO NOT WORK ON ANY OTHER SECTION IN THE TEST.

Section 2: Mathematical Reasoning

Time: 25 Minutes

20 Questions

(1–20)

Multiple Choice

Directions: Solve each problem in this section by using the information given and your own mathematical calculations, insights, and problem-solving skills. Then select the one correct answer of the five choices given and mark the corresponding circle on your answer sheet. Use the available space on the page for your scratch work.

Notes

1. All numbers used are real numbers.

2. Calculators may be used.

3. Some problems may be accompanied by figures or diagrams. These figures are drawn as accurately as possible EXCEPT when it is stated in a specific problem that a figure is not drawn to scale. The figures and diagrams are meant to provide information useful in solving the problem or problems. Unless otherwise stated, all figures and diagrams lie in a plane.

Data That Can Be Used for Reference

Area

rectangle $A = lw$

triangle $A = \frac{1}{2}bh$

circle $A = \pi r^2$ $C = 2\pi r$

Volume

rectangular solid $V = lwh$

right circular cylinder $V = \pi r^2 h$

Pythagorean Relationship

$a^2 + b^2 = c^2$

Special Triangles

30° – 60° – 90°

45° – 45° – 90°

A circle is composed of 360°

A straight angle measures 180°

The sum of the angles of a triangle is 180°

GO ON TO THE NEXT PAGE

1. What is 864,925 rounded to the nearest thousand?

   A. 865,925

   B. 860,000

   C. 865,000

   D. 864,900

   E. 864,000

2. If $x = 2$, then $3x^2 + (3x)^2 =$

   A. 24

   B. 30

   C. 36

   D. 48

   E. 72

3. If $(a + b) = -3$, then $(a + b)^3 =$

   A. −27

   B. −9

   C. −6

   D. 9

   E. 27

4. If the product of six integers is negative, then at most how many of the six integers could be negative?

   A. six

   B. five

   C. four

   D. three

   E. two

5. If the sum of three consecutive integers is 141, what is the largest of the three integers?

   A. 45

   B. 46

   C. 47

   D. 48

   E. 49

6. If $z/3 = 25$, then $5z =$

   A. 375

   B. 360

   C. 125

   D. 80

   E. 75

7. If $m^4 + n^4 = 0$, what is the value of $9m - 5n$?

   A. 9

   B. 5

   C. 4

   D. 0

   E. −1

8. If Marcos travels at an average speed of 55 miles per hour, how many hours would it take for him to travel d miles?

   A. $55d$

   B. $d/55$

   C. $55/d$

   D. $d + 55$

   E. $d - 55$

9. If $a + 5 = 3b$ and $a = 4b - 11$, what is the value of b?

    A.   13

    B.   6

    C.   −2

    D. −6

    E. −13

10. If the volume of a cube is 64, what is the area of one face of the cube?

    A. 96

    B. 64

    C. 32

    D. 16

    E.   8

Note: Figure not drawn to scale.

11. In the figure above, if $n = 50$, what is the value of m?

    A.   40

    B.   50

    C.   90

    D. 100

    E. 140

12. If x is an integer and $3x + 11$ is even, which of the following must be even?

    A. x

    B. $x + 1$

    C. x^2

    D. $2x + 1$

    E. x^3

13. If a rectangular box with dimensions z, $\frac{z}{2}$, and y has a volume of 12, what must y equal?

    A. 12

    B.   6

    C.   4

    D.   3

    E.   2

14. What is the value of the ratio of x to y if $xy = 21$?

    A. 21 to 1

    B. 7 to 3

    C. 3 to 7

    D. 1 to 21

    E. It cannot be determined from the information given.

GO ON TO THE NEXT PAGE

15. If the diameter of a circle P is 40 percent of the diameter of circle Q, then the area of circle P is what percentage of the area of circle $Q?$

   A. 16

   B. 20

   C. 40

   D. 80

   E. It cannot be determined from the information given.

16. If $x^5 = 9$ and $x^6 = y/11$, which of the following is an expression for x in terms of y?

   A. $^{9}y/_{11}$

   B. $^{11}y/_9$

   C. $y/_{99}$

   D. $^{99}/_y$

   E. $99y$

17. For how many integer values of x will the value of the expression $3x - 4$ be an integer greater than 4 and less than 250?

   A. 86

   B. 85

   C. 84

   D. 83

   E. 82

Note: Figure not drawn to scale.

18. In the figure above, if the area of $\triangle OXY$ equals the area of $\triangle WYZ$, which of the following are the coordinates of $W?$

   A. $(4, 4)$

   B. $(4, 5)$

   C. $(4, 6)$

   D. $(4, 8)$

   E. $(4, 10)$

19. Tickets numbered from 1 through 50 are placed in a container, and one ticket will be selected at random. What is the probability that the ticket selected will have a number on it divisible by 3?

   A. $^{3}/_{50}$

   B. $^{1}/_5$

   C. $^{3}/_{10}$

   D. $^{8}/_{25}$

   E. $^{1}/_3$

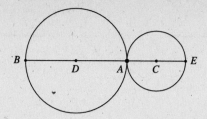

20. In the figure above, C and D are the centers of the two circles, and AD = AE. If the area of the smaller circle is 100π, what is the area of the larger circle?

A. 1600π

B. 800π

C. 400π

D. 200π

E. 100π

IF YOU FINISH BEFORE TIME IS CALLED, CHECK YOUR WORK ON THIS SECTION ONLY. DO NOT WORK ON ANY OTHER SECTION IN THE TEST.

Section 3: Verbal Reasoning

Time: 25 Minutes

25 Questions

(26–52)

Sentence Completion

Directions: In this section, choose the best answer for each question and blacken the corresponding space on the answer sheet.

Each blank in the following sentences indicates that something has been omitted. Consider the lettered words beneath the sentence and choose the word or set of words that best fits the whole sentence.

Example

With a million more people than any other African nation, Nigeria is the most _____ country on the continent.

A. impoverished

B. successful

C. populous

D. developed

E. militant

26. A kind and very modest philanthropist, Merrill donates money generously and _____ to many worthy causes.

A. cynically

B. commercially

C. blatantly

D. parsimoniously

E. unobtrusively

27. The farmers believed that their crop failures were caused by the influx of Easterners, so they steadfastly _____ the sale of land to the newcomers.

A. infringed

B. commuted

C. intensified

D. discouraged

E. exacted

28. Although most of the avalanches in Colorado occur in _____ mountain regions and pose no threat to human lives or property, the population _____ in some mountain counties has greatly increased the danger.

   A. obscure . . . decline

   B. populated . . . increase

   C. remote . . . explosion

   D. uninhabited . . . vacuum

   E. steep . . . deficiency

29. For almost a century, Maryland and Pennsylvania quarreled about their border, and even fought several small _____ about it.

   A. skirmishes

   B. dissents

   C. protests

   D. contractions

   E. invasions

30. The retiring judge's office shelves were filled with _____ of his years on the bench, including a _____ of the famous espionage trial over which he presided.

   A. exigencies . . . disclosure

   B. verdicts . . . daguerreotype

   C. legacies . . . archetype

   D. memorabilia . . . memento

   E. souvenirs . . . commentary

31. Edgar Lee Masters used to walk through cemeteries reading the _____ on the gravestones to find ideas for his poems.

   A. epithets

   B. illuminations

   C. epigrams

   D. illustrations

   E. epitaphs

32. Advances in the film industry depend on _____ developments in such fields as photography, projection, processing, recording, and sound reproduction.

   A. pictorial

   B. technological

   C. cinematic

   D. artistic

   E. financial

33. If a millionaire lives quietly and thriftily, he is called a miser, but if he spends his money freely, he is criticized for being _____ and _____.

   A. vulgar . . . penny-pinching

   B. extravagant . . . ostentatious

   C. self-centered . . . modest

   D. mean-spirited . . . selfish

   E. parsimonious . . . pretentious

34. Against the horrors of the Machine Age, Ruskin _____ a vision of the Middle Ages, the era of the independent artisan.

   A. championed

   B. denigrated

   C. excluded

   D. queried

   E. rejected

Section **3** Verbal Reasoning

GO ON TO THE NEXT PAGE

35. DNA samples now make positive identifications easy, so future wars will probably no longer produce _____
remains, and the traditional unknown
soldier will become _____.

   A. human . . . sacred

   B. unburied . . . commonplace

   C. unidentifiable . . . obsolete

   D. interred . . . revered

   E. incinerated . . . antiquated

Analogies

Directions: In each of the following questions, you are given a related pair of words or phrases. Select the lettered pair that *best* expresses a relationship similar to that in the original pair of words.

Example

HORSE : JOCKEY ::

   A. pool : swimmer

   B. race car : driver

   C. pilot : helicopter

   D. slope : skier

   E. mountain : climber

Ⓐ ● Ⓒ Ⓓ Ⓔ

36. PARASITE : HOST ::

   A. flea : dog

   B. tenant : landlord

   C. nest : tree

   D. moat : castle

   E. patron : event

37. SOFA : FURNITURE ::

   A. music : sculpture

   B. jewelry : bracelet

   C. pepper : condiment

   D. prisoner : jail

   E. poem : sonnet

38. CIRCUS : CLOWN ::

    A. concert hall : soloist

    B. zoo : veterinarian

    C. fish : aquarium

    D. shoe : foot

    E. museum : artist

39. ARCTIC : PALM ::

    A. mountain : snow

    B. ocean : wave

    C. jungle : jaguar

    D. atoll : lagoon

    E. rain forest : cactus

40. GRADUATE : MEASURING ::

    A. flour : sifting

    B. cash : charging

    C. window box : watering

    D. scythe : ploughing

    E. wedge : splitting

41. LIBERAL : REACTIONARY ::

    A. incidental : casual

    B. reticent : outspoken

    C. juicy : succulent

    D. deformed : monstrous

    E. aristocratic : royal

Critical Reading

Directions: Questions follow the passage below. Using only the stated or implied information in each passage and in its introduction, if any, answer the questions.

Questions 42-52 are based on the following passage.

Between 1840 and 1924, when the laws restricting Asian immigration were enacted, thousands of Chinese, Japanese, and Koreans migrated to the United States and
(5) Hawaii. In each case, immigration was prompted by active recruitment of labor for plantation, railroad, mining, or field work. And in each case, anti-Asian sentiment resulted ultimately in the passage of exclusion
(10) laws. Filipinos were permitted to immigrate until 1934, when they too were barred by law from further entry.

The relatively small Asian population consisted largely of laborers without the
(15) means or, in some cases, the inclination to return to their homelands. Partly because their time was consumed in struggles for a livelihood, the Asian point of view on the immigrant experience is rarely presented
(20) in writings in English or even in Asian languages. Some unknown immigrants carved poems in Chinese into the walls of the barracks on Angel Island, where they were held before being allowed to enter
(25) the United States between 1910 and 1940. Autobiographical information about a Japanese house servant and a Chinatown merchant was collected by Hamilton Holt, editor of *The Life Stories of Undistinguished*
(30) *Americans* (1906). And Carlos Bulosan, a self-taught Filipino farm worker, was able only because of the mandatory rest required by his tuberculosis to write his account of the life of the Filipino migrants in the
(35) American West immediately prior to the Depression. But with these exceptions, Asian immigrant workers vanished without leaving behind much written account of their individual lives in America. Although
(40) some letters and diaries written in Asian languages have survived earthquake, fire, and Japanese relocation, the general privation and loneliness of Asian immigrant life, sequestered as it was in field labor camps
(45) or urban ethnic enclaves, must have damp

GO ON TO THE NEXT PAGE

Section **3** Verbal Reasoning

ened the desire to communicate. In the face of pervasive American ignorance and antipathy toward Asians, an Asian writer could hardly know where to begin and (50) what audience to address. Moreover, since they were segregated from the mainstream of American social and economic life and prevented by law from becoming naturalized American citizens with voting and (55) civil rights, many early immigrants did not learn English and did not consider the culture it represented as something that belonged to them or to which they could contribute.

(60) Then, too, autobiographical writing and popular fiction were not in the tradition of the Asian cultures that produced the first immigrants. Even in the Philippines, where the American curricula and educational (65) system had been instituted after the Spanish-American War, the majority of peasants had not the privilege of schooling, and most of the Filipino immigrants were illiterate. In fact, labor recruiters, in search (70) of a docile labor force, preferred those who had little formal education. In China and Korea, writing and literature were the domain of the literati, who traditionally confined themselves to poetry and the (75) classical essay. Autobiography as such was virtually unknown, since for a scholar to write a book about himself would have been deemed egotistical in the extreme. Fiction was considered frivolous. Farmers (80) and peasants performed as storytellers, dramatic dancers, and singers, but rarely expressed themselves through the written word. And certainly they did not write autobiographies.

(85) Quite understandably, then, the earliest Asian-American writers were not representative of the general population of Asian Americans. Foreign students, scholars, and diplomats, who were, together with mer- (90) chants, exempted from the Asian exclusion

laws and who generally received better treatment in America than did Asian laboring people, comprise a disproportionately large part of the early Asian-American lit- (95) erary voice. Their writing is characterized by efforts to bridge the gap between East and West and plead for tolerance by making usually highly euphemistic observations about the West on one hand while (100) explaining Asia in idealized terms on the other. Since many of these early Asian writers in English felt that they themselves understood two points of view and, in some cases, two epochs — to them the (105) West stood for modernity and the East for tradition — they viewed themselves as straddling two worlds. Since they found that elements from two vastly different cultures could be combined within them- (110) selves, they concluded that there could be points of compatibility between other people of the two cultures. They saw themselves as ambassadors of goodwill to the West. Most of them, however, did not be- (115) lieve that social class distinctions could be bridged. Their writing is marked by dissociation from the Asian common people, whether in Asia or in the West, and even their pleas for racial tolerance are made (120) primarily on behalf of members of their own privileged class. They tended to accept discrimination against the poor and uneducated members of their own race as reasonable, questioning instead the logic of (125) discrimination against the educated elite.

42. This passage is primarily concerned with

A. anti-Asian sentiments in the United States in the late 19th and early 20th centuries.

B. the poor living conditions of early Asian immigrant laborers.

C. illiteracy among early Asian immigrants.

D. the reasons that early Asian immigrants left little record of their experiences.

E. the relationship between Asian laborers and educated Asian Americans.

43. The Asian exclusion laws mentioned in the first paragraph

A. barred the immigration of all Asians except Filipinos.

B. prohibited Asian immigrants from voting.

C. allowed only certain Asians to immigrate to the United States.

D. were enacted because Asian immigrants were taking jobs from U.S. citizens.

E. were responsible for discouraging Asian-American workers from writing about their experiences.

44. "Privation" in line 42–43 most nearly means

A. lack of comforts and necessities.

B. lack of educational opportunity.

C. inhumane treatment.

D. lack of privacy.

E. sterility.

45. All the following inferences can be drawn from the passage EXCEPT

A. many immigrant laborers were not taught English.

B. most Americans were not interested in reading about the immigrant laborers' experiences.

C. Asian laborers did not mix freely with American citizens.

D. Asian culture did not encourage the writing of novels and short stories.

E. Asian laborers were hostile to the United States and longed to return to their homelands.

46. The author cites *The Life Stories of Undistinguished Americans* because it

A. shows Asian laborers' low self-esteem.

B. includes information about two Asian-American workers.

C. includes the only existing writing by early Asian immigrants.

D. was edited by an American rather than an Asian.

E. sympathetically portrays the plight of the Asian immigrants.

47. According to the passage, one of the reasons so many of the early Asian immigrant laborers were uneducated was that

A. educated Asians disdained American culture and traditions and weren't interested in coming to America.

B. labor recruiters found it easy to dupe uneducated Asians with false promises.

C. formal education was considered unnecessary in most Asian countries.

D. labor recruiters thought uneducated workers would be less likely to cause trouble.

E. illiterate Asians agreed to come to the United States because they knew they would have more opportunities for an education than in their own countries.

GO ON TO THE NEXT PAGE

Section **3** Verbal Reasoning

48. "Enclaves" as it is used in line 45 most nearly means

    A. slums.

    B. ghettos.

    C. restricted areas.

    D. labor camps.

    E. tenements.

49. From the last paragraph of the passage, the reader can infer that early Asian-American writers who were educated

    A. were eager to be accepted in their new country.

    B. wrote works of no literary value.

    C. wrote works that were accepted readily by the American audience.

    D. portrayed their native countries more realistically than they portrayed America.

    E. wrote only autobiographies and other nonfictional works.

50. According to the author, educated Asian immigrants

    A. preferred the customs of America to the traditions of their homelands.

    B. urged American readers to be tolerant and understanding of the plight of immigrants.

    C. believed that in America, social class distinctions should disappear.

    D. felt that their education should exempt them from discrimination by Americans.

    E. adopted English as their written language as a sign of their commitment to America.

51. "Highly euphemistic observations" in line 98 most nearly means

    A. untruthful comments.

    B. observations in language designed to be inoffensive.

    C. seemingly profound statements that in fact contain little meaning.

    D. flowery, redundant compliments.

    E. observations designed to provoke intelligent discussions about the blending of two cultures.

52. Most of the early Asian-American writing that exists

    A. is not representative of the majority of early Asian immigrants.

    B. was written to protest racial discrimination.

    C. was intended for educated Asian audiences.

    D. is of no literary value or importance.

    E. was collected, edited, and published by American citizens.

IF YOU FINISH BEFORE TIME IS CALLED, CHECK YOUR WORK ON THIS SECTION ONLY. DO NOT WORK ON ANY OTHER SECTION IN THE TEST.

Section 4: Mathematical Reasoning

Time: 25 Minutes

20 Questions

(21–40)

Directions: This section is composed of two types of questions. Use the 25 minutes allotted to answer both question types. Your scratch work should be done on any available space in the section.

Notes

1. All numbers used are real numbers.

2. Calculators may be used.

3. Some problems may be accompanied by figures or diagrams. These figures are drawn as accurately as possible EXCEPT when it is stated in a specific problem that a figure is not drawn to scale. The figures and diagrams are meant to provide information useful in solving the problem or problems. Unless otherwise stated, all figures and diagrams lie in a plane.

Data That Can Be Used for Reference

Area

rectangle
$A = lw$

triangle
$A = \frac{1}{2}bh$

circle
$A = \pi r^2$
$C = 2\pi r$

Volume

rectangular solid
$V = lwh$

right circular cylinder
$V = \pi r^2 h$

Pythagorean Relationship

$a^2 + b^2 = c^2$

Special Triangles

$30° - 60° - 90°$

$45° - 45° - 90°$

A circle is composed of 360°
A straight angle measures 180°
The sum of the angles of a triangle is 180°

GO ON TO THE NEXT PAGE

Quantitative Comparison

Directions: In this section, you are given two quantities, one in column A and one in column B. You are to determine a relationship between the two quantities and mark

- **A.** if the quantity in column A is greater than the quantity in column B.
- **B.** if the quantity in column B is greater than the quantity in column A.
- **C.** if the quantities are equal.
- **D.** if the comparison cannot be determined from the information that is given.

AN **E** RESPONSE WILL NOT BE SCORED.

Notes

1. Sometimes, information concerning one or both of the quantities to be compared is given. This information is not boxed and is centered above the two columns.

2. All numbers used are real numbers. Letters such as a, b, m, and x represent real numbers.

3. In a given question, if the same symbol is used in column A and column B, that symbol stands for the same value in each column.

EXAMPLES		Answers
Column A	**Column B**	
E1 15	2^4	Ⓐ ● Ⓒ Ⓓ
E2 $x° \diagup\diagdown y°$ $x + y$	$90°$	Ⓐ Ⓑ ● Ⓓ
E3 $r \cdot s = 0$ r	s	Ⓐ Ⓑ Ⓒ ●

Column A	Column B

21. $1 - \frac{1}{30}$ | $\frac{9}{10} + \frac{1}{30}$

22. Gina's average speed, in miles per hour, if she jogged 15 miles in 3 hours | Lisa's average speed, in miles per hour, if she jogged 10 miles in 2 hours

The average (arithmetic mean) of r, s, and t is 87.

23. $r + s + t$ | 260

m and n are positive integers.

24. 3^m | 10^n

a, b, c, and d are four different negative integers.

25. $a + b + c + d$ | $abcd$

The lengths of the sides of a triangle are 10, 11, and l.

26. 21 | ℓ

Circle with center P

27. Length of $\overline{AB}$ | Length of $\overline{XY}$

Column A	Column B

28. x | y

$x + y < 0$

29. xy | 0

$a + 6 = b$
$a + b = 13$

30. $2a + 6$ | 13

$15 - x < 2$
$2y < 24$

31. x | y

M is the midpoint of $\overline{BC}$

32. The area of $\triangle ABM$ | The area of $\triangle AMC$

GO ON TO THE NEXT PAGE

Grid-In Questions

Directions: Questions 33–40 require you to solve the problem and enter your answer by carefully marking the circles on the special grid. Examples of the appropriate way to mark the grid follow.

Decimal point   Fraction bar

Answer: 1½

Do not grid in mixed numbers in the form of mixed numbers. *Always* change mixed number to improper fractions or decimals.

Change to 1.5   or   Change to ³⁄₂

Answer: ⁸⁄₉

Accuracy of decimals: Always enter the most accurate decimal value that the grid will accommodate. For example: An answer such as .8888 . . . can be gridded as .888 or .889. Gridding this value as .8, .88, or .89 is considered inaccurate and therefore *not acceptable*. The acceptable grid-ins of ⁸⁄₉ are

Be sure to write your answers in the boxes at the top of the circles before doing your gridding. Although writing out the answers above the columns is not required, it is very important to ensure accuracy. Even though some problems may have more than one correct answer, grid only *one answer*. Grid-in questions contain no negative answers.

Answer: 123

Space permitting, answers may start in any column. Each of the following grid-in answers is correct.

Note: Circles must be filled in correctly to receive credit. Mark only one circle in each column. No credit will be given if more than one circle in a column is marked; for example:

Answer: 258

No credit!

33. In the figure above, $x =$

34. If $\dfrac{m+n}{m} = \dfrac{10}{9}$, then $n/m =$

35. Set A consists of all multiples of 4 between 50 and 65. Set B consists of all multiples of 3 between 50 and 65. What is one possible number that is in Set A but NOT in Set B?

36. In a certain species of fish, 0.3 percent of a school are born with physical defects. If a school of fish contains 21 individuals with such defects, how many fish are in the school?

37. If $(2z + 5)(3z + 4) = az^2 + bz + c$ for all values of z, what is the value of b?

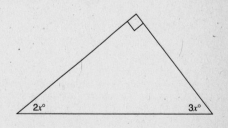

38. In the figure above, what is the value of x?

GO ON TO THE NEXT PAGE

39. What is the perimeter of the 12-sided figure above?

40. If $5x + 9y = 28$ and x and y are positive integers, what is the value of $x?$

IF YOU FINISH BEFORE TIME IS CALLED, CHECK YOUR WORK ON THIS SECTION ONLY. DO NOT WORK ON ANY OTHER SECTION IN THE TEST.

Section 5: Writing Skills

Time: 30 Minutes

39 Questions

(1–39)

Identifying Sentence Errors

Directions: The following sentences may contain one error of grammar, usage, diction, or idiom. No sentence will contain more than one error, and some have no error. If there is an error, it will be underlined and have a letter beneath it. Sections of the sentence that are not underlined cannot be changed. In selecting your answer, observe the requirements of standard written English.

*If there is an error, choose the one underlined part that must be changed to correct the sentence. If there is no error, choose **E**. Blacken the corresponding space on the answer sheet.*

Example

> The violinist and <u>her</u> <u>will audition</u> for the conductor <u>as soon as</u> they have
>   A   B   C
>
> <u>completed</u> their studies. <u>No error</u>
>   D   E
>
>

1. The report <u>written by</u> experts on Asia
           A
   <u>recommend</u> a large loan <u>from</u> the World
     B   C
   Bank <u>to repair</u> the roads battered by
        D
   floods. <u>No error</u>
          E

2. Everywhere you look in New York City,
   <u>one</u> sees the white-brick apartment
    A
   buildings <u>that sprang up</u> after <u>the war</u>
            B   C
   <u>like mushrooms.</u> <u>No error</u>
     D   E

3. In <u>virtual</u> every year, the young men
      A
   <u>set sail</u> for other islands <u>to participate</u> in
     B   C
   <u>a series of</u> gift exchanges. <u>No error</u>
     D   E

4. Last year, Americans <u>spent</u> millions <u>on</u>
                  A   B
   tobacco products, and despite the warnings <u>against smoking</u>, they <u>spend</u> even
        C   D
   more this year and next. <u>No error</u>
                       E

GO ON TO THE NEXT PAGE

5. Neither Henry James nor James Whistler, <u>both</u> great lovers of France,
A
<u>were able</u> to <u>earn a living</u> in Paris, and
B   C
<u>moved to</u> London. <u>No error</u>
D   E

6. <u>Walking on coral</u> from their earliest
A
years, the Kitawans <u>develop</u> soles
B
<u>as tough as leather</u> and <u>they find</u> the
C   D
tender feet of Westerners very odd.
<u>No error</u>
E

7. Edwards <u>is</u> a lazy journalist <u>who</u> will
A   B
<u>not</u> do hardly any work until a deadline
C
<u>approaches</u>. <u>No error</u>
D   E

8. The city <u>punishes</u> the self-employed <u>in</u>
A   B
not <u>being</u> a corporation <u>with</u> the unin-
C   D
corporated business tax. <u>No error</u>
E

9. Like <u>London's</u> subway system,
A
<u>that of Boston</u> is easy <u>to learn</u> and
B   C
expensive <u>to use</u>. <u>No error</u>
D   E

10. The <u>older</u> houses of the Florida Keys
A
<u>mirrors</u> a <u>multicultural legacy</u> of
B   C
Bahamian, New England, African,
<u>and Creole influences</u>. <u>No error</u>
D   E

11. Investment strategists <u>in</u> the New York
A
offices of Morgan Stanley <u>continue to</u>
B
<u>believe</u> that stocks are <u>the best possible</u>
C   D
investment. <u>No error</u>
E

12. <u>Like Shakespeare</u>, Whitman's writings
A
<u>continue</u> <u>to be</u> relevant <u>to</u> our culture.
B   C   D
<u>No error</u>
E

13. The large gilt mirror <u>above the fireplace</u>
A
<u>giving</u> the room <u>the atmosphere</u> of a
B   C
Viennese apartment <u>of the nineteenth</u>
D
<u>century</u>. <u>No error</u>
E

14. New York City is <u>more populous</u> than
A
<u>any one</u> of 30 states and <u>has</u> a budget
B   C
larger than <u>that of</u> 45. <u>No error</u>
D   E

15. It <u>comes as a surprise</u> to most American
A
tourists <u>to discover that</u> many a college
B
in Oxford University <u>were founded</u>
C
long before America <u>was discovered</u>.
D
<u>No error</u>
E

16. <u>Surprisingly</u>, Key West is <u>close</u> to
A   B
Havana, Cuba, by 60 miles <u>than</u> <u>it is</u> to
C   D
Miami, Florida. <u>No error</u>
E

17. Neither the Nixon nor the Reagan library <u>have</u> ever <u>requested to borrow</u>
     A   B
any FBI Watergate or Iran-contra <u>items</u>
                             C
<u>for use in</u> an exhibition. <u>No error</u>
 D   E

18. Almost everyone in the studio audience
<u>found</u> the situation hilarious except the
 A
other contestant <u>who</u> <u>was unable</u> to
               B   C
solve the puzzle and <u>I</u>. <u>No error</u>
                D   E

19. <u>A writer since the age of 16</u>, Barbara
               A
Pym <u>has been acclaimed</u> <u>for</u> "the best
        B   C
novelist <u>of her</u> generation." <u>No error</u>
        D   E

Improving Sentences

Directions: The following questions test correctness and effective expression. In selecting the answer, pay attention to grammar, diction, sentence structure, and punctuation.

In the following questions, part or all of each sentence is underlined. The (A) answer repeats the underlined portion of the original sentence, and the next four offer alternatives. Choose the answer that best expresses the meaning of the original sentence and at the same time is grammatically correct and stylistically superior. The correct choice should be clear, unambiguous, and concise.

Example

In her performance, Eartha Kitt sang songs <u>in English, in French, and she sang in Arabic.</u>

   A. in English, in French, and she sang in Arabic.

   B. in English and French, and she also sang in Arabic.

   C. in English and French, singing also in Arabic.

   D. in English, French, and Arabic.

   E. in English, in French, and Arabic.

Ⓐ Ⓑ Ⓒ ● Ⓔ

GO ON TO THE NEXT PAGE

20. The beginnings of van Dyke's short stories are <u>as good as, if not better,</u> his endings.

    A. as good as, if not better

    B. good as, if not better

    C. as good as, if not better than

    D. as good and better than

    E. as good and better as

21. To germinate properly, the seeds of the sweet pea must be planted <u>in either spring or fall.</u>

    A. in either spring or fall.

    B. in either the spring or in the fall.

    C. either in the spring or the fall.

    D. either the spring or in the fall.

    E. either in spring or the fall.

22. Bryant Park and Washington Square, Manhattan's finest squares, <u>lined with buildings whose architects</u> were aware that they were creating walls to enclose space.

    A. lined with buildings whose architects

    B. are lined by buildings whose architects

    C. are lined by architects with buildings that

    D. with buildings by architects who

    E. surrounded by buildings whose architects

23. <u>It is feared by many real estate agents</u> that the Internet will soon replace them.

    A. It is feared by many real estate agents

    B. It is the fear of many real estate agents

    C. By many real estate agents, it is feared

    D. Many real estate agents have the fear

    E. Many real estate agents fear

24. The anthropologist Scoditti set out to record the islanders' songs, to understand their ritual dances, <u>and he wanted to explain the symbolism</u> of their carvings.

    A. and he wanted to explain the symbolism

    B. also wanting to explain the symbolism

    C. explaining the symbolism

    D. and to explain the symbolism

    E. and explaining the symbolism

25. If the repairs of the rockets are completed by June, <u>the launch taking place in July.</u>

    A. the launch taking place in July.

    B. the launch having taken place in July.

    C. the launch will take place in July.

    D. the launch has taken place in July.

    E. the launch will have taken place in July.

26. A notorious speakeasy during Prohibition, <u>Ernest Hemingway made this saloon his favorite haunt</u>, and it is still a popular tourist attraction.

   A. Ernest Hemingway made this saloon his favorite haunt

   B. Ernest Hemingway's favorite was to haunt this saloon

   C. this saloon was Ernest Hemingway's favorite haunt

   D. the favorite haunt of Ernest Hemingway was this saloon

   E. this saloon became the favorite haunt of Ernest Hemingway

27. The visit to China of the Secretary of State, it is hoped, will lay the groundwork for the Premier's visit to Washington, <u>and this is when</u> the disarmament treaty will be signed.

   A. and this is when

   B. at which time

   C. which is when

   D. and that is when

   E. and this the time when

28. If one digs beneath the snow in the garden, <u>you may find</u> the scarlet flowers of the hardy cyclamen.

   A. you may find

   B. you may come upon

   C. you come across

   D. one may find

   E. one finds

29. Like New York City, the Internet has long traffic delays, easy access to pornography, and <u>there are far too many self-centered babblers.</u>

   A. there are far too many self-centered babblers.

   B. it also has far too many self-centered babblers.

   C. and far too many self-centered babblers.

   D. and there are too many self-centered babblers by far.

   E. and it has far too many self-centered babblers.

30. The knot garden, a blend of geometry and plants, <u>creates patterns to please the eye</u>.

   A. creates patterns to please the eye.

   B. creates patterns which pleases the eyes.

   C. create eye-pleasing patterns.

   D. create a pattern that pleases the eye.

   E. please the eye by creating a pattern.

31. John Adams and Thomas Jefferson were often bitter political adversaries, <u>and they maintained a personal relationship</u> that outlasted their rivalry.

   A. and they maintained a personal relationship

   B. but they maintained a personal relationship

   C. but a personal relationship was maintained by them

   D. so a personal relationship was maintained

   E. thus maintaining a personal relationship

GO ON TO THE NEXT PAGE

Section 5 Writing Skills

32. <u>Audubon recorded in watercolors not only</u> the birds of America but also the plants and the animals.

    A. Audubon recorded in watercolors not only

    B. Audubon's watercolors not only recorded

    C. Audubon's watercolors recording not only

    D. Audubon recorded not only in watercolors

    E. Audubon not only recorded in watercolors

33. Many large corporations support the literacy project, <u>they donate</u> materials developed by literacy experts to reading centers throughout the country.

    A. they donate

    B. they make donations of

    C. and they donate

    D. and donating

    E. to donate

Improving Paragraphs

Directions: The following passage is an early draft of an essay. Some parts need to be revised.

Read the selection carefully and answer the questions that follow. There will be questions about sentence structure, diction, and usage in individual sentences or parts of sentences. Other questions will deal with the whole essay or paragraphs and ask you to decide about organization, development, and appropriate language. Choose the answer that follows the requirements of standard written English and most effectively expresses the intended meanings.

After you have chosen your answer, fill in the corresponding space on your answer sheet.

Questions 34–39 are based on the following passage.

(1) I was born in California and my mother and father were born in Thailand. (2) Thailand used to be called Siam. (3) A few years ago they went to Thailand to visit my grandparents at the time when a new king was being crowned.

(4) My grandparents lived in a small town not far from the capital city, which is called Bangkok. (5) The coronation ceremony of a Thai king is very ancient. (6) It has a long history and has been passed down from very olden times. (7) On coronation day, a Brahmin poured holy water on the king's hands. (8) Then, after the ceremony the king could issue royal commands with the help of the Hindu gods Siva, Vishnu, and Brahma. (9) Later, Buddhist monks also participate in the coronation. (10) In modern times, the Representatives and Senators will also offer holy water to the king. (11) Thus, combining the religious and the political.

(12) Unlike the musical *The King and I,* Thailand today is a democracy, but it still has a king. (13) The coronation of the king combined the new democratic people plus religion and ancient ceremony. (14) Thus, Thailand honors the past and marches into the future.

34. Which of the following is the best version of sentences 1 and 2 (reproduced below)?

I was born in California and my mother and father were born in Thailand. Thailand used to be called Siam.

A. (As they are now)

B. I was born in California, and my mother and father were born in Thailand, which used to be called Siam.

C. I was born in California, but my parents were born in Thailand, which used to be called Siam.

D. Born in California, my parents are from Siam, which is now called Thailand.

E. I was born in California. My parents were born in Thailand. Thailand was formerly called Siam.

35. Which of the following is the best way to revise and combine sentences 5 and 6 (reproduced below)?

The coronation ceremony of a Thai king is very ancient. It has a long history and has been passed down from very olden times.

A. The coronation ceremony of a Thai king has a long ancient history and has been passed down from very old times.

B. The long ancient history of the coronation ceremony of a Thai king has been passed down from olden times.

C. A Thai king's coronation ceremony, passed down from ancient times.

D. The coronation ceremony of a Thai king has been passed down from ancient times.

E. Passed down from olden times, the ancient coronation ceremony of a Thai king has a long history.

36. Which of the following is the most effective version of the underlined portions of sentences 10 and 11 (reproduced below)?

In modern times, the Representatives and Senators <u>will also offer holy water to the king. Thus combining the religious and the political.</u>

A. (As it is now)

B. also offer holy water to the king. Thus combining the religious and the political.

C. also will offer holy water to the king. Thus, they combine religion and politics.

D. also offer holy water to the king, adding a political element to the religious.

E. combined religion and politics when offering holy water to the king.

GO ON TO THE NEXT PAGE

Section 5 Writing Skills

37. Which of the following sentences in the second paragraph can best be omitted or moved to a different paragraph in the essay?

A. the fourth

B. the seventh

C. the eighth

D. the ninth

E. the tenth

38. In the context of the third paragraph, which of the following is the best version of the underlined portion of sentence 12 (reproduced below)?

Unlike the musical The King and I, *Thailand today is a democracy* but it still has a king.

A. (As it is now)

B. Unlike the musical *The King and I,* Thailand today is democratic

C. Unlike the musical *The King and I,* modern Thailand is democratic

D. Unlike the country in the musical *The King and I,* Thailand today is democratic

E. Thailand today, unlike the musical *The King and I,* is a democracy

39. Of the following kinds of grammatical errors, which occur most often in this draft?

A. inconsistent verb tenses

B. sentence fragments

C. confusion of adjectives and adverbs

D. subject-verb agreement errors

E. errors of case in pronouns

IF YOU FINISH BEFORE TIME IS CALLED, CHECK YOUR WORK ON THIS SECTION ONLY. DO NOT WORK ON ANY OTHER SECTION IN THE TEST.

SCORING PSAT/NMSQT PRACTICE TEST

Answer Key

Section 1: Verbal Reasoning	Section 2: Mathematical Reasoning	Section 3: Verbal Reasoning	Section 4: Mathematical Reasoning	Section 5: Writing Skills
1. C	1. C	26. E	21. A	1. B
2. B	2. D	27. D	22. C	2. A
3. B	3. A	28. C	23. A	3. A
4. A	4. B	29. A	24. D	4. D
5. E	5. D	30. D	25. B	5. B
6. D	6. A	31. E	26. A	6. E
7. B	7. D	32. B	27. A	7. C
8. E	8. B	33. B	28. B	8. B
9. D	9. B	34. A	29. D	9. E
10. B	10. D	35. C	30. C	10. B
11. C	11. C	36. A	31. A	11. E
12. D	12. B	37. C	32. C	12. A
13. D	13. B	38. A	33. 85	13. B
14. A	14. E	39. E	34. 1/9 or .111	14. E
15. B	15. A	40. E	35. 52, 56, or	15. C
16. B	16. C	41. B	64	16. B
17. A	17. E	42. D	36. 7,000	17. A
18. B	18. C	43. C	37. 23	18. D
19. A	19. D	44. A	38. 18	19. C
20. C	20. C	45. E	39. 152	20. C
21. C		46. B	40. 2	21. A
22. D		47. D		22. B
23. C		48. B		23. E
24. E		49. A		24. D
25. B		50. D		25. C
		51. B		26. C
		52. A		26. B
				28. D
				29. C
				30. A
				31. B
				32. A
				33. C
				34. C
				35. D
				36. D
				37. A
				38. D
				39. A

ANALYZING YOUR TEST RESULTS

The charts on the following pages should be used to carefully analyze your results and spot your strengths and weaknesses. The complete process of analyzing each subject area and each individual problem should be completed for the practice test. These results should then be reexamined for trends in types of errors (repeated errors) or poor results in specific subject areas. *This reexamination and analysis is of tremendous importance to you in ensuring maximum test-preparation benefit.*

Verbal Reasoning Analysis Sheet

Section 1	Possible	Completed	Right	Wrong
Sentence Completion	6			
Analogies	6			
Critical Reading	13			
Subtotal	30			
Section 3	**Possible**	**Completed**	**Right**	**Wrong**
Sentence Completion	10			
Analogies	6			
Critical Reading	11			
Subtotal	27			
Overall Verbal Totals	52			

Mathematical Reasoning Analysis Sheet

Section 1	Possible	Completed	Right	Wrong
Multiple Choice	20			
Subtotal	20			
Section 4	**Possible**	**Completed**	**Right**	**Wrong**
Quantitative Comparison	12			
Grid-Ins	8			
Subtotal	20			
Overall Math Totals	40			

Writing Skills Analysis Sheet

Section 5	Possible	Completed	Right	Wrong
Identifying Sentence Errors	19			
Improving Sentences	14			
Improving Paragraphs	6			
Overall Writing Skills Totals	39			

You can now use the Score Range Approximator on page 394 to convert your raw scores to *approximate* scaled scores.

Analysis/Tally Sheet for Problems Missed

One of the most important parts of test preparation is analyzing *why* you missed a problem so that you can reduce the number of mistakes. Now that you have taken the practice test and checked your answers, carefully tally your mistakes by marking them in the proper column.

Reason for Mistakes					
	Total Missed	*Simple Mistake*	*Misread Problem*	*Lack of Knowledge*	*Lack of Time*
Section 1: Verbal					
Section 3: Verbal					
Subtotal					
Section 2: Math					
Section 4: Math					
Subtotal					
Section 5: Writing					
Total Math, Verbal, and Writing					

Reviewing the preceding data should help you determine *why* you are missing certain problems. Now that you've pinpointed the types of errors, focus on eliminating them.

PSAT/NMSQT Score Range Approximator

The following charts are designed to give you only an approximate score range, not an exact score. When you take the actual PSAT/NMSQT, you will see questions similar to those in this book; however, some questions may be slightly easier or more difficult. Needless to say, this may affect your scoring range.

How to approximate your score in Verbal Reasoning

1. Add the total number of correct responses for the two verbal sections.

2. Add the total number of incorrect responses (only those attempted or marked in) for those sections.

3. The total number of incorrect responses for the verbal sections should be divided by 4, giving you an adjustment factor (round off to the nearest whole number, if necessary).

4. Subtract this adjustment factor from the total number of correct responses to obtain a raw score.

5. This raw score is then scaled to a range of 20 through 80.

   For example:

   If the total number of correct answers was 30 of a possible 52

   and 20 problems were attempted but missed,

   dividing 20 by 4 gives an adjustment factor of 5.

   Subtracting this adjustment factor of 5 from the original 30 correct gives a raw score of 25.

   This raw score is then scaled to a range of 20 through 80.

6. Use the following table to match your raw score for Verbal Reasoning and the corresponding approximate score range:

Raw Score	Approximate Score
40–52	60–80
30–39	50–59
20–29	40–49
0–19	20–39

Keep in mind that this is only an *approximate* score range.

How to approximate your score in Mathematical Reasoning

1. Add the total number of correct responses for the two math sections.

2. Add the total number of incorrect responses for the multiple-choice questions.

3. The total number of incorrect responses for these multiple-choice questions should be divided by 4, giving you an adjustment factor for multiple choice (round off to the nearest whole number).

4. Total the incorrect responses for the quantitative comparison questions and divide this total by 3, giving you an adjustment factor for quantitative comparison (round off to the nearest whole number).

5. Add the adjustment factors for multiple choice and quantitative comparison, giving you a single adjustment factor.

6. Subtract this adjustment factor from the total number of correct responses to obtain a raw score.

7. This raw score is then scaled to a range of 20 through 80.

   For example:

   If the total number of correct answers was 20 of a possible 40,

   and 8 multiple-choice problems were attempted but missed,

   dividing 8 by 4 gives an adjustment factor of 2 for multiple choice.

   Now suppose that 6 quantitative comparison problems were attempted but missed.

   Dividing these 6 problems by 3 gives an adjustment factor of 2 for quantitative comparison.

   Adding the adjustment factors for multiple choice and quantitative comparison (2 + 2) gives you a single adjustment factor of 4.

   Subtracting this adjustment factor of 4 from the original 20 correct gives a raw score of 16.

   This raw score is then scaled to a range of 20 through 80.

   Note: The reason for this unusual calculation is that ¼ point is deducted for each incorrect multiple-choice question and ⅓ point is deducted for each incorrect quantitative comparison question. You receive no deduction for incorrect grid-in responses.

8. Use the following table to match your raw score for Mathematical Reasoning and the corresponding approximate score range:

Raw Score	Approximate Score
30–40	60–80
20–29	45–59
10–19	34–44
0–9	20–33

Keep in mind that this is only an *approximate* score range.

How to approximate your score in Writing Skills

1. Add the total number of correct responses for the Writing Skills section.

2. Add the total number of incorrect responses (only those attempted or marked in) for that section.

3. The total number of incorrect responses for the Writing Skills section should be divided by 4, giving you an adjustment factor (round off to the nearest whole number, if necessary).

4. Subtract this adjustment factor from the total number of correct responses to obtain a raw score.

5. This raw score is then scaled to a range of 20 through 80.

   For example:

   If the total number of correct answers was 25 of a possible 39

   and 12 problems were attempted but missed,

   dividing 12 by 4 gives an adjustment factor of 3.

   Subtracting this adjustment factor of 3 from the original 25 correct gives a raw score of 22.

6. Use the following table to match your raw score for Writing Skills and the corresponding approximate score range:

Raw Score	Approximate Score
30–39	63–80
20–29	50–62
10–19	40–49
0–9	20–39

Keep in mind that this is only an *approximate* score range.

COMPLETE ANSWERS AND EXPLANATIONS TO PSAT/NMSQT PRACTICE TEST

Section 1: Verbal Reasoning

Sentence Completions

1. **C.** The missing word should describe an object like a bed or chair. Only "inanimate" (without life) makes sense in this context.

2. **B.** The word needed here must accord with the words "inconsiderate" and "unhealthy" and refer to a man or woman. "Mordant," which means "caustic," does not quite fit this context, so the best choice is "shameful."

3. **B.** Any of the nouns except "placebos" might fit here, though **D** and **E** are less good than **A** or **B**. Neither "soporific" nor "somnolent" can work here, since a doctor would have some concern about the sleep-inducing properties. "Tonic" (invigorating) is clearly a bad choice, but "addictive" and "narcotics" make good sense of the sentence.

4. **A.** Since the second half of the sentence refers to the eleven different languages, the right answer must be "linguistic."

5. **E.** Since the rains have caused so many floods, the first adjective must be either **C** "massive" or **E** "unprecedented." The second word must mean something like "increased," but with only **C** and **E** to choose from, the answer must be "augmented."

6. **D.** The first adjective should mean something like "shocking"; of the five choices, either **B** "unusual" or **D** "audacious" is a possibility. The verb must mean something like "put together." Words like "confine" **A** and "combine" **C** would work, but these letters have already been eliminated. The best choice is "juxtapose" **D.**

Analogies

7. **B.** In all but **D**, the first term is a place where the second can be found, but only in **B** is the second term one who works in that place. In **D**, the place is the second term.

8. **E.** A "marathon" is an event in which a "runner" participates. Similarly, a "juror" participates in a "trial."

9. **D.** Something that is "brittle" is apt to "shatter"; something that is "porous" is apt to "leak."

10. **B.** To "embarrass" is to shame or make self-conscious, while to "mortify" is to humiliate with shame, that is, a more intense embarrassment. In the same way, to "delight" is more intense than to "please."

11. **C.** The first word here is a noun and the second a verb denoting the chief activity of the noun. A "chef"'s chief activity is to "cook"; an "idler" is someone who is idle, who "dawdles."

12. **D.** Here the first term is an adjective that describes a primary characteristic of the second term, a noun. A "hermit" is "solitary" as a "daredevil" is "intrepid," or fearless. Though many "grandparents" are "aged," many are not, and age is not the primary characteristic of a grandparent as solitude is of a hermit.

Critical Reading

13. **D.** The passage doesn't suggest a moratorium is needed **A;** in fact, it calls for further research. Nor does it suggest fears are "groundless" **B;** see lines 51–53. **C** is a minor point in the passage, and although the passage mentions research, it does not describe it **E.**

14. **A.** Uncontrolled gene transfer is the possibility that most concerns critics. Nothing indicates that **B** will occur, and **C, D,** and **E** are not specifically mentioned in the passage.

15. **B.** This is the best definition considering the context. The word can also mean **C,** but that definition is appropriate to conscious beings, not bacterial genes. **D** may seem to fit context, but it—like **A** and **E**—is not a correct definition of the word.

16. **B.** In lines 47–50, the passage specifically mentions the fragility of the altered bacteria. **C** and **E** are not mentioned. **D** is correct in only one instance; it is cited as an example. While the EPA is mentioned in the passage, nothing suggests it is reluctant **A.**

17. **A.** See lines 5–9. **C** is incorrect; altered bacteria may help clean up oil spills but they don't prevent them. **E** might be possible but is not mentioned as a benefit. The meaning of **B** is unclear, and **D** is simply incorrect.

18. **B.** Nowhere in the passage is it implied that the benefits are not worth the risks. In fact, the author clearly indicates that with further research, altered bacteria can be safely used. All of the other points are either implied or stated in the passage.

19. **A.** This is the best definition considering the context. Although **B** is also a correct definition, it clearly doesn't fit here. **E** is also a correct definition of the word but is not as appropriate as **A** for cloth (crinoline). **C** and **D** are simply incorrect definitions.

20. C. See lines 14–17. Although **B** might be true, it is not implied in the passage. Neither is **A**; in fact, the passage suggests that men felt women were unsuited for intellectual pursuits. **D** and **E** are simply inaccurate.

21. C. Note the root word "merit." In the context of the passage, "government" (**A** and **D**) is not appropriate; "system" is a better choice. Although a meritocracy excludes sex or race discrimination, it does discriminate on the basis of ability. Therefore, **B** is incorrect. **E** is irrelevant.

22. D. See lines 57–64. Although a contrast is drawn with business, it is not related to the rewards of a career in either field **C**. **B** is not specifically supported in the passage, while **E** is not addressed. **A** is incorrect; science may be a good field for women, but the passage indicates that it still does not offer them abundant opportunities.

23. C. The attitudes described in Passage 1 are behind the convictions and inherited ideas that, according to the passage, influence 20th century scientists (lines 57–64). Passage 2 suggests that although **B** *should* be true, it is not as of yet (lines 97–102). **A** is not accurate, according to Passage 2, and **D** is not addressed in the passage. The attitudes described in Passage 2 are not significantly different from those described in Passage 1 **E**.

24. E. The purposes of the passages are very different: Passage 1 is a historical account, while Passage 2 is arguing a point. Women's feelings aren't described in Passage 1 and are barely touched upon in Passage 2 **A**. The women referred to in Passage 1, while not encouraged by men to engage in intellectual pursuits, are not themselves described as anti-intellectual **B**. At first **C** may sound like a good answer, but Passage 2, for example, does include facts in the form of statistics. The future is not discussed in Passage 1 **D**.

25. B. Passage 1 doesn't address the attitudes of scientists apart from the attitudes of men in general, whereas Passage 2 specifically targets scientists. Both passages are concerned with social stereotypes **A, C,** and **E** are not covered in either passage, and **D** is touched on in Passage 1 but not in Passage 2.

Section 2: Mathematical Reasoning

Multiple Choice

1. **C.** In 864,925, the number in the thousands place is 4. Because the number immediately to the right of 4 is 5 or larger (9), round the thousands digit up to a 5, which yields 865,000.

2. **D.** If $x = 2$, then $3x^2 + (3x)^2 = 3(2^2) + (3 \cdot 2)^2$
$$= 3 \cdot 4 + (6)^2$$
$$= 12 + 36$$
$$= 48$$

3. **A.** If $a + b = -3$, then $(a + b)^3 = (-3)^3 = -27$.

4. **B.** Because the product of an odd number of negative integers is a negative integer, the maximum number of the six integers that could be negative is five.

5. **D.** Let $x = $ first integer

$x + 1 = $ second integer

$x + 2 = $ third integer

Since the sum of the three integers is 141,

$$x + x + 1 + x + 2 = 141$$
$$3x + 3 = 141$$
$$3x + 3 - 3 = 141 - 3$$
$$3x = 138$$
$$\frac{3x}{3} = \frac{138}{3}$$
$$x = 46$$

The largest integer is $x + 2 = 48$.

6. **A.** If $\frac{z}{3} = 25$, then multiplying both sides of the equation by 3 yields

$3 \cdot \frac{z}{3} = 3 \cdot 25$

$z = 75$

Hence $5z = 5 \cdot 75 = 375$

7. **D.** For any numbers m and n, $m^4 \geq 0$ and $n^4 \geq 0$.

Since $m^4 + n^4 = 0$, then both $m = 0$ and $n = 0$. Therefore $9m - 5n = (9)(0) - 5(0) = 0$.

8. **B.** Since Distance = Rate × Time,
$$\text{Time} = \frac{\text{Distance}}{\text{Rate}}$$
The distance that Marcos travels is d miles at a rate of 55 miles per hour. Hence the time it takes is $\frac{d}{55}$ hours.

9. B. Substituting $a = 4b - 11$ for a in the equation $a + 5 = 3b$, yields

$$4b - 11 + 5 = 3b$$
$$4b - 6 = 3b$$
$$4b - 6 - 3b = 3b - 3b$$
$$b - 6 = 0$$
$$b - 6 + 6 = 0 + 6$$
$$b = 6$$

10. D. The volume of a cube with side length x is x^3. If $x^3 = 64$, then $x = 4$. The area of any face of the cube is $x^2 = 4^2 = 16$.

11. C. Since the sum of the angles in any triangle must equal $180°$,

$$m + n + m - n = 180$$
$$2m = 180$$
$$\frac{2m}{2} = \frac{180}{2}$$
$$m = 90$$

Note: The given value of $n = 50$ is not needed to solve for m.

12. B. Since the sum of two odd integers is an even integer, and $3x + 11$ is even, then $3x$ must be odd. Since the product of two odd integers is an odd integer, then x must be an odd integer. Hence $x + 1$ must be an even integer.

13. B. The volume of a rectangular box is lwh. With the given dimensions and volume $V = lwh$

$$12 = (z)(\tfrac{2}{2})(y)$$
$$12 = 2y$$
$$\tfrac{12}{2} = \tfrac{2y}{2}$$
$$6 = y$$

14. E. There are many different values for x and y such that $xy = 21$. Therefore, there are many different values for the ratio of x to y, and thus the ratio cannot be determined from the information given.

15. A. The radius of circle P will also be 40% of the radius of circle Q. Because the area of any circle is πr^2, the radius will be used to compare the areas of the two circles. Since

$$40\% = .40 = .4$$

and $(.4)^2 = (.16) = 16\%$

the area of circle P will be 16% of the area of circle Q.

16. C. Since $x^6 = x^5 \cdot x = \frac{2}{11}$ and $x^5 = 9$,

$$9x = \frac{2}{11}$$

$$\tfrac{1}{9}(9x) = \tfrac{1}{9}\left(\frac{2}{11}\right)$$

$$x = \frac{2}{99}$$

17. E. For the expression $3x - 4$ to be greater than 4 and less than 250,

$$4 < 3x - 4 < 250$$

Add 4,

$$4 + 4 < 3x - 4 + 4 < 250 + 4$$

$$8 < 3x < 254$$

Divide by 3,

$$\tfrac{8}{3} < \tfrac{3x}{3} < \tfrac{254}{3}$$

$$2\tfrac{2}{3} < x < 84\tfrac{2}{3}$$

Since x is an integer, $x = 3, 4, 5 \ldots 82, 83, 84$. Hence there are 82 integer values of x.

18. C. In the figure, $0X = 2$ and $0Y = 3$, and the area of $\triangle X0Y$ is $\frac{1}{2}(0X)(0Y) = \frac{1}{2}(2)(3) = 3$.

For the area of $\triangle WYZ$ to be the same,

$$\tfrac{1}{2}(YZ)(WZ) = \tfrac{1}{2}(1)(WZ) = 3$$

$$\tfrac{1}{2}(WZ) = 3$$

$$2 \cdot \tfrac{1}{2}(WZ) = 2 \cdot 3$$

$$WZ = 6$$

Hence the coordinates of W are $(4, 6)$.

19. D. In the set of numbers from 1 to 50 inclusive, there are 16 numbers divisible by 3: $3, 6, 9, \ldots, 48$. Therefore, the probability that a ticket selected will have a number divisible by 3 is $\frac{16}{50} = \frac{8}{25}$.

20. C.

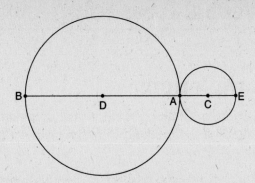

Since the area of the smaller circle is 100π and the area of any circle is πr^2, then

$$\pi r^2 = 100\pi.$$

$$\frac{\pi r^2}{\pi} = \frac{100\pi}{\pi}$$

$$r^2 = 100$$

So $r = 10$ is the radius of the smaller circle.

Since AD = AE, the diameter of the smaller circle is the same as the radius of the larger circle, so the larger circle's diameter is 20.

Hence the area of the larger circle

$$\pi r^2 = \pi\left(20^2\right)$$

$$= 400\pi$$

Section 3: Verbal Reasoning

Sentence Completions

26. **E.** The missing adverb must describe the giving of a man described as "kind and modest." Of the five choices, only "unobtrusively" (that is, "quietly") fits well.

27. **D.** Since the farmers dislike the Easterners, the missing verb should denote something like "refusal." The only possibility is "discouraged" **D.**

28. **C.** The first adjective could be "obscure" **A,** "remote" **C,** or "uninhabited" **D,** but the noun should denote a large or growing number of people who are threatened. The two possibilities are **B** and **C,** but **B** has been eliminated already.

29. **A.** The right answer must follow logically from the verb "fought" and also accord with the adjective "small." The best choice is "skirmishes," which is idiomatic and relevant.

30. **D.** The first missing noun cannot be **A,** but the four other choices are possible. The best choice for the second noun is "memento" (a keepsake, reminder, or souvenir). **B** is a remote possibility, but a "daguerreotype" is an early nineteenth-century photograph, surely long predating an espionage trial.

31. **E.** Options **B** and **D** make little sense. An "epithet" is a characterizing word or phrase, such as rosy-fingered (Dawn) or thunder-bearing (Jove). An epigram is a terse and witty saying. The best choice here is "epitaph," the inscription about the dead on a tomb or monument.

32. **B.** Only the more generalized "technological" could apply to all of the fields listed in this series. The words "pictorial" and "cinematic" fit several but not all of the terms, such as "sound reproduction."

33. **B.** The two terms should be critical ones that describe a free-spending person. Only **B** has two words that clearly qualify, "extravagant" and "ostentatious."

34. **A.** The context suggests a verb meaning "put forward" or "advocated." Of the five choices, only "championed" is plausible.

35. **C.** If identifications are now easy, there should "no longer" be remains that are "unidentified." And if there are no unknown soldiers, the traditional tomb will become "obsolete."

Analogies

36. **A.** A "parasite" is an organism that lives on another species (the "host"), as a "flea" lives on a "dog."

37. **C.** A "sofa" is one of many items of "furniture," as "pepper" is one of many "condiments" or seasonings.

38. **A.** The "circus" is the venue in which a "clown" performs, as a "concert hall" is the place where a "soloist" performs. The work of "artists" would be found in a "museum," but they do not practice their art there.

39. **E.** The first term here is a place, while the second is something that is very unlikely to be found there. Only the "cactus" (likely to be found in a desert) and the "rain forest" are analogous.

40. **E.** The difficulty in this question is determining the meaning of "graduate." The five answers make clear that the first term is the noun, not the verb. Here it must refer to containers used in laboratories to measure liquids, so the relationship is the noun is used to perform action. The best answer is a "wedge," a hard material used "splitting" wood.

41. **B.** A "reactionary" person is extremely conservative, the polar opposite of one who is "liberal." Similarly, the adjectives "reticent" (quiet) and "outspoken" are antonyms.

Critical Reading

42. **D.** The passage touches on **A, B, C,** and **E,** but its main emphasis is on the explanation of why so little writing was produced by the early Asian immigrants.

43. **C.** See lines 85–92. **A** is incorrect because most Filipinos were also barred by these laws in 1934. **D** is incorrect; the passage doesn't imply that this was the reason for passage of the laws. **B** and **E** are irrelevant, since the exclusion laws barred immigration.

44. **A.** The concept of lack, or absence, is central to the word. Therefore, **C** is incorrect. **B** is too limited. **D,** while it may sound correct, is not; "privacy" is not part of the definition of "privation." Also, in context, "lack of privacy" doesn't make sense. **E** is an incorrect definition and also doesn't fit the context.

45. **E.** Note (line 14) that some immigrants had no desire to return to their homelands. **A** (lines 53–54), **B** (lines 44–48), **C** (lines 42–43), and **D** (lines 58–61) are inferences that can be drawn from the passage.

46. **B.** The author cites the book as one of the few sources of autobiographical information about Asian immigrants. **D** is true but not the reason the author cites the book. **C** is incorrect because this isn't the only existing writing. The passage doesn't indicate whether the Asian workers are presented sympathetically or unsympathetically **E.** **A** is also incorrect; the title of the book is not related to Asian self-esteem.

47. D. See lines 66–69. The docility of the work force, not its gullibility, is cited; therefore **B** is not correct. **A** is clearly untrue; see the final paragraph of the passage. Nothing indicates whether either **C** or **E** is a true statement.

48. B. This is the best choice in this context. One meaning of "ghetto" is a section of a city where many members of a minority live—an "urban ethnic enclave." These enclaves are not necessarily slums **A** nor do they necessarily consist of tenements **E**. Neither **C** nor **D** fits the context here.

49. A. This inference can be drawn from lines 92–97. The passage does not imply that their works were of no value **B** nor that they were accepted by an American audience **C**. **D** is incorrect because the passage states that these writers described Asia in idealized—not realistic—terms. The inference in **E** is contradicted by the third paragraph of the passage.

50. D. See lines 116–121. The passage doesn't state that they "preferred" America **A** but rather that they felt able to combine the two cultures. **C** is contradicted in lines 116–121. **B** might seem a good choice, but see lines 114–116. Nothing in the passage suggests **E**.

51. B. At first glance, **A** may seem a good choice, but "euphemistic" does not mean untrue; it means disguising unpleasant truths by using inoffensive or "polite" terms (for example, "passed away" instead of "died"). **C**, **D**, and **E** are not supported by context nor are they correct definitions of the word.

52. A. See lines 82–85. **E** may be true, although the passage does not state this. **C** and **B** are contradicted (lines 92–97 and lines 116–121). The passage includes no value judgment on early Asian immigrant writing **D**.

Section 4: Mathematical Reasoning

Quantitative Comparisons

21. A. $\quad 1 - \dfrac{1}{30} = \dfrac{30}{30} - \dfrac{1}{30} = \dfrac{29}{30}$ $\qquad\qquad \dfrac{9}{10} + \dfrac{1}{30} = \dfrac{27}{30} + \dfrac{1}{30} = \dfrac{28}{30}$

$\qquad$ Hence, $1 - \dfrac{1}{30} > \dfrac{9}{10} + \dfrac{1}{30}$

22. C. average speed $= \dfrac{\text{distance}}{\text{time}}$

$\qquad$ Gina's avg. speed $= \dfrac{15\,\text{miles}}{3\,\text{hours}} = 5$ mph $\quad$ Lisa's avg. speed $= \dfrac{10\,\text{miles}}{2\,\text{hours}} = 5$ mph

$\qquad$ The average speed for each person is the same.

23. A. The average (arithmetic mean) of $r, s,$ and t is

$\qquad \dfrac{r+s+t}{3} = 87$

$\qquad$ Multiplying both sides by 3,

$\qquad 3 \cdot \dfrac{r+s+t}{3} = 3 \cdot 87$

$\qquad\quad r+s+t = 261 > 260$

24. D. Substitute some test values for m and n in 3^m and 10^n:

$\qquad$ If $m = 1$ and $n = 2$, then $3 < 10^2$

$\qquad$ If $m = 3$ and $n = 1$, then $3^3 > 10$

$\qquad$ Because the relationships differ depending on the values chosen, the comparison cannot be determined.

25. B. The sum of four different negative integers will always be a negative integer, and the product of four different negative integers will always be positive.

$\qquad$ Therefore, $a + b + c + d < abcd$.

26. A. The triangle inequality theorem states that the sum of any two sides of a triangle must be greater than the third side.

$\qquad$ Hence, $10 + 11 > l$

$\qquad\qquad\quad 21 > l$

27. **A.** $\overline{AB}$ is a diameter of the circle because it passes through the center P of the circle, and $\overline{XY}$ is a chord of the circle that does not pass through the center. Because any diameter of a circle is the longest chord of the circle, $\overline{AB} > \overline{XY}$.

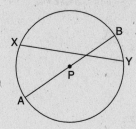

28. **B.** In any triangle, the larger of two angles is opposite the larger of two sides. Because $m + 1 > m,$ the angle opposite the side with length $m + 1$ is larger than the angle opposite the side with length m.

Hence, $y > x$.

29. **D.** Substitute some test values for x and y:

If $x = -2$ and $y = -3$, then $x + y < 0$ and $xy > 0$.

If $x = -5$ and $y = 2$, then $x + y < 0$ and $xy < 0$.

Because the relationships differ depending on the values chosen, the comparison cannot be determined.

30. **C.** $a + 6 = b$

$a + b = 13$

Adding both sides of the equations yields

$2a + b + 6 = b + 13$

$2a + b + 6 - b = b + 13 - b$

$2a + 6 = 13$

31. **A.** Solving $15 - x \qquad < 2$

$15 - x - 15 < 2 - 15$

$-x < -13$

$\dfrac{-x}{-1} > \dfrac{-13}{-1}$

$x > 13$

(*Note:* Inequality is reversed when dividing by a negative number.)

Solving $2y < 24$

$$\frac{2y}{2} < \frac{24}{2}$$

$$y < 12$$

Therefore, $x > y$.

32. C.

Because M is the midpoint of BC, BM = CM.

The area of $\triangle ABM = \frac{1}{2}\,bh = \frac{1}{2}\,(BM)(AB)$.

The area of $\triangle AMC = \frac{1}{2}\,bh = \frac{1}{2}\,(CM)(AB)$.

Because the heights are the same and the bases are equal in the two triangles, the areas of the triangles are equal.

Grid-Ins

33. Answer: 85

Because the three angles form a straight line

$$45 + x + 50 = 180$$

$$x + 95 = 180$$

$$x + 95 - 95 = 180 - 95$$

$$x = 85$$

34. Answer: ⅑ or .111

Because $\dfrac{m+n}{m} = \dfrac{10}{9}$

$$\dfrac{m}{m} + \dfrac{n}{m} = \dfrac{10}{9}$$

$$1 + \dfrac{n}{m} = \dfrac{10}{9}$$

$$1 + \dfrac{n}{m} - 1 = \dfrac{10}{9} - 1$$

$$\dfrac{n}{m} = \dfrac{10}{9} - \dfrac{9}{9}$$

$$\dfrac{n}{m} = \dfrac{1}{9} \text{ or } .111 \ldots$$

Note that answers ⅑ and .111 are correct, but .1 and .11 are *not* correct in this situation.

35. Answer: 52, 56, or 64

The multiples of 4 between 50 and 65 are

$A = \{52, 56, 60, 64\}$

The multiples of 3 between 50 and 65 are

$B = \{51, 54, 57, 60, 63\}$

The numbers in Set A but *not* in Set B are 52, 56, and 64. Note that although more than one answer is possible, you need to grid in only one of them for full credit.

36. Answer: 7,000

Let x = number of fish in the school

0.3 percent of x is 21

$$0.003x = 21$$

$$\dfrac{0.003x}{0.003} = \dfrac{21}{0.003}$$

$$x = 7,000$$

There are 7,000 fish in the school.

37. Answer: 23

Multiplying $(2z + 5)(3z + 4) = 6z^2 + 8z + 15z + 20$

$$= 6z^2 + 23z + 20$$

Because $(2z + 5)(3z + 4) = az^2 + bz + c$ for all values of z,

$$6z^2 + 23z + 20 = az^2 + bz + c$$

and

$$b = 23$$

38. Answer: 18

Because the sum of the angles in any triangle must equal 180°,

$$2x + 3x + 90 = 180$$
$$5x + 90 = 180$$
$$5x + 90 - 90 = 180 - 90$$
$$5x = 90$$
$$\frac{5x}{5} = \frac{90}{5}$$
$$x = 18$$

39. Answer: 152

The perimeter of this 12-sided figure is the same as the perimeter of a square with side length 30 plus four additional segments of length 8.

$$\text{Perimeter} = 4 \cdot 30 + 4 \cdot 8$$
$$= 120 + 32$$
$$= 152$$

The perimeter is 152 units.

40. Answer: 2

Since x and y are positive integers and $5x + 9y = 28$, the only possible values for y are 1, 2, and 3. If y were greater than 3, x would have to be a negative integer.

Substituting 1, 2, or 3 for y will show that $y = 2$ is the only value that will yield an integer value for x.

Hence, $5x + 9 \cdot 2 = 28$

$$5x + 18 = 28$$
$$5x + 18 - 18 = 28 - 18$$
$$5x = 10$$
$$\frac{5x}{5} = \frac{10}{5}$$
$$x = 2$$

Section 5: Writing Skills

Identifying Sentence Errors

1. **B.** Despite the distraction of the plural "experts," the subject here is the singular "report," so the verb should be the singular "recommends."

2. **A.** Since the sentence uses "you" in the first clause, it should continue to use "you," not "one."

3. **A.** The adverb "virtually," not the adjective "virtual," should modify the adjective "every."

4. **D.** The present tense "spend" makes no sense with the phrase "this year and next"; the verb should be in the future tense, "will spend."

5. **B.** With "neither . . . nor," the subject is singular, either James or Whistler, but not both. The parenthetical phrase using "both" does not change this fact, so the verb should be the singular "was able."

6. **E.** This sentence is correct. Though an opening participle may often dangle, this one does not.

7. **C.** Since "hardly" is a negative, the "not" makes a double negative; it should be omitted.

8. **B.** This is an error in idiom. The sentence should read "punishes for" rather than "punishes in."

9. **E.** The sentence is correct. "London's subway system" and "that of Boston" are properly parallel.

10. **B.** This is another error in agreement. The plural "houses" requires the plural verb "mirror."

11. **E.** There are no errors in this sentence.

12. **A.** This sentence should read either "Like Shakespeare's, Whitman's writing" or "Like Shakespeare, Whitman wrote" to maintain the logic of the comparison: writings to writings, or writer to writer.

13. **B.** As it stands, this is a sentence fragment, lacking a main verb. The participle "giving" should be "gives."

14. **E.** This sentence is correct.

15. **C.** The phrase "many a" introduces a singular noun ("many a man," not "many a men") so this singular subject requires the singular verb "was founded."

16. **B.** With "than," the adjective "close" should be in its comparative form, "closer."

17. **A.** This is another example of the use of "either . . . or" that requires a singular verb ("has").

18. **D.** The pronoun "I" is the object of the preposition "except," so the correct form is "except . . . me." It is easy to miss this error because the pronoun and the governing preposition are separated.

19. **C.** This is another idiom error. In this context, we say "acclaimed as."

Improving Sentences

20. **C.** There are two phrases here that must be complete, "as good as" and "if not better than." Of the choices here, only **C** is complete.

21. **A.** The original version is correct. With correlatives like "either . . . or," the same structure should follow each of the conjunctions. You could also write "either in spring or in fall," but the original version is more brief.

22. **B.** The original sentence is a fragment, lacking a main verb. **B** corrects this error. The choice of preposition ("with" or "by") is not important. Both **D** and **E** are also sentence fragments.

23. **E.** Although the original version of this sentence is grammatical, the more direct active voice is a more vigorous sentence using three fewer words.

24. **D.** This sentence is testing parallelism. It begins with two infinitives ("to record," "to understand") controlled by the verb "set out." The best version simply repeats the infinitive ("to explain").

25. **C.** The sentence, as it stands, is a fragment. The main clause needs an indicative verb in the future tense.

26. **C.** The phrase that begins this sentence dangles, and **A** and **B** make it appear that the "speakeasy" and "Hemingway" are the same. Though **E** is grammatical, the more concise **C** is the best choice here.

27. **B.** Three of the choices here use a pronoun ("this," "which," and "that") with no antecedent, that is, no specific noun or pronoun to refer to. Only **B** avoids this problem.

28. **D.** Both **D** and **E** avoid the shift from the pronoun "one" at the beginning to "you." Since the original sentence presents the finding as only a possibility, ("may") **D** is the better of the two choices since it does not change the meaning.

29. **C.** This is another test of parallelism with a series. Here the first two elements are noun phrases ("traffic delays," "access to pornography") that are objects of the verb "has." The parallel is a third object of this verb, "too many self-centered babblers." The introduction of a second verb breaks up the parallelism.

30. **A.** The original sentence is correct. All of the four other choices have agreement errors ("pleases," "create," "create," and "please").

31. **B.** To make sense, the sentence needs a conjunction like "but" that suggests a contrast between the first part ("adversaries") and the second ("personal relationship"). **B** is better than **C** because it avoids the wordier passive voice.

32. **A.** The original version is correct. It places the "not only" before "the birds," so that "not only" precedes the parallel phrase "the plants." **C** places the "not only" properly, but has no main verb.

33. **C.** As it stands, the sentence is run-on. The addition of "and" corrects the comma splice.

Improving Paragraphs

34. **C.** The best version subordinates the second sentence, avoiding the repetition of the word "Thailand." The "but" that replaces the "and" is a better choice of conjunction, since it emphasizes the difference between the two birthplaces. The participle in **D** is out of place, and **E** has too many short sentences.

35. **D.** The original here is wordy since "has a long . . . history," "ancient," and "has been passed down from very olden times" all say virtually the same thing. **C** is too short, since it is a fragment, lacking a main verb. The best choice here is **D**.

36. **D.** In both **A** and **B**, the second sentence is a fragment. The future tense in **C** and the past tense in **E** are awkward; both are inferior to **D**.

37. **A.** The second paragraph is about the coronation ceremony, but the fourth sentence is about the writer's grandparents. The sentence can be omitted or moved to the first paragraph, where it logically follows the third sentence.

38. **D.** Though it requires more words, only **D** avoids the illogical comparison of a country (Thailand) and a musical comedy (*The King and I*).

39. **A.** The recurrent error in this draft is the handling of verb tenses. They jump about with no apparent plan. The second paragraph, for example, moves from the present (5) to the past (7) back to the present (9) to the future (10).

The Final Touches

1. Make sure that you are familiar with the testing center location and nearby parking facilities.

2. Spend your last week of preparation primarily on reviewing strategies, techniques, and directions for each area.

3. Don't "cram" the night before the exam. It's a waste of time!

4. Remember to bring the proper materials to the test: identification, admission ticket, three or four sharpened Number 2 pencils, a watch, a good eraser, and a calculator.

5. Start off crisply, first working the answers you know and then coming back and trying the other questions.

6. If you can eliminate one or more of the choices, make an educated guess.

7. Mark in reading passages, underline key words, write out information, and make notations on diagrams. Take advantage of being permitted to write in the test booklet.

8. Make sure that you are answering "what is being asked" and that your answer is reasonable.

9. Using the Successful Overall Approaches (see Introduction) is the key to getting the answers right that you should get right — resulting in a good score on the SAT I and PSAT.

CliffsNotes

LITERATURE NOTES

Absalom, Absalom!
The Aeneid
Agamemnon
Alice in Wonderland
All the King's Men
All the Pretty Horses
All Quiet on the Western Front
All's Well & Merry Wives
American Poets of the 20th Century
American Tragedy
Animal Farm
Anna Karenina
Anthem
Antony and Cleopatra
Aristotle's Ethics
As I Lay Dying
The Assistant
As You Like It
Atlas Shrugged
Autobiography of Ben Franklin
Autobiography of Malcolm X
The Awakening
Babbit
Bartleby & Benito Cereno
The Bean Trees
The Bear
The Bell Jar
Beloved
Beowulf
The Bible
Billy Budd & Typee
Black Boy
Black Like Me
Bleak House
Bless Me, Ultima
The Bluest Eye & Sula
Brave New World
The Brothers Karamazov
Call of the Wild & White Fang
Candide
The Canterbury Tales
Catch-22
Catcher in the Rye
The Chosen
The Color Purple
Comedy of Errors...
Connecticut Yankee
The Contender
The Count of Monte Cristo
Crime and Punishment
The Crucible
Cry, the Beloved Country
Cyrano de Bergerac
Daisy Miller & Turn...Screw
David Copperfield
Death of a Salesman
The Deerslayer
Diary of Anne Frank
Divine Comedy-I. Inferno
Divine Comedy-II. Purgatorio
Divine Comedy-III. Paradiso
Doctor Faustus

Dr. Jekyll and Mr. Hyde
Don Juan
Don Quixote
Dracula
Electra & Medea
Emerson's Essays
Emily Dickinson Poems
Emma
Ethan Frome
The Faerie Queene
Fahrenheit 451
Far from Madding Crowd
A Farewell to Arms
Farewell to Manzanar
Fathers and Sons
Faulkner's Short Stories
Faust Pt. I & Pt. II
The Federalist
Flowers for Algernon
For Whom the Bell Tolls
The Fountainhead
Frankenstein
The French Lieutenant's Woman
The Giver
Glass Menagerie & Streetcar
Go Down, Moses
The Good Earth
Grapes of Wrath
Great Expectations
The Great Gatsby
Greek Classics
Gulliver's Travels
Hamlet
The Handmaid's Tale
Hard Times
Heart of Darkness & Secret Sharer
Hemingway's Short Stories
Henry IV Part 1
Henry IV Part 2
Henry V
House Made of Dawn
The House of the Seven Gables
Huckleberry Finn
I Know Why the Caged Bird Sings
Ibsen's Plays I
Ibsen's Plays II
The Idiot
Idylls of the King
The Iliad
Incidents in the Life of a Slave Girl
Inherit the Wind
Invisible Man
Ivanhoe
Jane Eyre
Joseph Andrews
The Joy Luck Club
Jude the Obscure
Julius Caesar
The Jungle
Kafka's Short Stories
Keats & Shelley
The Killer Angels
King Lear
The Kitchen God's Wife
The Last of the Mohicans

Le Morte Darthur
Leaves of Grass
Les Miserables
A Lesson Before Dying
Light in August
The Light in the Forest
Lord Jim
Lord of the Flies
Lord of the Rings
Lost Horizon
Lysistrata & Other Comedies
Macbeth
Madame Bovary
Main Street
The Mayor of Casterbridge
Measure for Measure
The Merchant of Venice
Middlemarch
A Midsummer-Night's Dream
The Mill on the Floss
Moby-Dick
Moll Flanders
Mrs. Dalloway
Much Ado About Nothing
My Ántonia
Mythology
Narr. ...Frederick Douglass
Native Son
New Testament
Night
1984
Notes from Underground
The Odyssey
Oedipus Trilogy
Of Human Bondage
Of Mice and Men
The Old Man and the Sea
Old Testament
Oliver Twist
The Once and Future King
One Day in the Life of Ivan Denisovich
One Flew Over the Cuckoo's Nest
100 Years of Solitude
O'Neill's Plays
Othello
Our Town
The Outsiders
The Ox-Bow Incident
Paradise Lost
A Passage to India
The Pearl
The Pickwick Papers
The Picture of Dorian Gray
Pilgrim's Progress
The Plague
Plato's Euthyphro...
Plato's The Republic
Poe's Short Stories
A Portrait of the Artist...
The Portrait of a Lady
The Power and the Glory
Pride and Prejudice
The Prince
The Prince and the Pauper
A Raisin in the Sun

The Red Badge of Courage
The Red Pony
The Return of the Native
Richard II
Richard III
The Rise of Silas Lapham
Robinson Crusoe
Roman Classics
Romeo and Juliet
The Scarlet Letter
A Separate Peace
Shakespeare's Comedies
Shakespeare's Histories
Shakespeare's Minor Plays
Shakespeare's Sonnets
Shakespeare's Tragedies
Shaw's Pygmalion & Arms...
Silas Marner
Sir Gawain...Green Knight
Sister Carrie
Slaughterhouse-Five
Snow Falling on Cedars
Song of Solomon
Sons and Lovers
The Sound and the Fury
Steppenwolf & Siddhartha
The Stranger
The Sun Also Rises
T.S. Eliot's Poems & Plays
A Tale of Two Cities
The Taming of the Shrew
Tartuffe, Misanthrope...
The Tempest
Tender Is the Night
Tess of the D'Urbervilles
Their Eyes Were Watching God
Things Fall Apart
The Three Musketeers
To Kill a Mockingbird
Tom Jones
Tom Sawyer
Treasure Island & Kidnapped
The Trial
Tristram Shandy
Troilus and Cressida
Twelfth Night
Ulysses
Uncle Tom's Cabin
The Unvanquished
Utopia
Vanity Fair
Vonnegut's Works
Waiting for Godot
Walden
Walden Two
War and Peace
Who's Afraid of Virginia...
Winesburg, Ohio
The Winter's Tale
The Woman Warrior
Worldly Philosophers
Wuthering Heights
A Yellow Raft in Blue Water